Regulating Paradise

Regulating Paradise

Land Use Controls in Hawai‘i

SECOND EDITION

David L. Callies

UNIVERSITY OF HAWAI‘I PRESS
Honolulu

© 2010 University of Hawai'i Press
All rights reserved
Printed in the United States of America

15 14 13 12 11   6 5 4 3 2

Library of Congress Cataloging-in-Publication Data

Callies, David L.
Regulating paradise : land use controls in Hawai'i / David L. Callies.—2nd ed.
p.   cm.
Includes bibliographical references and index.
ISBN 978-0-8248-3475-3 (pbk. : alk. paper)
1. Land use—Law and legislation—Hawaii.   I. Title.
KFH458.C35 2010
346.96904'5—dc22

2010018259

University of Hawai'i Press books are printed on acid-free
paper and meet the guidelines for permanence and durability
of the Council on Library Resources.

Designed by Santos Barbasa

Printed by The Maple-Vail Book Manufacturing Group

To Laurie, my wife and partner,
and for my grandchildren,
Kailani, Nainoa, and Makoa

Contents

Preface

This book is a long-overdue sequel to *Regulating Paradise,* published in 1984, which is both out of print and out of date. It reflects more of an emphasis on land use and development law at the expense of environmental law for two reasons. First, there has been a great deal of activity, both legislatively (statutes and ordinances) and judicially (Hawai'i state and relevant federal cases), particularly in the areas of land development conditions, creation of state agencies with land management or development functions (OHA, ATDC, for example), coastal zone management, and environmental impact assessment. Second, I no longer teach, research, or write in environmental law, and my colleague, Denise Antolini, who does, is writing her own book on Hawai'i environmental law. Therefore, while there is some overlap (we both give coastal zone management full chapter treatment, and I have a catch-all environmental law chapter as it specifically affects land use), in-depth treatment of such subjects as clean air, clean water, endangered species, and environmental impact assessment I gladly leave to Professor Antolini.

This book could not possibly have been written without the generous support of several groups and the dedicated research and drafting provided by a cadre of patient research assistants over the past three years. In the first category, my thanks to the Pacific Legal Foundation for its annual support for several years and additional contributions from Title Guaranty Escrow Services, the McNaughton Group, the Maryl Group, Castle & Cooke Hawai'i, Hawai'i Leeward Planning Conference, Outrigger Enterprises, the Lyle Anderson Group, and the Bill Mills Development Company, all through the Hawai'i Property Law Project. In the second category, my thanks for the splendid research contributions not only in the tedious tasks of checking sources and notes, but also in providing research memoranda and draft chapter additions: to my present research assistants Stephen Fischer, Mark Kaetsu, Kekoa Keiley, and Emily Klatt; and for past research contributions, Adrienne Saurez, Christopher Goodin, Jennifer Benck, Tina Wakayama, Glenn Sonoda, Marissa Lum, Rafael Renteria, Joe Dane, Madeline Reed, Sara Stringfellow, and Anna Fernandez. Also, my thanks to Princess Soares, my faculty-support staff specialist for her consistent help and unfailing good humor as we moved the book from draft (eight, at last count) to completion over the past eighteen months, and to my past staff specialist, Josephine Ah Ching. For reviewing early drafts of chapters, my thanks to Professors Denise Antolini and Kem Lowry; and for reviewing the entire manuscript on behalf of the University of Hawai'i Press, Dan Davidson and Professor Dan Tarlock. Drafts of many chapters were sent to and for the most part reviewed by the relevant government agencies, many of which made detailed and helpful suggestions. However, since many of the individual government reviewers asked to remain anonymous, all references to present and past public sector reviewers are omitted here, except where referenced in footnotes. My thanks to Lorenzo Trinidad for the Corky Trinidad editorial cartoons from the *Honolulu Star-Bulletin* that appear in this book. I've also been blessed again with superb editorial support from Ann Ludeman, managing editor at the University of Hawai'i Press, and the careful editing and suggestions of copy editor Lee S. Motteler. Finally, my eternal thanks for the years of support and encouragement of William H. Hamilton, director of the University of Hawai'i Press. I couldn't have done it without you, Bill.

Note on Style

In the text, diacritical marks in Hawaiian words and names follow modern usage (e.g., *'āina,* Hawai'i, Lāna'i, etc.). However, note that in state and county government agencies and offices, use of the marks is often considered optional. Also, to facilitate searching, the marks are omitted in court cases and Web site URLs throughout this volume. Titles of publications (articles, books, Web pages, etc.), where possible, follow the original.

Introduction

A "Baker's Dozen" Land Policy Agenda
for the Fiftieth State

Ua mau ke ea o ka ʻāina i ka pono—The life of the land is
perpetuated in righteousness.
   —Hawaiʻi state motto

Land use in Hawaiʻi continues to be the most regulated of all the fifty
states. According to many sources, going from raw land to the completion of a project may well average ten years, given that such raw land is
almost certainly classified by the State Land Use Commission initially as
either Conservation or Agriculture (still, between them, comprising 95

"ALL RIGHT, ALL OF YOU – GO AWAY! GO AWAY! …"

percent of the land area of the state). The costs associated with holding and developing land for so long are considerable, and this drives up the price of virtually anything connected with land development. It is no wonder that our housing prices, for example, are among the highest in the United States. Couple this regulatory scheme with increasingly large numbers of so-called public interest groups that lay claim both to stakeholder status in the land use process and a veto power over the ultimate decision, and we have an unhealthy brew that threatens the economic future of the Fiftieth State. Commenced in order to bring order and sense to the use and development of that most precious of Island commodities—land—the regulation of land use has become an enormously complex process, often equally frustrating to the public and private sectors alike.

Context: The Evolution of Land Use Controls in Hawai'i

The preoccupation with land management in Hawai'i goes well back in history, arguably dating from the semifeudal relationship of certain of Hawai'i's monarchs with their chief nobles (ali'i) to whom they parceled out land in ahupua'a, which usually extended from the uplands to the sea.[1] Thus, the roots of the statewide regulatory system are historical, which does much to explain the relatively easy acceptance of a strong regulatory regime without significant legal challenge: Management and disposal policies existed before a modern system of public land policy evolved. Indeed, this public land policy began to emerge shortly after what has been described as the chaotic conditions following the virtual destruction of ancient Hawaiian social and economic patterns in the middle of the nineteenth century.[2] This culminated—officially at least—in the division (mahele) of 1848, also known as the Great Mahele (or simply Mahele). Between 240 and 250 owners (konohiki) met with King Kamehameha to divide their lands formally into two groups: those belonging to the king and those belonging to the chiefs. The division was recorded in a Mahele Book between January 27 and March 7, 1848. By this process, the king obtained rights to about half the land in Hawai'i, which he immediately separated further into crown lands (his own)[3] and land for the government (the chiefs and the people) to be controlled by the legislature. The chiefs obtained title to land that the Mahele set aside for them by filing an appropriate claim with a land commission. Therefore, at the conclusion of the Mahele, land in Hawai'i was assigned to—but not necessarily owned by—three groups: the royal family (crown lands), the government, and the chiefs. In theory, each group's land was divided subject to the rights of those common people who were tenants thereon. However, unfamiliarity with European concepts of landownership, lack of concern and lack of understanding resulted in the loss of many of these rights in just a few years.[4]

In order to establish a more equitable pattern of landholding, there were several attempts to encourage "homesteading" acts both before and after Hawai'i became a territory of the United States in 1898. Although a few hundred people did acquire family farm-sized tracts, the increasingly entrenched position of the large landholders remained largely unchanged, thereby perpetuating the centralized character of land management but with different "managers."[5] In sum, the fact that land management (though not necessarily ownership) had passed to a "foreign" oligarchy from a native one in the space of a few decades may be significant, but it is not when viewed from the perspective of a land use management framework.[6] The centralizing influence remains, reinforced by the fact that government has also been highly centralized throughout much of Hawai'i's history.[7]

In theory, it was possible for this pattern to have been broken by federal land policies once Hawai'i became a territory, if the early attempts at "homesteading" had been continued by the federal government. They were not. Nearly 2 million acres, Hawai'i's public lands, were ceded to the U.S. government, some of it quickly set aside for military purposes.[8] This simply increased the tendency toward centralization of land management, despite sporadic attempts by both the federal government and a succession of governors in the first quarter of the twentieth century to resuscitate homesteading.[9] The result was a climate that heavily favored centralized land use management and control at the public sector level, which is just what occurred in the middle decade of the twentieth century.

In the years preceding 1961, when the State of Hawai'i passed its Land Use Law, the interests of the private landholding oligarchy and the centralized state government converged out of concern for the threat to agricultural land, the mainstay of the major private interests and the single most important factor in the Hawaiian economy.[10] Hawai'i's economic boom was beginning, along with land speculation and development. Presumably the state's four counties were unequal to the task of dealing with the problems generated by this rapid economic growth, having comparatively little planning expertise and few land use controls.[11] The stage was thus set for the passage of Hawai'i's landmark land use law, which resulted in the zoning of Hawai'i by a state agency in order to contain sprawl and preserve agricultural land. It is this law and its progeny upon which most commentators have chosen to dwell. This is but the tip of the iceberg, however. Hawai'i now labors under a plethora of local as well as additional state regulations that affect the use of land, public and private. Both traditional and unique zoning and subdivision schemes with multiple permits and conditions, all tied to tiers of local plans, vie for prominence with a host of regulations and standards issued pursuant to federal statutes that, directly or indirectly, further restrict the use of land.

Not nearly so widely publicized are the steadily increasing power and authority of Hawai'i's counties—in particular Honolulu and specialized state development corporations—over land use planning and control. The result is a comprehensive and detailed set of land use controls. Indeed, as the counties and their planning and zoning departments have grown in experience, skill, and size and as their plans and ordinances have become more sophisticated, the role of the state in land use decision making not clearly involving a statewide interest is steadily diminishing. Land use decisions are thus beginning to more nearly resemble the regional regulatory patterns of developed states on the mainland. The Islandwide jurisdiction of each of Hawai'i's four counties, together with the absence of any smaller units of local government, effectively prevents local decision making from becoming too parochial.

Nevertheless, Hawai'i's statewide land use law and the state plans that guide its implementation set the basic land use patterns for both private and public land in Hawai'i. They also provide the context for county land use regulation, since only in one of the state's four land use classifications may the counties exercise traditional local zoning and subdivision powers. All four counties have local land use powers and vigorously exercise them, not only through traditional zoning districts but also through a host of special and mixed uses and districts, some of which "overlay" traditional districts for historic, conservation, or aesthetic purposes. How these affect traditional private development "rights" is an increasingly important issue. So is the relationship of proliferating county plans to traditional local land control ordinances.

As the problems of land management in a developing state grow in complexity, so does the relationship of traditional land use controls with other related or special-purpose laws. Hawai'i has its share of specific state and local laws to protect historic sites and the natural environment. In addition to local responses to federal programs with the same goals, Hawai'i has its own set of historic preservation and environmental impact assessment laws directed at the review—but not always preservation—of historic and natural areas threatened with development. Special laws and state development corporations are also directed at special issues such as elimination of blight, redevelopment of commercial areas, and provision of reasonably priced housing.

The effect of land use laws on environmental laws is evident from the many land use implications of Hawai'i's response to the environmentally sensitive federal programs of the 1960s, 1970s, and 1980s. Of major importance to an island state are the federal coastal zone and flood hazard protection programs and the way they have been integrated into state and local land use controls. Following closely in importance are the plans and regulations required by federal endangered species habitat protection, clean air, and clean water laws and their effects on the siting of commercial, industrial, and large residential developments.

Finally, in states such as Hawai'i, both the state and the federal governments make their presence felt through land use and disposal policies. The unique historic posture of Hawai'i's "ceded lands" continues to affect how, when, and to whom the federal government "disposes" of certain of its holdings. Ceded lands and other sizable tracts also are largely exempt from local and state land use regulation unless there are significant spillover consequences on adjacent land.

A partial listing of major permits required for residential and resort development alone contains literally hundreds of entries. Government applies these regulations at both the county and state level, often with substantial federal encouragement. They apply to every aspect of the land use and development process, on virtually every square foot of beach, mountain, plateau, and valley, whether public or private, whether resort or residential, agricultural or urban. Thirteen particular issues—a baker's dozen—confront our island state, fifty years since Hawai'i voted overwhelmingly to join the Federal Union.

Land Development Conditions and the Use of Development Agreements

Coupled with the land development permit process as it presently exists, government imposes onerous conditions—often illegally—at the land reclassification stage that lack either nexus or proportionality to a particular development. It is fair to require the land development community to bear a proportionate share of the costs of public facilities such as public schools and parks and infrastructure such as streets and water and sewer systems generated by a new development. It is, however, neither fair nor legal to foist "catch-up" infrastructure or social costs upon a particular project that has virtually no effect upon such costs. A prime example is the current litigation in Maui County over a 50 percent workforce/affordable housing set-aside, imposed at the land classification stage on every form of development, including single-family detached. There is neither nexus nor proportionality. Every court that has rendered an opinion on such housing requirements has required such a connection, particularly and (for Hawai'i) most relevantly, the State of California and the Ninth Circuit Court of Appeals.[12]

However, by negotiating a development agreement between landowner and local government, as provided for by statute in Hawai'i (and California, among twelve other states that provide for such agreements), Hawai'i's counties could dispense with the twin requirements of nexus and proportionality, bargaining for substantial infrastructure and affordable/workforce housing from a developing landowner in exchange for "freezing" existing land development regulations and plans for a fixed period of years. Hundreds of such agreements have been negotiated in California under a similar statutory scheme and upheld by California courts on a regular basis. Indeed, such an agreement was the basis for a $50 million bypass highway and a 180-acre shoreline park, provided by a developer of resort-residential projects under a development agreement negotiated with the County of Hawai'i, in exchange for county guarantees that the landowner could take up to twenty years to complete the project as originally approved.

This is the second substantial advantage to the use of such agreements: the vesting of rights in the land developer to proceed with a project for whatever period of time he or she may negotiate in exchange for providing such "extra" public infrastructure/facilities. Multiphase developments in particular are at risk in the event of a change in county administration from an approving to a disapproving county council. The common law of vested rights (including estoppel for the most part) in Hawai'i requires that a developer acquire a "last discretionary permit" and then spend substantial sums of money or otherwise demonstrate good faith reliance on that permit before acquiring a right to continue with the development in the face of a law, plan, or policy that renders it illegal. Negotiating a development agreement freezes—but does not change in any way—existing plans, regulations, ordinances, or policies that permit such a development and renders laws to the contrary "void."

Affordable Housing: Barriers, Workforce Housing, and Inclusionary Zoning

The resolution of Hawai'i's affordable housing crisis is a critical issue for statewide concern. Mandatory set-asides of so-called workforce housing units—even if constitutional, which they probably are not (see preceding section on land development conditions)—cannot realistically provide so much as a partial solution, dependent as they are on a robust development economy: no development, no set-asides. Moreover, except when levied at an almost certainly unconstitutionally high level, such set-asides provide very little housing. Thus, for example, a recent study of low-income housing production in Massachusetts finds that of fourteen thousand such units provided over a decade, less than 10 percent—a mere fourteen hundred—came from set-asides. A far more productive solution is a combination of government subsidy—either construction of such houses or providing fully infrastructured land to the private sector for such construction—coupled with the lowering of regulatory barriers (both administrative and substantive) to such housing, as advocated by the U.S. Department of Housing and Urban Development and our State Task Force on Regulating Barriers to Affordable Housing. Among the solutions proposed decades ago in states such as New Jersey are using expedited permits and the increased use of manufactured housing (including so-called mobile homes), much of which is virtually indistinguishable today from traditionally constructed housing on-site.

Right to Exclude

There is a growing—and deeply flawed—sense of entitlement to cross private land to reach beaches, trailheads, and other public resources that is shared by many members of the public and various levels of government. Let's be clear: With few exceptions, this is common-law trespassing. The right to exclude others from one's land is a fundamental attribute of the fee simple ownership of land, and it has three times in the past twenty-five years been held by the U.S. Supreme Court to be a fundamental U.S. Constitutional right. It is on this ground that owners of land fronting undeniably public beaches have every right to gate

private access ways to the beach and private residential communities
have every right to gate the entrance to their private streets. Nor may
government require such an access as a condition of land development,
as at least three state supreme courts have clearly held. There are only
two exceptions: (1) those who have successfully trespassed for enough
years that they have acquired what the law calls an easement by prescrip-
tion, and (2) Native Hawaiians who can demonstrate that such access is
a traditional and customary right.

If that access is so important to the public at large, then government can easily and relatively inexpensively condemn an easement
for the public across any land it chooses. As the iconic justice Oliver
Wendell Holmes Jr. of the U.S. Supreme Court wrote in a landmark
opinion nearly a century ago, "We are in danger of forgetting that a
strong public desire to improve the public condition is not enough to
warrant achieving the desire by a shorter cut than the constitutional way
of paying for the change."[13]

Eminent Domain after *Kelo v. New London*

Following Hawai'i's famous *Hawaii Housing Authority v. Midkiff* decision
rendered by the U.S. Supreme Court in 1984,[14] there is virtually nothing
left of the Fifth Amendment requirement that government condemn
land only for a public use. So long as the announced public purpose
(no longer only use by the public) was conceivable and possible, even if
it never came to pass, a unanimous Court agreed it was constitutional.
Thus it came as no surprise that, based largely on that decision, the U.S.
Supreme Court upheld the condemnation of two private houses by a
city redevelopment agency in order to make way for "economic revitalization" in a depressed city on the Atlantic coast.[15] While the Court left
it open to the states to tighten public use standards and raise the bar for
public use determinations (and dozens did so, either by constitutional
or statutory amendment following the *Kelo* decision),[16] Hawai'i is so far
not among them.

Thus, it is worth loudly applauding the increasing use of public purchase—either through bargain and sale or through eminent
domain (compulsory purchase)—of private lands deemed important to
preserve for public benefit and use. Prime examples are the community
coalitions brought together to purchase large tracts of land in Pūpūkea
and Waimea Falls Park and the use of the state's Legacy Lands funds
to contribute a public portion of the purchase price. Also potentially

important—with reservations—is the increased activity of the Office of Hawaiian Affairs (OHA) in the acquisition of large acreages ostensibly to preserve the Hawaiian values for which OHA was created.

The U.S. Supreme Court did, however, leave one small sliver of a remedy for private landowners who can successfully show that the use of eminent domain by government is actually to benefit another private party and that the stated public purpose is a sham: pretextuality. If, for example, government were to condemn one discount store in a shopping center at the request of another discount store for the purpose of eliminating competition, a claim of future blight elimination would not meet the public use/public purpose test. The Hawai'i Supreme Court decided that county condemnation of land for a public bypass road that a developer agreed to construct in order to relieve congestion on an existing public highway could be characterized as pretextual and sent the case back to the trial court to hear more evidence.[17] While one may applaud the concept, its execution in the context of these facts has been mystifying condemnation attorneys all over the country.

Open Space: Use of Rural and Agricultural Lands and Definition of Farm Dwellings

Our famous Land Use Law provides little concrete guidance about what constitutes sufficient agricultural use and farm dwellings to qualify as permitted uses in the State Agricultural Classification. Moreover, all four of Hawai'i's counties have for two decades permitted so-called fake farms—large-lot residential developments with some associated agricultural uses either on or off such large lots—and they have done so with no significant objection either from the Land Use Commission or the State Legislature. It should therefore have surprised no one that the much maligned Hōkūli'a resort residential development on the Big Island sought and successfully obtained county permits to commence such development on state agriculturally classified land. Nor did the settlement of the ensuing litigation before the State Supreme Court could render a decision contribute to any certainty. The Hōkūli'a developer simply followed the practice in the industry as the Court has previously held it was entitled to do, all in accordance with a well-drafted and executed development agreement. The attempt to change the rules in the middle of the game (as was duly noted and reported in the *Wall Street Journal*) sent a most unfortunate message to developers both in and out of the state about the security of land entitlements in Hawai'i.

In addition, there is the matter of open space preservation. The current Important Agricultural Lands statute has the capacity to do much to ease the necessary conversion of poor agricultural land (recall that our State Land Use Law specifically permits so classifying land even if it is lava covered or so thinly soiled that it is demonstrably useless for agricultural purposes) to some kind of economically beneficial use (as required by the Fifth Amendment to the U.S. Constitution as interpreted by the U.S. Supreme Court in *Lucas v. South Carolina Coastal Council*) in exchange for virtual permanent classification of important—translate "useable for agricultural purposes"—agricultural land in agricultural districts. However, the notion persists that agricultural land can continue to be regulated for open space preservation under the guise of protecting conservation and agricultural values even when neither is transparently possible.

So it is also with the state's conservation zone. An example stems from the application of the U.S. Endangered Species Act to that zone. The act is designed to protect plant and animal species listed by the U.S. Fish and Wildlife Service as endangered. Despite propaganda by various environmental activist groups, the listing goes well beyond cute-looking wolf or fox cubs, lovely wildflowers, or stands of stately redwoods. The list in Hawai'i also includes tiny blind cave spiders and cephalopods. It is to protect the latter that nearly one-quarter of the island of Kaua'i was originally designated as "critical habitat" by the Fish and Wildlife Service in the 1990s. While the federal statute by its terms prohibits only certain federal activity in such designated habitat, our State Land Use Law requires the State Land Use Commission to designate land in the restrictive Conservation District for the protection of endangered species and then requires the State Department of Land and Natural Resources, through its governing Land Board, to place such land in the most restrictive of its four subdistricts. The result is almost certainly to prevent all economically beneficial use of such land. This is not only just plain wrong, but it is also almost certainly unconstitutional as a regulatory taking of private land without compensation, as more fully described below.

Regulatory Takings after *Lingle v. Chevron*

While the 2005 *Lingle v. Chevron* case was about gas stations and gas prices, a unanimous U.S. Supreme Court took the occasion to deliver a tutorial on takings jurisprudence, both regulatory and physical. In particular, the Court reiterated two key standards applicable to land development regulations, whether at the state or county level, based on previous holdings:

> (1) If a regulation deprives a landowner of "all economically beneficial use," then the Court will treat it as if government condemned the property. There is no defense of necessity or harm prevention available. Only if government is codifying common law nuisance or basing its law on some "background principle of a state's law of property" such as custom or public trust can government escape the requirement to pay the landowner for that deprivation.[18]
>
> (2) If a regulation only partially deprives a landowner of economically beneficial use, then the court must examine the character of the governmental regulation and its economic effect on the landowner, and in particular whether the law frustrates the distinct or reasonable investment-backed expectations of the regulated landowner.[19]

An example under Honolulu's Land Use Ordinance occurs with respect to development in that ordinance's Preservation 2 (P-2) zoning category. As noted above, it is not constitutional for a regulation to deprive a landowner of all economically beneficial use of his or her land. However, the only permitted uses in this P-2 zone are vacation cabins and golf courses. But a small tract of P-2 cannot support the latter, and the former are permitted only as accessory uses to outdoor recreational principle uses. Indeed, the use of a ridge parcel so classified for vacation cottages has been denied by the director of the Department of Permitting and Planning on just such grounds: They appear to be a principal use rather than an accessory use, and the parcel is too small to support a golf course. The situation raises total regulatory takings problems, as a matter of constitutional law. The same is almost certainly true for the state conservation zone (over 40 percent of the state land area), in which virtually no economically beneficial uses are permitted.

The Nature and Practice of Redevelopment at HCDA, ATDC, HFDC, and HHL

While Hawai'i has no local governments or special municipal districts besides our four counties, the state does have several special-purpose redevelopment agencies provided for by state statute. Each has a partic-

ular purpose as defined in the statute creating it. Each has considerable
freedom from county—and in some instances state—land use controls.
Each is charged with developing land. None has fully realized its goals.
Hawaiian Home Lands (HHL) is perhaps the oldest of the four. Its purpose is to redevelop and develop land for the housing of Native Hawaiians. Until recently, there was very little substantive progress partly due
to lack of infrastructure on its assigned land. HHL now appears to be
moving briskly—for Hawai'i—toward producing housing. However, a
major issue is the extent to which it may ignore state and local land use
controls. A recent State Supreme Court case found that an environmental impact statement review is applicable to HHL projects because
it does not significantly affect the land. Apparently, police power regulations apply to HHL only if they do not significantly affect the land. Presumably, therefore, State Land Use Commission, Department of Land
and Natural Resources, and county zoning regulations are inapplicable,
rendering HHL free to develop land any way it chooses.

Perhaps the state development corporation with the greatest
promise and effect is the Hawai'i Community Development Authority
(HCDA). Its statutory purpose is not solely to develop land, such as the
Kaka'ako waterfront, but also to provide for affordable housing. Also
statutorily free of county land use controls, HCDA is required to regulate the use of land within its jurisdiction by means of detailed development plans and regulations conforming to such plans. After nearly
thirty years, much of Kaka'ako remains underdeveloped and precious
little affordable housing has been created, perhaps not surprising given
the prime nature of the real estate in that area. Interference by the State
Legislature has not helped. Thus, a carefully planned and fully complying mixed-use project with significant environmental cleanup and
Native Hawaiian performing arts facilities was pulled from HCDA and
canceled by the State Legislature after years of hearings, planning, and
effort largely due to the efforts of a small but focused band of surfers,
environmentalists, and residents. The development community, both
locally and out of state, thereby learned (or relearned) once again two
lessons about development or redevelopment in Hawai'i: (1) Entitlements are worth very little in the face of minority opposition, even after
full compliance with our myriad land plans and laws, and (2) Hawai'i
has so many "stakeholders" wielding a veto over development that the
process takes years, with no certainty about outcomes.

The Aloha Tower Development Corporation (ATDC), on the other
hand, has only one legislative purpose in life: to redevelop unused and

derelict piers on either side of the Aloha Tower Marketplace. In this it has been an abysmal failure. The sole response to its request for proposals to develop about a third of the piers and land under its jurisdiction came to naught when ATDC radically changed the rules in the middle of preconstruction implementation, effectively terminating its best opportunity for such redevelopment since the marginally successful Aloha Tower Marketplace. An arbitrator awarded the developer nearly $2 million in damages, finding that ATDC bargained in bad faith. So far, the state has simply refused to pay the award.

Cultural Sensitivity, Burials, and Land Development

There is a sense among certain participants in the Hawaiian Renaissance that, like many groups in the environmental community with whom they are often allied, stakeholding is a given, and it means the power to veto. Contrast the long delay in the Honolulu complex that was to house the "first" Whole Foods Market in Hawai'i with the "backup" smaller store, commenced about a year later, now thriving in Kahala Mall, resulting from the discovery of human—and likely Native Hawaiian—remains. Note also the difficulties a well-off landowner presently faces in building a single-family home on a single lot on Kaua'i. No one suggests that human remains, regardless of ancestry, be treated in the cavalier fashion allegedly displayed by some contractors for the Hōkūli'a project on the Big Island following the discovery of bones in broken lava tubes (and for which Hōkūli'a has paid dearly, even after putting a *kiawe* wood gated perimeter around each such "find" at considerable cost, both in terms of land and construction costs, in addition to providing access, the necessity for which the formerly hidden nature of the burials belies). However, one suspects the perversion of the flawed process for dealing with burials under applicable statutes—which were rushed onto the books with little critical examination—for other motives and on other bases, such as in order simply to delay or stop the process of land development.

Further, there is the brouhaha over telescopes and other such uses largely under the auspices of the University of Hawai'i atop Mauna Kea. One of the two or three best sites in the world for astronomical observations (witness the tens of millions of dollars foreigners are not only willing to invest in equipment, but also the millions to share a few precious nights of already-leased "viewing time" with existing lessees), it is in danger of losing its status as some Native Hawaiian groups insist the site be treated as "sacred."[20]

What Triggers an Environmental Assessment under HEIS

In common with many states, Hawai'i has an environmental assessment statute requiring an initial evaluation of the environmental impacts of certain proposed developments, leading to a formal environmental impact statement if the assessment demonstrates such a need. The requirements are procedural: Regardless of the results of such an environmental review, the applicable statute does not prohibit the project's going forward. To paraphrase a federal court describing the result under the federal environmental policy act upon which our state statute is based, the law does not prohibit an environmental blunder; it simply renders that blunder knowledgeable.

It is thus little short of amazing that our State Supreme Court has applied this lengthy, expensive, and time-consuming requirement to sweep within its terms entire projects on hundreds of acres when the sole "trigger"—use or sale of state land—amounts to a culvert under a state highway. The court seems unable either to reasonably apply a de minimis standard or to refrain from legislating from the bench. There is nothing in either the Hawai'i Environmental Impact Statement (HEIS) law or its legislative history to demonstrate any legislative intent to sweep with such a large broom. The HEIS law desperately needs amending by the Legislature.

The "Third Rail": OHA, Ceded Lands, Crown Lands, and T&C Rights

Claims of Native Hawaiians to certain lands ceded by the government that succeeded Queen Lili'uokalani to the United States upon annexation of Hawai'i as a territory of the United States at the end of the nineteenth century have roiled the state for at least the past two decades. The nub of the issue is whether the United States had sufficient title to such lands to return them legally to the State of Hawai'i shortly after statehood, and if so, whether the state was the proper returnee. Many Native Hawaiians maintain that the queen's government was illegally overthrown, the transfer of ceded lands to the United States was also illegal, and therefore the transfer back to the state is legally ineffective as well. The State of Hawai'i takes issue with at least the last two assertions and maintains that in any event the vote for statehood cured past legal problems, if any. The state has been negotiating, largely with a state entity, the Office of Hawaiian Affairs (OHA), on the matter of title to and income from ceded lands for the past ten years. OHA rejected most settlement offers and appeared determined to maintain an all-or-nothing position. The matter came to something of a head following a decision by the State Supreme Court, largely if not exclusively based upon the Apology Resolution passed by Congress during the Clinton administration, forbidding the state to deal in ceded lands until Native Hawaiian claims are resolved, which could be years or decades. Given that the Apology Resolution is supposed by many to have no legal effect—

indeed, at least one member of our senatorial delegation so stated on
the floor of the Senate—and the resolution also so states, it is hardly
surprising that the state and many of its citizens strongly disagreed with
both the decision and its basis, resulting in a successful petition for a
hearing before the U.S. Supreme Court. Early in 2009 the Court ruled,
in a relatively brief but surprisingly unanimous opinion, that the Apology Resolution is just that: an apology, without so much as a scintilla of
legal effect on the rights of Native Hawaiians. Acknowledging that there
may well be moral obligations resulting from the manner in which the
territorial government was established following the precipitous ending
of the Hawaiian monarchy, the Court disposed of any notion that the
resolution conferred any rights against the federal or the state government. The Court also strongly hinted that the conferring of statehood,
after a popular vote overwhelmingly favoring it, might well dispose of
many claims as a matter of law. While there is some sentiment for finding independent state grounds to prevent the sale of ceded lands until
the resolution of Native Hawaiian claims, and while there are presently
bills in the State Legislature that may, with certain exceptions, so provide, these are by no means free from legal issues; legal challenges are
a virtual certainty, likely on Fourteenth Amendment due process and
equal protection grounds. There is also the small matter of the state/
federal admission legislation, which places the ceded lands in trust for
five purposes: education, agriculture, public improvements, public use,
and Native Hawaiians. In an unpublished memorandum (and presumably unanimous) opinion fifteen years ago, the State Supreme Court
handily disposed of the notion that any of the five purposes takes precedence over all of the other four and specifically held that the state
could dispose of ceded lands so long as the proceeds were traceable
and accounted for among the said five purposes or beneficiaries. It is
difficult to see what, on the legal landscape, has changed, except for the
Apology Resolution, now legally a very dead letter.

Covenanted Communities: Local Government
by Contract in Hawai'i

The problems and opportunities created by covenanted communities
and their explosive growth in Hawai'i are staggering. On the one hand,
the absence of units of local government prevalent in virtually all of the
other fifty states—cities, villages, towns, and school and park districts—
removes local government activity effectively from all but the regional

level. Our local government consists solely of our four counties with islandwide (multiple islands in the case of Kaua'i and Maui Counties) regional rather than local interests. O'ahu's toothless neighborhood boards have proven to be pale shadows of government entities with little power beyond holding hearings on proposed developments and making (usually ignored) recommendations to the county governments, which actually make decisions.

Enter the covenanted community. An outgrowth of private land development restrictions placed on the residential subdivision approval process and created by means of the basic CCRs—covenants, conditions, and restrictions—which attach to most residential land developments beyond a handful of lots, the covenanted community has virtually supplanted local government in such areas as design control, land development control, public safety, and recreational facilities. Gates, guards, and patrols substitute for police protection. Detailed design, siting, landscaping, and height restrictions supplant local zoning—even to the point of deciding who may live in such communities based on age and whether pets will be allowed or cars parked in driveways. Private pools, parks, and playgrounds cater to the closed and often gated membership owners. "Taxes" are levied in the form of annual assessments to pay for the above. The result is a microcosm of a community (though some on the U.S. mainland sprawl over dozens of square miles, complete with restaurants and shopping centers) catering to the needs of its members, just as villages and towns do on the U.S. mainland.

All such obligations are "voluntarily" assumed, and the communities and their governing boards are private, so there is virtually no required due process, either substantive or procedural, to guard against neighborhood board excess. Indeed, even an elected board is no certainty until the particular development is "built out," often leaving critical decisions about community design and exceptions in the application thereof to a single developer representative. Courts usually apply a "business judgment" rule in the event of a challenge to the authority of such boards or individuals, meaning that in the absence of demonstrated and egregious bad faith, such decisions are legally unassailable.

The Endangered State of Comprehensive Plans and Planning

Hawai'i is—or was—a land planning state. There is a statutory state plan, functional plans, county comprehensive general and development plans, and neighborhood plans, all calling for certain uses of land

and all theoretically with the force of law. Indeed, the Hawai'i Supreme Court so held in two 1989 decisions.[21] It is not so today.

First, the State Legislature confounded its own agency, the Hawai'i Community Development Authority (HCDA), by reversing the approval of a carefully designed land development project replete with Native Hawaiian cultural performance venue and massive privately funded environmental cleanup of the site, all in accordance with a carefully drafted plan and after months of hearings on both plan and project. It then stripped the same HCDA of its authority to undertake or approve most development in that part of its jurisdiction—Kaka'ako—closest to Ala Moana Boulevard, also as set out in the aforesaid plan.

Second, our State Water Commission and Supreme Court unaccountably dispensed with the mandatory language in both a state water plan and applicable county general and development plans to radically alter the assignment of water rights from the Windward side of O'ahu to the Leeward side. In so ignoring the plans, the Court favored Native Hawaiian and water conservation uses over economic uses—an inversion of the applicable statutory hierarchy as set out in the state Water Code.[22]

Most recently, a coalition of groups has attacked a multiphase residential project in the 'Ewa District, even though the City and County of Honolulu plans for such a project have been in place for some time. So far, the State Land Use Commission has rejected the landowner's petition for the necessary boundary amendments from agriculture to urban use classification, on the plausible ground that the application fails adequately to address with precision the timing of the development phases. While the project is proposed on useful—and presently used for—agricultural land, five former Honolulu planning directors have publicly written in a daily newspaper to point out that the apparent conflict between housing and agriculture was thoughtfully and carefully considered and resolved in official plans and planning. Whither do planning plans and planning go in today's Hawai'i?

"McMansions" and the Zoning Envelope

There are in addition several issues that cry out for resolution or attention connected with zoning ordinances in Hawai'i, particularly in Honolulu. Perhaps the most intractable (and unforeseeable) is connected with the national trend (until recently) toward demolishing perfectly good but older houses in order to build much larger ones, generally to take advantage of a perceived good location that would support more expensive housing. Some of the dwellings—dubbed "McMansions"— are erected in formerly pleasant (from an aesthetic perspective, at least) neighborhoods and are considerably out of scale with nearby residences and the neighborhood generally. Kahala is a prime example. Less obvious but equally tragic is the demolition of the typical bungalow of 1,000–1,500 square feet in Kaimuki and its replacement with blocky two- and three-story multigeneration houses containing upwards of 3,000 square feet. Both are perfectly legal, since the front and side yard requirements in both neighborhoods can legally support vastly larger structures within the bulk regulation-bounded "zoning envelope." And the aesthetic (or lack thereof) nature of the new houses is not governed by zoning regulations because there is no special design overlay district to add aesthetic architectural feature requirements. Nor are there private restrictive design covenants such as one might find in newer, upper-end housing developments such as Hawai'i Loa Ridge and Wai'alae Iki 4 and 5. Some out-of-state jurisdictions have begun to save such housing stock and neighborhoods by means of maximum house size ordinances, and at least one has been upheld on the U.S. mainland.[23]

Notes

1. Jon Chinen, *The Great Mahele: Hawaii's Land Division of 1848*, Honolulu: University of Hawai'i Press, 1958 at 3–6.

2. Robert H. Horwitz, Judith B. Finn, Louis A. Vargha, and James W. Ceaser, *Public Land Policy in Hawaii: An Historical Analysis*, Report No. 5. Honolulu: University of Hawai'i, Legislative Reference Bureau, 1969.

3. Presently the subject of debate is whether they were held for himself or in trust for his people; *see* Jon M. Van Dyke, *Who Owns the Crown Lands of Hawai'i?* Honolulu: University of Hawai'i Press, 2007.

4. Ralph S. Kuykendall, *The Hawaiian Kingdom 1778–1854: Foundation and Transformation*, Honolulu: University of Hawai'i Press, 1938 at 287–291.

5. Horwitz et al., supra note 2.

6. Tom Dinell, "Land use zoning in a developing state: A brief critique of Hawaii's Land Use Law," 2 THIRD WORLD PLAN. REV. 195–197 (1980).

7. Id. at 197; Fred P. Bosselman and David L. Callies, *The Quiet Revolution in Land Use Control*, prepared for the Council on Environmental Quality, Washington, D.C.: U.S. Government Printing Office, 1973.

8. Horwitz et al., supra note 2.

9. Id.

10. Bosselman and Callies, supra note 7.

11. Dinell, supra note 6; Phyllis Myers, *Zoning Hawaii: An Analysis of the Passage*

and Implementation of Hawaii's Land Classification Law, Washington, D.C.: Conservation Foundation, 1976 at 19–20.

12. *Commercial Builders of N. Cal. v. Sacramento,* 941 F.2d 872 (9th Cir. 1991); *Bldg. Indus. Ass'n of Cent. Cal. v. City of Patterson,* 171 Cal. App. 4th 886 (2009); *San Remo Hotel v. City & County of San Francisco,* 41 P.3d 87 (Cal. 2004).

13. *Penn. Coal Co. v. Mahon,* 260 U.S. 393 (1922).

14. *Haw. Hous. Auth. v. Midkiff,* 467 U.S. 229 (1984).

15. *Kelo v. City of New London,* 545 U.S. 469 (2005). For extensive comment, *see* Dwight H. Merriam and Mary Massaron Ross, *Eminent Domain Use and Abuse:* Kelo *in Context,* Chicago: ABA Publishing, 2006.

16. For extensive listing and discussions, *see* David L. Callies, *Public Use and Public Purpose, After* Kelo v. New London. Newark, N.J.: LexisNexis, 2008.

17. *County of Hawaii v. C&J Coupe Family Ltd.,* 120 Haw. 400, 208 P.3d 713 (2009).

18. *Lucas v. S.C. Coastal Council,* 505 U.S. 1003 (1992).

19. *Penn Cent. Transp. Co. v. New York,* 438 U.S. 104 (1978).

20. The U.S. Supreme Court has repeatedly set limits on the reach of "cultural sensitivity," making it clear that religious practice does not justify fencing off every bit of land that some group claims has religious significance. See Eric Felton, "Save the Planet? Even the Indians Have Reservations," the *Wall Street Journal,* Oct. 30, 2009, at W11.

21. *Kaiser Hawaii Kai Dev. Co. v. City & County of Honolulu,* 70 Haw. 480, 777 P.2d 244 (1989); *Lum Yip Kee Ltd. v. City & County of Honolulu,* 70 Haw. 179, 767 P.2d 815 (1989).

22. *See* David L. Callies and Calvert G. Chipchase, "Water regulation, land use and the environment," 30 U. Haw. L. Rev. 49 (2007).

23. *See Rumson Estates, Inc. v. Mayor & City Council of Fair Haven,* 828 A.2d 317 (N.J. 2003).

Chapter 1

State Land Use Controls

Hawai'i is unique among the fifty states in its comprehensive statewide land use controls. The State Land Use Commission (LUC) manages a system of land district classification distinct from but overlaying the county zoning schemes. Actions by state agencies—which are required for the approval of the multitude of permits required for virtually any large land use project—must also theoretically meet the requirements of the statutory state comprehensive plan.

Hawai'i's Land Districts

Land in Hawai'i is divided into four use districts: urban, rural, agricultural, and conservation.[1] The LUC is responsible for grouping contiguous parcels of land into these districts according to the present and foreseeable use and character of the land. The urban district includes lands that are in urban use and will be for the foreseeable future.[2] The rural district is designed for land with small farms and low-density residential lots.[3] The agricultural district consists of land theoretically used for farming and ranching,[4] and after recent amendments it includes a new, statutorily defined subdistrict: "Important Agricultural Lands" (IAL). The LUC, Hawai'i's four counties, and private landowners are currently identifying and classifying IALs. Finally, the conservation district includes land in areas formerly classified as forest and water reserve zones, open spaces, water sources, wilderness, and scenic and historic areas.[5] Land within the conservation district is further divided into five subzones: protected, limited, resource, general, and special.[6]

Presently, about 48 percent of Hawai'i's land area is designated conservation, 47 percent agricultural, 5 percent urban, and less than half a percent rural.[7] This last classification is expanding—largely from the agricultural districts—to accommodate rural residential development in the wake of the lengthy litigation over large-lot resort-residential development on agricultural-zoned land on the island of Hawai'i between 1995 and 2005.[8] Given the steady demand for residential, commercial, and resort/residential real estate in Hawai'i, coupled with the comparatively tiny percentage of land classified urban or rural (approximately 5 percent), landowners expend much time and energy seeking to reclassify agricultural (and occasionally conservation) land into one or the other development-oriented districts.

This district classification system is akin to a zoning scheme, although, as described in chapter 2, Hawai'i's four counties retain most of the regulatory authority to further classify land in the urban district for typical urban uses. As described below, only low-density residential use is permitted (jointly by the LUC and the counties) in the rural and agricultural districts, and virtually no economically beneficial uses at all are permitted in the conservation district, much of which is publicly owned. In sum, the counties control uses within the urban district, the counties and the state jointly control uses in the agricultural and rural districts, and the state controls uses in the conservation district.

Permitted uses in agricultural districts include the cultivation of crops, orchards, and forests; animal husbandry, fish farming, wind farms, solar energy facilities (in land designated to have limited farming potential), scientific monitoring stations not equipped for use as a residence, agricultural tourism on working farms, and open-area recreational facilities.[9] Employee housing, mills, storage facilities, and other buildings related to farming are permitted for "[b]ona fide" agricultural uses.[10] Land currently or previously used by a sugar or pineapple plantation may contain housing for employees or former employees.[11] Construction of single-family homes is also permitted on lots in the agriculture district subdivided before June 4, 1976.[12] The subdivision of agricultural land, especially prime agricultural land with high-quality class A or B soil, is subject to special requirements, such as that the use of the land be primarily agricultural.[13] Aside from specified exceptions, residential uses beyond "farm dwellings" are theoretically prohibited. In practice, however, all four of Hawai'i's counties have for decades permitted large-lot residential subdivisions so long as there is some demonstrable agricultural use on a lot or on common open space, largely because of inadequate statutory and common law definitions of "farm buildings" and agricultural use.[14] Golf courses and golf driving ranges are not permitted "open space recreational" uses unless approved by a county before July 1, 2005.[15] An LUC survey of land parcels in the agricultural division of Hawai'i County revealed that 78 percent are smaller than 5 acres, each averaging 1.24 acres in size and altogether totaling only 89,095 acres.[16] By statute, the agricultural district specifically includes lands "not suited for agriculture," such as lava flow land and desert, lending credence to the suspicion in some quarters that, particularly with the demise of plantation agriculture, the district has become a de facto open space district.[17]

The rural districts may contain low-density residential uses, agricultural uses, golf courses and related facilities, and public utilities.[18] The density of dwellings in rural districts generally must not exceed one per half acre, though variances may be granted for "good cause."[19] Although only a tiny fraction of state land is now classified as rural, this is changing as landowners take advantage of 2008 amendments to the Land Use Law and seek to reclassify agricultural land to rural for large-lot residential development projects. There is increasing state and county resistance to all but truly agricultural uses in the large agricultural district, following several long and costly lawsuits challenging residential use on land classified agricultural.[20]

Once so classified by the LUC, urban districts are wholly controlled by the counties; all uses permitted by county ordinances or zoning rules are permitted in urban districts.[21]

Conservation districts are specially protected by the state and are governed by the State Department of Land and Natural Resources (DLNR). The state seeks to "conserve, protect, and preserve the important natural resources of [Hawai'i] through appropriate management and use to promote their long-term sustainability and the public health, safety and welfare."[22] Consequently, virtually no structural development is permitted in the conservation district (except an occasional single-family house, as noted below), a change from the practice of the LUC in the 1960s and 1970s, when both a golf course and a college campus were developed on conservation district land.[23]

DLNR further divides the conservation district into subzones that permit different uses: (1) Protective; (2) Limited; (3) Resource; (4) General; or (5) Special.[24] The Protective subzone is intended to protect valuable watersheds, historic sites, and the ecosystems of native species.[25] A few activities, such as removing dead nonnative or small trees, do not require a permit (removing a hazardous tree, on the other hand, requires submitting documentation). Most uses, however, will require documentation of the need and/or a permit. Permitted uses include nature reserves and scenic areas; restoring fishponds; agriculture and a single-family residence when such a use was "historically, customarily, and actually found on the property"; public facilities such as transportation systems, water systems, and recreational facilities; and the maintenance, replacement, operation, and renovation of existing structures. Subdivision (not to be confused with residential development) may be approved when it "serves a public purpose and is consistent with the objectives of the [Protective] subzone."[26]

The Limited subzone is intended to prevent uses where "natural conditions suggest constraints on human activities" to prevent erosion, floods, or buildup in areas vulnerable to natural disasters.[27] It includes all the permitted land uses in the Protective category. Additional permitted land uses are a small amount (less than one acre) of agriculture with a permit, or a larger amount with both a permit and a management plan; botanical gardens, erosion control devices, landscaping, and single-family residences in floodplains or coastal high-hazard areas that conform to flood control regulations.[28]

The Resource subzone consists mainly of parkland, land suitable for lumber, and land suitable for recreational outdoor activities such as hiking and fishing, offshore islands, and sandy beach areas.[29] Permitted uses are astronomy facilities, commercial forestry, artificial reefs, mining, and single-family homes, in addition to the uses permitted in the Protective and Limited subzone.

The General subzone is dedicated to open space where no conservation uses are defined yet urban use is not desirable.[30] The subzone thus accommodates open space (but no golf courses) and other land uses "which are consistent with the objectives of the general subzone."[31] Finally, the Special subzone is for areas "possessing unique developmental qualities" complementary to natural resources in the surrounding area.[32] This classification allows a unique use on a specific site. Examples include Koko Head's Sea Life Park for recreational, education, and commercial purposes; Kāneʻohe's Haka site for cemetery purposes; and Honolulu's Kapakahi Ridge for nursing or convalescent home purposes.[33]

In agricultural and rural districts, a landowner who wishes to make use of the land for "certain unusual and reasonable uses" in a manner not enumerated by statute may petition for a special permit from the relevant county planning commission (for land under fifteen acres) or from both the county planning commission and the LUC (for land over fifteen acres).[34] Although the counties and the state share jurisdiction over land use in the rural and agricultural districts, it is each county's responsibility to enforce the State Land Use Law in both.[35] Alternatively, a conservation district landowner wishing to make any use of his or her land must submit a Conservation District Use Application (CDUA) to the Department of Land and Natural Resources.[36] The special permit and CDUA processes are described below. Besides permits, a landowner also has the option of requesting that his or her land be reclassified from one district to another (a so-called boundary amendment) or, within the conservation district, from one subzone to another, to allow for his or her proposed use. The Hawai'i Legislature has also enacted new legislation that fast-tracks and streamlines reclassification of agricultural land to the other districts in exchange for designating other land IAL. Finally, a landowner may petition the LUC for a "declaratory order" interpreting its rules regarding the permissible uses of the landowner's land. These processes are also described below.

The Special Use Permit Process

Within agricultural and rural districts, Hawai'i's Land Use Law specifically permits a landowner to seek a "special permit" for uses otherwise not permitted. The county planning commissions have jurisdiction over such special use permits—for "certain unusual and reasonable uses"— within these districts for parcels less than fifteen acres in size.[37] For parcels more than fifteen acres, or land designated IAL, special permits are subject to the approval of both the relevant county planning commission and the LUC.[38] Criteria for determining that a use is "unusual and reasonable" are the following: (1) The use is not contrary to the objectives of the LUC statute and administrative rules (which are not explicitly stated in the statute); (2) the use would not "adversely affect" surrounding property; (3) the use would not "unreasonably burden public agencies" to provide infrastructure such as roads and sewage systems; (4) whether "unusual conditions, trends, and needs have arisen since district boundaries and rules were established"; and (5) whether the land in question is "unsuited for the uses permitted within the district."[39] The state attorney general has also opined that the purpose of a special use permit is to "provide a landowner relief in exceptional situations that would not change the essential character of the district nor be inconsistent therewith, and is basically analogous to a variance."[40]

The fifth factor is illustrated by much land covered by lava flows being classified within the "agricultural" district, a classification theoretically designated for land with a "high capacity" for cultivation. In the agricultural district, special permits may be issued for land uses supporting ecotourism related to the preservation of threatened or endangered species. Moreover, although the counties generally prescribe uses in the rural district, there is one circumstance under which the LUC has jurisdiction: A landowner seeking a variance from the statutory minimum lot size requirement must also apply for a special permit from the LUC.[41]

To approve a special use permit, the relevant county planning commission must determine, by majority vote, that the use would promote the effectiveness and objectives of the land use statute.[42] The commission may impose conditions upon issuance of the special use permit— including, for example, time limits.[43] Overuse is discouraged, and the Hawai'i Supreme Court has specifically held that such permits may not be used to circumvent the need for a boundary amendment, particularly for large and intrusive projects.[44] However, the same Court permitted a golf course by special permit, even though the Land Use Law specifically forbade them in the agricultural district where the applicant planned to develop it.[45]

Several cases have further defined what is permitted under the Land Use Law. In *Curtis v. Board of Appeals*, a cellular phone tower was not considered a "communications equipment building" or a "utility line," both of which would be permitted uses of right in an agricultural district.[46] Noting that such an expansionary reading of the term "utility line" would frustrate the State Land Use Law's goals of protection and rational development, the Hawai'i Supreme Court found telecommunications towers and antennas "novel and unique use[s]" requiring a special permit absent enumeration in the statute.[47] Later, in *T-Mobile USA, Inc. v. County of Hawaii Planning Commission*, the Court allowed a "stealth antenna" concealed completely within a false chimney and with all related equipment kept in a garage.[48] In distinguishing from *Curtis*, the Court pointed out that the entire structure would be concealed in a chimney and garage— both structures being permitted uses—and that the concealed antenna would not undermine the State Land Use Law's objectives.[49]

The Conservation District Use Application Process

The DLNR controls uses within the conservation district, and in order for landowners to make use of their conservation land, they must go through the DLNR Conservation District Use Application (CDUA) permitting process. First, however, the owner must go through the county Special Management Area (SMA) review process (described more fully in chapter 8). The county must either determine (1) that the proposed land use is outside the SMA or (2) that the proposed land use is exempt. Otherwise, the landowner must include the SMA permit in the CDUA application. Next, the landowner must include basic information about himself, a description of the land, and plans for the proposed use, including maintenance and management plans, a filing fee, and a draft environmental assessment (briefly described in chapter 9) of the proposed use.

Finally, landowners must indicate for which of the following permits they are applying: (1) a departmental permit, (2) a board permit, (3) an emergency permit, (4) a temporary variance, (5) a nonconforming use, (6) a site plan approval, or (7) a management plan.[50] The type of permit required is determined by the subzone in which the land is located and the use proposed.[51] For example, a landowner with land in the protective subzone who wishes to post signs should apply for a site plan approval, while a landowner with land in the limited subzone who wishes to create botanical gardens must have a management plan in place and obtain a board permit.

A public hearing is required for any application involving land uses for commercial purposes, changes in identified uses, uses in the protective subzone, and proposed land uses affecting the public interest.[52] The applicant for a CDUA has the burden of demonstrating that the proposed land use will be "consistent with the purpose of the conservation district" and subzone in which the use will occur, that it will comply with Coastal Zone Management statutes and rules, will not cause "substantial adverse impact to existing natural resources" within the region or community but that it will at the very least preserve "natural beauty and open space characteristics" of the land, and that it will fulfill the general catch-all requirement that the proposed use not materially harm "public health, safety, and welfare."[53] Subdivision of land is not allowed to increase the "intensity" of land uses in the conservation district.[54]

Conservation District Subzone Reclassification

If the use to which a landowner wishes to put conservation land would otherwise be prohibited within the relevant subzone, the landowner may request to have the land reclassified to a subzone that permits the use.[55]

The conservation district subzone reclassification process requires the
landowner to propose an administrative rule change, which is processed
as an amendment to the DLNR's regulations.[56] To consider a reclassification request, the DLNR requires information on the landowner and
property, including geographic, climatic, hydrological, and biological
characteristics, as well as historic properties located in the area, scenic
or visual resources, infrastructure evaluations, and a review of the property's characteristics in relation to subzone objectives.[57]

District Boundary Amendment

A landowner denied a use within a designated district may petition
the LUC to reclassify the land into a more intensive use district—for
example, from conservation or agriculture to urban—through a District
Boundary Amendment (DBA). The LUC processes all DBAs for conservation land as well as for parcels larger than fifteen acres in urban, rural,
and agricultural districts. The relevant county planning commission
processes applications for DBAs of parcels less than fifteen acres in the
rural, urban, and agricultural districts. After proper notice and the filing of the petition and fees, the LUC holds a "contested case" hearing.[58]
Thus, DBAs are generally considered to be nonlegislative acts, though
whether such a conclusion would or should be applied to DBAs resulting from five-year reviews of state boundary classifications is dubious, as
this would reflect a policy determination of a more general nature than
a DBA petition.[59]

The LUC uses the following criteria in determining whether to
reclassify the subject land: whether reclassification is in accordance with
the goals, objectives, and policies of the Hawai'i State Plan (discussed
infra); district standards; impact upon habitat and historical, natural,
or cultural resources, particularly the cultural resources of the Native
Hawaiians;[60] consequences for natural resources relevant to Hawai'i's
economy; whether there is a commitment of state funds; employment
opportunities and economic development; housing opportunities for
all income levels; the county general plan and all community or community development plans relating to the land subject to the reclassification petition; and the representations and commitments made by
the petitioner.[61] The LUC must also closely scrutinize reclassifications
of intensively cultivated agricultural lands under the recently enacted
Important Agricultural Lands statute.[62] The LUC may approve the reclassification if it will not impair nearby agricultural production or is neces-

sary for urban growth. The overall standard for approving DBAs is, by a clear preponderance of the evidence, whether the DBA is reasonable, does not violate the statute that governs land districts, and is consistent with the Hawai'i State Plan.[63] Six affirmative votes from the nine-member LUC are necessary to approve a DBA, and the LUC may choose to impose conditions that run with the land. The LUC may impose sanctions for failing to observe conditions, including downzoning land to "uphold . . . the intent and spirit" of the statute and "assure substantial compliance with representations made by the petitioner."[64] Thus, for example, the LUC has threatened to return land classified urban to its former agricultural classification for failure of the landowner-developer to commence development in a timely manner.[65] Whether it may legally do so depends largely upon how one views the nature of the boundary amendments. Cases and commentators are by and large critical of such "rezonings" merely for failure to proceed with a particular project.[66]

The LUC approves most petitions for DBAs.[67] Every five years, the Office of Planning (OP) is required to review all DBAs in the state,[68] an obligation which it has rarely met, particularly in the past fifteen years; OP last undertook such a review in 1991. This lack of overall boundary review has probably contributed to the LUC's tendency to focus on individual parcels to the detriment of a statewide overview.

Several Hawai'i cases further interpret and elaborate upon the LUC's obligation under the Land Use Law. First, under *Kilauea Neighborhood Ass'n v. Land Use Commission*, the LUC must make specific findings with regard to each criterion for reclassifying district boundaries when approving a District Boundary Amendment.[69] Second, according to *Ka Paakai o ka Aina v. Land Use Commission*, in approving a DBA, the LUC must take into account the impact of reclassification on Native Hawaiian rights.[70] Specifically, the Hawai'i Supreme Court held that the LUC may not delegate to a landowner its constitutional and statutory obligation to protect Native Hawaiian customary rights and must make specific findings and conclusions regarding the following:

> (1) the identity and scope of valued cultural, historical, or natural resources in the petition area, including the extent to which traditional and customary native Hawaiian rights are exercised;
> (2) the extent to which those resources, including traditional and customary native Hawaiian rights, will be affected or impaired by the proposed action; and

(3) the feasible action, if any, to be taken by the [LUC] to reasonably protect native Hawaiian rights if they are found to exist.[71]

The *Ka Paakai o ka Aina* decision has been criticized for misunderstanding the responsibility of the LUC in the DBA process. A DBA provides a landowner with considerable discretion in future uses of the land, making it often impossible to so much as speculate about the effects of a DBA on Native Hawaiian—or any other—rights or resources, given the variety of possible uses of land that may result from such a DBA. Moreover, many such uses are impossible without county concurrence or approval.

Declaratory Orders

Any interested person may also petition the LUC to issue a declaratory order.[72] A declaratory order indicates how the LUC would interpret its own rules with regard to a particular parcel and use within it. After receiving a petition for a declaratory order, the LUC may deny the petition, issue a declaratory order, or set a hearing, which may or may not be of the contested case variety required for DBAs.[73] The LUC will not issue declaratory orders for questions that are speculative or hypothetical, for petitions in which the petitioner would not have standing in a judicial action, for questions affecting the interests of the LUC in pending litigation, or questions beyond the LUC's jurisdiction.[74]

Important Agricultural Lands

The State Legislature created a major new land subclassification, IAL, via amendments to the Land Use Law in 2005. Recognizing a "substantial interest" in the survival of the agricultural industry in Hawai'i, these amendments sought to provide incentives to landowners to preserve lands capable of producing high yields for agricultural purposes, even if the lands were not currently put to such use.[75] The designation is thus a carrot to landowners to preserve large blocks of contiguous fertile land from creeping urbanization and fragmentation. Among other stated aims, the law seeks to "ensure that uses on important agricultural lands are actually agricultural uses"[76] and attempts to avoid their development as large-lot residences with little actual agricultural use, as illustrated by the so-called fake farm phenomenon that brought luxury homes to lands designated for agriculture. The first IAL designation by the LUC occurred in March of 2009, when approximately 3,770 acres on Kaua'i owned by a subsidiary of Alexander & Baldwin were reclassified.

IAL designation criteria include whether the land is already used for farming, the quality of the soil, the sufficiency of water and infrastructure (including convenience of transportation of agricultural goods), and whether the land is associated with traditional Native Hawaiian agriculture, such as taro farming.[77] The designation is fairly flexible: An IAL candidate need not meet every criterion.[78] Indeed, a parcel meeting *any* of the criteria must receive "initial consideration."[79] The LUC also requires a certification issued by the Department of Agriculture as to the quality of the land to be designated IAL; at a minimum, the land must have "sufficient quantities of water to support viable agricultural production" and "contribute . . . to maintain[ing] a critical land mass important to agricultural productivity."[80]

The classification process begins with either (1) a petition from a landowner or (2) county action. A two-thirds majority of the LUC is required to designate lands IAL at the request of a landowner.[81] In the second category, the county must make designations based on maps and in consultation with landowners and various interest groups. The county departments must include the position of the owners of the land to be designated in their final recommendation, along with comments from other interest groups, the viability of existing agribusinesses, and its conformity with the criteria. The county council ultimately makes the decision, which is reviewed by the LUC.[82] Lands designated as IALs are eligible for incentive programs, including grant assistance, tax offsets, enhanced access to water, and agricultural training.[83]

IALs are subject to extra considerations and requirements for special use permits, rezoning, and district boundary amendments. Like land areas greater than fifteen acres, such actions pertaining to IALs require processing by both the LUC and the relevant county.[84] The state must find that the public benefit from the proposed action is justified by a need for additional land for nonagricultural purposes, that the action will not harm existing agricultural enterprises, and that the proposed action has "no significant impact upon the viability" of neighboring agricultural operations that may share marketing or infrastructure costs.[85] Absent a landowner request, the IAL designation may also be removed if, through no fault of the landowner, there is no longer a sufficient supply of water to allow profitable farming.[86] IAL maps must be reviewed at least once a decade, but not more often than once every five years.

In 2008, incentives to classify land as IAL commenced in earnest with the adoption of additional statutory amendments. The amendments enact the incentives noted above, expanding on the promised tax credits, providing for the state to guarantee loans by commercial lenders to agricultural producers, and mandating priority processing for agricultural permits. Moreover, the amendments allow the building of farm dwellings, but only if used exclusively by employees who actively work on the land and immediate family members. Such dwellings cannot occupy more than 5 percent of the total IAL or fifty acres, whichever is less. No residential subdivisions are permitted, but farmers may cluster dwellings together to preserve agricultural space. These portions of the 2008 amendments are uncontroversial.

Of greater importance to land use is a reclassification land swap: In exchange for landowner designation of large tracts of contiguous arable land, the LUC will by a declaratory order facilitate the reclassification of a smaller amount of agriculture district land to urban, conservation, rural, or a combination thereof. The land to be so reclassified need not be contiguous with the proposed IAL, though it must be in the same county. This reclassification may apply to up to 15 percent of the land; thus at least 85 percent of the land must be designated IAL. If landowners seek less than 15 percent of the land to be reclassified rural, urban, or conservation, they earn a "credit" for the difference. The credit is valid for ten years but may not be transferred to another person.[87]

Procedurally, a landowner petitioning to reclassify land IAL may, within that petition, seek the above-described land swap reclassification. The LUC will review the suitability of the reclassification to urban, rural, or conservation and may include "reasonable conditions" in the declaratory order.[88] If it fails to approve either reclassification—the IAL designation or the land swap designation—the petition is denied entirely.[89] Additionally, land swap reclassifications to the urban district must be consistent with the relevant county general development plan. What distinguishes the land swap from a more conventional DBA— besides a presumably greater propensity on the part of the LUC for approval—is that the new law contains no provision for a contested case hearing. This accelerates the reclassification process by avoiding the delays associated with the public review process otherwise required under the ordinary system for DBAs. Land swap reclassification approval is conditioned only upon meeting the suitability requirements and a two-thirds vote by the LUC.[90] The LUC possesses "the sole authority to interpret the adopted map boundaries delineating the [IAL]."[91] Of course, land so reclassified is still subject to permitting requirements associated with the reclassified district, county plans, and county zoning restrictions.

Land use is restricted by more than just district boundaries, however. State agencies making land use decisions must conform their rulings to the overall theme, goals, objectives, and policies of the comprehensive State Plan, enacted as a statute.

Act 100: The State Plan as Law

Hawai'i is unique among the fifty states in having converted its State General Plan into a statute—Act 100—which made it the first state to enact a comprehensive state plan. The writing of the plan into the statutory code transformed what is in most states a policy document into a set of preeminent legal requirements.[92] Its passage by the Ninth State Legislature in 1978 represented not only a milestone for the state—indeed, the governor ranked it second only to the State Constitution in importance—but also for the nation.[93] Moreover, a State Land Use Law amendment to LUC standards for deciding boundary amendments—providing no such boundary amendment can be adopted unless it is in conformance with the State Plan—adds considerably to the State Plan's legal significance in Hawai'i.[94]

The State Plan

The culmination of efforts having begun in 1975, the State Plan is the product of three years of intense work by the Department of Planning and Economic Development (now the Department of Business, Economic Development & Tourism (DBEDT)) that included an inventory of goals, objectives, and policies; a statewide household survey; technical studies; issue papers; public workshops and hearings; the creation of a policy council; and intense lobbying in the legislature. Its major areas of concentration were the following: population; the economy (tourism, defense and other federal spending, the sugar and pineapple industries, diversified agriculture, and potential new areas such as motion picture production); the physical environment; facility systems (water supply, transportation, energy, public utility facilities, solid and liquid waste disposal); and sociocultural advancement (housing, health, education, social services, leisure activities, public safety, and cultural heritage).

The Hawai'i State Plan is divided into three major parts: overall theme, goals, objectives, and policies; planning coordination and implementation; and priority guidelines.[95] The Findings and Purposes statement of the act sets out the rationale for the plan:[96]

> The legislature finds that there is need to improve the planning process in this State, to increase the effectiveness of government and private actions, to improve coordination among different agencies and levels of government, to provide for wise use of Hawai'i's resources and to guide the future development of the State.[97]

> The purpose of this chapter is to set forth the Hawai'i state plan that shall serve as a *guide* for the future long-range development of the State; identify the goals, objectives, policies and priorities for the State; *provide a basis* for determining priorities and allocating limited resources, such as public funds, services, human resources, land, energy, water, and other resources; improve coordination of federal, state, and county plans, policies, programs, projects, and regulatory activities; and to establish a system for plan formulation and program coordination to provide for an integration of all major state, and county activities.[98]

The all-important implementation strategy is accomplished through several mechanisms. To begin, a policy council of state, county, and public representatives was established to advise the legislature and reconcile conflicts between the agencies and plans described below. DBEDT provides technical assistance to the policy council, particularly by performing statewide policy analysis and reviewing recommendations on all State Plan matters. Twelve state functional plans[99] define, implement, and conform to the overall theme, goals, objectives, policies, and priority guidelines of the State Plan.[100] County general plans (general and development) must indicate desired population and physical development patterns for each county and regions within the county and further define the overall theme, goals, objectives, policies, and priority guidelines of the State Plan.[101] State programs must conform to both the State Plan (and apply its priority guidelines) and to approved state functional plans.[102] Therefore, while the county general plans must *take into account* state functional plans and vice versa, both functional plans and county general plans must *conform* to the State

Plan.[103] Finally, priority guidelines address areas of statewide concern.[104] For example,

> Protect and enhance Hawai'i's shoreline open spaces and scenic resources.[105]

> Utilize Hawai'i's limited land resources wisely, providing adequate land to accommodate projected population and economic growth needs while insuring the protection of the environment and the availability of the shoreline, conservation lands and other limited resources for future generations.[106]

> Encourage urban growth primarily to existing urban areas where adequate public facilities are already available or can be provided with reasonable public expenditures, and away from areas where other important benefits are present, such as protection of important agricultural land or preservation of lifestyles.[107]

That part of the State Plan dealing with implementation—and especially conformance—is the most significant for the purpose of land use control. This is so because the State Plan in theory requires "conformance" to its policies, goals, objectives, and priority guidelines across virtually the whole spectrum of state land use actions. However, in 1984 the legislature defined "conformance" as a weighing of the overall theme, goals, objectives, and policies and a determination that an action, decision, rule, or state program is both consistent with the overall theme and fulfills one or more of the goals, objectives, or policies.[108] Under this new definition, conformance becomes relatively easy to accomplish—and nearly impossible to contest. This is particularly true now that the term "guidelines" has replaced "directions" in "statutory directions." "Guidelines" now means merely a "stated course of action which is desirable and should be followed unless a determination is made that it is not the most desirable in a particular case; thus a guideline *may be deviated from without penalty or sanction.*"[109]

STATE ACTIVITIES

Nevertheless, the State Plan requires that all state programs be in conformance with its theme, goals, objectives, policies, and priority guidelines as well as with its twelve functional plans: "The formulation, administration, and implementation of state programs shall be in conformance with the overall theme, goals, objectives, and policies and shall utilize as guidelines the priority guidelines contained within this chapter, and the state functional plans approved pursuant to this chapter."[110] These state programs include but are not limited to those programs involving coordination and review; research and support; design, construction, and maintenance; services; and regulatory powers.[111] State programs that exercise coordination and review functions include but are not limited to the state clearinghouse process, the capital improvements program, and the Coastal Zone Management program. State programs that exercise regulatory powers in resource allocation include but are not limited to the land use and management programs administered by the Land Use Commission and Board of Land and Natural Resources.[112] State programs "shall further define, implement, and be in conformance with the overall theme, goals, objectives, and policies, and shall utilize as guidelines both the priority guidelines contained within this chapter, and the state functional plans approved pursuant to [the statute]."[113]

Certain programs relating to budget review and land use control are particularly singled out as "implementation mechanisms" for conformance with the overall theme, State Plan goals, objectives, and policies. These are program appropriations, capital improvement project (CIP) appropriation, budgetary review and allocation, "land use decision-making processes of state agencies" (such as the LUC and the Board of DLNR) and "all other regulatory and administrative decision-making processes of state agencies."[114] Thus, the state's major land use decision-making body—the LUC—is to some extent bound by the State Plan and its subordinate functional plans in land reclassification (e.g., DBA) decisions. The State Land Use Law provides decision-making criteria—such as the "extent to which the proposed reclassification conforms" to the State Plan—that the LUC must consider in making DBA decisions.[115] A more detailed look at these statutory guidelines is discussed supra in the section on the DBA process.

THE FUNCTIONAL PLANS

While broad policies are sketched in the State Plan, it is the functional plans to which state and county agencies were originally to look for guidance. The State Plan provides for the preparation of twelve such plans addressing different policy areas: education, employment, health, housing, human services, agriculture, conservation lands, energy, historic preservation, recreation, tourism, and transportation.[116] Ten plans were adopted in 1984 by concurrent resolution.[117] Five plans were revised in 1989,[118] and seven plans were revised in 1991.[119] The functional plans must define, implement, and conform to the overall theme, goals, objectives, policies, and priority guidelines contained within the statute.[120] In the same paragraph, Act 100 directs that "county general plans and development plans shall be taken into consideration in the formulation of state functional plans."[121] The State Plan also sets out basic requirements for the functional plans: "The functional plan shall identify priority issues in the functional area and shall contain objectives, policies, and implementing actions to address those priority issues."[122]

Originally, the responsibility for preparing each functional plan was assigned to named state agencies such as the DLNR and the former DPED, but the duty of maintaining and creating guidelines for the revisions of the functional plans was transferred back to the Hawai'i Office of Planning from the Department of Budget and Finance in 2001.[123] The State Functional Plans have "languished" since they were last updated in 1991.[124]

All the State Functional Plans have the same framework. Each plan has three chapters. Chapter I, the first five or so pages of each plan, is an introduction and is largely the same in each State Functional Plan. It follows a basic introduction with the purpose, role, theme, advisory committee, and review, revision, and coordination processes of the State Functional Plans. Chapter II addresses the approach to the specific functional plan's issues. It consists of a long-term philosophy statement, an overview of the specific functional plan, the objectives and scope of the functional plan, the coordination of the specific functional plan with other State Functional Plans, and the issue areas addressed in the functional plan.[125]

For example, in the State Conservation Lands Functional Plan (SCLFP),[126] Chapter II articulates the overall theme and goals of the Hawai'i State Plan, describes how further growth in the population and economy of Hawai'i is inevitable but must be balanced with Hawai'i's need to minimize the negative effects on the natural environment, and states what must be done to meet these statewide concerns. The brief overview indicates that the plan addresses issues concerning the aquaculture industry and continued efforts to broaden public use of natural resources and lands, while protecting and preserving land from overuse. The objective of the SCLFP is to provide for a management program balancing the use and protection of the state's natural resources. The majority of the responsibility lies with the state, although federal,

private, and county assistance will also play roles. The SCLFP is closely
related to other State Functional Plans that are concerned with the use
of natural resources and/or environmental protection, including the
Energy, Health, Historic Preservation, and Recreation Plans. These
plans include many complementary as well as competing interests. The
plan is then divided into three issue areas directly related to planning
and management: (I) inventories of resources and background information and basic research; (II) management; and (III) education and
public information.

Chapter III is the bulk of each functional plan. This chapter is
particularly significant, as it declares the objectives, policies, and implementing actions of the functional plan. Each issue area listed in Chapter
III has several main objectives. Each objective has multiple related policies, and each policy has one or more corresponding implementation
actions. For instance, in Chapter III of the State Conservation Lands
Functional Plan, Issue Area I is first stated. Then the first of two objectives of Issue Area I is listed: establishment of databases for inventories
of existing lands and resources. It is followed by the first of five policies within the section: Develop and maintain a centralized statewide
database of conservation areas and natural resources. A corresponding implementation action is then stated: Develop a centralized land
inventory and natural resource database in conjunction with the State
Geographic Information System. A lead organization, assisting organizations, a start date, a total budget estimate, a target location, and comments are set forth with each implementing action.

County Plans

Finally, county general plans and development plans are integrated
with State Functional Plans. These plans "shall further define the overall theme, goals, objectives, policies, and priority guidelines" of the
State Plan,[127] and the formulation, amendment, and implementation of
such plans "shall *take into consideration* statewide objectives, polices, and
programs stipulated in state functional plans."[128] This directive is particularly critical to the county land use regulatory scheme, since most
county land use control schemes are tied so directly to their general or
development plans that land use changes made contrary to those plans
are invalid. Thus, for example, in the City and County of Honolulu City
Charter, a provision requires all local zoning and subdivision ordinances
to conform to local development plans.[129]

All of these detailed development plan elements must further define the provisions of the State Plan and take into consideration state-wide objectives, policies, and programs stipulated in State Functional Plans approved in consonance with this chapter. County general plans and the more detailed development plans are to (1) be formulated with input from the state and county agencies as well as the general public, (2) take into consideration the State Functional Plans, and (3) be formulated on the basis of sound rationale, data, analyses, and input from the state and county agencies and the general public.[130] This would be, for example, where a county council's findings stated that studies were made, public hearings were held, field investigations were conducted, public testimony was considered, and findings were made that the amendment to the development plan was consistent with policies and objectives of the development and general plans, and that the ordinance did not violate the State Planning Act requirement that county development plans be formulated with input from state and county agencies and the general public and on the basis of sound rationale, data, and analyses.[131] However, Act 100 also makes its own specific requirements with respect to both the manner of formulation and the contents of county general and development plans, providing that any amendment to the county general plan of each county shall not be contrary to the county charter.[132]

While there have been no substantive amendments to the state planning system or its plans since the 1990s, a Hawai'i 2050 task force was established to review the State Plan and other fundamental components of community planning and to develop recommendations on creating the Hawai'i 2050 sustainability plan for future long-term development of the state.[133] The Hawai'i 2050 Sustainability Plan was submitted for review in early 2008.[134] Paralleling the studies that went into the process to develop the State Plan, the goals are divided into the economy, the physical environment, and physical, social, and economic well-being.[135]

The Sustainability Plan is advisory only, but it contains a number of specific goals and proposals. It proposes an implementing entity, "the Sustainability Council," a nonregulatory body that would "promote sustainability, determine intermediate and long-term benchmarks, measure success, coordinate cross-sector efforts and dialogue, and report to government and private sector leaders on progress."[136] The plan purports to provide "over-arching State goals" to guide the counties in developing sustainable practices. Of the nine "priority actions" for which the plan suggested benchmarks, two have major implications for land use: (1) increasing affordable housing; the plan estimates that

between 2007 and 2011, there is a need for 23,000 affordable housing units; and (2) increasing production of local foods and products.[137]
The state's use of incentive programs and regulations to encourage
agriculture will likely continue to have land use implications for the
foreseeable future.

Hawai'i's land use system and complicated interlocking planning
schemes are still evolving. The release of the Hawai'i 2050 Sustainability
Plan, though it speaks mainly in generalities, is the first return to comprehensive state planning since the early 1980s. The Sustainability Plan
may mark the beginning of a revival of state comprehensive planning.
Recent legislation reveals a renewed interest in land use issues by the
State Legislature and a willingness to try new ideas. The agricultural
land swap scheme promises new opportunities for rational development
of Hawai'i's islands.

Notes

1. HAW. REV. STAT. § 205-2(a) (2008). For a brief overview of the Land Use
Law and its districts, see David Kimo Frankel, *Protecting Paradise: A Citizen's Guide to
Land & Water Use Controls in Hawaii*, Kailua: Dolphin Printing & Publishing, 1997 at
407.
2. HAW. REV. STAT. § 205-2(a)(1).
3. Id. § 205-2(a)(2).
4. Id. § 205-2(a)(3).
5. Id. §§ 205-2(a)(4), -2(e).
6. HAW. CODE R. § 13-5-10 (Weil 2005).
7. *See* State of Hawai'i, Department of Business, Economic Development &
Tourism, *State of Hawai'i Data Book 2007* (2008) at table 6.04. Land classified as rural
may increase as landowners increasingly use it for small residential estates formerly
permitted in the agricultural district.
8. *Kelly v. 1250 Oceanside Partners*, Civ. No. 00-1-0192K (D. Haw. Sept. 9, 2003)
(Findings of Fact, Conclusions of Law, Order Regarding Trial on Count IV of the
Fifth Amended Complaint); *Kelly v. 1250 Oceanside Partners*, Civ. No. 00-1-0192K (D.
Haw. Mar. 14, 2006) (Fourth Amended Final Judgment). The litigation was settled
by the parties before the Hawai'i Supreme Court had the opportunity to rule on the
lawfulness of such residential development and the meaning of "farm dwelling."
9. HAW. REV. STAT. § 205-2(d) (2008).
10. Id. §§ 205-2(d)(7), -4.5.
11. Id. § 205-4.5(a)(12).
12. Id. § 205-4.5(b).
13. Id. § 205-4.5(f).
14. See, for example, the factual context in *Save Sunset Beach Coal. v. City &
County of Honolulu*, 102 Haw. 465, 78 P.3d 1 (2003).
15. HAW. REV. STAT. 205-4.5(d) (2008).

16. Rory Flynn, "Seeing through the fog of 'fake farms,'" HAW. REP., Jan. 30, 2007, http://www.hawaiireporter.com (type "Fog of Fake Farms" into the search box) (last visited Jan. 13, 2010). *See also* Adrienne Suarez, Comment, "Avoiding the next Hokulia: The debate over Hawaii's agricultural subdivisions," 27 U. HAW. L. REV. 441 (2005). For a decidedly contrary view, see Nathan Roehrig, Comment, "Urban type residential communities in the guise of agricultural subdivisions," 25 U. HAW. L. REV. 199 (2002).

17. HAW. REV. STAT. § 205-2(d) (2008). *See* Norman Cheng, Comment, "Is agricultural land in Hawaii 'ripe' for a takings analysis?" 24 U. HAW. L. REV. 121 (2001).

18. HAW. REV. STAT. § 205-5(c) (2008).

19. Id.

20. *See Kelly,* supra note 8; *Save Sunset Beach,* supra note 14.

21. HAW. CODE R. § 15-15-24 (Weil 2005).

22. HAW. REV. STAT. § 183C-1 (2008).

23. Madalyn Purcell, Comment, "Residential use of Hawaii's conservation district," 14 U. HAW. L. REV. 633 (1992).

24. HAW. CODE R. § 13-5-10(b) (Weil 2005).

25. Id. § 13-5-11.

26. Id. § 13-5-22.

27. Id. § 13-5-12.

28. Id. § 13-5-23.

29. Id. § 13-5-15.

30. Id. § 13-5-14.

31. Id. § 13-5-25.

32. Id. § 13-5-15.

33. Id. at Ex. 2.

34. HAW. REV. STAT. § 205-6 (2008).

35. Id. § 205-12, Opinion of the Attorney General 70-22. *See also County of Hawaii v. Ala Loop Homeowners,* 120 Haw. 256, 203 P.3d 676 (2009).

36. HAW. CODE R. § 13-5-30(b) (Weil 2005).

37. HAW. REV. STAT. § 205-6 (2008).

38. HAW. CODE R. § 15-15-95 (Weil 2005).

39. Id. § 15-15-95(b).

40. HAW. REV. STAT. § 205-6 (2008), Opinion of the Attorney General 63-37; *Neighborhood Bd. No. 24 (Waianae Coast) v. State Land Use Comm'n,* 64 Haw. 265, 639 P.2d 1097 (1982) (recognizing the undesirability of "unlimited use of the special permit to effectuate essentially what amounts to a boundary change" that "would undermine the protection from piecemeal changes to the zoning scheme guaranteed landowners by the more extensive procedural protections of boundary amendment statutes").

41. HAW. REV. STAT. § 205-2(c) (2008).

42. Id. § 205-6(c) (2008).

43. Id.; HAW. CODE R. §§ 15-15-95, -96 (Weil 2005).

44. *Neighborhood Bd. No. 24,* supra note 40.

45. *Mahaulepu v. Land Use Comm'n,* 71 Haw. 332, 790 P.2d 906 (1990); *see* Douglas Ushijima, Note, "*Mahaulepu v. Land Use Comm'n*: A symbol of change; Hawaii's

Land Use Law allows golf course development on prime agricultural land by special use permit," 13 U. Haw. L. Rev. 205 (1991).

46. *Curtis v. Bd. of Appeals*, 90 Haw. 384, 978 P.2d 822 (1999); Haw. Rev. Stat. § 205-4.5(a)(6) (2008).

47. *Curtis*, supra note 46 at 397, 978 P.2d at 835.

48. *T-Mobile USA, Inc. v. County of Haw. Planning Comm'n*, 106 Haw. 343, 351, 104 P.3d 930, 938 (2005).

49. Id. at 354, 104 P.3d at 941.

50. Haw. Code R. § 13-5-30(b) (Weil 2005).

51. Id.§ 13-5-30(c).

52. Id. § 13-5-40.

53. Id. § 13-5-30(c).

54. Id. § 13-5-30(c)(7).

55. Id. § 13-5-16(a).

56. Id. § 13-5-16(c).

57. Id. § 13-5-16(b).

58. *See Town v. Land Use Comm'n*, 55 Haw. 538, 524 P.2d 84 (1974).

59. *See*, e.g., *Fasano v. Bd. of County Comm'rs of Wash. County*, 507 P.2d 23 (Or. 1973).

60. *See Ka Paakai o ka Aina v. Land Use Comm'n*, 94 Haw. 31, 7 P.3d 1068 (2000).

61. Haw. Rev. Stat. § 205-17 (2008).

62. Id. § 205-41.

63. Id. §§ 205-4, -16.

64. Id. § 205-4(g); *see also Lanai Co. v. Land Use Comm'n*, 105 Haw. 296, 97 P.3d 372 (2004).

65. Taylor Hall, "Big Island project may get second chance," Honolulu Advertiser, June 6, 2009, at B-5.

66. *See*, e.g., *Scrutton v. County of Sacramento*, 79 Cal. Rptr. 872 (Ct. App. 1969). *See also* the much-critical Illinois case of *Goffinet v. County of Christian*, 356 N.E.2d 442 (Ill. 1976).

67. Comment of Don Davidson, chief exec. officer, Land Use Comm'n (Nov. 10, 2008).

68. Haw. Rev. Stat. § 205-18 (2008).

69. *Kilauea Neighborhood Ass'n v. Land Use Comm'n*, 7 Haw. App. 227, 751 P.2d 1031 (1988).

70. *Ka Paakai*, supra note 60.

71. Id. at 47, 7 P.3d at 1084.

72. Haw. Code R. § 15-15-98(a) (Weil 2005).

73. Id. § 15-15-100.

74. Id. § 15-15-102.

75. Haw. Rev. Stat. § 205-41 (2008).

76. Id. § 205-43.

77. Id. § 205-44(c).

78. Id. § 205-44(a).

79. Id.

80. Id. § 205-44(c)(5), (7).

81. Haw. Const. art. XI, § 3 (requiring a two-thirds majority for reclassification or rezoning action).

82. Haw. Rev. Stat. §§ 205-47, -49 (2008).

83. Id. § 205-46.

84. Id. § 205-3.1.

85. Id. § 205-50.

86. Id. § 205-50(g).

87. Id. § 205-45(h)(2).

88. Id. § 205-45(e).

89. Id.

90. Id. § 205-45(e)(3).

91. Id. § 205-49(c).

92. *See* Todd W. Eddins and Jerilynn S. Ono Hall, "*Kaiser Hawaii Kai Development Co. v. City and County of Honolulu*: Zoning by initiative in Hawaii," 12 U. Haw. L. Rev. 181 (1990) (analyzing the Hawai'i Supreme Court's ruling, where the Court held that initiative proposals adopted by the electorate to downzone two tracts of land from residential to preservation were invalid, and the impact of the decision on the future of zoning by initiative).

93. George R. Ariyoshi, *Hawaii 2050*, Haw. Bus., May 2006, http://www.hawaiibusiness.com/Hawaii-Business/May-2006/Hawaii-2050/ (last visited Dec. 14, 2009).

94. Haw. Rev. Stat. § 205-16 (2008).

95. Id. §§ 226-2, -51, -101.

96. *See* Lynton Keith, "The Hawaii State Plan revisited," 7 U. Haw. L. Rev. 29 (1985) (reviewing the origin and content of the State Plan, the State Plan process, the amendments to the State Plan made by the 1984 State Legislature, and the uses of the plan); Michael B. Dowling and Joseph A. Fadrowsky III, "*Dolan v. City of Tigard*: Individual property rights v. land management systems," 17 U. Haw. L. Rev. 193 (1995) (analyzing relevant parts of the *Dolan* Court's reasoning for its decision and examination of a "new" test for exactions and surveying the initial response to *Dolan* by various federal and state courts and endeavors to predict the impact of the decision of future litigation, especially within the context of the land management system in Hawai'i); Alan F. Smith, "Uniquely Hawaii: A property professor looks at Hawaii's Land Law," 7 U. Haw. L. Rev. 1 (1985).

97. Haw. Rev. Stat. § 226-1 (2008).

98. Id.

99. State Functional Plans include education, employment, health, housing, human services, agriculture, conservation lands, energy, historic preservation, recreation, tourism, and transportation. The ten plans that were adopted in 1984 differ from the current twelve plans.

100. Haw. Rev. Stat. § 226-52(a)(3) (2008).

101. Id. § 226-52(a)(4).

102. Id. § 226-59.

103. Id. §§ 226-55, -52(a)(4).

104. Id. § 226-101.

105. Id. § 226-104(b)(13).

106. Id. § 226-104(b)(12).

107. Id. § 226-104(b)(1).
108. Id. § 226-2.
109. Id.
110. Id. § 226-59.
111. Id. § 226-52(a)(5).
112. Id.
113. Id. § 226-52(a)(5).
114. Id. § 226-52(b)(2).
115. Id. § 205-17.
116. Information obtained from the State of Hawai'i Office of Planning, June 2, 2006.
117. Plans adopted in 1984 include conservation lands, energy, higher education, health, historic preservation, housing, recreation, tourism, transportation, and water resources development. Since the amendments, water resources development is no longer a functional plan.
118. Plans that were revised in 1989 are education, employment, health, housing, and human services.
119. Plans that were revised in 1991 are agriculture, conservation lands, energy, historic preservation, recreation, tourism, and transportation.
120. HAW. REV. STAT. § 226-52(a)(3) (2008).
121. Id.
122. Id. § 226-55(b).
123. Hawai'i Sustainability Task Force, "Hawai'i 2050 Sustainability Plan: Charting a course for Hawai'i's sustainable future" (2008) at 83, *available at* http://www. hawaii2050.org/images/uploads/Hawaii2050_Plan_FINAL.pdf (last visited Dec. 16, 2009) (hereinafter "Hawai'i 2050 Sustainability Plan").
124. Id.
125. Some functional plans, such as the Historic Preservation State Functional Plan (1991), do not have an overview, objectives and scope section, or a section on the coordination with other State Functional Plans, in Chapter II. However, all State Functional Plans have the long-term philosophy statement and a main section on what issues are addressed in the specific functional plan.
126. State of Hawai'i, Department of Land and Natural Resources, *The Hawaii State Plan: Conservation Lands State Functional Plan* (1991) (in accordance with section 226 of the Hawaii Revised Statutes).
127. HAW. REV. STAT. § 226-52(a)(4) (2008).
128. Id. § 226-58(a). *See also Lum Yip Kee Ltd. v. City & County of Honolulu*, 70 Haw. 179, 767 P.2d 815 (1989), where the City Council's action in amending development plans was consistent with policies and objectives of State Functional Plans, the ordinance did not violate the State Planning Act requirement that counties "take into consideration state functional plans in formulating and amending development plans." For an extended discussion of the relationship between county, general, and development plans in a different context, see David L. Callies and Calvert G. Chipchase, "Water regulation, land use and the environment," 30 U. HAW. L. REV. 49 (2007).
129. HONOLULU, HAW., REV. ORDINANCES § 6-1511 (2001).

130. HAW. REV. STAT. § 226-2 (2008); *Kaiser Hawaii Kai Dev. Co. v. City & County of Honolulu*, 777 P.2d 244 (Haw. 1989).

131. HAW. REV. STAT. § 226-58 (2008); *Lum Yip Kee*, supra note 128.

132. HAW. REV. STAT. § 226-58(a) (2008).

133. 2050 Sustainability Plan for Hawaii, Act 8, 2005 Haw. Laws 1st Sp. Sess. (effective July 1, 2005); HAW. REV. STAT. § 226-1 (2008).

134. Hawai'i 2050 Sustainability Plan, supra note 133.

135. HAW. REV. STAT. § 226-4 (2008).

136. Hawai'i 2050 Sustainability Plan, supra note 133 at 3.

137. Id. at 63–67.

Chapter 2

Local Planning and Zoning

> Zoning reached puberty in company with the Stutz Bearcat
> and the speakeasy. F. Scott Fitzgerald and the Lindy Hop
> were products of the same generation. Of all these phe-
> nomena of the twenties, only zoning has remained viable a
> generation later.
>
> —Babcock, *The Zoning Game*[1]

Although the legal and planning literature of the 1970s was filled
with gleeful requiems for local zoning, the "ancien régime" of land use
controls is not only alive but increasingly robust even after decades of
neglect.[2] Local zoning never really declined except in the perception
of commentators on the land use scene. Cities—where the vast majority of people live and work and where, therefore, land use decisions
most directly affect the public's way of life—never abandoned zoning.[3]
While states and federal agencies may have promoted, often successfully, regional and statewide land use management and control systems
as an added—sometimes even superseding—layer of control upon local
governments, these were in addition to rather than a substitute for local
zoning. In a sense, then, the ancien régime was not overthrown but
circumscribed—applied to urban areas, addressing primarily local concerns—with the exception of Hawai'i, which chose to zone the entire
state in 1961 through its Land Use Law.

The history of zoning nationally is adequately treated in a number
of articles, books, and treatises,[4] appearing to have sprung from the
need to uniformly control nuisance and, whether or not concomitantly,
to protect property values.[5] It first appeared in recognizable form during the latter part of the nineteenth century and in the early part of
the twentieth, although its antecedents precede the beginnings of the
United States. Its efficacy could have been blunted by an unexpected
linkage between regulation and taking in the 1922 case of *Pennsylvania
Coal Co. v. Mahon*, in which the U.S. Supreme Court held that a regulation, if it went too far, could result in a "taking" under the Fifth Amendment to the U.S. Constitution, for which compensation would have to

be paid.[6] "Taking" in this context means the regulation of land so heavily that the owner is left with virtually no permissible uses; this "regulatory taking" issue continues to bedevil land use regulation.[7] However, a few years later, in the landmark *Euclid* case, the U.S. Supreme Court ultimately held that the dividing of a city or village into use zones and the permitting or prohibiting of various uses and classes of uses therein were constitutional,[8] though such zoning as applied in a given case might be found unconstitutional.[9] Thereafter, zoning swept the country, spreading to every major city in the United States.[10] By 1930, forty-seven states had adopted zoning enabling legislation in accordance with the federal Standard Zoning Enabling Act, and 981 municipalities, representing 67 percent (or 46 million) of our urban population, had adopted the zoning ordinance as the latest and most useful technique to control the use of land.[11]

The Basics of Zoning

As the *Euclid* case made abundantly clear, while the so-called fact basis of zoning may well have as its aim the abatement of nuisance and protection of property, zoning is firmly rooted in police power—the power to regulate for the protection of the health, safety, morals, and welfare of the people.[12] In most jurisdictions, including Hawai'i, that power is delegated from the state—the repository of police power—to units of local government through a zoning enabling act. The act is usually based on the Standard Zoning Enabling Act produced by the U.S. Department of Commerce in 1926. Such acts permit but do not require local governments to divide the land area in their jurisdictions into districts (or zones) and to list permitted uses, permitted height and density (known as bulk regulations), and conditional uses for each. The map upon which the districts are drawn is called the "zoning map," a copy of which must usually be kept in the offices of the local government unit, to be marked with each change in district boundaries and each exception or variance granted.

The lists of uses, bulk regulations, definitions, administrative procedures, and so forth are collectively called the "text." The map and text are used in tandem; each zoning district on the map has a corresponding list of permitted uses within the text. The list of permitted uses, including permitted accessory, temporary, and special or conditional uses, is exhaustive. An accessory use might be a garage, while a temporary use may refer to a fruit stand or construction shed. A special or conditional use is one permitted in a district but only subject to certain articulated conditions. For example, a neighborhood grocery may be permitted in a residential area provided it is screened, has no electric signs, and is open only at certain hours. The point of imposing such conditions is to preserve the character of the area, minimizing the negative side effects of otherwise necessary or desirable uses. Each district also has a set of bulk regulations limiting, for example, the size of the lot per unit, the permitted height of principal and accessory structures, minimum yard requirements, and off-street parking and loading requirements.

There are essentially three broad categories of uses—residential, commercial, and industrial—though "mixed use" and "overlay" districts are increasingly common as well. Except for such mixed use areas, districts are generally categorically exclusive: Homes are not permitted in commercial or industrial districts, factories are not permitted in residential or commercial districts, and so forth. The districts theoretically follow a use-intensity pattern, so that low-density residential uses do not abut industrial or even intensive commercial uses. Thus, a ring of garden or medium-rise apartment buildings in a high-density residential zone might appropriately separate single-family homes in a low-density residential zone from a shopping center, as they do in Honolulu's Mānoa Valley around the Mānoa Marketplace.

There is also a section in the text treating uses that were permitted as of some past date but fail to conform to the existing land use regulations for the district, called collectively "nonconformities." Most courts have held that it is an unconstitutional confiscation of property to require the immediate termination of what had previously been a lawful use of property after a zoning change renders that use prohibited in that district. Some jurisdictions, including Hawai'i, use "amortization"— the termination of a nonconforming use after the end of an arbitrarily determined useful life.[13] Local governments employ this technique most often in eliminating low-investment nonconforming uses, such as signs and billboards, or to terminate what they consider particularly noxious uses, such as junkyards.

Finally, there are administrative regulations setting out how the zoning ordinance restrictions on a particular parcel of land may be changed. The principal agencies for administration of a local zoning ordinance are (1) a zoning officer or administrator, (2) the zoning board of appeals, (3) the local legislative body, and (4) the planning commission.

The zoning administrator is generally responsible for seeing that the provisions of the zoning ordinance are carried out. He receives complaints of violations and issues zoning certificates if so required by ordinance. He also grants or denies certain special use requests. In Honolulu, that officer is the director of the Department of Planning and Permitting (DPP). The zoning administrator's decisions may be appealed to a board of appeals, alternatively known as a zoning board of adjustment. Generally, this board also hears all requests for variances or exceptions from the terms of the zoning ordinance (except in Honolulu, where, by charter amendment, the DPP director hears and decides all variances). The local legislative body is responsible for enacting the zoning ordinance in its original form (usually upon recommendation of a zoning commission appointed for the purpose) and for adopting amendments. Amendments, usually reviewed first by a recommending body such as the planning commission, take two forms: textual and map. The latter, in which land is reclassified ("rezoned") from one district to another, is by far the most common. Finally, a planning commission, an appointed body, is constituted for the purpose of advising on the planning aspects of land use changes. The commission usually reviews requests for amendments and special uses, reviews (and in some cases approves) subdivision plats, holds public hearings, and occasionally provides planning recommendations on variance and special or conditional use requests.

The Place of Planning in Land Use Controls

In theory at least, land use regulations should follow comprehensive planning. Indeed, such was the original philosophy behind zoning in the United States. In 1928, the U.S. Department of Commerce promulgated the Standard City Planning Enabling Act, which contemplated the establishment of a planning commission for each adopting city, whose duty it was to produce a "master plan"—a comprehensive scheme of development—for the physical development of the city. However, the plan was to be advisory to the governing body of the city.[14] The statutes of many states permit the formulation of such a plan by a planning board or commission. Many of these same states then require its adoption by local legislative bodies. A few (e.g., Hawai'i, California, Oregon, Florida) require conformance to these plans once they are adopted.

However, not many court decisions have advanced the cause of mandatory planning before zoning. While observing that good planning is important as a requisite or even a prerequisite to effective land use controls, the judiciary has often interpreted planning requirements so broadly as to make them nearly meaningless. The following New Jersey court's characterization of the plan-zoning ordinance link is typical: "No doubt good housekeeping would be served if a zoning ordinance followed and implemented a master plan . . . but the history of the subject dictated another course. . . . A plan may be readily revealed in an end-product—here the zoning ordinance—and no more is required by statute."[15] Given such interpretations, comprehensive planning is often advisory.

The Enabling Act

The state enabling legislation grants to Hawai'i's four counties the power to zone, primarily as a tool to implement "a long-range comprehensive general plan prepared or being prepared to guide the overall future development of the county."[16] The manner and method of administration and enforcement is left wholly to the discretion of the counties, except that nonconforming uses may be terminated only through amortization and then only in commercial, industrial, apartment, and resort districts.[17] As noted above, amortization of nonconformities has been upheld in several states, provided the period after which the use must end is reasonable. Reasonableness is generally a function of the owner's investment in the structure or use and the structure's age in relation to its predetermined useful life. Additionally, the enabling legislation permits (but does not require) minor rezonings—"non-significant changes"—by administrative bodies (such as zoning boards or planning commissions) or officers (such as the director of Planning and Permitting in Honolulu), even though courts regard even minor rezonings as legislative acts requiring the passage of an ordinance by a county council.[18]

Finally, Hawai'i is one of the first states in the nation to require local governments to permit two dwelling units per lot in all residence zones.[19] Called "*ohana* zoning," the law was passed in 1981[20] principally to help alleviate Hawai'i's acute housing shortage and to permit extended families to live on the same lot, even if the lot was zoned for single-family residences. A county may forbid such second dwellings only if public facilities (water, sewer) are inadequate or bulk requirements (yard, setback, height) are potentially infringed.

County Charter Provisions

The charters of Hawai'i's four counties all provide for zoning, yet they do so in different ways and with different implications, particularly in terms of the legal effect of plans on the zoning ordinance. Those portions of the counties' zoning powers that are enshrined in the charters may not be altered by the county councils, either by ordinance or resolution. The State Constitution provides that charters may be amended only by general law of the legislature or by vote of the people of the county.[21] County charter provisions also deal with the relationship of planning to zoning. This issue is best analyzed on a county-by-county basis.

HONOLULU

The charter of the City and County of Honolulu ties zoning to planning very closely. Indeed, zoning (and subdivision) must conform to so-called regional (sub-island) development plans in order to be valid at all.[22] These development plans were adopted in 1982 and "amended" (replaced, actually) between 1999 and 2004,[23] eliminating both the original detailed maps and site-specific text that allegedly too much resembled zoning maps and ordinances.[24] The Honolulu City Council passed (by resolution) a general plan in 1977 and amended it in 1997, but it is largely advisory under the present charter. It is, however, a guide that certain state agencies are required by statute to consider or conform to, as described in chapter 1.[25] Designed to cover a wide range of objectives, the Honolulu General Plan is largely aspirational and strives to "set forth the city's objectives and broad policies for the long-range development of the city," addressing general social, economic, environmental, and design needs.[26] It includes within its purview policy and development objectives "to be achieved for the general welfare and prosperity of the people and the most desirable population distribution and regional development pattern."[27] The development plans indicate geographically where future development is planned and where it is not;[28] they are supposed to implement the general plan's goals. There has been considerable debate in Honolulu over what the county's eight development plans *should* contain. However, the charter is quite clear as to what they are and what they *must* contain: "'Development plans' shall consist of conceptual schemes for implementing and accomplishing the development objectives and policies of the general plan within the city. A development plan shall include a map, statements of standards and principles with respect to land uses, statements of urban design principles and controls, and priorities as necessary to facilitate coordination of major development activities."[29]

The development plans and maps (which "shall not" be detailed in the manner of zoning maps) must describe the desired urban character and the significant natural, scenic, and cultural resources for the several parts of the city to a degree that is sufficient to serve as a policy guide for more detailed zoning maps and regulations and public and private sector investment decisions.[30] For example, the Primary Urban Center Plan contains chapters on downtown's current role in Oʻahu's development pattern, on the plan for future development of the area, including plans to protect and enhance "natural, cultural and scenic resources," on transportation, on infrastructure, and on public facilities.[31] All Oʻahu Regional Development Plans are available on the Department of Planning and Permitting Web site.[32]

Based on this language, some commentators have suggested that all existing zoning must also conform to any new development plans that are adopted. Moreover, in a series of cases, the Hawaiʻi Supreme Court has held that (1) zoning must conform to plans;[33] (2) in case of contradiction between plans and zoning designation, the more restrictive of the two controls present land use;[34] and (3) both plan map and zoning map amendments are legislative acts.[35] While it is not clear whether the Honolulu City Council is required to rezone all land to accord with the development plans, in 1966 the Court also held that zoning ordinances passed or amended after such plans are passed but contrary to their provisions are void.[36] Under the current revised charter, a landowner may seek a development plan amendment and a zoning map amendment concurrently. The Honolulu City Council presently hears and decides all such amendment requests at one "annual review," so as to adequately consider their cumulative effect on the development plans.

MAUI

Like Honolulu, Maui County's plans are binding. Although Section 8-8.5 of the Maui County Charter—the general and community planning provision—says nothing about land use changes and development proposals having to conform to either the general plan or the area-specific community plans,[37] Section 2.80B.030.B of the Maui County Codes states, "All agencies shall comply with the general plan. Notwithstanding any other provision, all community plans, zoning ordinances, subdivision ordinances, and administrative actions by agencies shall conform to the general plan. Preparation of County budgets and capital improvement programs shall implement the general plan to the extent practicable. The community plans authorized in this chapter are and shall be part of the general plan of the County, as provided by section 8-8.5 of the charter."[38] Thus, while the ordinance continues to emphasize the general plan as a guide, it nevertheless requires that local zoning and subdivision regulations conform to that guide.[39] There is nothing prospective about this language. The Maui ordinance provides that both past and present zoning and subdivision ordinances have to conform to its plans, which requires therefore that all existing ordinances be changed as well.[40] However, as this language is contained in an ordinance, not a charter, it can easily be amended.

The Maui General Plan is primarily a statement of policies. It consists of two parts: (1) a set of objectives expressing the common wishes and aspirations of the county residents and (2) policies that will have to be carried out in order to attain each objective.[41] Together, the objectives and policies of this plan provide a framework for the specific decisions that the county will be required to make in the future.[42] They are carried out through an implementation program.[43]

The detailed community plans are required to be far more specific. The community plans created and revised by the citizen advisory committees must set forth, in detail, land uses within the community planning regions of the county. The objectives of each community plan must implement the policies of the general plan. Each community plan must include implementing actions that clearly identify priorities, timelines, estimated costs, and the county department accountable for the completion of the implementing actions.[44]

Moreover, once adopted into the county code (by ordinance), the community plans are incorporated into and made a part of the general plan, so that they are supposed to be as binding as the general plan with respect to local zoning and subdivision ordinances: "The community plans authorized in this chapter are and shall be part of the general plan of the County, as provided by section 8-8.5 of the charter."[45] Furthermore, Section 8-8.5 of the Maui County Charter states, "The community plans generated through the citizen advisory councils and accepted by the planning commission, council, and mayor are part of the general plan."[46] Thus, the charter also specifically ties the community plans to the general plan.

KAUAʻI

The relationship of planning to zoning on Kauaʻi is relatively straightforward. The Kauaʻi Charter requires the County Council to adopt a general plan setting forth in graphic and textual form policies to govern

the future physical development of the county: "Such plan may cover
the entire county and all of its functions and services or may consist
of a combination of plans covering specific functions and services or
specific geographic areas which together cover the entire county and
all of its functions and services. The general plan shall serve as a guide
to all future council action concerning land use and development
regulations, urban renewal programs and expenditures for capital
improvements."[47]

Based upon this language in the Kaua'i Charter, it is unlikely that
local zoning and subdivision regulations could be required to conform
to the Kaua'i General Plan. Because the charter further provides that
relatively detailed development plans merely implement the guidelike
general plan (a provision that the Maui Charter lacks), it is also unlikely
that development plans would be construed to supersede past or future
zoning and subdivision regulations, even though the charter requires
both the general and development plans to be adopted by ordinance
and not by resolution.[48]

HAWAI'I

Hawai'i County, on the other hand, clearly means for its zoning and
subdivision codes to conform to its planning schemes—in this case, its
general plan—at least prospectively:

> (a) The council shall enact zoning, subdivision, and such
> other ordinances which shall contain the necessary provisions
> to carry out the purpose of the general plan.
> (b) No public improvement or project, or subdivision or
> zoning ordinance, shall be initiated or adopted unless the same
> conforms to and implements the general plan.[49]

The requirements for the Hawai'i general plan are specifically spelled
out in the county code, making it possible for its contents to be relatively detailed. These include a "statement of development objectives,
standards and principles with respect to the most desirable use of land"
in the county and identifying those uses as "residential, recreational,
agricultural, commercial, industrial and other purposes," which are to
be "consistent with the proper conservation of natural resources and
the preservation of . . . natural beauty and historical sites."[50] Details for
the use of land are to address such issues as the most desirable population density; a system of roads and public access to shorelines and other

open spaces; locations and improvements of public buildings; location and the extent of public utilities and terminals; the extent and location of public housing projects; adequate drainage facilities and control; and air pollution.[51] Anything not covered in detail is provided for in a more general statement recognizing that the County Council may address "such other matters as may . . . be beneficial to the social, economic, and governmental conditions and trends . . . of the county . . . to promote the general welfare and prosperity of its people."[52] The Hawai'i County Plan, like those of Honolulu, Maui, and Kaua'i, is adopted into its code by ordinance.[53]

County Zoning in Hawai'i

County zoning in the State of Hawai'i may be said to be a mixture of innovation and "Euclidian" zoning. Euclidean zoning (after the landmark *Euclid* case) is a convenient nickname for traditional as-of-right or self-executing zoning (that is, no special permissions are needed) in which district regulations are explicit; residential, commercial, and industrial uses are segregated; districts within categories such as "residential" are cumulative ("higher" uses such as single-family residences are permitted in "lower" use zones, such as those for apartments); and bulk and height controls are imposed.[54] It also results in the least guidance for landowners because of its many required reviews and often imprecise standards, particularly in its "overlay" zones.

Honolulu County: The Demise of Euclidean Zoning?

The City and County of Honolulu's Land Use Ordinance (LUO) contains many—but not all—of the zoning requirements of the city and county. The rest are found in the charter. While clearly retaining many standard Euclidean zoning features, both contain many elements, such as special permit zones and overlays, that make Honolulu's zoning requirements the most technical and thorough of the four counties.

The Zoning Districts

The LUO divides the land area of O'ahu into twenty-four districts, each with its own set of permitted uses, restrictions, and standards. These are in turn grouped into eleven broad categories: preservation, agricultural, country, residential, apartment, apartment mixed use, resort, business, business mixed use, industrial, and industrial-commercial mixed use as follows:[55]

Preservation
        Restricted   P-1
        General   P-2
        Military and Federal   F-1

Agricultural
        Restricted   AG-1
        General   AG-2

Country   C

Residential   R-20, R-10, R-7.5, R-5,
                                    R-3.5

Apartment
        Low-density   A-1
        Medium-density   A-2
        High-density   A-3

Apartment Mixed Use
        Low-density   AMX-1
        Medium-density   AMX-2
        High-density   AMX-3

Resort   Resort

Business
        Neighborhood   B-1
        Community   B-2

Business Mixed Use
        Community   BMX-3
        Central   BMX-4

Industrial
        Limited   I-1
        Intensive   I-2
        Waterfront   I-3

Industrial-Commercial Mixed Use   IMX-1

Each district carries with it certain typical standards relating to permitted uses, bulk of structures, required yards, and the like, all theoretically designed to protect the health, safety, welfare, and morals of its inhabitants. While certain regulations apply generally to all districts, the LUO is so organized that, once a landowner locates a parcel of property on the zoning map of Oʻahu, a general idea of what is permitted in the zoning "envelope" surrounding that parcel is easily found by looking up that district in the text of the LUO. The zoning map, prepared by the director of the Department of Planning and Permitting, is available for public inspection—and purchase—at the Office of the City Clerk; it is also available online.[56] In the event of conflict between the map and the text of any ordinance, the text prevails.[57]

An example of how the LUO works is the A-1 apartment district.[58] First, the following principal uses permitted in that district are listed in Table 21-3 (the Master Use Table), most of which are generally permitted, with additions, in the rest of the apartment districts as well (an example of cumulative zoning):[59]

Boarding facilities
Consulates
Duplex units
Detached one-family dwellings
Detached two-family dwellings
Multifamily dwellings
Public uses and structures
Type A utility installations

The Master Use Table also lists special accessory uses. An accessory use is, inter alia, "clearly incidental to and customarily found in connection with the principal use."[60] Accessory uses include home occupations and receive-only antennas.[61]

Also listed are uses and structures that are permitted only upon the fulfillment of certain conditions (these conditions and permits for use are discussed later in the section on zoning administration). One such category of conditional uses includes group living facilities, special needs housing for the elderly, use of historic structures, neighborhood grocery stores, day care facilities, meeting facilities, elementary, intermediate, and high schools, joint use of parking facilities, off-site parking facilities, Type B utility installations, and joint developments.[62] Special uses are also permitted only upon certain conditions but differ in that they are less permanent or less obtrusive than conditional uses. An example of special uses includes language schools.[63]

Second, the area, yard, and bulk regulations set out size limitations on principal structures and indicate where accessory structures may or may not be located in relation to required front, side, and rear yards.[64] A separate table in this section contains the intensity-of-use ratio known as the "floor area ratio" or FAR. Briefly, FAR refers to the ratio of floor area to land area permitted, expressed as a percent or decimal.[65] Thus, a floor area ratio of .5 would mean that on a ten thousand square-foot lot, the maximum floor space permitted would be five thousand square feet. Additional height and yard limits would also apply, but usually application of the FAR results in a structure smaller than would otherwise be permitted within such height and yard limitations. The consideration of such regulations creates what is commonly called the "zoning envelope" within which a permitted building must fit.

The Special Districts

That zoning in large cities is substantially changed from the heyday of Euclidean zoning is clear.[66] The most obvious change is the trend toward permitting: Instead of the traditional zoning district listing ranges of permitted uses on a parcel so zoned, a special zone is set out in the zoning ordinance and a permit to develop a particular project is issued in accordance with certain standards and goals; little is permitted automatically. The Honolulu LUO contains a classic example of this trend, particularly in its planned unit development regulations and special design district regulations.

Special Design Districts

An increasingly common approach to the regulation of development through zoning is to require that development of any kind be allowed only by special permit in certain areas. While a few communities appear to require practically all development to go through such a permitting process (for example, Irvine, California), the Honolulu LUO requires it only by means of its special design district (SDD) designation. There are now seven special design districts in the City and County of Honolulu: the Hawai'i Capitol Special District, the Diamond Head Special District, the Punchbowl Special District, the Chinatown Special District, the Thomas Square/Honolulu Academy of Arts Special District, the Waikīkī Special District, and the Hale'iwa Special District.[67] All but the Waikīkī District are "overlay" districts: The regulations applicable in such districts are in addition to—or "overlay"—the standards and requirements in the traditionally mapped zoning district upon which they are superimposed.

The establishment of a special design district is a multistep process.[68] First, the department discusses the proposal with the applicant and may assign a project manager to review the proposal.[69] Additionally, the applicant must present the project to the relevant neighborhood board.[70] Once these steps have been completed, the proposal is submitted to the director of DPP, pertinent governmental agencies, and the Design Advisory Committee for review and comment.[71] The director of DPP must then either deny the application or submit a report and proposed ordinance to the planning commission.[72] Within forty-five days of receiving the proposal, the planning commission must hold a public hearing; within thirty days of the public hearing, the planning commission must forward the director's report and proposed ordinance to the Honolulu City Council. The council then holds a public hearing and may approve, conditionally approve, or deny the proposed ordinance.[73]

If the district is established, the DPP director creates a design control system for all development in the district, promulgating "regulations which provide guidance for the design of new development and the renovation of existing development."[74] All development in an SDD is classified as major, minor, or exempt. Major and minor projects require special district permits in order to proceed.[75]

Changing Districts and Uses

The name of the game in zoning is change.[76] Change is accomplished through amendments, special and conditional uses, and variances, with procedures within the City and County of Honolulu contained in both the LUO and the Honolulu Charter. Key actors in these processes are the Honolulu City Council, Planning Commission, Zoning Board of Appeals (ZBA), and the director of the DPP.

Administration and Administrative Appeals

The formulation of general and development plans, as well as the administration of the zoning and subdivision ordinances of the City and County of Honolulu, are both largely in the hands of the director of DPP.[77] Thus, the DPP director receives nearly all applications for land use changes and the initial interpretive and information requests. Appeals from the final decisions of the director and in the general administration of the ordinance go to the ZBA. The ZBA will sustain an appeal only in the event of an erroneous finding of fact by the director or upon a finding that the director acted in an "arbitrary or capricious manner or had manifestly abused his discretion."[78]

Amendments and Public Hearings

There are three classes of amendments set out in the LUO: changes in zoning (so-called map amendments or rezonings) or amendments to the LUO (so-called text amendments); establishment of special design districts; and the creation of planned unit developments. All require the adoption of an ordinance by the Honolulu City Council.[79] In all categories, it is critical to follow the procedural timetable. A missed deadline can result in a procedural defect that may require starting all over again.

Whether map or textual, a landowner requesting an amendment must first present the request before the neighborhood board of the project's district.[80] After presentation, the applicant submits the request for an amendment to the DPP director, in whom the city charter vests the power to prepare zoning amendments.[81] The director then requests written comments and recommendations on the rezoning from pertinent governmental agencies, community organizations, and other interested parties during a forty-five-day comment period.[82] If the director chooses to proceed with a rezoning request, he submits a report and proposed ordinance to the Planning Commission for further review[83] within ninety days of acceptance of the initial completed request.[84]

The Planning Commission is specifically provided for by the charter.[85] Consisting of nine members, it not only advises the mayor, council, and the director of DPP and reviews local plans, but it is also vested by the charter with the authority to review subdivision and zoning ordinances and amendments.[86] Upon receiving the report of the DPP director in regard to a proposed amendment, the commission must hold a public hearing within forty-five days and transmit the proposed amendment (with its recommendations and those of the DPP director) "through the mayor to the Council for its consideration and action" within thirty days of the close of the public hearing.[87] The council must then hold another public hearing and either approve, approve with modifications, or reject the proposed amendment within ninety days after receiving the proposal from the commission. If the council fails to act, such inaction signifies rejection.[88]

Throughout the proceedings, it is clear that the council has the "last word," and therefore it is reasonable to assume that the process up to the point of the council hearing and consideration is advisory only. Indeed, the Hawai'i Supreme Court has so held, rejecting contentions that formal administrative procedures apply to either the DPP or the planning commission's processes.[89]

One of the thorniest issues in the council hearing process is how much the amendment can be changed by the council after the hearing without triggering the need for a new hearing. While presumably it could not substitute another amendment entirely, it is surely not necessary to rehear an amendment proposal after the insertion of every new comma. Indeed, the Hawai'i Supreme Court has held that the raising of a height limit in the special Hawai'i Capitol District by sixty feet (from 250 to 310 feet) after public hearing was not sufficiently significant to require a new hearing.[90] While agreeing that the council could not adopt a proposal different from the one "noticed" for public hearing merely because the changes were "advocated or discussed at a public hearing," the Court declared that it would have to be "fundamentally different from that proposed [so] as to amount to a new proposal" in order to require a re-notice and rehearing.[91] How the Court would decide a more complex matter, such as changes to development plans after council hearing, remains to be seen.

A final point on the amendment process is that some courts have held that map amendments involving relatively small land parcels should be treated as judgelike or quasijudicial determinations, even when made—as in Honolulu—by a legislative body such as the City Council.[92] With largely local effects and often with contestants arguing for and against, the proceeding does more closely resemble the judicial process rather than the public-policy and general-applicability character of legislation and the legislative process. The results of such a determination would be significant in the judicial process: Issues in appeals from legislative determinations are tried in court de novo (all over again), while administrative appeals are reviewed based solely on the record already made before administrative bodies or legislative bodies acting in nonlegislative capacities (as in the granting of shoreline management permits in Honolulu). The Hawai'i Supreme Court has expressly held that rezoning is a legislative act.[93] While legislative decisions are, in accordance with appropriately drafted enabling provisions, traditionally subject to referenda, quasijudicial decisions traditionally are not.[94] The U.S. Supreme Court, however, recently decided that both legislative and administrative acts are subject to the referendum process in *City of Cuyahoga Falls v. Buckeye Community Hope Foundation.*[95] Although it remains unlikely that zoning by initiative and referendum in Hawai'i will be revived (because of the *Nukolii* and *Hawaii Kai* decisions discussed above), the federal *Buckeye* decision throws this area of the law into confusion.

Conditional Zoning: Reclassification/Development

Conditions on rezoning and conditions on development proceed from different bases in law and policy. The purpose of placing conditions on the land reclassification or rezoning process at common law is to prevent the use of land in a fashion inconsistent with the overall zoning scheme or development plan for the area. Honolulu specifically provides for conditions on rezoning in its LUO:[96] Before the enactment of a zoning change, the City Council may impose conditions on the applicant's use of property. The stated rationale is to protect the public from "potentially deleterious effects" of the proposed use and to fulfill the need for "public service demands created by the proposed use."[97] The LUO further provides that the required conditions be formally recorded in a so-called unilateral agreement.[98] Some observers argue that is a fundamentally flawed process for at least two reasons. First, there is no reason why the two purposes set out in the LUO cannot be accomplished by other more traditional and defensible means: Providing for infrastructure and public facilities is usually accomplished through the development or subdivision exaction or impact fee, discussed in chapter 3. Protecting the public from deleterious effects of a use is usually accomplished either by removing the use from the zoning district or by making it a special or conditional use, approved according to strict standards and by permit only by a zoning administrative officer after a hearing—but without a zone change. Second, critics also suggest that the method of memorializing the conditions—the unilateral agreement—is both illegal and a contradiction in terms. Under basic contract law theory, there is no such thing as an enforceable "unilateral" agreement: An *agreement* presumes at least two parties and, to be enforceable, "consideration"—a bargained-for benefit—must flow both ways. A "unilateral" agreement is thus lacking the required reciprocity element, as the applicant is making a one-sided promise and receiving nothing in exchange.

There are also more general problems with Honolulu's conditional zoning. Related to or often treated the same as contract zoning, the practice comes dangerously close to bargaining away the police power of local government. In most jurisdictions, this kind of conditional zoning is considered illegal, unless (as with development agreements discussed in chapter 3) there is a statutory basis for the practice.[99] Moreover, it is difficult to know what is or is not permitted in a mapped zone classification if zoning approvals are regularly hedged with conditions on approval, such as the common limiting of existing uses to fewer than those permitted in the new zone classification under the local zoning ordinances.[100] Such limitations rarely have anything to do with the appropriateness of the use in the district. Rather, community and/or government opposition—either to most of the uses permitted in the zoning ordinance in that district or to the particular use, without conditions governing how the use is to be carried out—is among the salient reasons for conditioning the rezoning. If the concerns are legitimate, then perhaps the controversial other uses should be removed from the zoning classification as uses "of right" and permitted only upon certain articulated conditions, thereby leveling the playing field for all participants in the zoning game. Otherwise, the zoning ordinance itself becomes something of a *shibai* (pretense).

Special and Conditional Uses

The city may impose conditions on land use changes without resort to conditional zoning, however, as it can now process special and conditional uses. Provisions in the LUO specifically address such conditional permissions, each of which could, by the process of text amendment discussed above, be expanded to cover any situation to which conditional zoning might be applied. The difference is that the City Council is not involved in the special or conditional use process, except to the extent that it originally—or in the future (by way of text amendment)—lists in each zoning district classification the special or conditional uses that might be approved, according to the process described below.

The conditional use permit is the broader of the two categories. Like the approval of planned developments and major projects in council-established SDDs, conditional use permit applications are issued by the director of the DPP.[101] In deciding such applications, the director is guided by the standards set out for such conditional uses generally—and by specific uses in particular—as set out in the LUO in Article V and the list, if any, of conditional uses appended to or contained in the LUO sections applicable to particular zone district classifications. The director may also vary the application of dimensional and bulk standards (yard, lot dimension, height) in permitting such uses.[102]

64 Regulating Paradise

Special use permits can be granted for uses of a less permanent or intrusive nature. Reflecting that lower level of potential impact, no hearing is required; application to the DPP director is sufficient.[103] As with conditional uses, the special use permit is restricted to those special uses set out as permitted in the various zoning district classifications. While some of the uses permitted in this category are both permanent and consequential (such as private vacation cabins), most are temporary in nature, such as produce stands and construction trailers.[104]

Variances

The DPP director has the authority to soften the application of the precise zoning ordinance requirements under extraordinary circumstances by "varying" applicable building and use requirements. According to the charter, an applicant's success in obtaining such variances is based upon convincing the director of "unnecessary hardship":

> (1) the applicant would be deprived of the reasonable use of such land or building if the provisions of the zoning code were strictly applicable;
> (2) the request of the applicant is due to unique circumstances and not the general conditions in the neighborhood, so that the reasonableness of the neighborhood zoning is not drawn into question; and
> (3) the request, if approved, will not alter the essential character of the neighborhood nor be contrary to the intent and purpose of the zoning ordinance.[105]

Variances have become increasingly difficult to obtain. If the director denies the variance, the landowner may appeal to the ZBA, which holds another hearing on the variance and determines whether or not the action of the director was clearly erroneous, arbitrary or capricious, or an abuse of discretion.[106] Because legal standards are applied, an applicant's success is largely dependent on legal research and supplying past cases in which variances were granted under similar circumstances.

Nonconformities

Nonconformities violate either present structural or present use requirements. Counties may not pass zoning ordinances that eliminate single-family or duplex residential and agricultural uses as nonconforming.[107]

Somewhat different rules apply to nonconforming structures. In Honolulu, while nonconformities may not be expanded, moved, or structurally altered, the nonconforming use of part of the structure may be expanded under certain circumstances. Moreover, the use of the structure may change to other nonconforming uses "of the same nature and general impact,"[108] and the structure itself may be repaired so long as the work is limited to an enumerated list of "ordinary repairs"[109] (up to 10 percent of its value in any twelve-month period), thereby extending its life indefinitely. The repairs permitted are unlimited if they are for the purpose of "strengthening or restoring to a safe condition" a structure declared to be unsafe by an appropriate official. The structures must cease to be used in a nonconforming fashion if use is discontinued for twelve consecutive months or for any eighteen months in three years.[110] If the nonconforming structure is damaged or destroyed beyond 50 percent of its replacement cost, then it must be reconstructed in a conforming fashion only.[111] Under the Honolulu LUO, nonconforming uses of land (as opposed to structures) may neither be enlarged, moved about, nor expanded, and nonuse for six consecutive months or for a total of twelve months in any three-year period will result in termination.[112]

MAUʻI COUNTY: UNREFINED EUCLIDIAN

With the exception of its historic preservation provision, Maui's zoning scheme is traditionally Euclidian.[113] Like the County of Hawaiʻi, Maui appears to have some virtually unclassified ("interim zone") areas.[114] The districts set out in the ordinance are for the most part both less complicated and less finely tuned than those in Honolulu, reflecting Maui County's less-developed and more rural character.

The Zoning Districts
Maui is divided into twenty-six zoning districts:[115]

A. Residential districts:
    1. R-1 6,000 square feet,
    2. R-2 7,500 square feet,
    3. R-3 10,000 square feet;

B. Multiple-family districts:
    1. Two-family district (duplex district),
    2. Apartment districts;

C. Hotel districts;

D. Business districts:
     1. B-1 neighborhood business district,
     2. B-2 community business district,
     3. B-3 central business district,
     4. B-R resort commercial district,
     5. B-CT business country town district;

E. Industrial districts:
     1. M-1 light industrial district,
     2. M-2 heavy industrial district;

F. Airport district;

G. Agricultural district;

H. Off-street parking and loading;

I. Planned development;

J. Civic improvement district;

K. Park districts:
     1. PK-1 neighborhood park district,
     2. PK-2 community park district,
     3. PK-3 regional park district,
     4. PK-4 golf course park district;

L. Rural districts:
     1. RU-0.5 rural district,
     2. RU-1 rural district;

M. Open space districts:
     1. OS-1 passive open space district,
     2. OS-2 active open space district.

One or two points are worth elaborating. First, the planned development "district" is not a traditional zoning district at all but an overlay district.[116] Thus, densities permitted therein depend upon which of the five residential district regulations apply to the Planned Unit Development (PUD).[117] Moreover, the PUD regulations specifically provide that "[a]ll other regulations shall be the same as those for the particular district in which the planned development is located."[118] On the other hand, a planned development may be located in just about any district—residential, duplex, apartment, hotel, business, and industrial. Such districts and the regulation of uses therein are the responsibility of the County Planning Commission, not the County Council.[119] Maui uses a three-step approval process for PUDs: approval, sketch plan, and unified site and building program.[120] The incentive for undertaking planned development on Maui is a series of density and related bonuses designed to reduce development costs.[121]

Of particular interest in Maui County is the "projects district" established in 1974.[122] Its purpose is "to provide for a flexible and creative planning approach rather than specific land use designations, for quality developments."[123] A design proposal for the project area is required prior to development.[124] In return, the owner/developer retains a degree of flexibility much like that for planned development.[125] Unlike general PUDs, however, such districts are specifically identified on the Wailuku-Kahului General Plan.[126] As with planned development zones, both the zoning ordinance and the subdivision requirements remain applicable to developments within the project district, except to the extent that their provisions are modified by or inconsistent with the project district provisions. As with PUDs, the Planning Commission approves creation of these districts.[127]

Maui has also established civic improvement districts for the purpose of "encouraging, securing and maintaining the orderly and harmonious appearance, attractiveness and aesthetic development of structures and developments in such districts in order that the most appropriate use and value thereof be determined and protected and that the public health, safety and general welfare be preserved."[128] A "precise plan" for any such district must be adopted by the County Council upon Planning Commission recommendation. The plan describes the area included, together with applicable standards of design.[129] From there on, an advisory committee, appointed by the mayor (with approval of the council), regulates development by reviewing developer/applicant plans and approving, modifying, or rejecting in accordance with the standards contained in the plans.[130] For example, the Nāpili Bay Civic Improvement District on West Maui's Gold Coast was established in 1971 through the use of this procedure.[131] Among the design and land use

standards described in its precise plan were prohibitions on building
height and total floor area, directives about the construction and style
of buildings, restrictions on signs and advertisements, and instructions
about the availability of off-street parking.[132]

Finally, the interim zoning district as it operates in Maui County is
worth noting.[133] When the permanent zoning ordinance was enacted
in 1971, there were portions of the county that were left unclassified.
To regulate land use in such areas (Makawao, Lahaina, Hāna, Lānaʻi,
and Molokaʻi), the county enacted an interim zoning ordinance.[134]
Many parts of Molokaʻi and the Kula district on Maui remain in such
an "interim zone," in which only residential uses are permitted. Land
newly classified as urban by the State Land Use Commission is also often
temporarily placed in this zone.[135]

Administration

As in Honolulu, administration of the zoning ordinance in Maui
County is largely the responsibility of the Maui County Council, Planning Commission, Board of Variances and Appeals, and an administrative officer, the planning director. Zoning changes are ultimately the
responsibility of the council, whether or not they initiate the process.[136]
In addition to granting variances,[137] the board acts on all appeals pertaining to the zoning ordinance and the decisions of the planning
director.[138] The Maui Charter provides for the planning director to
prepare and revise the general plan and proposed zoning ordinances
and maps.[139] The charter also provides for the Planning Commission
to review, hold hearings upon, and make findings on the general plan
and zoning ordinances.[140] The Maui zoning ordinance allows review of
subdivision plans by the director of public works.[141] However, the zoning
ordinance delegates to the Planning Commission, however, the responsibility to prepare a master plan or plans of the urban areas.[142] But the
commission is left out of the community development plan formulation
process; it is responsible only for reviewing and making findings and
recommendations on revisions to enacted community development
plans proposed by the planning director or by the council.[143]

Conditional Zoning

In 1980, Maui enacted a comprehensive conditional zoning amendment whereby a property owner may substantially improve the chances
of obtaining an otherwise "iffy" rezoning if the applicant agrees in
advance to certain conditions calculated to mitigate public service bur-

dens and protect the public against deleterious uses that might result.[144] Formal, written agreement to such conditions as the county imposes might precede consideration of the rezoning request itself, but even the execution of a separate and unilateral agreement by a landowner to abide by such conditions will not bind the county to pass the requisite rezoning amendment. Similar to Honolulu's scheme, the conditions are then enumerated in a "unilateral agreement" running in favor of the council, to be recorded with the Bureau of Conveyances, assuring that any subsequent purchaser of the land has notice of them. The legal terminology applied to such conditions or declarations of covenants is that they "run with the land," though whether they will be subsequently enforceable is an unsettled question in Hawai'i. It may depend more on the nature of the covenants and who seeks enforcement, rather than on anything the County of Maui may have in mind.

KAUA'I COUNTY: A NON-EUCLIDIAN APPROACH

Kaua'i appears to be the only one of Hawai'i's four counties in which a comprehensive plan preceded zoning. Consequently, Kaua'i's General Plan—and in particular its first goal, to maintain the concept of Kaua'i as the Garden Isle—has probably had a greater influence on the later-adopted Comprehensive Zoning Ordinance (the Kaua'i CZO) than the plans of the other three counties. As a result, the Kaua'i CZO varies from the standard Euclidean ordinance of the other counties. It is primarily a density-based rather than lot/use-based ordinance.

Districts, Uses, and Automatic Rezonings

The Kaua'i CZO is organized into six major-use categories with fourteen districts and two overlay categories with nine districts, all of which are drawn on zoning maps depicting the seven planning areas into which the county has been divided: Kapa'a-Līhu'e, Kōloa-Po'ipū, Hanapēpē, Waimea, Hanalei, Kīlauea, and Kaua'i-Ni'ihau.[145] These districts are as follows:[146]

Residential	R: R-1, R-2, R-4, R-6, R-10, R-20
Resort	RR: RR-10, RR-20
Commercial	C
Neighborhood Commercial	CN
General Commercial	CG
Industrial	I
Limited Industrial	IL

General Industrial	IG
Agricultural	A
Open	O
Special Treatment	ST
Public Facilities	ST-P
Cultural/Historic	ST-C
Scenic/Ecological	ST-R
Constraint	S
Drainage	S-DR
Flood	S-FL
Shore	S-SH
Slope	S-SL
Soils	S-SO
Tsunami	S-TS

The special treatment and constraint categories are overlay districts. Thus, underlying mapped district classifications govern use therein except as modified by whatever special treatment and constraint zone conditions are applied by "overlaying" the special zones on top of the mapped zones.[147]

Kaua'i also uses conditional zoning extensively.[148] Aside from providing for the imposition of conditions on any zone change for both health/safety and public improvement/heritage protection, the Kaua'i CZO also lists the kinds of conditions that may be imposed.[149] It further provides for "automatic" zone changes whenever specified conditions occur.[150]

The practice of automatic zone changes may seem a bit dubious, because zoning in Hawai'i is a legislative act and so, therefore, is rezoning. Rezoning arguably automatically deprives a property owner of the usual due process involved in rezoning a parcel of land, and some states therefore forbid the practice altogether. Others, however, permit automatic rezoning under very limited circumstances, comparing it to a special use with conditions.[151] The breach of a condition of such a special use permit causes the permit to automatically expire, leaving the owner with the underlying zoning. This special use procedure is superior both administratively and legally.

Kaua'i requires a zoning permit for residential,[152] commercial,[153] industrial,[154] resort,[155] agricultural,[156] open space[157] development, and conditional use.[158] It thus utilizes permit zoning as opposed to the standard zoning envelope model where many uses are permitted as "of right" in each district. There are usually four classes of zoning permits available for each development type.[159] This zoning permit system is closely tied to (1) the size of the project and (2) its location in or out of one of the two classes of overlay districts: constraint and special treatment.[160] An applicant for a zoning permit files an application with the county planning department, showing, among other things, existing and proposed structures.[161] Whether the planning director or the Planning Commission issues the permit depends upon which of the four classes of permit is required; this in turn depends upon the size of the development and its location in or out of an overlay or constraint zone.[162]

Use permits are required for a variety of uses. For example, fifteen individual uses require a use permit in commercial districts, from animal hospitals and automobile sales to warehouses and schools.[163] Such permits are granted only if the proposed use is compatible within the district and not detrimental to the health, safety, peace, morals, comfort, and general welfare of the community, will cause no substantial harmful environmental consequences, and will be consistent with the general plan.[164] The commission or the director may impose a variety of conditions on the permit pertaining to such a location, amount, type, and time of construction, amount and type of traffic, appearance of the building, and landscaping.[165]

Permitting in a special treatment or constraint district depends upon the nature and location of a proposed development. In these overlay districts, the underlying standard zoning district requirements— residential, commercial, agricultural, open space, industrial—apply, except as their special requirements impose further restrictions.[166] There are three special treatment districts: Public Facilities (ST-P), Cultural/Historic (ST-C), and Scenic/Ecologic Resources (ST-R).[167] In addition to zoning permit requirements, use permits are required for nearly all "uses, structures or development" in a special treatment district.[168]

Constraint districts, which are more traditional overlay districts, contain restrictions directed at alleviating specific physical site development problems—or preventing development where such problems are too severe.[169] There are six such districts, designed to deal with drainage, flood, tsunami, steep slope, shoreland protection, and unsuitable soil problems.[170] The flood, shore, and tsunami district regulations track various state and federal requirements, which are discussed in chapter 6 on coastal zone management and chapter 7 on flood hazards.

Kaua'i's permit system is particularly strong in its approach to preserving agriculture and open space. In the agriculture district, no structures other than agricultural buildings and single-family residences are permitted without a use permit.[171] Moreover, a use permit allows only the applicant an animal hospital, a church, a school, commercial recreation, or similar structure as determined by the planning director.[172] Even if a use permit is issued, subdivision is limited (in order to "limit, retard, and control such subdivision of agricultural land that will destroy agricultural stability and potential"[173] and to "avoid dissipation of agricultural land"[174]) according to a sliding scale that ties the number and size of the subdivided lots to the size of the original parcel.[175] Thus, a parcel of ten acres or less can be divided into one-acre parcels,[176] but a parcel between thirty and fifty acres may be divided into only five-acre parcels.[177] However, while at least one dwelling unit may be constructed on each parcel of one acre or larger, three additional acres per parcel are needed for each additional dwelling unit on the same parcel, up to a maximum of only five dwelling units per parcel, regardless of its size.[178] The open space district is designed principally for the preservation of environmentally critical land or water areas and the regulation of development in hazard zones.[179] As in the agriculture zone, the generally permitted uses are structurally limited to agricultural buildings and single-family residences.[180] Land coverage is limited to 10 percent of a lot or parcel.[181] Density is limited according to the underlying State Land Use Commission classification.[182] Thus, the limit is one dwelling unit per acre on land classified urban (provided the slope is no greater than 10 percent), one dwelling unit per three acres if it is designated rural (or if the slope exceeds 10 percent in urban), and one dwelling unit per five acres on agricultural land.[183]

Both districts may be subject to Kaua'i's "agricultural park" ordinance passed in 1974, whereby an area of at least 350 acres in either the agricultural or open space zone may become a sort of agricultural, development-free horizontal condominium.[184] The purpose of the ordinance was apparently to prevent development of agricultural land and to keep it available to small farmers.[185]

Administration

The permit/performance nature of the Kaua'i CZO obviates much "normal" zoning administration. A few points of difference from standard practice in Hawai'i in the variance and amendment process are worth noting, however.

The variance on Kaua'i has two extraordinary features. First, the

zoning ordinance not only fails to recite the usual hardship requirement, it also expressly rejects financial hardship as a "permissible basis
for the granting of a variance." This rejection is preceded by an unusu-
ally articulate list of factors and restrictions on the granting of variances.[186] Second, the variance request is processed, heard, and decided
not by a zoning board of appeals but by the Planning Commission.[187]
This is most unusual, as the hearing of variances is generally regarded
as a quasijudicial proceeding for which an appeals board is usually
uniquely qualified. On the other hand, as Kaua'i has tended toward a
permit-oriented performance land use control scheme, and as the Planning Commission has a substantial administrative, quasijudicial role by
hearing permit requests under the scheme, it is less illogical that it, as
another appointed body, be entrusted with responsibility for variances
as well.

The amendment process also contains some novel facets. The
Planning Commission not only receives and processes amendment
applications,[188] but it also holds the sole hearing on such applications.[189]
This is a laudable piece of economy. The practice (as in Honolulu) of
holding another hearing before the council is unnecessary. However,
the CZO also provides that should the commission disapprove of a proposed amendment, its decision is final, except that its decision may be
appealed to the council, which must then hold a hearing before deciding the fate of the amendment.[190] It is not altogether clear why the Planning Commission is given authority to make final decisions on generally
legislative matters. The providing of an appeal to the council does not
really save this process. Identical procedures for both negative and positive decisions of the Planning Commission on proposed amendments
would be more consistent, even if it is the intent that the commission
have more than the usual advisory role to the council on amendment
matters.

Hawai'i County: A Traditional Approach

The County of Hawai'i zoning ordinance is more traditional than those
of the other three counties. With the exception of two overlay districts,
the zones are textbook-typical. There is a host of permitted uses in each
district, permitted automatically and without the need for, say, the use
permit usually required in Kaua'i or the potential restrictions of a special design or historic, scenic, and cultural districts in Honolulu. There
is, however, a rigorous and comprehensive planning review process
applicable to many of the districts.

The Zoning Districts
Hawai'i County divides land into seventeen districts:[191]

RS, single-family residential districts
RD, double-family residential districts
RM, multiple-family residential districts
RCX, residential-commercial mixed use districts
RA, residential and agricultural districts
FA, family agricultural district
A, agricultural districts
IA, intensive agricultural districts
V, resort-hotel districts
CN, neighborhood commercial districts
CG, general commercial districts
CV, village commercial districts
MCX, industrial-commercial mixed use districts
ML, limited industrial districts
MG, general industrial districts
O, open districts
Special districts

Each district lists uses permitted of right, followed by standard bulk limitations on these uses (yard, height, and so forth), density of coverage, and the like.

Plan approval may also be required for any variance or conditional use permit.[192] No hotel or condominium may obtain plan approval unless it is approved in accordance with project procedures.[193] A detailed site plan must be filed with the director of planning (who heads the Department of Planning), who must deny, approve, or defer it subject to conditions, according to detailed site planning criteria.[194] The director's decisions are appealable only to the Hawai'i County Board of Appeals.[195]

The director is also authorized to continually review any multiphase project, raising the potential of a stop-order in the event of violations.[196] Thus, while the uses permitted are determined by the district regulations, the manner in which the uses are developed is controlled by the director and Board of Appeals in most zoning classifications.

Aside from a relatively straightforward agricultural district, there is also an intensive agricultural district for the preservation of agricultural lands that have "high yields of crops."[197] There is also an open district "to protect investments which have been or shall be made in reliance upon the retention of such open use."[198] Growing plants (if it does not impair a view), golf courses, historical sites, private recreation, and public parks are the principal permitted uses.[199]

Planned Development and Other Special Approvals

The most refreshing aspect of the County of Hawai'i's planned development regulations is that they appear to permit commercial and industrial as well as residential developments.[200] Moreover, planned developments are permitted as special use rather than as a new district classification,[201] thereby avoiding any potential problems of automatic "reverting" to the former zone classification in the event that the planned development permit is violated. However, no planned development is permitted in any district unless the uses proposed are permitted either of right or conditionally in the zoning district where the property is situated.[202] Thus a rezoning will often be required before a planned unit development is approved.[203] This two-step process provides additional guarantees to property owners who have relied on existing zoning to develop their property, but it is nevertheless cumbersome for planned developments.

Hawai'i's charter shifts the power to hear and decide variances from the Planning Commission to the director, but only "as provided by law."[204] It is therefore not altogether clear that the director is authorized to hear variance requests until "conforming" legislation has been passed by the council. The charter further provides that the decision of the director may be appealed to the Board of Appeals.[205] The zoning code presently provides that "a variance shall not allow the introduction of a use not otherwise permitted within the district."[206] This language would appear to foreclose the granting of the notorious use variance.

Conclusion

Local zoning among the counties in Hawai'i is both similar and diverse. Some of the most innovative and procedurally direct land use procedures in the country—as well as some of the most traditional—are written into the four county codes. If the name of the zoning game is change, then Hawai'i is playing the game, with major code revisions about to begin or already commenced in all four counties. In particular, major revisions or additions to the all-important detailed plans (which often take precedence over subsequent zoning amendments) are proceeding in the two most heavily developed of the four counties—Honolulu and

Maui. While nationally known for its state land use schemes, Hawaiʻi is also a laboratory for innovative and complex local land use controls. As a result of recent decisions by Hawaiʻi's Supreme Court,[207] such controls will be strictly enforceable as well.

Notes

1. Richard F. Babcock, *The Zoning Game: Municipal Practices and Policies*, Madison: University of Wisconsin Press, 1966.
2. "The ancien regime being overthrown is the feudal system under which the entire pattern of land development has been controlled by thousands of individual local governments, each seeking to maximize its tax base and minimize its social problems, and caring less what happens to all the others." Fred P. Bosselman and David L. Callies, *The Quiet Revolution in Land Use Control*, prepared for the Council on Environmental Quality, Washington, D.C.: U.S. Government Printing Office, 1972; *see*, e.g., Clifford L. Weaver and Richard F. Babcock, *City Zoning: The Once and Future Frontier*, Chicago: APA Planners Press, 1979; David L. Callies, "The quiet revolution revisited," 46 J. AM. PLAN. ASS'N 135 (1980).
3. David L. Callies, "The quiet revolution revisited: A quarter century of progress," 26 URB. LAW. 197 (1994); *see also* Weaver and Babcock, supra note 2.
4. E.g., Seymour I. Toll, *Zoned American*, New York: Grossman Publishers, 1969; Charles M. Haar and Michael C. Wolf, *Land-Use Planning: A Casebook on the Use, Misuse, and Re-Use of Urban Land*, 4th ed. Boston: Little, Brown & Co., 1989; Charles M. Haar and Jerold S. Kayden, eds., *Zoning and the American Dream: Promises Still to Keep*, Chicago: Planners Press, 1989; Dwight Merriam, *The Complete Guide to Zoning*, New York: McGraw-Hill, 2005; Michael Allan Wolf, *The Zoning of America: Euclid v. Ambler*, Lawrence: University Press of Kansas, 2008.
5. *See*, e.g., David L. Callies, *Euclid* (ch. 12), *in* Gerald Korngold and Andrew P. Morris, eds., *Property Stories*, 2d ed., New York: Foundation Press, 2009; Babcock, supra note 1, at ch. 7 ("The Purpose of Zoning"); John Delafons, *Land-Use Controls in the United States*, 2d ed., Cambridge: MIT Press, 1969; John F. Garner and David L. Callies, "Planning law in England and Wales and in the United States," 1 ANGLO-AM. L. REV. 292 (1972); Alfred Bettman, "The constitutionality of zoning," 37 HARV. L. REV. 834 (1924).
6. *Penn. Coal Co. v. Mahon*, 260 U.S. 393, 415 (1922).
7. David L. Callies, "Takings: Physical and regulatory," 15 ASIA PAC. L. REV. 77 (2007); Robert Meltz, Dwight H. Merriam, and Richard M. Frank, *The Takings Issue: Constitutional Limits on Land Use Control and Environmental Regulation*, Washington D.C.: Island Press, 1998; Thomas E. Roberts, ed., *Taking Sides on Takings Issues*, Chicago: ABA Press, 2003. For a recent summary of regulatory takings law, see *Lingle v. Chevron U.S.A. Inc.*, 544 U.S. 528 (2005).
8. *Vill. of Euclid v. Ambler Realty Co.*, 272 U.S. 365 (1926).
9. Two years after *Euclid* foreclosed the possibility of facially challenging the constitutionality of zoning, a landowner succeeded in an as-applied challenge in *Nectow v. City of Cambridge*, 277 U.S. 183 (1928). *See* Wolf, supra note 4, and Callies, *Euclid*, supra note 5.

10. Except Houston, still unzoned—but nevertheless regulated—today. *See* Bernard H. Siegan, "Non-zoning in Houston," 13 J.L. & ECON. 71 (1970).

11. Haar and Wolf, supra note 4, at 204.

12. Garner and Callies, *Planning Law in England,* supra note 5, at 306; Callies, *Euclid,* supra note 5; Wolf, *The Zoning of America,* supra note 4.

13. *See,* e.g., *City of Los Angeles v. Gage,* 274 P.2d 34 (Cal. Ct. App. 1954); *Art Neon Co. v. City & County of Denver,* 488 F.2d 118 (10th Cir. 1973); *Modjeska Sign Studios v. Berle,* 373 N.E.2d 255 (N.Y. 1977).

14. *See* Haar and Wolf, supra note 4, § 6, at 344–345; *but see,* e.g., David L. Callies, Robert H. Freilich, and Thomas E. Roberts, *Cases and Materials on Land Use,* 5th ed., St. Paul: West, 2008, at 458–471 (discussing plans that have the force and effect of law).

15. *Kozesnik v. Twp. of Montgomery,* 131 A.2d 1, 7–8 (N.J. 1957).

16. HAW. REV. STAT. § 46-4(a) (2009). Hawai'i has none of the local government units—cities, villages, towns—that other states have.

17. Section 46-4(a) of the Hawaii Revised Statutes states, "The council of any county shall prescribe rules, regulations, and administrative procedures and provide personnel it finds necessary to enforce this section and any ordinance enacted in accordance with this section. The ordinances may be enforced by appropriate fines and penalties, civil or criminal, or by court order at the suit of the county or the owner or owners of real estate directly affected by the ordinances."

18. Id.

19. Id. § 46-4(c).

20. Jody Lynn Kea, Comment, "Honolulu's Ohana Zoning Law," 13 U. HAW. L. REV. 505 (1991).

21. HAW. CONST., art. VIII, §§ 1 and 2.

22. City and County of Honolulu, *Revised Charter of the City and County of Honolulu,* § 6-1511 (2000): "Public improvement projects and subdivision and zoning ordinances shall be consistent with the development plan for that area, provided that the development plan amendments and zoning map amendments may be processed concurrently." *See* Charles C. Goodin, "The Honolulu development plans: An analysis of land use implications for Oahu," 6 U. HAW. L. REV. 33 (1983).

23. City & County of Honolulu, Department of Planning and Permitting, *Development/Sustainable Communities Plan,* http://www.honoluludpp.org/planning/ DevSustCommPlans.asp (click on region, then on cover for dates) (last visited Nov. 11, 2009).

24. *See* David L. Callies and Calvert G. Chipcase, "Water regulation, land use and the environment," 30 U. HAW. L. REV. 49 (2007).

25. Id.

26. Honolulu, *Charter,* § 6-1508 (2000).

27. Id.

28. *Development/Sustainable Communities Plan,* supra note 23.

29. Honolulu, *Charter,* § 6-1509.

30. Id.

31. City & County of Honolulu, Department of Planning and Permitting, *Primary Urban Center Development Plan,* http://honoluludpp.org/planning/ DevSust_PrimaryUrbanCenter.asp (last visited Nov. 11, 2009).

32. *Development/Sustainable Communities Plan,* supra note 23.

33. *Lum Yip Kee, Ltd. v. City & County of Honolulu,* 70 Haw. 179, 767 P.2d 815 (1989).

34. *Save Sunset Beach Coal. v. City & County of Honolulu,* 102 Haw. 465, 78 P.3d 1 (2003).

35. Id.

36. *Dalton v. City & County of Honolulu,* 51 Haw. 400, 462 P.2d 199 (1966).

37. County of Maui, *Charter of the County of Maui,* § 8-8.5 (2003).

38. County of Maui, *Maui County Code,* § 2.80B.030.B (2003).

39. Id.

40. Id.

41. County of Maui, *General Plan* (1990).

42. Id.

43. Id.

44. Maui, *Charter,* § 8-8.5.5, *available at* http://www.co.maui.hi.us/index.asp?NID=736.

45. Maui, *County Code,* § 2.80B.030.B.

46. Maui, *Charter,* § 8-8.5.6.

47. County of Kaua'i, *Kauai County Charter,* § 14.06 (1969, as amended).

48. Id. § 14.07. "Development plan" means a relatively detailed scheme for the replacement or use of specific facilities within the framework of the general plan. Id. § 14.08.

49. County of Hawai'i, *Hawaii County Charter,* § 3-15 (2000).

50. Id.

51. Id.

52. Id.

53. Id.

54. Michael J. Meshenberg, *The Language of Zoning: A Glossary of Words and Phrases,* Chicago: American Society of Planning Officials, 1976 at 14. Contrast this basic form of zoning with that recommended by the American Planning Association's "Growing Smart" project, which culminated in model state and local language in 2002, and the recommendations incorporating "New Urbanism" in Robert Freilich and S. Mark White, *21st Century Land Development Code,* Chicago: APA Planners Press, 2008.

55. City & County of Honolulu, Department of Planning & Permitting, *Land Use Ordinance,* § 21-3.10 (2003), *available at* http://www.co.honolulu.hi.us/refs/roh/21_990.pdf (last visited Nov. 21, 2009) (hereinafter "Honolulu LUO").

56. City & County of Honolulu, Department of Planning & Permitting, *Interactive GIS Maps and Data,* http://gis.hicentral.com/ (last visited Nov. 21, 2009).

57. *See* Honolulu LUO § 21-3.30(b)(1).

58. Id. § 21-3.80.

59. Id. at Table 21-3.

60. Id. § 21-10.1.

61. Id. at Table 21-3.

62. Id.

63. Id.

64. Id. § 21-3.80-1; Table 21-3.3.

65. Id. § 21-10.1.

66. *See*, e.g., Weaver and Babcock, supra note 2.

67. *See* Honolulu LUO, §§ **21-9.30** (Hawai'i Capitol), **-9.40** (Diamond Head), **-9.50** (Punchbowl), **-9.60** (Chinatown), **-9.70** (Thomas Square/Honolulu Academy of Arts), **-9.80** (Waikīkī), and **-9.90** (Hale'iwa).

68. Id. § 21-2.40-2(a)(2).

69. Id. § 21-2.40-2(b)(1).

70. Id. § 21-2.40-2(b)(2).

71. Id. § 21-2.40-2(c).

72. Id. § 21-2.40-2(c)(8).

73. Id. § 21-2.70.

74. Id. § 21-9.20-1. Development in a special design district may be subject to additional approvals based on ownership; for example, development along the Waikīkī Beachwalk area is subject to initial approval of Outrigger Hotels, which developed the beachwalk. Thus an applicant would first have to meet Outrigger Hotels' design criteria before review by the urban design review board.

75. Id. §§ 21-2.40-1, -2.

76. *See* Babcock, *The Zoning Game*, supra note 1.

77. Honolulu, *Charter*, § 6-1503 (2000); Honolulu LUO, § 21-1.30 (2003).

78. Honolulu, *Charter*, § 6-1516.

79. Honolulu LUO, § 21-2.40-2 (2003).

80. Id. § 21-2.40-2(b)(2); City & County of Honolulu, Department of Planning & Permitting, *Zone Change Application Instructions*, http://www.honoluludpp.org/downloadpdf/planning/ZoneChangeApp.pdf (last visited Nov. 21, 2009). Presentation before the neighborhood board may be waived by the board or deemed waived if the board fails to provide an opportunity for presentation within sixty days of the applicant's request. Additionally, a preapplication meeting involving "informal review of the proposed rezoning" and discussion of "development plan consistency" is technically required even before the neighborhood board meeting, unless waived by the DPP.

81. Honolulu, *Charter*, § 6-1503.

82. Honolulu LUO, § 21-2.40-2(c)(4).

83. Id. § 21-2.40-2.

84. Id. § 21-2.40-2(c)(8).

85. Honolulu, *Charter*, §§ 6-1505, 6-1506 (2000).

86. Id. § 6-1506. It may also perform "such other related duties as may be necessary to fulfill its responsibilities under this charter or as may be assigned by the mayor or the council." Id.

87. Honolulu LUO, § 21-2.70(b)(1)(A).

88. Id. § 21-2.70(b)(3).

89. *See Kailua Cmty. Council v. City & County of Honolulu*, 60 Haw. 428, 591 P.2d 602 (1979); *Life of the Land, Inc., v. City Council of Honolulu*, 61 Haw. 390, 606 P.2d 866 (1980).

90. *Carlsmith, Carlsmith, Wichman & Case v. CPB Props., Inc.*, 64 Haw. 584, 645 P.2d 873 (1982).

91. Id. at 594, 645 P.2d at 880.

92. *See*, e.g., *Fasano v. Bd. of County Comm'rs of Wash. County*, 507 P.2d 23 (Or. 1973).

93. *See Save Sunset Beach,* supra note 34, at 473, 78 P.3d at 9.
94. *See, e.g., City of Eastlake v. Forest City Enters.,* 426 U.S. 668 (1976).
95. *See City of Cuyahoga Falls v. Buckeye Cmty. Hope Found.,* 538 U.S. 188, 199 (2003).
96. Id.
97. Honolulu LUO, § 21-2.80(c).
98. Id. § 21-2.80(e).
99. *See* Callies et al., *Cases and Materials on Land Use,* supra note 14. Development agreements authorized by statute are a way around the problem of bargaining away police power, as discussed at the end of chapter 3.
100. For cases criticizing this practice, *see Carlino v. Whitpain Investors,* 453 A.2d 1385 (PA 1982), and *Cederberg v. City of Rockford,* 291 N.E.2d 249 (Ill. App. Ct. 1973).
101. Honolulu LUO, §§ 21-2.40-1, -2.
102. Id.
103. Id.
104. Id. at table 21-3 and art. V.
105. Honolulu, *Charter,* § 6-1517 (2000).
106. Id. §§ 6-1516, -1517.
107. HAW. REV. STAT. § 46-4(a) (2009).
108. Honolulu LUO, § 21-4.110(c)(4).
109. Id. § 21-4.110(c)(3).
110. Id. § 21-4.110(c)(2).
111. Id. § 21-4.110(b)(1).
112. Id. § 21-4.110.
113. *See* infra chapter 8; *see also* Maui, *County Code,* at art. III.
114. Maui, *County Code,* at art. I.
115. Id. § 19.06.010.
116. Id. at art. II, § 19.32.
117. Id. § 19.32.040.F ("Overall dwelling unit density shall be determined by dividing the total number of dwelling units by the net land area. Net land area shall be total lot area minus the area of dedicated streets and other dedicated areas").
118. Id. § 19.32.050.
119. Id. § 19.32.020.
120. Id.
121. Id. § 19.32.040.
122. Id. § 19.58.010 (Dec. 2007), (Ord. 787 § 1, 1974).
123. *Id.* § 19.45.010.B.
124. Id. § 19.45.040(C)(1) ("All applications shall include . . . [a] description of the proposed project district, including land uses, densities, infrastructural requirements, development standards, and a conceptual map showing the project district boundaries, and the acreages of land involved").
125. Id. § 19.45.010.
126. Id. § 19.74.78-81; Maui County Council, *Wailuku-Kahului Community Plan,* pt. III.C., at 19 (2002), http://www.co.maui.hi.us/documents/Planning/Long%20Range%20Division/Community%20Plans/wailuku.pdf (last visited Nov. 21, 2009).
127. Maui, *County Code,* § 19.45.050.

128. Id. § 19.34.010.
129. Id. § 19.34.020.
130. Maui, *Charter*, § 8-8.5 (Jan. 2003).
131. Maui, *County Code*, § 19.60.020 (Dec. 2007).
132. Id. § 19.60.030.
133. Id. § 19.02.020.
134. Id. § 19, art. I.
135. Personal communication, Lee Ohigashi, deputy corp. counsel, County of Maui, Jan. 1981.
136. Maui, *County Code*, § 19.510.040(A)(4) (Dec. 2007).
137. Id. § 19.520.050.C; Maui, *Charter*, § 8-8.7 (Jan. 2003).
138. Maui, *County Code*, § 19.520.040.
139. Maui, *Charter*, § 8-8.3.
140. Id. § 8-8.4.
141. Id. § 8-5.3 (amended 2006).
142. Maui, *County Code*, § 19.510.080.B.2 (Dec. 2007).
143. Maui, *Charter*, § 8-8.5.
144. Maui, *County Code*, § 19.40.010.
145. County of Kaua'i, *Comprehensive Zoning Ordinance*, § 8-2.3 (2004 Supp.).
146. Id. § 8-2.2 (2001); *see also* id. § 8-3.2(a) ("Types of Residential Districts").
147. Id. § 8-1.3(j).
148. Id. § 8-2.2(c)(1).
149. Id. § 8-2.2(c)(2).
150. Id. § 8-2.2(c)(3).
151. E.g., *Goffinet v. County of Christian*, 357 N.E.2d 442 (Ill. 1976).
152. Kaua'i, *Comprehensive Zoning Ordinance*, § 8-3.9 (2004 Supp.).
153. Id. § 8-5.6.
154. Id. § 8-6.6.
155. Id. § 8-4.6.
156. Id. § 8-7.8.
157. Id. § 8-8.7.
158. *See* id. §§ 8-3.4 (residential), -4.4 (resort), -5.4 (commercial), -6.4 (industrial), -7.3 (agricultural), and -8.3 (open). It should be noted that the Kaua'i CZO does not refer to these uses as "conditional"; rather the sections are titled, for example, in commercial districts, "Uses and Structures in Commercial Districts That Require a Use Permit." Id. § 8-5.4.
159. *See*, e.g., id. §§ 8-3.9 (residential), -5.6 (commercial), -6.6 (industrial), and -4.6 (resort).
160. *See* id. § 8-6.6(a)(1): "A Class I Permit must be obtained for construction or development on a parcel where: (A) the parcel is not located in a Constraint or Special Treatment District and is not larger than fifteen thousand (15,000) square feet."
161. Id. § 8-19.2(3).
162. *See*, e.g., id. § 8-19.3(b): "The Planning Director or his designee shall check the application to determine whether the construction, development, activity or use conforms to the standards established by this Chapter."
163. Id. § 8-5.4.

164. Id. § 8-20.5(a).

165. Id. § 8-20.5(b).

166. *See* id. § 8-1.3(j) (explaining that overlay districts impose "additional special regulations").

167. Id. § 8-9.2.

168. *See* id. § 8-9.3.

169. Id. § 8-10.1.

170. Id. § 8-10.2.

171. Id. § 8-7.2.

172. Id. § 8-7.3.

173. Id. § 8-7.4(a)(1).

174. Id. § 8-7.4(a)(2).

175. Id. § 8-7.4(a)(4).

176. Id. § 8-7.4(b)(1)(A).

177. Id. § 8-7.4(b)(1)(D).

178. Id. § 8-7.5(2).

179. Id. § 8-8.1.

180. Id. § 8-8.2.

181. Id. § 8-8.5(a)(1).

182. Id. § 8-8.5(b).

183. Id. §§ 8-8.5(b), 8-8.5(b)(1).

184. County of Kaua'i, *Kauai County Code*, § 9A-1.2(1) (1987).

185. Id. § 9A-1.1.

186. Kaua'i, *Comprehensive Zoning Ordinance*, § 8-21.2 (2004 Supp.).

187. Id. § 8-21.1.

188. Id. § 8-22.2.

189. Id. § 8-22.3.

190. Id. § 8-22-6.

191. County of Hawai'i, *Hawaii County Code*, § 25-3-1 (1983).

192. Id. § 25-2-71.

193. Id. § 25-6-43.

194. Id. § 25-2-72.

195. Id. § 25-2-58.

196. Id. § 25-2-34.

197. Id. § 25-5-80.

198. Id. § 25-5-160.

199. Id. § 25-5-162.

200. Id. § 25-6-10.

201. *See* id. § 25-6-3.

202. Id. § 25-6-5.

203. Id.

204. Hawai'i, *Charter,* § 6-4.2(h).

205. Id.

206. Hawaii, *County Code,* § 25-2-50.

207. *Save Sunset Beach,* supra note 34.

Chapter 3

Subdivisions, Land Development Conditions, and Development Agreements

I. SUBDIVISIONS

The subdivision approval process represents one of the most relevant of land use control techniques. It is exercised at the county level, enabled through legislation at the state level, and is a prerequisite for virtually all single-family residential development as well as a significant portion of new multifamily, commercial, and industrial development whenever a landowner-developer divides land into more parcels. Generally characterized by preliminary and then final plan or plat approval, it is at this stage in the land development process that county government often requires a series of land development conditions (exactions, dedications, impact fees) precedent to permission to develop.[1] Such land development conditions trigger analysis of case law relating to when government can legally impose such conditions. Hawai'i has no substantive case law on such conditions (in this, it is virtually alone among states with significant development).[2] However, the U.S. Supreme Court has set down tests requiring nexus and proportionality in order for such land development conditions to pass constitutional muster, as discussed in the following sections in this chapter. Of course, to the extent a county and a landowner negotiate and execute a development agreement, as permitted by state statute in Hawai'i, the nexus and proportionality tests are inapplicable.[3] This chapter therefore also discusses development agreements, even though such agreements can and should be negotiated, if at all, far earlier in the land development process than at the point of subdivision regulation and control. This chapter also discusses the applicability of the concept of vested rights, given that the vesting of rights to complete a land development project is what often attracts a landowner-developer to the development agreement process.

Hawai'i: Of Mandatory Dedications and Open Space

The State of Hawai'i has required subdivision exactions for decades. It does so by statute, directing each county to require and set standards for the dedication of land for parks and playgrounds in their respective subdivision ordinances. The county may take money in lieu of land, or it may take a combination of land and money. Credit against the required dedication or money must be given both for privately owned parks and for lands previously dedicated.[4] The counties have responded in various ways to this park/playground dedication scheme.

Honolulu

While the subdivision ordinance is ultimately passed by the City Council (which also considers any amendments), it is initially prepared by the director of the Department of Planning and Permitting (DPP) and reviewed (public hearing, findings, and recommendations) by the Planning Commission. However, review of subdivisions themselves, as well as the promulgation of rules and regulations governing such approach, is up to the DPP director. The rules prohibit the subdividing of land, the selling or advertising of any interest in land located in a subdivision (that is, a lot), or the recording of a plat or subdivision unless a final plan has been approved by the director. Moreover, no roadway may be opened or building occupied until the director approves the public improvements required by the rules and regulations.[5] Appeals from the director's decisions are heard by the Zoning Board of Appeals.[6]

Honolulu follows a traditional two-step process in the review of subdivisions. An applicant files twenty copies of the preliminary map with the DPP's Subdivision Branch, which reviews the application for conformance with the Subdivision Rules and Regulations.[7] Requirements for the preliminary map include detailed location and dimensions of each lot; location and dimension of existing and proposed streets; slope and contour lines; location of landmarks and flood/inundation zones; proposed use (residence, park, public building, etc.) of each lot; and existing and proposed infrastructure (sewer, water, landscaping).[8] Copies of the map are distributed to other county and state agencies for review and comment while the DPP conducts its own review.[9] The Subdivision Branch will ultimately accept or reject the application in its entirety. If accepted, it is next reviewed by the Subdivision Committee, which meets weekly. The committee looks for any issues that stand out on the

application beyond mere conformance issues and makes a recommendation to the DPP director.

Next, the DPP director makes a preliminary map decision on the
basis of the committee's recommendation.[10] The director has very little
discretion in preliminary map approval, which signifies that the preliminary map conforms to the rules and regulations promulgated.[11] The
director's approval is generally accompanied by requirements or conditions, such as the dedication of land for streets and parks (roads, streets,
drainage, sewers, water, landscaping) or the construction or guaranteed
construction (by performance bond) of certain improvements. These
required improvements are coordinated through the relevant DPP
branch or other agency, which will upon improvement completion submit a letter of work certification to the DPP director. After preliminary
map approval, a developer may be able to obtain permits for model
homes; however, no interest may be sold with mere preliminary map
approval.

Finally, after all such improvements have been completed and
within one year of the date of preliminary map approval (unless
extended), the applicant must submit fifteen copies of the final map.
The DPP director has forty-five days to act on the final map, which decision is purely ministerial in nature. The sole question is whether or not
the final map conforms to the previously approved preliminary map,
and thus whether the required improvements have been completed.[12]

Honolulu has responded to the state's dedication of land for parks
and playgrounds requirements by including detailed provisions in its
subdivision code that extend beyond subdivisions to multifamily buildings: "Every subdivider as a condition precedent to (1) the approval of
a subdivision by the director, or (2) issuance of a building permit for
multiple family development by the Building Department, shall provide
land in perpetuity or dedicate land for park and playground purposes,
for the joint use by the occupants of lots or units in subdivisions as well
as by the public."[13] In single-family and duplex zoning districts, 350
square feet per unit must be dedicated.[14] In multifamily districts, the
requirement is 110 square feet per dwelling unit or 10 percent of the
maximum permitted floor area, whichever is less.[15]

Since the state statute permits money payment in lieu of the land
dedication requirement, the Honolulu subdivision code so provides.[16]
If the city receives cash instead of land, the money goes into a revolving
fund for parks and playgrounds, to be paid out within five years either
for the purchase of land for new or expanded parks/playgrounds, the

purchase of park/playground equipment, or the improvement of existing facilities. Regulations set out standards for the minimum size of a
parcel acceptable for dedication (two and a half acres in a residential
district, ten thousand square feet in apartment districts).[17] Priority is first
given to establishing or expanding parks and playgrounds within one-
half mile, one mile, and then two miles of the project site.[18] Honolulu
permits credits against the aforementioned requirements primarily for
private parks and playgrounds. These private facilities must be owned
and maintained by the owner and occupants of the subdivision.[19]

Kaua'i

Kaua'i's ordinance is similar both in form and content to the one
described above for Honolulu, with a few exceptions. Kaua'i also uses
a two-step review process in which copies of a preliminary subdivision
map are distributed to various county and state agencies before being
reviewed by the Planning Commission for tentative approval. Twelve copies of the map must be filed with the Planning Department and should
include the tax map key, subdivision name, the names and locations of
adjoining subdivisions, streets, and sewers, the proposed lot and street
layout of the subdivisions, the number and size of lots, the location of
flood or tsunami hazards, and so forth.[20] The various government agencies have thirty days to review the preliminary subdivision map before
they must submit their review to the planning director. The planning
director then prepares a subdivision report for the Planning Commission. At this time, the Planning Commission must approve, approve
with conditions, or disapprove the preliminary subdivision map.[21] After
tentative approval is granted, the subdivider must then submit six copies of grading plans, construction plans, and specifications showing
details and road construction, drainage structures, sewers, water mains,
and all other utilities proposed to be constructed in the subdivision.[22]
The Department of Public Works and Department of Water approve
the construction plan and submit their recommendations of approval
to the Planning Commission,[23] which is then responsible for the subdivision map's final approval.[24] In granting final approval, the Planning
Commission must determine whether the final subdivision map substantially conforms to the terms, conditions, and format of the preliminary
subdivision map, the construction plans, and whether the applicant
has satisfied all other requirements imposed by law. The commission
has forty-five days to act, or the map is deemed to be approved.[25] The

Planning Commission also has the power to grant modifications to the subdivision code in particular cases, similar to variances in practice.[26]

One of the requirements for subdivision is parks and playgrounds.[27] However, unlike Honolulu, Kauaʻi uses a population density standard to compute the amount of land to be dedicated for park and playground purposes: one and three-quarter acres per thousand "or fraction thereof."[28] As population is difficult to predict until after the development is completed, Kauaʻi's subdivision code provides the following estimates: 3.5 persons per single-family or duplex unit and 2.1 persons per multifamily dwelling unit.[29]

The manner in which a developer may pay money in lieu of dedicating land is also different. The value of the land to be developed is used as a basis to calculate the amount of money to be paid: the "raw" land plus 50 percent of the difference between that raw land value and the prospective fair market value as improved for development purposes.[30] While the money must be used for park and recreational facilities within the district where the subdivision will be developed, it is up to the county engineer to decide precisely how it is spent within that district.[31] Finally, while credit for private parks is permitted (as the state statute requires), there is a limit of 50 percent on such credit. Thus all subdivisions will have contributed to or developed truly public park and recreational facilities.[32]

Maui

The Maui subdivision provisions, like those of Kauaʻi, are found principally in a separate subdivision code. That ordinance appears to be administered solely by the planning director, who approves both preliminary and final subdivision plans. An applicant may appeal the director's decision to the Zoning Board of Adjustment and Appeals, which may also vary the subdivision ordinance's provisions.[33]

An applicant must first submit nine copies (or more if requested) of the preliminary map to the Department of Planning.[34] Within five days of submission, the planning director must distribute copies for review and comment to the director of water supply, the director of public works, the sanitary engineer, and—if the proposed subdivision is near a current or proposed state highway—the district engineer.[35] Other agencies, including the Department of Environmental Management, Department of Fire and Public Safety, and the Maui Electric Company may be consulted at the director's discretion.[36] The director's review period follows, with a decision on the preliminary map required within forty-five days, or if the project is to be processed as an affordable housing project, thirty days.[37]

The final map must be complete within one year of the preliminary map's approval; a missed deadline results in the preliminary map being deemed null and void.[38] However, a developer may request an extension in writing, which may be granted for good cause, so long as the request is made more than fifteen days before the one-year deadline.[39] When the final map is ultimately submitted, ten copies must be provided, which are again distributed to various interested agencies[40] for examination of whether the final map is "substantially similar to the approved preliminary plat, that the plat is technically correct, as well as to verify the information on the final plat by entering upon the respective subdivision."[41] A provision in the ordinance requires the director to notify the developer as to any errors or omissions within twenty days of submission, to afford the developer an opportunity to correct the final map.[42]

As in Honolulu and Kaua'i (and pursuant to state statutory requirements), Maui requires dedication of land for parks and playgrounds (or money in lieu thereof) as a condition for subdivision plat approval.[43] The amount of land required is tied to the number of lots in the subdivision: 500 square feet per lot, in excess of three, resulting from the subdivision; or 250 square feet per lot for residential workforce housing.[44] In the event the director chooses to permit the contribution of money in lieu of land, the director may require (1) payment, as calculated according to a formula in the ordinance,[45] (2) a combination of payment and land to be dedicated,[46] or (3) improvement to parks and playgrounds in the community plan area where the subdivision is located.[47]

Hawai'i

The Hawai'i subdivision ordinance also follows the two-part plan approval process characteristic of the other counties. As on Maui, it is the director of the Department of Planning who approves preliminary and final plats of subdivision. The subdivider must submit eight copies of a written application for subdivision, a preliminary plat, and other supplementary material required to describe the nature and objectives of the proposed subdivision.[48] Copies are then distributed to county and state agencies (the manager of the Department of Water Supply, the director of public works, the State Department of Health, and—if the proposed subdivision is near a state highway—the district engineer) for their review[49] and then sent back to the Planning Department for tentative approval within forty-five days of the applicant's initial submission.[50] After the director and the relevant officers have reviewed the plat, the director may defer action pending further review, give tentative approval of the preliminary plat as submitted or modified, or disapprove the preliminary plat, stating the reasons in writing.[51] If conditions are attached, the subdivider has three years to complete them. The director may grant an extension of no more than two years.[52] If the conditions are not fulfilled by the end of the three-year period, the approval of the preliminary plat expires; however, approval may be renewed provided that the preliminary map is still in conformance with current code and rule requirements.[53]

One year after tentative approval of the preliminary plat, the subdivider must prepare and complete the final plat.[54] Within thirty days of receipt, the director must again distribute copies to the relevant agencies.[55] Ultimately, final approval is a ministerial function; the director must simply determine if the subdivider has complied with all the conditions for approval. If the director disapproves the plat, the grounds for disapproval must be filed in the records of the Planning Department. However, no plat can be disapproved by the director without giving the subdivider an opportunity to correct errors on the plat map.[56] Like Kaua'i, Hawai'i County allows for subdividers to apply for variances from the provisions of the Subdivision Code.[57]

Like the other counties, Hawai'i requires the dedication of parkland by subdividers.[58] Subdividers are required to dedicate land, pay a fee, or a combination of both.[59] The amount of land to be dedicated is at least five acres for every one thousand people in the district.[60] Fees in lieu of land dedication are determined by fair market value at the time of filing.[61] The Hawai'i Subdivision Code also includes requirements for subdivisions in Safety Flood Hazard Districts,[62] plantation community subdivisions (subdivision on lands formerly owned by sugar plantations and developed into housing and community buildings for employees of the plantation),[63] farm subdivisions (subdivision of agricultural lands, provided that structures for residential occupancy or habitation are prohibited, in order to encourage landowners to provide agricultural lands for farm leasing),[64] standards for determining preexisting lots,[65] and regulations regarding the review by Hawai'i County for condominium property regimes.[66]

In sum, the four counties are largely responsible for the implementation of subdivision control in Hawai'i. The four subdivision

ordinances are similar in structure and control; however, all respond
to the mandatory park and recreation land dedication requirement
imposed by statute in substantially different ways. Only one county—
Kaua'i—ensures that a percentage of truly public area will be provided
by the erstwhile subdivider. None of the counties address the phasing
and timing of development and infrastructure improvements through
their subdivision codes in the manner of, say, Ramapo, New York, as set
forth in the landmark *Golden v. Town of Ramapo*.[67] This "sequencing" is
addressed—briefly—in the various county development plans[68] as well
as in the Revised Ordinances of Honolulu.[69] It is an important element
in the public management and control of land. Without the provision
of public improvements and the sequencing or timing of development
to coincide with those improvements, the planning for both public and
private development becomes increasingly divorced from practice.

II. LAND DEVELOPMENT CONDITIONS

For decades, local government has charged land developers for a part
of the cost of public facilities, at least with respect to those facilities
intrinsic to the development, in the form of subdivision dedications
and fees. Initially "charged" as the price of drawing and recording the
simpler and cheaper subdivision plat in place of the lengthy, tedious,
and easily flawed metes and bounds description for land development,
these fees and dedications soon became part of the regulatory land
use process, exercised by local government under police power for the
health, safety, and welfare of the people, often as a method to control
or manage growth.[70] Hawai'i has so "charged" developers at both the
state and county land use regulatory levels, both at the filing of land
use reclassification and at the time of development approval, in both
the subdivision process described in the preceding section and at the
coastal zone special or shoreline management permit stage of development. As appears below, both are theoretically governed by the state
impact fee statute. This is not so, in fact.

By justifying land development dedications and fees as police
power regulations rather than "voluntary" costs of using the subdivision
process, local governments invite judicial scrutiny under the takings
clause of the Fifth Amendment to the U.S. Constitution, which permits
the taking of private property for public use only upon payment of just
compensation. While early cases by and large upheld such intrinsic

dedications and fees, the more recent charges of "impact fees" for the shared construction by several land developments of large and expensive public facilities (such as municipal wastewater treatment plants and sanitary landfills) outside or extrinsic to the development upon which the fee is levied have led knowledgeable courts to scrutinize the connection between these fees and the need generated by the charged development for the particular facility in question.[71] It is generally agreed that the law applicable to impact fees, exactions, and in lieu fees, as well as to compulsory dedications, is the same, given that they all represent land development conditions levied at some point in the land development process, such as subdivision plat approval, shoreline management permit, building permit, occupancy permit, or utility connection.[72] Therefore, except where the text specifically makes such distinctions, the terms are used here interchangeably.

The major legal issue with respect to fees, dedications, and exactions is the connection or "nexus" to the land development. Without this nexus, such land development regulations are generally unconstitutional takings of property without compensation, particularly after the U.S. Supreme Court decisions in *Nollan v. California Coastal Commission*[73] and *Dolan v. City of Tigard.*[74]

As the history and cases make abundantly clear, such land development conditions are development driven; that is, to be valid they must be collected (and exactions and dedications required) for, and only for, public facilities and infrastructure for which land development causes a need.[75] Courts uniformly strike down—usually as an unauthorized tax—land development conditions that are not so connected. Generally, this includes attempts to remedy existing infrastructure deficiencies[76] or to provide for operation and maintenance of facilities.[77] Of course, if payment for a public facility or its construction or dedication is in part fulfillment of a landowner's contractual obligations under a development agreement between landowner and local government, then the legal issues and analysis are entirely different and the need for nexus and proportionality, at least as a matter of constitutional law, disappears.[78] Parts of this chapter discuss this issue in more detail.

Nexus, Proportionality, and Takings: The Federal Constitutional Standard

While much of the recent case law dealing with such conditions and exactions has developed from challenges to the impact fee, the language is applicable to all three. To be enforceable and valid, an impact fee must be levied upon a development to pay for public facilities, the need for which is generated, at least in part, by that development.[79] This is the so-called rational nexus test developed by the courts in Florida and other jurisdictions that have considered such fees and exactions.[80] First proposed in 1964,[81] it became the national standard by the end of the 1970s.[82]

The test essentially has two parts. First, the particular development must generate a need to which the amount of the exaction bears some rough proportionate relationship. Second, the local government must demonstrate that the fees levied will actually be used for the purpose collected.[83] This test was confirmed and made applicable to all land development conditions by a decision of the U.S. Supreme Court in 1987. Decided on the last day of the Court's 1987 term, *Nollan v. California Coastal Commission*[84] deals ostensibly with beach access. Property owners sought a coastal development permit from the California Coastal Commission to tear down a beach house and build a bigger one. The commission granted the permit only upon condition that the owner give the general public the right to walk across the owner's backyard beach area, an easement over one-third of the lot's total area. The purpose, the commission said, was to preserve visual access to the water, which was impaired by the much bigger beach house. The Court, however, held that—assuming the commission's purpose to overcome the psychological barrier to the beach created by overdevelopment was a valid one—it could not accept that there was any *nexus* between these interests and the public lateral access or easement condition attached to the permit.[85] It would be an altogether different matter if there were an "essential nexus" between the condition and what the landowner proposes to do with the property.[86]

The *Nollan* Court did not discuss the required degree of connection between the exaction imposed and the projected impacts of the proposed development. This issue was left open until the U.S. Supreme Court's 1994 decision in *Dolan v. City of Tigard.*[87] Florence Dolan owned a plumbing business and electrical supply store located in the business district of Tigard, Oregon, along Fanno Creek, which flowed through the southwestern corner of the lot and along its western boundary. Dolan applied to the city for a building permit to double the size of the store and pave the thirty-nine-space parking lot. To mitigate the impact of increased runoff from her property that would result from her expansion plans, the commission required that Dolan dedicate to the city the portion of her property lying within the hundred-year flood plain along Fanno Creek for a public greenway. To mitigate the impact of increased traffic and congestion caused by an increase in visitors to her store, the commission also required that Dolan dedicate an additional fifteen-foot strip of land adjacent to the floodplain as a public pedestrian/bicycle pathway.

In *Dolan*, the Supreme Court added a second test beyond nexus: whether the degree or amount of the exactions demanded by the city's permit conditions were sufficiently related to the projected impact of the development proposed. The Court coined the term "rough proportionality" to describe the required relationship between the exactions and the projected impact of the proposed development.[88] Although "no precise mathematical calculation is required, the city must make some sort of individualized determination that the required dedication is related both in nature and extent to the impact of the proposed development."[89] The Court reviewed the exactions (the two required dedications, of the public greenway and the pedestrian/bicycle pathway) and found that the city had not met its burden of demonstrating the required proportionality.

In sum, *Nollan* and *Dolan* require that to pass constitutional muster, land development conditions imposed by government

> 1. Must seek to promote a legitimate state interest;
> 2. Must be related to the land development project upon which they are being levied by means of a rational or essential nexus;
> 3. Must be proportional to the need or problem that the land development project is expected to cause, and the project must accordingly benefit from the condition imposed.

Under the first standard, legitimate state interest, government may require a landowner to dedicate land (or interests in land) or contribute money for public projects and purposes, such as public facilities and, in most jurisdictions, public housing. Under the second standard, essential nexus, government must find a close connection between the need or problem generated by the proposed development and the land or other exaction or fee required from the landowner/developer. Thus, for example, a residential development will in all probability generate a need for public schools and parks. A shopping center or hotel in all probability will not. Both will generate additional traffic and therefore generate a need for more streets and roads. Under the third standard, proportionality, a residential development of, say, three hundred dwelling units may well generate a need for additional classroom space but almost certainly not a new school or school site. On the other hand, such a residential development of several thousand units would, when constructed, likely generate a need for a new school and school site, depending upon the demographics of the new residents.

Ignoring the foregoing raises a presumption, as a matter of both law and policy, that the impact fee is nothing more than a revenue-raising device, either for a facility that has nothing to do with the land development upon which the fee is raised or for undetermined fiscal purposes generally. In either case, the "fee" is then presumed to be a tax. This characterization as a tax is almost always fatal to an impact fee, since most local governments have very little specific authority from the state to tax beyond the property tax and, occasionally, a sales or income tax. Since an impact fee is none of the above, and since all local government taxes must be supported by specific statutory authority, such a fee is almost always declared illegal.[90]

Applicability of *Nollan* and *Dolan* to Land Development Conditions Generally

A number of courts have struck down land development conditions for failure to comply with *Nollan*'s and *Dolan*'s three-part test. An excellent example is the Eighth Circuit Court decision in *Christopher Lake Development Co. v. St. Louis County*,[91] in which the court applied *Dolan* to strike down a county drainage system requirement.[92] The county granted the owner of forty-two acres preliminary development approval for two residential communities on the condition that the owner provide a drainage system for an entire watershed. Citing *Nollan* for the nexus test, the court held that although "the County's objective to prevent flooding may be rational, it may not be rational to single out the Partnership to provide the entire drainage system."[93] The court then found such a requirement disproportionate to the drainage problems resulting from the proposed development: "[F]rom our review of the record, the County has forced the Partnership to bear a burden that should fairly have been allocated throughout the entire watershed area. A strong public desire to improve the public condition will not warrant achieving the desire by a shorter cut than the constitutional way of paying for the change."[94] As for a remedy, the court said, "We believe that the Partnership is entitled to recoup the portion of its expenditures in excess of its pro rata share and remand to the district court to determine the details and amounts."[95]

What if a city or other local agency requires payment of an impact fee or imposes some other sort of development condition not requiring the dedication of land? Does the *Nollan/Dolan* nexus test apply? The California Supreme Court said yes in *Ehrlich v. City of Culver City*.[96] The *Ehrlich* court held that there was no ascertainable difference between a fee and a dedication. Other courts have also applied *Nollan/Dolan* beyond dedications to monetary exactions. Thus, the Ninth Circuit, in *Garneau v. City of Seattle*,[97] specifically applied the doctrine of those cases to other than physical dedications, even though it found them inapplicable for other reasons, as discussed below.[98] While noting that the case before it was not appropriate for setting out precise rules, nevertheless an Oregon appellate court held in *Clark v. City of Albany*[99] that "[t]he fact that *Dolan* itself involved conditions that required a dedication of property interests does not mean that it applies only to conditions of that kind."[100]

LEGISLATIVE DECISIONS

Many courts have ruled that the heightened scrutiny of *Nollan/Dolan* is inapplicable to legislated impact fees and exactions. The *Ehrlich* case discussed above is one of those cases. There, the court held that if a city bases a development or impact fee on an ordinance or rule of general applicability, the fee will be within the city's police power and will not be subject to the heightened constitutional scrutiny of the *Nollan/Dolan* nexus test, though there must be *some* connection between the fee and the proposed project. Also, in *Home Builders Ass'n v. City of Scottsdale*,[101] the Arizona Supreme Court specifically refused to apply heightened scrutiny to Scottsdale's water resource development fee, deciding that *Nollan/Dolan* was inapplicable to generally legislative fees of this type.[102] The Fifth Circuit also declined to apply such scrutiny to a challenge to a general zoning ordinance prohibiting trailer coaches on any lot in the city except trailer parks, in *Texas Manufactured Housing Ass'n v. City of Nederland*.[103]

However, some courts share the puzzlement of Justice Thomas in his dissent from a denial of a petition for certiorari in *Parking Ass'n of Georgia, Inc. v. City of Atlanta*:[104]

> It is not clear why the existence of a taking should turn on the type of governmental entity responsible for the taking. A city

council can take property just as well as a planning commission can. Moreover, the general applicability of the ordinance
should not be relevant in a takings analysis. . . . The distinction
between sweeping legislative takings and particularized administrative takings appears to be a distinction without a constitutional difference.[105]

Citing Justice Thomas' certiorari petition dissent in *Parking Ass'n of Georgia*, an Illinois appellate court disagreed that a municipality could "skirt
its obligation to pay compensation . . . merely by having the Village
Board of trustees pass an 'ordinance' rather than having a planning
commission issue a permit."[106] Oregon appellate courts have also consistently applied *Nollan/Dolan* to legislative and quasijudicial exactions
alike, whether required by a zoning ordinance or not.

Critical as the takings/nexus issue is, there are other legal requirements for attaching conditions to the development of land. Among
these are the need for authority to levy such dedications, fees, and other
exactions in the form of enabling legislation and local ordinances to
avoid the charge that they are "ad hoc"; and the need to expend the fee,
whether "in lieu" of a dedication requirement or an impact fee, within
a reasonable period of time after collection. These issues are discussed
below in the context of impact fees in Hawai'i.

Impact Fees in Hawai'i

Hawai'i has its own impact fee statute.[107] Recall that impact fees are not
taxes; consequently, in order to justify payment the government must
show a direct connection between the fee and a service or benefit to
the area being developed.[108] Moreover, there must be proportionality
between the amount of the fee and the benefit conferred to the development.[109] This is reflected in the statute's definition of "impact fees,"
which limits the fee's use to "all or a portion of the public facility capital
improvement costs required by the development from which it was collected," restricting the funds to that particular development.[110]

The statute lays out a clear methodology for determining impact
fees.[111] The county must first approve a needs assessment study to identify the public facilities to be benefited by the impact fees.[112] The study
must be conducted by an "engineer, architect, or other qualified professional" and must include the "data sources and methodology" upon
which the study is based.[113] The needs can be assessed for either future

or existing improvements.[114] Second, the cost must be proportional to the improvement; additionally, the developer should only pay his pro rata share.[115] The final step is ensuring that the impact fee is "fair and reasonable."[116] This step is primarily concerned with ensuring that the developer only pays a fee that is "substantially related to the needs arising from the development," as well as proportionate to the burden the newly developed property will create.[117] In determining whether a fee is a "proportional share" of the improvement costs, the statute lists seven factors.[118] Consideration of these factors is necessary to ensure that the new development pays only for its own relative increase in the burden on the community.[119]

Under the Hawai'i statute, in order to impose an impact fee the local government must demonstrate that the fee will benefit the development being charged.[120] "Collection and expenditure of impact fees assessed, imposed, levied, and collected for development shall be reasonably related to the benefits accruing to the development."[121] To ensure that the fees are reasonably related, the statute sets out several requirements. First, impact fees must be deposited in a separate account or fund;[122] this allows for better oversight of impact fee expenditures.[123] Second, the collection and expenditure of the impact fee must be "localized"; that is, there must be geographically limited benefit zones to ensure that the fees being spent are used to construct facilities from which the paying development can benefit (however, "benefit zones" are not required if the development can still enjoy a reasonable benefit without such boundaries).[124] Third, collection of the fee is predicated upon the creation of a plan that identifies the planned improvements to the development, based on the needs or anticipated needs of the development.[125] This is essentially a capital improvement plan within a needs assessment study, the purpose being to identify necessary improvements and list anticipated funding sources (of which impact fees would be one).[126] The fourth requirement requires that the fees be spent on the kind of public facilities for which the fees were originally collected.[127] Last, the collecting county must spend or encumber the impact fee within six years of its collection.[128] Those fees that are not spent within six years of their collection are refunded to the developer (or his successor) with any accrued interest.[129] Similarly, if an improvement project is terminated, the fee must be refunded to the developer as well[130] (since there is no longer any reasonable benefit being conferred upon the development).[131]

Hawai'i also has a statutory impact fee that applies only to schools.

In 2007, the State Legislature adopted a provision whereby any "new residential developments within designated school impact districts shall provide land for schools or pay a fee in lieu of land proportionate to the impacts . . . on existing school facilities."[132] Act 245 requires that no new residential development in a designated school impact district "shall be issued a residential building permit or condominium property regime building permit until the department of education provides written confirmation that the permit applicant has fulfilled its school impact fee requirements."[133]

The State School Board must first designate a school impact district for impact fee purposes. In order to designate such a district, the department must prepare a written analysis that contains a map delineating the boundaries of the impact areas as well as analysis to support the need for new or expanded school facilities construction within the next twenty-five years based on growth, density, demographics, and other criteria. After a school impact district is so designated, it then must prepare an impact fee analysis, taking into account factors such as "student generation rates" and enrollment capacity, and then based on such factors determine the appropriate impact fee to assess.[134]

From the developer's standpoint, any residential development within a school impact district that requires a county subdivision approval, a building permit, or a condominium property regime approval "shall be required to fulfill the land requirement and vertical construction requirement of the department."[135] However, certain developments are exempt: All nonresidential development, those that will pay the transient accommodation tax, or "any form of housing permanently excluding school-aged children, with the necessary covenants or declarations of restrictions recorded on the property" are not subject to this section.[136] Whether land is dedicated or a fee in lieu is paid largely depends on the size of the development. For example, in fulfilling the land requirement, contemplated developments of greater than or equal to fifty units entail either payment, land dedication, or a combination, whereas units less than fifty require only the fee in lieu.[137]

While HRS § 46-141-48 lays out a state policy regarding impact fees, many of Hawai'i's counties already have such ordinances in place, pursuant to their authority under the counties' state-delegated police powers.[138] Consequently, Hawai'i's Impact Fee Law merely provides a guideline to the counties as to the applicability, calculation, and administration of impact fees.[139] So far, however, none of the counties has modified its local impact fee ordinances to follow the state statute. The primary binding requirement the Impact Fee Law imposes over the counties is that county ordinances cannot require a development "to pay or otherwise contribute more than a proportionate share of public facility capital improvements."[140]

Of particular concern in Hawai'i is the increasing governmental tendency to attach mandatory affordable or workforce housing requirements to land use approvals. However, unless local government can demonstrate a clear rational and proportional nexus between market price and the imposition of below-market cost housing set-asides, it may not require them at any stage in the land development process. What scant precedent exists for imposing such exactions on residential developments does so only when the local government requiring such exactions provides a series of meaningful bonuses to help offset the cost of the mandatory affordable housing set-asides. As to the imposition of such costs on nonresidential development, local government must demonstrate that it generates a need for such housing, generally of the workforce variety, and that the amount to be set aside is proportionate to that need. As one commentator recently noted in the commercial housing set-aside context, "A number of cities have adopted exaction programs that require downtown office and commercial developers to provide housing for lower-income groups or to a municipal fund for the construction of such housing. [Such] programs satisfy the nexus test only if the municipality can show that downtown development *contributes to the housing problem the linkage exaction is intended to remedy.*"[141]

As noted in a standard treatise on land use, "There is some authority for the use of set-asides and other housing exactions and fees to provide needed low income housing, but whether this is a sufficient basis for nexus, let alone proportionality, to stave off a constitutional challenge, is not clear."[142] Indeed, as another treatise observes, "When the provision of lower-income housing is not linked to housing subsidies, *zoning incentives may be necessary to absorb losses incurred by the developer on the lower-income units. Density bonuses are a possibility, and the ordinance can also relax sited development requirements.*"[143]

Before addressing the constitutional issues of nexus and proportionality, there is the initial question of authority for housing set-asides or exactions. Thus, for example, Hawai'i's impact fee statute, does not apply to housing linkage fees, and, indeed, expressly excludes such fees from the authority granted to Hawai'i's four counties to levy impact fees for public facilities.[144] The relevant statute states that "impact fees may be imposed only for those types of public facility capital improvements specifically identified in a county comprehensive plan or a facility needs assessment study."[145] However, it defines "impact fees" as "the charges imposed upon a developer by a county or board to fund all or a portion of the *public facility capital improvement costs* required by the development from which it is collected, or to recoup the cost of existing public facility capital improvements made in anticipation of the needs of a development."[146] That same section also defines "public facility capital improvement costs" and explains that such costs "do not include expenditures for *required affordable housing*."[147] Moreover, Section 46-143(c) imposes nexus *and* proportionality requirements, providing that "[a]n impact fee shall be substantially related to the needs arising from the development and shall not exceed a proportionate share of the costs incurred or to be incurred in accommodating the development."[148] It is therefore not at all clear that Hawai'i's counties have the power or authority to require workforce (affordable) housing as a condition of land development approval.

While Hawai'i courts have not ruled on this issue, a Virginia court has done so. In *Kansas-Lincoln, L.C. v. Arlington County Board*[149] the court found that the county did not have the authority to include a requirement that a developer provide affordable housing as part of the land development process at the zoning stage, nor did it have the authority to require an affordable housing contribution as part of the site plan approval process:[150]

> There is no authority for the County Board to require site plan
> applicants to make affordable housing contributions to the
> County Housing Reserve Fund or provide affordable hous-
> ing units as part of the County's site plan approval process.
> Moreover, the County is not authorized to require site plan
> applicants who seek to provide affordable housing through
> the bonus density program to also make a contribution to the
> affordable housing fund as that requirement is specifically
> prohibited by Va. Code § 15.2-2304.[151]

The court found that the requirement was outside the legislative authority granted to Arlington County by the Virginia General Assembly and was, therefore, illegal and invalid.

As to the constitutional issues (nexus and proportionality), *Nollan's* nexus test, or its close equivalent, applies to linkage fees. For example, in *Commercial Builders of N. Cal. v. Sacramento*,[152] the Ninth Circuit held that an ordinance that imposed a linkage "fee in connection with the issuance of permits for nonresidential development of the type that will generate jobs,"[153] (in other words, a workforce-affordable housing requirement) was constitutional under *Nollan*.[154] Plaintiffs challenged the ordinance directly on *Nollan* grounds: lack of nexus or connection between the development and the affordable housing condition. First, the court addressed the holding of *Nollan*: "*Nollan* holds that where there is no evidence of a nexus between the development and the problem that the exaction seeks to address, the exaction cannot be upheld."[155]

The court then explained that "the [o]rdinance was implemented only after a detailed study revealed a substantial connection between development and the problem to be addressed."[156] The court related at some length what the City of Sacramento did to establish the "substantial connection between the development and the problem" of affordable housing. First, it commissioned a study of the need for low-income housing, the effect of nonresidential development on the demand for such housing, and the appropriateness of exacting fees in conjunction with such developments to pay for housing. The study:

> Estimat[ed] the percentage of new workers in the developments that would qualify as low income workers and would require housing. [The study] also calculated fees for development. . . . Also as instructed, however, in the interest of erring on the side of conservatism in exacting the fees, it reduced the final calculation by about one-half. *Based upon this study,* the City of Sacramento enacted the Housing Trust Fund Ordinance [which] . . . included the finding that *nonresidential* development is 'a major factor in attracting new employees to the region' and that the influx of new employees '*creates a need for additional housing in the City.*' *Pursuant to these findings,* the Ordinance imposes a fee in connection with *the issuance of permits* for *nonresidential* development *of the type that will generate jobs.*[157]

Consequently, the court found "that the nexus between the fee provision here at issue, designed to further the city's legitimate interest in housing, and the burdens caused by commercial development is sufficient to pass constitutional muster."[158]

Even courts that decline to apply heightened scrutiny to legislatively imposed fees nonetheless apply some form of *Nollan*'s essential nexus test. For instance, in *San Remo Hotel L.P. v. City & County of San Francisco*,[159] although the California Supreme Court reaffirmed that legislatively imposed, ministerial impact fees are not subject to the tests in *Nollan* or *Dolan*,[160] it nonetheless required that there "be a 'reasonable relationship' between the fee and the deleterious impacts for the mitigation of which the fee is collected."[161]

In sum, there are virtually no instances of courts countenancing naked linkage or affordable housing set-aside requirements on residential developments without substantial bonuses, usually consisting of significant density increases. Indeed, a recent report from a nonprofit coalition on housing in California concludes that most California local governments with inclusionary affordable housing programs provide a range of substantial density bonuses and other advantages to developers required to provide affordable housing, and the average percentage of such housing requirements is closer to 10 percent, with 20 percent being at the high end of the spectrum. This experience is replicated in other surveys of other jurisdictions.

As to workforce housing exactions or set-asides on commercial development, the principal—indeed virtually the only—federal case approving such set-asides did so only after the local government requiring such set-asides engaged in thorough and detailed studies of the workforce jobs required and generated by the proposed commercial development, which requirements were then cut in half. If government wishes to enact such an ordinance mandating affordable housing set-asides or fees on commercial development (not zoning, but actual development), then it should consider the basis upon which the Ninth Circuit Court of Appeals upheld such an ordinance passed by the City of Sacramento, and it should also:

1. Undertake a detailed study of the precise need for workforce housing;
2. Work on a project-by-project basis;
3. Calculate the precise fee or set-aside each project requires;
4. Cut that fee in half before applying it to a given project;
5. Provide meaningful density bonuses, expedited permitting, and grants.

III. DEVELOPMENT AGREEMENTS

As noted in the previous section on land development conditions, none of the legal issues are relevant if the landowner and local government execute a development agreement requiring certain contributions, dedications, and so forth from a landowner-developer. While there are additional legal issues associated with development agreements, they have been broadly upheld in those states that provide for them by statute (particularly in California, where more than a thousand have been negotiated and executed) and in another state (Nebraska) where there is no such specific statutory authorization. However, as with land development conditions, Hawai'i has no reported cases dealing with development agreements, even though its authorizing statute has been in effect since 1985. Therefore, the summary below cites only two cases from other jurisdictions.

Developers and local governments face two difficult problems in the land development approval process. Local governments are unable to exact dedications of land or fees of the "impact" or "in-lieu" variety without establishing a clear connection or nexus between the proposed development and the dedication or fee.[162] The developer is usually unable to "vest" or guarantee a right to proceed with a project until that project is commenced.[163] The situation in Hawai'i is particularly complex. Vested rights—or the point at which a development may proceed in the face of a newly enacted land use regulation that would, if applied, hinder or halt the project completely—are a commonly litigated issue across the country and in Hawai'i. Two decades ago, Honolulu's use of an interim development control (in essence, a moratorium on development during which time the land was reclassified as what was then called a historic, cultural, scenic district [HCSD]) prompted precedent-setting litigation on the issue of vested rights. In two cases, decided in 1979 and 1980, both involving the nonprofit environmental group Life of the Land and the Honolulu City Council, the Hawai'i Supreme Court attempted to deal with the issue of a developer's right to proceed with a multistory condominium project despite the passage of an HCSD ordinance forbidding its construction.[164] In *Life of the Land I*, the Court hearkened back to two earlier opinions in which it had required developers to show that they had been given assurances by appropriate local government officials that they could proceed because the development met applicable zoning regulations and that they had a right to rely on such assurances.[165] Good-faith expectancy that a permit to build would be used would not be enough. Moreover, the Court held that money damages would be an inappropriate remedy even if rights had vested. It reasoned that development rights were acquired when the property was purchased and, furthermore, that money expended in reliance on these rights—for architectural drawings and site planning—vested those rights to proceed. In *Life of the Land II*, however, the Court backtracked somewhat by deciding vested rights were not even implicated. It held that the city was simply prevented from enforcing the HCSD ordinance because the pattern of meetings and assurances given the developer caused him to justly rely on the city's representatives; thus, the city was "equitably estopped" from enforcing the ordinance. The city arguably never meant to apply the new HCSD ordinance to his development anyway.[166]

A year later came the row on the island of Kaua'i over a resort development known as Nukoli'i at Hanamā'ulu. There, despite considerable public opposition in the form of a petition drive to place before Kaua'i's voters a rescission of the zoning permitting Nukoli'i's condominiums and hotel, the development partnership began construction of the condominiums based upon an apparently validly granted zoning classification permitting such development. The developer proceeded even though the petition had been certified (approved for voting) and the proposition to rescind was placed on the ballot. To no one's surprise, the proposition passed. Still the partnership continued to build, commencing hotel construction. After the zoning was ultimately rescinded, the partnership claimed that the right to finish construction had vested, taking advantage of the part of Kaua'i's charter initiative provision that expressly forbids such votes to affect vested rights. While the circuit court upheld the developer, the Hawai'i Supreme Court reversed the decision and ordered the cancellation of building permits and the halting of all construction activities.[167] The Court held that once the referendum was certified, the holding of the referendum itself was the last step (before building permits could issue) in the development permit process, which the developer needed to obtain vested rights.[168] It also decided that, unless no economic uses were left, a landowner's property could not be "taken" by regulation.

The decision was initially predicted to increase the popularity of initiative and referendum in Hawai'i. However, six years later, the State Supreme Court held in another landmark case that zoning by initiative is not allowed in Hawai'i. In *Kaiser Hawaii Kai Development Co. v. City &*

County of Honolulu,[169] the Hawaiʻi Supreme Court held that "[z]oning by initiative is inconsistent with the goal of long-range comprehensive planning"[170] and invalidated an initiative downzoning a parcel of land. It is likely that the Hawaiʻi Supreme Court would also invalidate zoning by referendum if it were ever presented with the question of whether such zoning is also inconsistent with the goal of long-range comprehensive planning.[171] Thus, despite the *Nukolii* decision, zoning by initiative and referendum is unlikely to play a role in the future in Hawaiʻi.

The development agreement offers a solution to both landowner-developer and local government. Usually authorized by statute, a well-structured agreement can be drafted to deal with a variety of common issues that arise in the land development process between landowner and local government.[172]

A major issue for government under the "vested rights" problem is whether the local government has bargained away its police power by entering into an agreement under which it promises not to change its land use regulations during the life of the agreement. Specific statutory authorization is helpful so as to make clear that these agreements effectuate public purposes recognized by the state. Thirteen states have so far adopted legislation enabling local governments to enter into development agreements with landowner-developers.[173] The dominant view is that development agreements, drafted to reserve some governmental control over the agreement, do not contract away police power but rather constitute a valid present exercise of that power. Thus, a recent California appeals court upheld a development agreement that was challenged directly on "surrender of police power" grounds, holding that a "zoning freeze in the Agreement is not . . . a surrender or abnegation [of the police power]."[174] In *Santa Margarita Area Residents Together v. San Luis Obispo County Bd. of Supervisors,* an area residents' association contended that because San Luis Obispo County had entered into a development agreement for a project before the project was ready for construction, freezing zoning for a five-year period, the county improperly contracted away its zoning authority.[175] In holding for the county, the court noted that land use regulation is an established function of local government, providing the authority for a local government to enter into contracts to carry out the function. The county's development agreement required that the project be developed in accordance with the county's general plan, did not permit construction until the county had approved detailed building plans, retained the county's discretionary authority in the future, and allowed a zoning freeze of limited duration only. The court found that the zoning freeze in the county's development agreement was not a surrender of police power but instead "advance[d] the public interest by preserving future options."

A second issue in the "vested rights" category is whether a city council, in exercising its power to contract, can make a contract that binds its successors. One of the clearest rejections of the application of reserved power and bargaining away police power comes from the wide-ranging Nebraska Supreme Court opinion upholding development agreements in *Giger v. City of Omaha*.[176] The objectors to the agreement claimed that development agreements were a form of contract zoning. However, the Nebraska Supreme Court preferred to characterize such agreements as a form of conditional zoning that actually increased the city's police power, rather than lessened it, by permitting more restrictive zoning (attaching conditions through agreement) than a simple rezoning to a district in which a variety of uses would be permitted of right.[177]

A Statutory Checklist

The Hawai'i statute contains minimum standards for describing the basic character of a proposed development subject to a development agreement.

1. Enabling Ordinance

A preliminary issue is whether an enabling statute is sufficient to grant local government the authority to enter into development agreements. There is some authority for requiring a local government to pass an enabling ordinance setting out the details of development agreement procedures and requirements. Thus, the Hawai'i statute appears to require that local governments desiring to negotiate development agreements first pass a local resolution or ordinance to that effect.[178] In Hawai'i,.the State Legislature has delegated the authority to the county to enter into development agreements—provided, however, that the county first passes an enabling ordinance establishing the procedures that the county executive branch must follow. All of Hawai'i's four counties have drafted them.

2. Approval and Adoption

Although one governmental body may enter into the negotiation stage of the development agreement, another may be authorized to approve the final product. In Hawai'i, for example, the mayor is the designated negotiator, with the final agreement presented to the county legislative body (county council) for approval. If approved, the council must then adopt the development agreement by resolution.[179]

3. Conformance to Plans and Other Reviews

Development agreements must often comply with local government plans as a condition of enforceability, either by statute or because of the rubric that the zoning bargained for must accord with comprehensive plans. The development agreement statute in Hawai'i so requires.[180] The importance of the plan is demonstrated by the Idaho Supreme Court in *Sprenger, Grubb & Associates, Inc. v. City of Hailey*.[181] There, the court upheld a rezoning over the objections of the developers of property subject to what the court called a "development agreement" (arguably an annexation agreement), on the ground that the applicable plan was sufficiently broad in that it supported the contested downzoning.[182] Largely to the same effect is a recent California court of appeals decision where the existence of and need to conform to applicable plans was critical in upholding a development agreement in the face of a broad and direct challenge to such agreements generally.[183]

4. The Legislative/Administrative Issue

One of the thorniest problems in land use regulation is whether the amendment or changing of such a regulation is legislative or quasijudicial/administrative.[184] Legislative decisions such as zoning amendments are subject to initiative and referendum, whereas in most jurisdictions, quasijudicial decisions such as the granting of a special use permit are not. Legislative decisions such as rezonings are, when appealed, usually heard de novo, whereas quasijudicial decisions such as the granting of a special use permit are decided on the record made before the permitting agency, usually under a state's administrative procedure code.[185] How to characterize the development agreement is different in California and Hawai'i: In the former, it is a legislative act,[186] whereas it is an administrative act in the latter.[187]

5. Public Hearing

Another issue arising frequently is whether a public hearing is required before a development agreement can be executed, and if so, what proceedings are required. Hawai'i explicitly requires that a public hearing be held prior to adoption of the development agreement.[188]

6. Binding of State and Federal Agencies

Another issue arising frequently is the binding inclusion of state or federal agencies. Hawaiʻi seeks to bind them and appears to authorize state and federal agencies to join in development agreements.[189]

7. Amendment or Cancellation of the Agreement

Generally, mutual consent of both parties is needed to amend or cancel the agreement.[190] In Hawaiʻi, if the proposed amendment would substantially alter the original agreement, a public hearing must be held.[191]

8. Breach

There are essentially two kinds of breaches that commonly occur during the period of an agreement: change in land use rules by local government and failure to provide a bargained-for facility, dedication, or hookup by either party.

a. When Local Government Changes the Land Development Rules

Recall that the overriding concern of the landowner in negotiating a development agreement is the vesting of development rights or the freezing of land development regulations during the term of the agreement. Whether these regulations are changed just prior to the execution of the agreement and whether the landowner may need further permits that are not subject to a particular agreement raise different but related questions. Here, we deal only with the effect on the landowner and the agreement should the local government change development regulations during the term of the agreement. Development agreement statutes usually contemplate such a freeze.[192]

The Hawaiʻi statute clearly and unequivocally provides that regulations and ordinances passed or promulgated after the execution of a development agreement are "void" unless necessary to prevent a danger to the health and safety of residents.[193] The California Supreme Court, in *City of West Hollywood v. Beverly Towers*,[194] made it abundantly clear in a footnote that landowner protection from development regulation changes is a major factor in executing development agreements: "Development agreements . . . between a developer and a government limit the power of that government to apply newly enacted ordinances to ongoing developments. Unless otherwise provided in the agreement, the rules, regulations, and official policies governing permitted uses, density, design, improvement, and construction are those in effect when the agreement is executed."[195]

The purpose of a development agreement, said the court, was "to allow a developer who needs additional discretionary approvals to complete a long-term development project as approved, regardless of any intervening changes in local regulations."[196]

The few courts that have dealt with local government changes in land use regulations have no difficulty in finding them inapplicable to the property subject to the agreement, provided the agreement itself is binding. Thus, in *Meegan v. Village of Tinley Park*,[197] the Illinois Supreme Court held that the original zoning of the subject property was valid during the term of the annexation agreement and any change by the village was void during that time. Indeed, since the village's attempted zoning change was void, said the court, there was no breach by the village.[198]

On the other hand, careful drafting is necessary to avoid the later application of land development regulations of a different sort than those contemplated in the agreement. Thus, in the California case of *Pardee Construction Co. v. City of Camarillo*,[199] the court held applicable to the subject property a transportation impact fee on the ground that it was different from the land development regulations listed in the agreement as frozen. While this seems to require a certain amount of prescience from the landowner at first blush, a local government can hardly be estopped from exercising its police power in enforcing a new breed of land development regulations that were not contemplated years before by either party as being included under the authority of its police power. *Country Meadows West Partnership v. Village of Germantown* represents a different perspective, where the court struck down the village's imposition of a new impact fee against a subdivider, holding that because of a subdivision agreement between the village and the subdivider, the latter was not obligated to pay the impact fee.[200]

Most development agreement statutes either contain a limitation on the duration of such agreements,[201] or they provide that the agreement must recite one.[202]

b. Nonperformance of a Bargained-for Act: Dedications, Contributions, and Hookups

Equally common is the failure of a landowner or local government to live up to the other terms of the agreement, generally by failing to provide a public facility or money therefor or by refusing to provide utility services to the subject property.[203] Under such circumstances, the courts have been strict in forcing the parties to live up to their bargains, even when unusual difficulties would appear to render such performance nearly impossible. Thus, in the California case of *Morrison Homes Corp. v. City of Pleasanton*, the court of appeals directed the local government to provide sewer connections to the landowner's property, as agreed in an annexation agreement, even though a superior governmental entity—a state regional water quality control board—ordered the local government not to do so.[204] After deciding that the agreement did not amount to the city's illegally contracting away its police power, the court stated, "The onset of materially changed conditions is not a ground for voiding a municipal contract which was valid when made, nor is the contracting city's failure to have foreseen them.[205]

Limits on Local Government Conditions, Exactions, and Dedications Pursuant to Development Agreements

While every governmental action must be invested with a public purpose, there are few conditions, exactions, or dedications that a local government may not legitimately bargain for in negotiating such agreements. Certainly, local governments may require landowners and developers to make reasonable contributions toward whatever services and other resources the government will need to provide as a result of an annexation or development.[206] But this is so under existing law on development conditions and exactions entirely apart from such agreements.[207] The question is whether the local government may go further since the development agreement is in theory a voluntary agreement that neither government nor landowner is compelled to either negotiate or execute. So long as the agreement is in fact voluntary, the answer is almost certainly yes.[208]

The Hawai'i development agreement statue provides that "Public benefits derived from development agreements may include, but are not limited to, affordable housing, design standards, and on- and off-site infrastructure and other improvements. Such benefits may be negotiated for in return for the vesting of development rights for a specific period." [209] According to one commentator,

> the government can require the developer to provide public
> benefits unrelated to the proposed project in exchange for the
> municipality granting her the right to develop. . . . [T]he stat-
> ute leads municipalities to believe that the granting of develop-

ment rights confers a governmental benefit on the developer. This is not the case. *Nollan* clearly holds that "the right to build on one's own property—even though its exercise can be subjected to legitimate permitting requirements—cannot remotely be described as a "governmental benefit."[210]

However, while it is true that the right to develop on one's own land is not a governmental benefit, the right to develop is not the bargaining chip being tendered by the government in a development agreement. The authorities cited in support of the above-quoted argument concern exactions imposed as required conditions to development. In the case of a development agreement, the municipality is not granting the landowner the right to develop nor imposing conditions on such development but instead is promising to protect the developer's investment by not enforcing any subsequent land use regulation that may burden the project. The developer does not require any such guarantee to exercise his right or privilege to build and may certainly choose to avail himself of such a guarantee and to negotiate for it. It could be argued that the development agreement does indeed convey a "governmental benefit" upon the developer, since "[i]t is well established that there is no federal Constitutional right to be free from changes in land use laws."[211] The municipality should therefore be free to negotiate its best terms in exchange for the benefit conferred, regardless of nexus. Because development agreements are adopted as a result of negotiations between a local government and a developer, they are not subject to either nexus or proportionality requirements imposed either by the *Dolan* or *Nollan* decisions or by any state court decisions.[212]

IV. HAWAI'I'S BUILDING CODE

Finally, a brief look at Hawai'i's Building Code and its provisions is helpful, as compliance with the code is a subsequent form of land use regulation to be dealt with after a successful subdivision process.

Building codes protect the health and safety of citizens by creating a uniform standard for construction at a state level, allowing building owners, designers, contractors, and code enforcers within the state to apply consistent standards.[213] Thus a code functions to require adequate access to buildings, ensure structural integrity, and make sure structures have adequate electric, plumbing, sewage disposal, and protection,

particularly in case of severe weather or natural disaster.[214] Traditionally, Hawai'i's counties were allowed to promulgate their own building
codes—which tracked various versions of the Uniform Building Code
dating back to 1991[215]—independent of one another.[216] This lack of uni-
formity had resulted in fragmented building requirements throughout
the state, which in turn created public health and safety concerns while
also posing a major problem to those "involved in building ownership,
design, construction, and insurance."[217]

To remedy such inconsistencies, the State Building Code Council
(administered under the Department of Accounting and General Services) was created in 2007 to "establish and implement" a State Building Code.[218] The council is comprised of a building official from each
county, the comptroller of the Department of Accounting and General
Services, and representatives from the State Fire Council, State Health
Department, Department of Labor and Industrial Relations, the Structural Engineers Association of Hawai'i, and the American Institute of
Architects.[219] In addition to continuously working to keep the code
updated, the council must also provide educational and technical training and assistance to affected agencies.[220] This assistance may include
"services or grants at the state and county levels relating to the implementation and enforcement of the state building code."[221]

The code regulates all substantial construction in Hawai'i, including the "construction, alteration, movement, enlargement, replacement,
repair, equipment, use and occupancy, location, maintenance, removal
and demolition of every building or structure or any appurtenances
connected or attached to such buildings or structures."[222] Accessibility,
structural integrity, hurricane and high-wind standards, fire safety, electrical standards, and plumbing and sewage standards are also regulated.
Finally, the code acknowledges and establishes procedures for designing
and constructing indigenous Hawaiian architectural structures, authorizing both the use of certain building materials as well as allowable uses.[223]

The content of the code is also specified by the act. The code must
include the following: the latest edition of the fire code as adopted
by the State Fire Council, the latest edition of the Uniform Plumbing
Code, the latest edition of the International Building Code, Hawai'i
design standards for emergency shelters that are hurricane resistant
and nationally recognized code provisions that include standards for
residential and hurricane resistance, residential construction, fires,
elevators, electrical, plumbing, mechanical, flood and tsunami, existing
buildings, energy conservation, and on-site sewage disposal.[224]

It is worth noting that the State Building Code is a guideline for the counties, and the counties are allowed to amend the state model without state approval.[225] However, if a county does not amend the statewide model code within two years, the state code becomes the county's code for the interim until the county adopts any amendments.[226] The county also has the right to control and implement all administrative, permitting and enforcement, and inspection procedures.[227]

Hawai'i Administrative Rules Title 3 Chapter 180 (Draft 2009) will adopt the State Building Code as required by Haw. Rev. Stat. § 107-25 (2009) under the authority of Haw. Rev. Stat. § 107-29 (2009). The State Building Code is modeled after the International Building Code, 2006 edition. "Detached one- and two-family dwellings and multiple single-family dwellings (townhouses) not more than three stories above grade plane in height" may be exempt if the county adopts the international residential code that will then govern.[228] "Existing state-owned buildings undergoing repair, alterations or additions and change of occupancy shall be permitted to comply with the existing Building Code, provided the extent of work does not exceed 50% of the appraised value of the building."[229] Existing buildings can continue the use or occupancy that existed at the time of the adoption of the Building Code as long as the use was legal at the time of adoption and the "use does not constitute a hazard to the general safety and welfare of the occupants and the public."[230]

Notes

1. Such land development conditions can of course be levied at virtually any stage of the land development process—as opposed to rezoning, at which stage such conditions are almost certainly unconstitutional—and in Hawai'i the counties levy such conditions legally at other stages of the development process as well, most commonly at the Special Management Area permit stage under the local implementation of the Hawaii Coastal Zone Management Act, discussed in chapter 5. Of course, land outside the county-designated landward portion of the coastal zone does not require such a permit for development, and so, obviously, land development conditions could not be imposed at that stage of the land development process.

2. Although the federal district court has ruled on certain ripeness issues in connection with a mandatory housing set-aside in the course of disposing of motions for summary judgment in *Kamaole Pointe Dev. LP v. County of Maui*, 2008 WL 5025004 (D. Haw. Nov. 25, 2008). For discussion of state common law on such land development conditions, see David L. Callies, Daniel J. Curtin, and Julie A. Tappendorf, *Bargaining for Development: A Handbook on Development Agreements, Annexation Agreements, Land Development Conditions, Vested Rights, and the Provision of Public Facilities,*

Washington, D.C.: Environmental Law Institute, 2003 and Arthur C. Nelson, Liza K. Bowles, Julian C. Juergensmeyer, and James Nicholas, *A Guide to Impact Fees and Housing Affordability*, Washington D.C.: Island Press, 2008.

3. Callies et al., *Bargaining for Development*, supra note 2.
4. HAW. REV. STAT. § 46-6(c).
5. HONOLULU, HAW., REV. ORDINANCES §§ 22-3.9, -3.8(a) (2007) (hereinafter "Honolulu Ord.").
6. Id. § 22-3.7(a).
7. City & County of Honolulu, Department of Planning & Permitting, *Guidelines on Processing a Subdivision Application* (Rev. 2005), http://honoluludpp.org/downloadpdf/engineering/subappguide.pdf. (last visited Nov. 24, 2009).
8. City & County of Honolulu, Department of Planning & Permitting, *Subdivision Rules and Regulations*, § 2-201 (1973).
9. Id. §§ 2-202, -203.
10. Id. § 2-203.
11. Id. §§ 2-203, 3-303.
12. Honolulu Ord. § 22-3.6 (2007). At least one state court outside Hawai'i has held that once a preliminary plat or plan is approved, local government is obligated, as a ministerial act, to approve the final plat or plan. *Youngblood v. Bd. of Supervisors*, 586 P.2d 556 (Cal. 1978).
13. Honolulu Ord. § 22-7.3.
14. Id. § 22-7.5(c)(1).
15. Id. § 22-7.5(c)(2).
16. Id. § 22-7.3(a).
17. Id. § 22-7.5.
18. Id. § 22-7.6(d). Regional parks are given last priority. Id.
19. Id. § 22-7.8(c).
20. County of Kaua'i, *Kauai County Code* § 9-3.3 (2006).
21. Id. § 9-3.4(b).
22. Id. § 9-3.5(a).
23. Id. § 9-3.7(d).
24. Id. § 9-3.8(d)(3).
25. Id.
26. Id. § 9-4.1.
27. Id. § 9-2.8.
28. County of Kaua'i, *Subdivision Ordinance*, § 9-2.8.
29. Id. § 9-2.8(d)(2).
30. Id. § 9-2.8(e)(1).
31. Id. § 9-2.8(e)(3)(A).
32. Id. § 9-2.8(f)(1).
33. County of Maui, *Maui County Code*, §§ 18.36.010, 18.36.020.
34. Id. § 18.08.020(A).
35. Id. § 18.08.090(A), (B).
36. County of Maui, Department of Public Works, *Subdivision Processing Guidelines* (Rev. 2008), http://www.co.maui.hi.us/documents/Public%20Works/DSA/Subdivision%20Section/processing%20guidelines_rev0708.PDF. (last visited Nov. 24, 2009).

37. Maui, *County Code*, § 18.08.100(A)(1), (2).
38. Id. § 18.12.010.
39. Id. § 18.12.060(A).
40. Id. § 18.12.070.
41. Id.
42. Id.
43. Id. § 18.16.320(B)(1).
44. Id. § 18.16.320(B)(2)(c).
45. Id. § 18.16.320(c)(1). In-lieu Payment and Dedication. In lieu of providing land in perpetuity or dedicating land, the director of parks and recreation shall require the subdivider to

> 1. Pay to the County a sum of money equal to the number of square feet that would have been required by subsection (B)(2)(c) of this section, multiplied by average of the following values, determined at subdivision approval, in accordance with the most recent certified assessment for real property tax purposes in the respective community plan area where the subdivision is located:
>> a. The average value per square foot of lands classified as improved residential;
>> b. The average value per square foot of lands classified as unimproved residential; and
>> c. The average value per square foot of lands classified as apartment.

Id. § 18.16.320(C)(1).

46. Id. § 18.16.320(C)(2).
47. Id. § 18.16.320(C)(3). The value of such improvements shall be at least equal to the sum of money required to be paid pursuant to this section.
48. County of Hawai'i, *Hawaii County Code*, § 23-58(a) (2005).
49. Id. § 23-61.
50. Id. § 23-62(a).
51. Id. § 23-62(a).
52. Id. § 23-62(d).
53. Id.
54. Id. § 23-67.
55. Id. § 23-73.
56. Id. § 23-74.
57. Id. § 23-14.
58. Id. § 8-5.
59. Id.
60. Id. § 8-6(a). Population density is calculated at single-family dwellings and duplexes at 3.5 persons/unit and multiple-family dwellings at 2.1 persons/unit. Id. § 8-6(b).
61. Id. § 8-8.
62. Id. §§ 23-99 through 23-102.
63. Id. § 23-103 through 23-111.
64. Id. § 23-112 through 23-116.

65. Id. § 23-117 through 23-120.

66. Id. § 23-121 through 23-143.

67. *Golden v. Planning Bd. of Town of Ramapo*, 285 N.E.2d 291 (N.Y. 1972). There, New York's highest court upheld subdivision regulations that prohibited the building of more than four houses in an area that was determined to be inadequately served by water, sewer, power, and fire protection service. The landowner either waited for *Ramapo* or built the services at their own cost. For discussion and criticism of *Ramapo* and sequencing/control generally, *see* Randall W. Scott, David J. Bower, and Dallas D. Miner, *The Management and Control of Growth: Issues, Techniques, and Trends*, Washington, D.C.: Urban Land Institute, 1974, at chapters 8 and 9; Fred. P. Bosselman, "Can the town of Ramapo pass a law to bind the rights of the whole world?" 1 FLA. ST. U. L. REV. 234 (1973).

68. See, for example, the two development plans for the City and County of Honolulu governing the urban core and 'Ewa districts.

69. Honolulu Ord. § 24-1.9.

70. Robert H. Freilich, *From Sprawl to Smart Growth*, Chicago: American Bar Association, 2000; Julian Conrad Juergensmeyer and Thomas E. Roberts, *Land Use Planning and Control Law*, 2d ed., St. Paul: West, 2002; Robert H. Freilich and David W. Bushek, eds., *Exactions, Impact Fees and Dedications: Shaping Land-Use Development and Funding Infrastructure in the* Dolan *Era*, Chicago: State and Local Government Law Section, ABA, 1995; David L. Callies, Robert H. Freilich,and Thomas E. Roberts, *Cases and Materials on Land Use*, 5th ed., St. Paul: West, 2008; Robert H. Freilich and Michael M. Shultz, *National Model Subdivision Regulations: Planning and Law*, Chicago: APA Planners Press, 1995, at 1–6; Daniel R. Mandelker, *Land Use Law*, 4th ed., Charlottesville, VA: LEXIS, 1997; Susan P. Schoettle and David G. Richardson, "Nontraditional uses of the utility concept to fund public facilities," 25 URB. LAW. 519, 519–522 (1993); Frona M. Powell, "Challenging authority for municipal subdivision exactions: The ultra vires attack," 39 DEPAUL L. REV. 635, 635–636 (1990); Julian Conrad Juergensmeyer and Robert M. Blake, "Impact fees: An answer to local government's capital funding dilemma," 9 FLA. ST. U. L. REV. 415 (1981); Thomas M. Pavelko, "Subdivision exactions: A review of judicial standards," 25 J. URB. & CONTEMP. L. 269 (1983); James E. Frank and Robert M. Rhodes. eds., *Development Exactions*, Washington, D.C.: Planners Press, 1987. The British also continue to experiment with land development conditions. *See*, e.g., Tom Cornford, "Planning gain and the government's new proposals on planning obligations," 2002 J. PLAN. & ENV'T. L. 796; David L. Callies and Malcolm Grant, "Paying for growth and planning gain: An Anglo American comparison of development conditions, impact fees and development agreements," 23 URB. LAW. 221 (1991).

71. Ira M. Heyman and Thomas K. Gilhool, "The constitutionality of imposing increased community costs on new suburban residents through subdivision exactions," 73 YALE L.J. 1119 (1964); *see also* John D. Johnston, Jr., "Constitutionality of subdivision exactions: The quest for a rationale," 52 CORNELL L.Q. 871 (1967).

72. *Bd. of County Comm'rs of Boulder Co. v. Homebuilders Ass'n of Metro. Denver*, No. 95SC479, 1996 WL 700564 at *4 (Colo. 1996) (citing Donald G. Hagman and Julian Conrad Juergensmeyer, *Urban Planning and Land Development Control Law*, 2nd ed., St. Paul: West, 2002, § 9.8); Frank and Rhodes, *Development Exactions*, supra note 70, at 3–4.

73. 483 U.S. 825 (1987).

74. 512 U.S. 374, (1994). For a recent commentary, *see* J. David Breemer, "The evolution of the nexus test," 59 WASH. & LEE L. REV. 373 (2002).

75. James C. Nicholas, "Impact exactions: economic theory, practice, and incidence," 50 LAW & CONTEMP. PROBS. 85 (1987); James C. Nicholas, Arthur C. Nelson, and Julian Conrad Juergensmeyer, *A Practitioner's Guide to Development Impact Fees*, Chicago: Planners Press, 1991, at 37–38; David L. Callies, ed., *Takings: Land Development Conditions and Regulatory Takings after Dolan and Lucas*, Chicago: ABA, 1996.

76. *Marblehead v. City of San Clemente*, 277 Cal. Rptr. 550 (1991).

77. But *see Bloom v. City of Fort Collins*, 784 P.2d 304 (1989).

78. Callies and Grant, "Paying for growth and planning gain," supra note 70, at 239–250.

79. David L. Callies, "Impact fees, exactions and paying for growth in Hawaii," 11 U. HAW. L. REV. 295 (1989); Brian W. Blaesser and Christine M. Kentopp, "Impact fees: The second generation," 38 WASH. U.J. URB. & CONTEMP. L. REV. 55 (1990); Julian Conrad Juergensmeyer, *Funding Infrastructure: Paying the Costs of Growth Through Impact Fees and Other Land Regulation Charges*, Lincoln Institute of Land Policy Monograph 85-5 (Feb. 1985); Callies et al., *Cases and Materials on Land Use*, supra note 70, at chapter 4.

80. *See*, e.g., *Hernando County v. Budget Inns of Fla., Inc.*, 555 So.2d 1319 (Fla. Dist. Ct. App. 1990); *Frisella v. Town of Farmington*, 550 A.2d 102 (N.H. 1988); *Baltica Constr. Co. v. Planning Bd. of Franklin Twp.*, 537 A.2d 319 (N.J. App. 1987); *Batch v. Town of Chapel Hill*, 387 S.E.2d 655 (N.C. 1990); *Unlimited v. Kitsap County*, 750 P.2d 651 (Wash. App. 1988).

81. Heyman and Gilhool, "The constitutionality of imposing increased community costs, supra note 71; *see also* Fred P. Bosselman and Nancy Stroud, "Legal aspects of development exactions, in *Development Exactions*, Chicago: Planners Press, 1987.

82. *See* Bosselman and Stroud, "Legal aspects," supra note 81, at 74.

83. Fred P. Bosselman and Nancy E. Stroud, "Mandatory tithes: The legality of land development linkage, 9 NOVA. L.J. 381, 397–399 (1985); *see also Holmdel Builders Ass'n v. Twp. of Holmdel*, 583 A.2d 277 (N.J. 1990).

84. 483 U.S. 825 (1987).

85. Id. at 838–839. For full discussion, *see* Callies and Grant, "Paying for growth and planning gain," supra note 70.

86. 483 U.S. 836–837. *See also* Bosselman and Stroud, "Mandatory tithes," supra note 83; Callies, "Impact fees," supra note 79; Brenda Valla, "Linkage: The next stop in developing exactions," 2 GROWTH MGMT STUD. NEWSL. No. 4, June 1987, at 4; Jerold S. Kayden and Robert Pollard, "Linkage ordinances and traditional exactions analysis," 50 LAW & CONTEMP. PROBS. 127 (Winter 1987); Rachelle Alterman, "Evaluating linkage and beyond," 32 WASH. U. J. URB & CONTEMP. L. 3 (1988); Callies et al., *Cases and Materials on Land Use*, supra note 70. But *see Holmdel Builders Ass'n v. Twp. of Holmdel*, 583 A.2d 277 (N.J. 1990) (upholding impact fees for housing as functional equivalents of mandatory set-asides, which the court had already approved under New Jersey's constitutionally based "fair share" doctrine).

87. 512 U.S. 374 (1994).

88. After coining the term "rough proportionality," the Court, in its majority opinion, never used that term again when it applied its decision to the facts; instead it continued to use the words "required reasonable relationship" or "reasonably related." Notably, the Court rejected stricter standards as the constitutional norm. *See Herron v. Mayor & City Council of Annapolis*, 388 F. Supp. 2d 565, 570–571 (D. Md. 2005).

89. *Dolan v. city of Tigard*, 512 U.S. 374, 395–396 (1994).

90. *See*, e.g., *Town of Longboat Key v. Lands End Ltd.*, 433 So.2d 574 (Fla. Dist. Ct. App. 1983); *Lafferty v. Payson City*, 642 P.2d 376 (Utah 1982); *Home Builders Ass'n of Cent. Ariz., Inc. v. Riddel*, 510 P.2d 376 (Ariz. 1973). *See generally* Juergensmeyer, *Funding Infrastructure*, supra note 79; Robert Mason Blake and Julian Conrad Juergensmeyer, "Impact fees: An answer to local governments' capital funding dilemma," 9 FLA. ST. U. L. REV. 415 (1981).

91. 35 F.3d 1269 (8th Cir. 1994).

92. Id. at 1274–1275.

93. Id.

94. *Christopher Lake*, 35 F.3d at 1275 (quoting *Dolan v. City of Tigard*, 512 U.S. 374, 396 [1994]).

95. Id.

96. 12 Cal. 14th 854 (1996). The Supreme Court of California recently reaffirmed the Ehrlich approach in *San Remo Hotel, L.P. v. City and County of San Francisco*, 41 P.3d 87, 104 (Cal. 2002).

97. 147 F.3d 802 (9th Cir. 1998).

98. Id. at 809-811.

99. 904 P.2d 185 (Or. Ct. App. 1995).

100. Id. at 189.

101. 930 P.2d 993 (Ariz. 1997).

102. Id. at 999–1000; *cf. GST Tucson Lightwave, Inc. v. City of Tucson*, 949 P.2d 971, 978–979 (Ariz. Ct. App. 1997) (deciding that *Nollan/Dolan* was inapplicable to a "franchise or license issued by a municipality to use public rights-of-way").

103. 101 F.3d 1095, 1105 (5th Cir. 1996).

104. 515 U.S. 1116 (1995).

105. Id. at 1117–1118.

106. *Amoco Oil Co. v. Village of Schaumburg*, 661 N.E.2d 380, 389–390 (Ill. App. Ct. 1995); *Twin Lakes Dev. Corp. v Town of Monroe*, 801 N.E.2d 821 (N.Y. 2003) (applying *Nollan* and *Dolan* to a fixed subdivision in lieu fee).

107. HAW. REV. STAT. § 46-141 et seq.

108. James C. Nicholas and Dan Davidson, *Impact Fees in Hawaii: Implementing the State Law*, Honolulu: Land Use Research Foundation, 1993, at 5.

109. Id.

110. HAW. REV. STAT. § 46-141. "Impact fees" means the charges imposed upon a developer by a county or board to fund all or a portion of the public facility capital improvement costs required by the development from which it is collected or to recoup the cost of existing public facility capital improvements made in anticipation of the needs of a development.

111. Nicholas and Davidson, *Impact Fees in Hawaii*, supra note 108 at 12.

112. HAW. REV. STAT. § 46-143(a): "A county council or board considering

the enactment or adoption of impact fees shall first approve a needs assessment study that shall identify the kinds of public facilities for which the fees shall be imposed. The study shall be prepared by an engineer, architect, or other qualified professional and shall identify service standards levels, project public facility capital improvement needs, and differentiate between existing and future needs."

113. HAW. REV. STAT.§ 46-143(a) and (b). Part (a) is set out supra note 112, and part (b) provides that "The data sources and methodology upon which needs assessments and impact fees are based shall be set forth in the needs assessment study."

114. Nicholas and Davidson, *Impact Fees in Hawaii*, supra note 108 at 12.

115. HAW. REV. STAT.§ 46-143(c): "The pro rata amount of each impact fee shall be based upon the development and actual capital cost of public facility expansion, or a reasonable estimate thereof, to be incurred."

116. Nicholas and Davidson, *Impact Fees in Hawaii*, supra note 108 at 12.

117. Id. at 12–13; *see also* HAW. REV. STAT.§ 46-143(d).

118. The Hawai'i Code provides the following:

> An impact fee shall be substantially related to the needs arising from the development and shall not exceed a proportionate share of the costs incurred or to be incurred in accommodating the development. The following seven factors shall be considered in determining a proportionate share of public facility capital improvement costs:
>
> (1) The level of public facility capital improvements required to appropriately serve a development, based on a needs assessment study that identifies:
>> (A) Deficiencies in public facilities;
>> (B) The means, other than impact fees, by which existing deficiencies will be eliminated within a reasonable period of time; and
>> (C) Additional demands anticipated to be placed on specified public facilities by a development;
>
> (2) The availability of other funding for public facility capital improvements, including but not limited to user charges, taxes, bonds, intergovernmental transfers, and special taxation or assessments;
>
> (3) The cost of existing public facility capital improvements;
>
> (4) The means by which existing public facility capital improvements were financed;
>
> (5) The extent to which a developer required to pay impact fees has contributed in the previous five years to the cost of existing public facility capital improvements and received no reasonable benefit therefrom, and any credits that may be due to a development because of such contributions;
>
> (6) The extent to which a developer required to pay impact fees over the next twenty years may reasonably be anticipated to contribute to the cost of existing public facility capital improvements through user fees, debt service payments, or other payments; and any credits that may accrue to a development because of future payments; and
>
> (7) The extent to which a developer is required to pay impact fees

as a condition precedent to the non-site related public facility capital
improvements, and any offsets payable to a developer because of this
provision.
HAW. REV. STAT.§ 46-143(d) (Westlaw 2007).

119. Nicholas and Davidson, *Impact Fees in Hawaii*, supra note 108 at 14 ("The impact fees charged to the new development must be based on the needs attributable to the new development").

120. Id.

121. HAW. REV. STAT. § 46-144.

122. Id. § 46-144(1).

123. Nicholas and Davidson, *Impact Fees in Hawaii*, supra note 108 at 15.

124. HAW. REV. STAT.§ 46-144(2).

125. Id. § 46-144(3).

126. Nicholas and Davidson, *Impact Fees in Hawaii*, supra note 108 at 15.

127. HAW. REV. STAT. § 46-144(4).

128. Id. § 46-144(5).

129. Id. § 46-145(a).

130. Id. § 46-145(b).

131. Nicholas and Davidson, *Impact Fees in Hawaii*, supra note 108 at 15.

132. H.B. 19, 24ᵗʰ Leg., Reg. Sess., § 302A-A (Haw. 2007).

133. HAW. REV. STAT. § 46-142.5 (2009).

134. H.B. 19, 24ᵗʰ Leg., Reg. Sess., § 302A-D (Haw. 2007).

135. Id. § 302A-C(a).

136. Id. § 302A-C(b).

137. Id. § 302A-F(b).

138. Id. at 34 (citing Kudo 1988 and Callies 1989).

139. Id.

140. HAW. REV. STAT. § 46-148.

141. Mandelker, *Land Use Law*, supra note 70, § 9.23 (emphasis added).

142. Patrick J. Rohan, *Zoning and Land Use Controls*, New York: Matthew Bender & Co., 2006 at § 9.06.

143. Daniel R. Mandelker, *Land Use Law*, 6th ed., New York: Matthew Bender & Co., 2006 at § 2.27 (emphasis added).

144. HAW. REV. STAT. §§ 46-141 to 148 (2006).

145. Id. § 46-142(b) (2006).

146. Id. § 46-141 (emphasis added).

147. Id. (emphasis added). The legislative history of HAW. REV. STAT. § 46-141 does not explain what is meant by "required affordable housing."

148. Id. § 46-143 (c).

149. 66 Va. Cir. 274 (Cir. Ct. 2004).

150. Id. at 286.

151. Id.

152. 941 F.2d 872 (9th Cir. 1991).

153. Id. at 873.

154. Id. at 875.

155. Id. at 875.

156. Id.
157. Id. at 873 (emphasis added).
158. Id.
159. 41 P.3d 87 (Cal. 2002).
160. Id. at 102–103.
161. Id. at 103 (citations omitted).
162. For more detailed treatment on this subject, *see* David L. Callies, D. Curtin, and Julie A. Tappendorf, *Bargaining for Development*, Washington, D.C.: Environmental Law Institute, 2003, at art. III; David L. Callies and Julie A. Tappendorf, "Unconstitutional land development conditions and the development agreement solution: Bargaining for public facilities after Nollan and Dolan," 51 Case W. Res. L. Rev. 663 (2001); Judith Welch Wegner, "Moving toward the bargaining table: Contract zoning, development agreements, and the theoretical foundations of government land use deals," 65 N.C. L. Rev. 957, 1017–1020 (1987) (describing the "rational nexus" test adopted by a majority of jurisdictions to assess the reasonableness of provisions requiring exactions of property in development agreements and the expansion of the doctrine governing exactions to address the use of "impact fees"); Lyle S. Hosoda, "Development agreement legislation in Hawaii: An answer to the vested rights uncertainty," 7 U. Haw. L. Rev. 173 (1985); David L. Callies, ed., *Takings: Land-Development Conditions and Regulatory Takings after Dolan and Lucas*, Chicago: ABA, 1996, at chapters 4, 9, 10, 11.
163. *See* John J. Delaney, "Vesting verities and the development chronology: A gaping disconnect?" 3 Wash. U. J.L. & Pol'y 603, 607–608 (2000) (noting that many states require action such as construction or expenditure of funds in reliance on a development permit for the permit to be valid).
164. *Life of the Land, Inc. v. City Council of Honolulu*, 61 Haw. 390, 606 P.2d 866 (1980); *Life of the Land, Inc. v. City Council of Honolulu*, 60 Haw. 446, 592 P.2d 26 (1979).
165. *Allen v. City and County of Honolulu*, 58 Haw. 432, 571 P.2d 328 (1977); *Denning v. County of Maui*, 52 Haw. 653, 485 P.2d 1048 (1971).
166. For an extended discussion of these cases and their implications, see David L. Callies, "Land use: Herein of vested rights, plans and the relationship of planning and controls," 2 U. Haw. L. Rev. 167 (1979).
167. *County of Kauai v. Pac. Standard Life Ins. Co.*, 65 Haw. 318, 653 P.2d 766 (1983).
168. For an excellent checklist and discussion, *see* Donald G. Hagman, "Estoppel and vesting in the use of multi-land permits," 11 Sw. U. L. Rev. 545 (1979).
169. 70 Haw. 480, 777 P.2d 244 (1989).
170. Id. at 484, 777 P.2d at 247.
171. Id. at 485, 777 P.2d at 247–248.
172. *See generally* Eric J. Johnson and Edward H. Ziegler, eds., *Development Agreements, Analyses, Colorado Case Studies, Commentary*, Denver: Rocky Mountain Land Use Institute, 1993; Douglas R. Porter and Lindell L. Marsh, eds., *Development Agreements, Practice, Policy and Prospects*, Washington D.C.: Urban Land Institute, 1989; David J. Larsen, *Development Agreement Manual: Collaboration in Pursuit of Community Interests*, prepared for the League of California's Institute of Local Self-Government, 2002. For commentary on the British experience with development agreements,

see Callies and Grant, "Paying for growth and planning gain," supra note 70. For sample development and annexation agreements, *see* Callies et al., *Bargaining for Development,* supra note 2.

173. *See generally,* Johnson and Ziegler, supra note 165; Porter and Marsh, supra note 165; Larsen, *Development Agreements Manual,* supra note 165. For commentary on the British experience with development agreements, see Callies and Grant, "Paying for growth and planning gain," supra note 2. See Appendix XVI for a checklist on drafting agreements, and Appendices XI, XIV, and XV for sample development and annexation agreements, all in Callies et al., *Bargaining for Development,* supra note 2.

174. *Santa Margarita Area Residents Together v. San Luis Obispo County Bd. of Supervisors,* 100 Cal. Rptr. 2d 740, 748 (Ct. App. 2000).

175. Id.

176. 442 N.W.2d 182 (Neb. 1989).

177. Id. at 192. The court reasoned: "In sum, we find that there is not clear and satisfactory evidence to support the appellants' contention that the city has bargained away its police power. The evidence clearly shows that the city's police powers are not abridged in any manner and that the agreement is expressly subject to the remedies available to the city under the Omaha Municipal Code. Further, we find that the agreement actually enhances the city's regulatory control over the development rather than limiting it." Id.

178. The Hawai'i code provides the following:

> General authorization. Any county by ordinance may authorize the executive branch of the county to enter into a development agreement with any person having a legal or equitable interest in real property, for the development of such property in accordance with this part; provided that such an ordinance shall:
>
> (1) Establish procedures and requirements for the consideration of development agreements upon application by or on behalf of persons having a legal or equitable interest in the property, in accordance with this part;
>
> (2) Designate a county executive agency to administer the agreements after such agreements become effective.
>
> (3) Include provisions to require the designated agency to conduct a review of compliance with the terms and conditions of the development agreement, on a periodic basis as established by the development agreement; and
>
> (4) Include provisions establishing reasonable time periods for the review and appeal of modifications of the development agreement.
>
> Negotiating development agreements. The mayor or the designated agency appointed to administer development agreements may make such arrangements as may be necessary or proper to enter into development agreements; provided that the county has adopted an ordinance pursuant to section 46-123. The final draft of each individual development agreement shall be presented to the county legislative

body for approval or modification prior to execution. To be binding on the county, a development agreement must be approved by the county legislative body and executed by the mayor on behalf of the county. County legislative approval shall be by resolution adopted by a majority of the membership of the county legislative body. HAW. REV. STAT. §§ 46-123, -124.

179. Id. § 46-124.

180. *See* id. § 46-129: "No development agreement shall be entered into unless the county legislative body finds that the provisions of the proposed development agreement are consistent with the county's general plan and any applicable development plan, effective as of [the effective date on] the development agreement."

181. 903 P.2d 741 (Idaho 1995).

182. Id. at 750: "The Council's conclusion that the 'downsizing' . . . is consistent with Hailey's comprehensive plan is not clearly erroneous, and is affirmed."

183. *See Santa Margarita Area Residents Together v. San Luis Obispo County Bd. of Supervisors*, 100 Cal. Rptr. 2d 740 (2000).

184. *See*, e.g., *Town v. Land Use Comm'n*, 54 P.2d 84, 90–91 (Haw. 1974) (holding a reclassification of land by a state land use commission to be quasijudicial); *Fasano v. Bd. of County Comm'rs*, 507 P.2d 23, 26 (Or. 1973) (holding a rezoning to be the same, despite the general rule that such "rezonings" are generally held to be legislative in character).

185. *See* Juergensmeyer and Roberts, *Land Use Planning and Control Law*, supra note 70, §§ 531, 538; *see also* David L. Callies, Nancy C. Neuffer, and Carlito P. Caliboso, "Ballot box zoning: Initiative, referendum and the law," 39 WASH. U.J. URB. & CONTEMP. L. 53 (1991).

186. *See Santa Margarita Area Residents Together v. San Luis Obispo County Bd. of Supervisors*, 84 Cal. App. 4th 221, 227 (2000).

187. *See* HAW. REV. STAT. § 46-131: "Each development agreement shall be deemed an administrative act of the government body made party to the agreement."

188. *See* id. § 46-128: "No development agreement shall be entered into unless a public hearing on the application thereof first shall have been held by the county legislative body."

189. The Hawai'i Code reads, "In addition to the county and principal, any federal, state, or local government agency or body may be included as a party to the development agreement. If more than one government body is made party to an agreement, the agreement shall specify which agency shall be responsible for the overall administration of the agreement." HAW. REV. STAT. § 46-126(d).

190. *See* CAL. GOV'T CODE § 65868 (West 1997): "A development agreement may be amended, or canceled, in whole or in part, by mutual consent of the parties to the agreement or their successors in interest"; HAW. REV. STAT. § 46-130 (1993): "A development agreement may be amended or canceled, in whole or in part, by mutual consent of the parties to the agreement, or their successors in interest."

191. *See* HAW. REV. STAT. § 46-130: "[I]f the county determines that a proposed amendment would substantially alter the original development agreement, a public

hearing on the amendment shall be held by the county legislative body before it consents to the proposed amendment."

192. For example, the California code reads as follows:

> Unless otherwise provided by the development agreement, rules, regulations, and official policies governing permitted uses of the land, governing density, and governing design, improvement, and construction standards and specifications, applicable to development of the property subject to a development agreement, shall be those rules, regulations, and official policies in force at the time of execution of the agreement. A development agreement shall not prevent a city, county, or city and county, in subsequent actions applicable to the property, from applying new rules, regulations, and policies which do not conflict with those rules, regulations, and policies applicable to the property as set forth herein, nor shall a development agreement prevent a city, county, or city and county from denying or conditionally approving any subsequent development project application on the basis of such existing or new rules, regulations, or policies.

CAL. GOV'T CODE § 65866 (West 1997).

193. HAW. REV. STAT. § 46-127(b).

194. 805 P.2d 329 (Cal. 1991).

195. Id. at 334 n.6. *See also* Daniel J. Curtin Jr., "Protecting developers' permits to build: Development agreement in practice in California and other states," 18 ZONING & PLAN. L. REP. 85, 85092 (1995) (discussing various tests for determining when a developer's rights have vested and local government is estopped "from enacting or applying subsequent zoning changes to prevent the completion of the project or substantially reduce the return upon the developer's investment").

196. *City of W. Hollywood v. Beverly Towers*, 805 P.2d 329, 334–335 (Cal 1991).

197. 288 N.E.2d 423 (Ill. 1972).

198. Id. at 426; *cf. Cummings v. City of Waterloo*, 683 N.E.2d 1222, 1230 (Ill. App. Ct. 1997) (holding that the city's amendment to its zoning ordinance that was contrary to the provisions of an annexation agreement was unenforceable against property subject to the annexation agreement).

199. 690 P.2d 701 (Cal. 1984).

200. The Hawai'i Code reads, "In addition to the county and principal, any federal, state, or local government agency or body may be included as a party to the development agreement. If more than one government body is made party to an agreement, the agreement shall specify which agency shall be responsible for the overall administration of the agreement." HAW. REV. STAT. § 46-126(d).

201. *See, e.g.*, 65 ILL. COMP. STAT. 5/11-15.1-1 (West 1993): "The agreement shall be valid and binding for a period of not to exceed 20 years from the date of its execution."; id. 5/11-15.1-5: "Any annexation agreement executed prior to October 1, 1973 . . . is hereby declared valid and enforceable as to such provisions for the effective period of such agreement, or for 20 years from the date of execution thereof, whichever is shorter."

202. *See, e.g.*, CAL. GOV'T CODE § 65865.2 (West 1997): "A development agree-

ment shall specify the duration of the agreement. . . ."; HAW. REV. STAT. § 46-126 (1993): "A development agreement shall . . . (4) Provide a termination date. . . ."

203. For other items bargained for and litigated, *see Van Cleave v. Vill. of Seneca*, 519 N.E.2d 63, 64 (Ill. App. Ct. 1988) (exemptions from real estate taxes) and *O'Malley v. Village of Ford Heights*, 633 N.E.2d 848, 849 (Ill. App. Ct. 1994) (exemption from environmental ordinances, which did not survive legal challenge).

204. 130 Cal. Rptr. 196 (Ct. App. 1976); but *cf. Keystone Bituminous Coal Ass'n v. DeBenedictis*, 480 U.S. 470, 492 (1987) (upholding governmental refusal to perform development agreement when health and safety issue is involved); *Goldblatt v. Town of Hempstead*, 369 U.S. 590, 593–594 (1962) (same).

205. *Morrison Homes Corp. v. City of Pleasanton*, 130 Cal. Rptr. 196, 202 (Ct. App. 1976).

206. *See*, e.g., *Vill. of Orlando Park v. First Fed. Sav. & Loan Ass'n*, 481 N.E.2d 946, 950 (Ill. App. Ct. 1985): "Additional positive effects of such agreements include controls over health sanitation, fire prevention and police protection, which are vital to governing communities."

207. *See* David L. Callies, "Exactions, impact fees and other land development conditions," *in Zoning and Land Use Controls*, ch. 9 (Eric Damian Kelly, ed., 2001); *see also Dolan v. City of Tigard*, 512 U.S. 374, 391 (1994) (holding that the Takings Clause of the Fifth Amendment requires that "the city must make some sort of individualized determination that the required dedication is related both in nature and extent to the impact of the proposed development"); *Nollan v. Cal. Coastal Comm'n*, 483 U.S. 825, 834–34 (1987): "We have long recognized that land-use regulation does not effect a taking if it substantially advances legitimate state interests and does not deny an owner economically viable use of his land. . . . [A] broad range of governmental purposes and regulations satisfies these requirements" (internal quotations omitted).

208. *See City of Annapolis v. Waterman*, 745 A.2d 1000, 1025 (Md. 2000) (conditions agreed to by the subdivider as part of an earlier subdivision agreement were not an unconstitutional taking of the subdivider's property). For a contrary view that would impose the same strict nexus and proportionality requirements upon such agreements as upon "freestanding" local government development dedications, exactions, and other conditions, *see generally* Sam D. Starritt and John J. McClanahan, "Land-use planning and takings: The viability of conditional exactions to conserve open space in the Rocky Mountain west after *Dolan v. City of Tigard*," 114 S. Ct. 2309 (1994), 30 LAND & WATER L. REV. 415 (1995).

209. HAW. REV. STAT. § 46-121.

210. Michael H. Crew, "Development Agreements after *Nollan v. California Coastal Commission*", 483 U.S. 825 (1985), 22 URB. LAW. 23, 34 (1990) (quoting *Nollan v. Cal. Coastal Comm'n*, 483 U.S. 825, 833 (1987)).

211. *Lakeview Dev. Corp. v. City of South Lake Tahoe*, 915 F.2d 1290, 1295 (9th Cir. 1990).

212. *See Leroy Land Dev. Corp. v. Tahoe Reg'l Planning Agency*, 939 F.2d 696 (9th Cir. 1991) (holding settlement agreement not subject to *Nollan*); *see also* Callies and Tappendorf, "Unconstitutional land development conditions," supra note 155.

213. 2007 Haw Sess. Laws, Act 82.

214. HAW. REV. STAT. § 107-25.

215. Janis L. Magin, "Hawaii edges closer toward unified State Building Code," PAC. BUS. NEWS, Mar. 2, 2007, http://pacific.bizjournals.com/pacific/stories/2007/03/05/focus1.html (last visited Nov. 22, 2009).

216. 2007 Haw Sess. Laws, Act 82.

217. Id.

218. HAW. REV. STAT. §107-22(a).

219. Id.

220. HAW. REV. STAT. §107-24(g).

221. Id.

222. HAW. CODE R. § 3-180-7 (Draft 2009).

223. Id. § 3-180-54 (Draft 2009).

224. HAW. REV. STAT. § 107-25 (LexisNexis 2009).

225. Id. § 107-28(a).

226. Id. § 107-28(b).

227. Id. § 107-26.

228. HAW. CODE R. § 3-180-7 (Draft 2009).

229. Id.

230. Id. § 3-180-10 (Draft 2009).

Chapter 4

Public Lands in Hawai'i

The Impact of State and Federal
Ownership and Management

Federal and state governments and their agencies own a staggering 48 percent of Hawai'i's land. The federal government owns or leases roughly 19 percent, or nearly 800,000 acres, and the Hawai'i State government owns 28 percent, or nearly 1,116,000 acres.[1] While much of this land is in undevelopable park and reserve, management policies in federal and state statutes—especially those pertaining to the state's public lands—permit a variety of private residential and commercial uses on these public lands. Moreover, federal land management and disposal policies affect the use of nearby private land in significant ways. Those aspects of public land policy that affect private uses on or near public lands are an indirect but potent tool for the management of private lands.

The State: Private Use on Public Lands

As noted, the State of Hawai'i owns slightly more than a million acres of land, about one-third of the land area of Hawai'i.[2] While much of the land is virtually unusable in an economic sense—mountain, wetlands, and the like—a significant percentage is nevertheless both developed and developable. Aside from the development for residential purposes of Hawaiian Home Lands,[3] the state has produced a detailed set of legislative guidelines that govern what residential and commercial use and disposal can be made of Hawai'i's state-owned land.[4] Most of these are enforced by the Department of Land and Natural Resources (DLNR) through its governing Board of Land and Natural Resources (hereinafter the Land Board).[5]

The Land Board has general power to deal with state public land, including leases and, under certain conditions, disposal for private use.[6] It places all public lands in one of thirteen classifications: intensive agricultural; special livestock; pasture; commercial timber; quarry; mining; recreational; watershed; residential; commercial and industrial; hotel, apartment, and motel; resort; and unclassified.[7] Aside from lands specifically set aside by the governor with the prior approval of the Land Board, all lands must be so classified prior to lease or sale.[8] State policy expresses a clear preference for leases,[9] which are restricted to a term not to exceed sixty-five years.[10] Moreover, such leases are unavailable to persons with delinquent financial obligations to the state.[11] They are not transferable or assignable, except by devise, bequest, or intestate succession, and even then only provided that the Land Board approves of the assignment or transfer and it is made in accordance with current industry standards.[12]

The Land Board imposes additional conditions on commercial leases. A business lease requires a "development plan which provides for careful placement of complementary enterprises consistent with county zoning requirements," and "wherever possible" the Land Board controls "the landscaping and architecture of the enterprises and protect[s] the public against the creation of nuisances of smoke, soot, irritating odors and gases and harmful wastes."[13] Leases for hotel and resort uses may be granted if the Department of Business, Economic Development, and Tourism finds that the land "possesses the amenities for a successful hotel and resort development and that the advantages of its placement for such use outweigh those inherent in free public use in its natural state."[14] Moreover, whenever the land being leased is "adjacent to any beach, waterway, or historic monument or landmark," the lease is subject to public right-of-way or public access that must be available "at all times."[15]

Public land for commercial, industrial, and other business uses, as well as hotel and resort uses, may be sold to private parties with the prior approval of the governor and the State Legislature.[16] When public land is sold for a hotel or resort, development plans must be submitted and the Land Board must make several findings: (1) the land is suitable for resort development; (2) its use will "promote the economic development of the State"; (3) the development is compatible with the developments in the area and is consistent with good, sound planning; and (4) the sale, as opposed to lease, is "absolutely necessary to give the purchaser self-sustaining economic operations."[17]

The Land Board applies somewhat different regulations to residential development on public land. It acts very much like a combination developer and county planning agency. It determines the demand for house lots in an area, investigates costs, places the development adjacent to an existing urban center "wherever possible," and subdivides and improves in conformity with local zoning and subdivision requirements.[18] To avoid speculation, the Land Board requires the lessee or purchaser of a residential lot to build on it within three years.[19] A purchaser of such a lot may not sell it for ten years unless it has first been offered to the Land Board.[20]

The Land Board may also make special provisions for persons who qualify for public housing or are unable to afford to buy or rent housing.[21] Included are persons whose land has been recently condemned but whose compensation award is insufficient to purchase other housing and "low-rent housing" residents or prospective residents who might otherwise be discouraged from increasing their income for fear of becoming ineligible for subsidized housing.[22] For this class of applicants, the Land Board may subdivide and lease lots of between five thousand and fifteen thousand square feet and lease them for an initial fifty-five-year term for the construction of a house.[23] A prospective lessee under this program must have a gross annual family income of less than $20,000 and no other residential land holdings.[24] The lessee is entitled to purchase the lot at its fair market value after ten years, provided a house is built.[25] The Land Board may also lease public lands to an eleemosynary organization that has been certified to be tax exempt, for nominal consideration without recourse to public auction.[26]

This scheme is subject to further Land Board regulation if any of the developed land is located in the State Conservation District as determined by the Land Use Commission. The Land Board must then regulate private development in accordance with statutory authority set out in the Land Use Law and its Regulation no. 4, as discussed in chapter 1.[27] Concessions may also be operated on public property. A "concession" is the grant of the privilege to "conduct operations involving the sale of goods, wares, merchandise, or services to the general public including but not limited to food and beverage establishments, retail stores, motor vehicle rental operations under HRS section 437D, advertising, and communications and telecommunication services, in or on buildings or land under the jurisdiction of any government agency."[28] Concessionaires may also operate a parking lot on property owned by the state and use, for compensation, space on public property to display advertising.

The State Park System and Public Use

Hawai'i's State Park System consists of fifty-five state parks totaling nearly twenty-six thousand acres on the five major islands.[29] The parks are managed by DLNR's Division of State Parks, which is authorized by statute to make rules governing the use and protection of the system.[30] Commercial use of state park land may be conducted only according to the provisions of a permit, contract, license, lease, concession, or other written agreement with the Land Board.[31] Thus, for example, commercial filming, photography, and videotaping on state public land requires a written permit approved by the board.[32] The Land Board issues permits governing the use of public facilities and areas within state parks for (1) camping, (2) lodging, (3) group use, and (4) special use.[33] Group use permits are issued for any group larger than twenty-five members.[34] Special use permits are issued for all types of uses other than camping, lodging, and group uses that are considered compatible with the functions and purposes of each individual area, facility, or unit of the premises.[35] Examples include weddings, community events, and scientific research.[36]

The Land Board may directly lease land to any eleemosynary or religious organization for campsites or sites for youth athletic or educational activities in a state park area without a public auction.[37] It may also lease lands within a state park or forest reserve for recreation-residence use for a period not to exceed twenty years.[38] For example, the state leased land for private cabins in Koke'e State Park on the island of Kaua'i. Such leases are coveted because the cabins are located in remote forest areas, high in the mountains of the northwest corner of Kaua'i.[39] Some of the leases have been held by Kaua'i's most powerful political and business leaders and wealthy kama'āina families for many years.[40] In the 1850s, Valdemar Knudsen, whose descendants would become major landowners in Kōloa, leased two parcels in Koke'e from the Kingdom of Hawai'i and built a home on one of them.[41] That first house opened the way for campsites that eventually turned into sites for the 118 cabins that exist today.[42]

However, animosity between DLNR and lessees began in 1985, when thirty-seven families lost their leases in an auction.[43] Although the state had intended the auction to provide more opportunities for local families, it in fact allowed off-island and out-of-state residents to bid successfully for the lots.[44] Some longtime leaseholders who lost their leases tore down their cabins or removed them from DLNR sites before new lessees could move in,[45] despite contrary provisions in some leases.[46]

In January 2005, the staff of the State Parks Division of DLNR recommended that the Land Board consider a proposal to hire a vendor through a bid process to manage the recreational cabins.[47] The units could be either rented or leased on a short-term basis.[48] In 2006, cabin leaseholders sued the state when DLNR moved to auction the cabins, arguing that they owned the cabins and land outright.[49] While a Kaua'i circuit court ruled in favor of the state, the litigation stalled the auction.[50] In 2008, the State Legislature passed a bill requiring DLNR to renegotiate market-rate leases directly with cabin occupants.[51] DLNR has since entered into new twenty-year leases with cabin occupants.[52] A provision in the new leases requires the tenants to acknowledge that the state owns the land under their structures. The new law also requires DLNR to auction vacant cabins first to neighbor island residents, then to other state residents, and only then to others.[53]

In 2001, the Land Board drafted a master plan for the Koke'e and Waimea Canyon State Park complex.[54] Over the past twenty years, the state has collected between $4 and $5 million in lease revenue from cabin owners but has lost approximately $500,000 from defaulted leases.[55] DLNR plans to turn the 6,200-acre park complex into a "recreational facility of the 21st century."[56] The plan addresses preservation of natural, cultural, and recreational resources, other users and uses, maintenance of trails, and infrastructural needs.[57] It also includes a review of leases for 118 private cabins in the park.[58]

Federal Lands: The Use and Disposal of a Scarce Commodity

The U.S. government once owned 80 percent of the land in the United States.[59] It still owns a whopping 653 million acres, or approximately one-third of the total land area.[60] Against this backdrop, it is not surprising that the federal government owns or leases nearly 20 percent of the land in Hawai'i. The majority of federal land is either controlled by the military or is designated as relatively remote national parks or national wildlife refuges.[61] Some of that land, however, is in prime scenic or development locations, such as Pearl Harbor, Ka'ena Point, Fort DeRussy, and Bellows Beach. The use and disposal of federal land and its effect on both public and private land use has been the subject of much comment.[62] However, it is not the purpose of this chapter to deal extensively with the vast subject of federal public lands policy but with selected effects of federal land use decisions on land development in Hawai'i.[63]

Much of the land that was eventually to become the vast majority of federal land called "the public domain" was acquired through fortuitous purchases. Alaska, the Louisiana Purchase, and the Gadsden Purchase—totaling 54 percent of the land area of the United States—come most readily to mind.[64] The land was for the most part acquired during a decidedly expansionist period in U.S. history. The major thrust of legislation and other programs governing land use was to put as much public land as possible rapidly and expeditiously into private hands. The wholesale giveaways that characterized the first half of the eighteenth century and much of the nineteenth did not abate until the first part of the twentieth century with the creation of the U.S. National Park System, followed by national forests, reserves, and a host of other federal land classifications designed to hold and conserve, rather than dispose of, public land.

A concomitant development was the reemergence of the public trust doctrine. Various state governments were directed by the courts to hold certain public lands in trust for "the people"—variously defined. The result was not only a slowdown but also a change in the manner of disposition. Leasing and other less-than-fee disposals took the place of the outright transfers of ownership that were so popular in the nation's first 150 years.[65]

Ceded Lands in Hawai'i

The federal government's potential for affecting land use in Hawai'i through disposal of land it now holds in the state is significant. Some of that land, much of it in critical locations, must be returned to the state at no cost if it is declared "surplus."[66] This is in part because federal public lands in Hawai'i have never been part of the public domain from which so many grants to private interests elsewhere have come over the past two centuries. Congress administers public domain lands primarily under the U.S. Constitution, Article IV, section 3, clause 2, which grants it power to dispose of and make all needful rules and regulations respecting territory or property belonging to the United States.[67] Although Hawai'i had achieved territorial status toward the end of the period when the federal government gave away land, it was still over half a century before Hawai'i became a state.[68] Partly as a consequence of an additional fifty-year period between U.S. settlement and annexation and partly because of the ending of the public domain acquisition period in U.S. history, Hawai'i's land never did become part of the public domain. Thus, while the resolution of annexation declared the republic's relinquishment of sovereignty and the cession and transfer to the United States "the absolute fee and ownership of all public, government, or Crown lands, public holdings" and other public property "of every kind and description belonging to the government of the Hawaiian Islands," it also expressly declared such land to be other than in the public domain.[69] Finally, the resolution specified that all but armed forces uses must be for the benefit of the inhabitants of the Hawaiian Islands:

> [t]hat the existing land laws of the U.S. relative to public lands shall not apply to such land in the Hawaiian Islands, but the Congress of the U.S. shall enact special laws for their management and disposition: *Provided,* That all revenue from or proceeds of the same, except as regards such part thereof as may be used or occupied for the civil, military, or naval purposes of the U.S., or may be assigned for the use of the local government shall be used solely for the benefit of the inhabitants of the Hawaiian Islands for educational and other public purposes.[70]

It is clear from the legislative history of the Admission Act of 1959 by which Hawai'i became a state that Congress meant to perpetuate this exceptional status.[71] First, Hawai'i was to be the successor in title to the lands and properties held by the territory prior to admission. Second, the federal government turned over to the new state substantial land it owned—with the notable exception of the ceded lands.[72] Third, the act set up a procedure by which these ceded lands would be returned to the state as well:

> (e) Within five years from the date Hawaii is admitted into the Union, each Federal agency having control over any land or property that is retained by the United States pursuant to subsections [ceded lands] shall report to the President the facts regarding its continued need for such land or property, and if the President determines that the land or property is no longer needed by the United States it shall be conveyed to the State of Hawaii.

(f) As used in the Act, the term "lands and other properties" includes public lands and other public property, and the term "public lands and other public property" means, and is limited to, the lands and properties that were ceded to the United States by the Republic of Hawaii under the joint resolution of annexation approved July 7, 1898 (30 Stat. 750), or that have been acquired in exchange for lands or properties so ceded.[73]

For purposes of disposal, the critical section of the Admission Act is the above-quoted subsection 5(e). The necessity for an extension of the five-year deadline soon became obvious. Between 1960 and 1964, the federal government returned a measly six hundred acres.[74] The slow pace of the return led directly to the enactment of the Ceded Lands Act of 1963, the history of which clearly declares the intent of Congress to promptly return all surplus ceded lands to the state as rapidly as possible.[75]

After tracing the various laws by which ceded lands were acquired by the United States, the act states that whenever such lands are determined to be surplus property by the Administrator of General Services (Administrator) with the concurrence of the head of the department or agency exercising administration or control over such lands and property, they "shall be conveyed to the State of Hawaii by the Administrator subject to the provisions of this Act."[76] The lands are conveyed to the state free of charge, unless improved with buildings or structures, in which case the improvements must be paid for or relocated: "If (1) the state refuses to pay for the improvements and (2) the administrator determines that relocation and removal are not feasible, then the obligation to transfer the land to the state ceases, and the value of the land only must be turned over to the state upon subsequent disposal."[77]

Finally, the lands and proceeds therefrom are to be held in "public trust:" "Any lands, property, improvements, and proceeds conveyed or paid to the State of Hawaii under section 1 of this Act shall be considered a part of public trust . . . and shall be subject to the terms and conditions of the trust."[78]

The present state of ceded lands in Hawai'i raises several critical questions:

1. At what point are such lands "surplus" so that they must be transferred to the state?

2. To whom or what should ceded lands be transferred (so far, they have been transferred to the state)?

3. Once such transfer takes place, what may be done with them?

CEDED LANDS: AT WHAT POINT SURPLUS?

Both the Admission Act and the 1963 Ceded Lands Act make clear that whoever (the president or the General Services administrator) eventually makes the transfer, the lands must first be declared "surplus."[79] Moreover, whichever agency of the federal government administers or controls the land must concur with such declaration of surplus.[80] Unfortunately, there is no express requirement in either act that there be a regular review of agency needs leading to a declaration of "surplus." Indeed, language requiring such a review every five years was apparently rejected by Congress during the course of hearings on the Ceded Lands Act.[81]

Shortly after Hawai'i achieved statehood, however, the Federal Office of Management and Budget—to whom the president delegated his authority to declare surplus ceded lands—did issue guidelines, which provide that a parcel of ceded land would not be retained when

1. It is not being used by the controlling agency and there are no firm plans for future use;

2. The costs of operation and maintenance are substantially higher than for other suitable properties of equal or less value which are, or can be made, available to the Federal Government without direct cost;

3. It is being leased to private individuals or enterprises and there are no firm plans for future Federal use; or

4. It is being used by the Government to produce goods or services which are available from private enterprise, except when it is demonstrated clearly in each instance that it is not in the public interest to obtain such requirement from private enterprise.[82]

These are, however, guidelines only, and there is apparently still some confusion over whether the federal government adheres to them, especially after the 1963 Ceded Lands Act amended the Admission Act.[83] Hawai'i was unsuccessful in its early attempt to obtain a favorable court decision setting out conditions under which the General Services administrator must declare ceded lands to be surplus. In 1963, the U.S. Supreme Court dismissed on procedural grounds the only suit that has so far reached it on this issue: "We have concluded that this is a suit against the U.S. and, absent its consent, cannot be maintained by the State."[84] A later attempt to obtain that consent failed.[85] However, pursuant to executive orders issued in the 1970s, the U.S. Department of Defense took great pains to inventory and analyze the ceded lands under its control.[86] The result was a recommendation that nearly three thousand acres be released to the state.[87]

A classic example of the reluctance of the federal government to release ceded lands to the state is Bellows Air Force Base, located on two and a half miles of sandy beach on the southeast coast of Oʻahu. Of the 1,495 acres that comprise the base, 1,457 are ceded lands. Aside from certain military transmitter facilities—which may soon be consolidated with facilities off the base—the major if not sole use for Bellows appears to be a semiannual amphibious training exercise utilizing approximately six hundred acres.[88] Other facilities include beach cottages, the use of which can hardly be described as "mission related"—the usual test for the need of facilities—an armory, and a nine-vehicle maintenance facility.[89] In fairness to the U.S. Air Force, Bellows Beach is open to the general public on weekends and holidays, and seventy-seven acres of ceded land were released at the Waimanalo end of the base in 1974.[90] Nevertheless, the federal government has consistently turned aside state requests to either release or lease the rest.[91]

THE CEDED LANDS AND PUBLIC TRUST

The Admission Act broadened considerably the "public trust" purposes for which ceded lands, once acquired by the state, could be used:

> The lands granted to the State of Hawaii . . . together with proceeds from the sale or other disposition of such lands and the income therefrom, shall be held by said State as public trust for the support of the public schools and other public educational institutions, for the betterment of the conditions of native Hawaiians, as defined in the Hawaiian Homes Commission Act, 1920, as amended, for the development of farm and home ownership on as widespread a basis as possible for the making of public improvements, and for the provisions of lands for public use. Such lands, proceeds, and income shall be managed and disposed of for one or more of the foregoing purposes in such manner as the constitution and laws of said State may provide, and their use for any other object shall constitute

a breach of trust for which suit may be brought by the U.S. The schools and other educational institutions supported, in whole or in part, out of such public trust shall forever remain under the exclusive control of said State; and no part of the proceeds or income from the lands granted under this Act shall be used for the support of any sectarian or denominational school, college, or university.[92]

While the state must therefore use the proceeds from the ceded lands for the five listed purposes in section 5(f)—(1) the support of public education; (2) the betterment of the conditions of Native Hawaiians; (3) the development of farm and home ownership; (4) the making of public improvements; and (5) the provision of lands for public use—the language of section 5(f) allows the state to choose the manner in which the proceeds are allocated among the listed purposes.

DLNR administers ceded lands that are eventually released to the state.[93] DLNR has been criticized for its management of and accounting for land and resources under its control generally and for ceded lands in particular. Apparently, funds generated by use or sale of formerly ceded lands sometimes ended up in (or were transferred to) the state's general fund rather than a special public trust fund.[94]

The stakes in such funds are high. Native Hawaiian groups and supporters successfully persuaded the 1978 Constitutional Convention to create the Office of Hawaiian Affairs (OHA), which is run by a generally elected board.[95] In 1980, the State Legislature amended a 1979 statute implementing OHA's constitutional creation by reserving "twenty percent of all funds derived from the public land trust, described in section 10-3" for OHA.[96] Despite the specified percentage, this reservation was far from clear in ultimately resolving OHA's pro rata share of the funds from ceded lands, resulting in more than two decades of controversy between OHA and the state. OHA's claim to profit or revenues from potential projects on ceded lands—upon which, for example, Aloha Tower and its multimillion dollar redevelopment at Honolulu Harbor sits—may have far-reaching effects not only on Native Hawaiians but also on the success of such development projects.

In 1995 OHA challenged the state's transfer of ceded lands until its multiple claims were resolved.[97] In a sharp reversal of an earlier memorandum opinion,[98] the Hawai'i Supreme Court enjoined the state from transferring any such lands until claims were resolved, citing a Clinton-era "Apology Resolution" as the principle basis for its decision.[99] The state promptly sought review by the U.S. Supreme Court, joined by twenty-nine other states that filed friend-of-the-court briefs supporting review. The U.S. Supreme Court granted review in September of 2008 and unanimously reversed the Hawai'i Supreme Court, specifically holding that the Apology Resolution was just that—an apology that could form no basis for legal action.[100]

FEDERAL LANDS AND STATE/LOCAL LAND USE CONTROLS

Of potentially equal significance in Hawai'i is the current federal policy of disposing of so-called surplus property aside from ceded lands. Within limits, the federal government may dispose of such property any way it chooses. It appears that disposal is part of an overall federal program to raise revenue. One such property is the Fort DeRussy site in Waikīkī. Surrounded on three sides by high-rise condominium and hotel developments, with unobstructed ocean view and access on the fourth side, the multiacre site is virtually free of development. It also has the last significant beachfront open space in Waikīkī. While the federal government has in the past expressed interest in selling it for development, city and state administrators have consistently declared their intent to retain it as open space. Indeed, a mayor of Honolulu once threatened to zone it for low-density development in order to frustrate federal plans.[101]

Recent federal court decisions, however, raise doubts about the power of Honolulu to regulate land use on federal land in the face of a contrary federal policy. In 1966, the U.S. Supreme Court held a state statute providing for the rounding up of stray burros on federal land to be unenforceable in view of a federal statute managing them and prohibiting such action, on the ground that when Congress passes legislation pertaining to federal property, state law "must recede."[102] Based on that decision, a federal appeals court in California—which has federal jurisdiction over Hawai'i—decided in 1979 that Ventura County's zoning laws prohibiting oil exploration without a permit were inapplicable to private oil companies with federal permission to explore and drill on federal land: "the federal government has authorized a specific use of federal lands, and Ventura cannot prohibit that use, either temporarily or permanently, in an attempt to substitute its judgment for that of Congress."[103]

However, in 1987's *California Coastal Commission v. Granite Rock Company*,[104] in which a company mining on federal land in California similarly sued to prevent the Coastal Commission from imposing state permitting requirements on the project,[105] the U.S. Supreme Court distinguished between environmental and land use regulations such as zoning.[106] The Court reasoned that "[l]and use planning in essence chooses particular uses for land; environmental regulation, at its core, does not mandate particular uses of land but requires only that, however the land is used, damage to the environment is kept within prescribed limits."[107] The Court then held that reasonable state *environmental* regulation is not preempted on federal land.[108] Thus, because the commission was not exercising "land use authority" by attempting to determine *if* federal land could be used for mining, but rather was using its "environmental authority" to regulate *how* mining was conducted, the Court held that the commission's permitting requirements were not preempted.[109] Therefore, even if the idea of city regulation resurfaces, Honolulu's land use controls may be difficult to apply to properties such as Fort DeRussy so long as the federal government retains any rights in that land.

In conclusion, public lands and their use and misuse will continue to affect land development in Hawai'i for some years. The subject of ceded lands and their release and development was a major item on the agenda of the Native Hawaiian Study Commission, which was reconstituted in 1981, though its recommendations were advisory only.[110] The importance of ceded lands continues unabated today. Measured against recent experience and current trends, the future does not bode particularly well for immediate return to Hawai'i of its remaining ceded lands. However current, the concern over ceded lands is but a part of the larger issue of use and management of public lands, which can proceed regardless of local land use controls, whether or not a particular federal or state administration chooses to subject itself to such local zoning. The agencies that oversee this use and development are largely their own masters, and the result for land use in Hawai'i is not always predictable. It may be more prudent to raise the need for a determination of consistency of such development with Hawai'i's federally approved Coastal Zone Plan as required under both federal and State Coastal Zone Management Acts (see chapter 6).

Federal Land Policy and Management: Public Lands

Although the term "public lands" has various meanings under different statutes and circumstances, it generally refers to government lands that are open to public sale or other disposition under general laws and that are not held back or reserved for a governmental or public purpose.[111] The phrase "public lands" is usually synonymous with "public domain."[112]

In public lands law, "disposal" commonly refers to the final, irrevocable act by which the right of a person, purchaser, or grantee attaches, and an equitable right becomes complete to receive legal title by patent or some other appropriate mode of transfer.[113] It is the policy of the United States that any disposal of public land take place according to uniform statutory procedures requiring consistency with the prescribed mission of the department or agency involved and reserving to Congress the power to review disposals in excess of a specified acreage.[114] The Federal Land Transaction Facilitation Act,[115] enacted in 2000, provides both for the identification of and decision-making criteria regarding the disposal of public lands, as well as the identification and acquisition of inholdings and other land that would improve the resource management ability of land management agencies and adjoining landowners, while allowing for the least disruption of existing land and resource management programs.

TRANSFORMATION AND PRIVATE INTERESTS IN PUBLIC LANDS

For nearly a century, this country's federally owned lands were valuable chiefly for their natural resources that could be removed by private commodity interests.[116] Traditionally, federal land managers favored commodity uses such as timber, grazing, and mining operations.[117] In recent years, however, public lands have undergone a fundamental change and are now dominated by recreational and preservation uses.[118] Indeed, various parties have sought to acquire some inholdings not for development purposes but for conservation.[119] Thus in Hawai'i, DLNR and the Trust for Public Land, a national nonprofit organization, purchased Moanalua Valley from a private party to "benefit the people . . . as an open space, a gathering place."[120] This shift is reflected in basic economics.[121] The hundreds of billions of dollars spent each year on outdoor recreation have surpassed mining, timber harvesting, and grazing as an economic force on Western public lands.[122] There has also been a marked increase in recreational visitors to public lands.[123] In 1995, the U.S. Forest Service recorded 345 million visitor days on National Forest land, which represents a 1,161% increase since 1950.[124] The Bureau of Land Management's (BLM) adjusted visitor days rose 176% from 1982 to 1996, and the National Park Service recorded a visitation level of nearly 270 million visits in 1995, a 711% increase since 1950.[125]

The increase in preservation use is in large part due to the conservation movement. Since the conservation movement mobilized enough political strength to institutionalize the national park concept in the National Park Service Organic Act of 1916, a series of statutory mandates provides for the preservation of public lands.[126] The Organic Act describes the Park Service's dual and sometimes conflicting mandate to provide for recreational use, while at the same time preserving resources "unimpaired for the enjoyment of future generations."[127] In 1940, an executive order created the Fish and Wildlife Service (FWS) by merging the Bureau of Fisheries of the Commerce Department with the Division of Biological Survey of the Department of Agriculture.[128] Since then, FWS has become an increasingly important preservation and recreation resource on federal lands.[129] The National Wildlife Refuge System Administration Act of 1966 authorized FWS to administer the wildlife refuges.[130] Then the Wilderness Act of 1964 signaled a heightened commitment to preservation, setting in motion a process that transferred millions of acres from extractive uses to recreation and the preservation of wildlife.[131] Finally, in 1975 the Federal Land Policy and Management Act required BLM to adopt a multiple-use management policy with recreation, wildlife preservation, and aesthetics as statutorily mandated uses.[132]

The National Park System

A major portion of federal lands in Hawai'i is designated national parks. Both the expansion of uses associated with such parks and the attempts by the federal government to regulate private land adjacent to park boundaries in order to protect federal interests in the parks have major land use implications for private landowners.

The National Park System of the United States comprises 391 areas covering more than 84 million acres in every state except Delaware; there are no national parks in the District of Columbia or in the territories of American Samoa, Guam, Puerto Rico, and the Virgin Islands.[133] The National Park Service (NPS) manages the parks. Created on August 25, 1916, when President Woodrow Wilson signed the National Park Service Organic Act (Organic Act),[134] NPS is a federal bureau within the Department of the Interior responsible for protecting national parks and monuments:[135]

> The Service thus established shall promote and regulate the
> use of Federal areas known as national parks, monuments and

> reservations . . . by such means and measures as conform to
> the fundamental purpose of the said parks, monuments and
> reservations, which purpose is to conserve the scenery and the
> natural and historic objects and the wild life therein and to
> provide for the enjoyment of the same in such manner and by
> such means as will leave them unimpaired for the enjoyment
> of future generations.[136]

The act leaves two questions unanswered: (1) whether the authority under the act extended to both public and private holdings within
the park's physical domain; and (2) whether the authority extended
outside of park boundaries to include the right to regulate private and
public lands.[137] Judicial interpretation of the Property Clause of the
U.S. Constitution has extended NPS's regulatory authority to both public and private holdings.[138] However, this authority includes only that
power necessary to enact regulations that govern private inholdings or
public lands if those regulations are proper and realistically related to
congressional intent.[139] While it is fairly well settled that NPS can regulate activities within park boundaries regardless of whether the activities
take place on public or private holdings, it is less clear whether NPS can
regulate outside of park boundaries.[140]

In its 1980 *State of the Parks Report*, NPS reported that "more than 50
percent of the reported threats were attributed to sources or activities
located external to the parks, particularly industrial and commercial
development projects on adjacent lands; air pollutant emissions, often
associated with facilities located considerable distances from the affected
parks; urban encroachment; and roads and railroads."[141] Further studies
have demonstrated that a multitude of development activities external
to national parks are impacting and threatening to engulf them, causing severe damage to the values and resources within the parks that they
were created to preserve.

The secretary of the Interior is authorized to publish rules and
regulations as deemed necessary or proper for the use and management of the national parks.[142] Federal regulations allow a park superintendent to issue permits "to authorize an otherwise prohibited or
restricted activity or impose a public use limit."[143] Such special permits
allow private use on official park lands. There are two instruments
that may be used to authorize a special park use: (1) a special use
permit or (2) a right-of-way permit.[144] A special use permit is issued
by a superintendent or individual or organization to allow the use of

NPS–administered resources and to authorize activities that require a permit.[145] A right-of-way permit is issued by a regional director to authorize any new utilities, including water conduits, on NPS lands.[146] NPS also issues other permits and signed agreements including but not limited to research, collection, and use of natural and cultural resources.[147]

Finally, the director may lease any property (except nonhistoric land) if the lessee meets the following restrictions:

> (a) The lease will not result in degradation of the purposes and values of the park area;
>
> (b) The lease will not deprive the park area of property necessary for appropriate park protection, interpretation, visitor enjoyment, or administration of the park area;
>
> (c) The lease contains such terms and conditions as will assure the leased property will be used for activity and in a manner [. . .] consistent with the purposes established by law for the park area in which the property is located;
>
> (d) The lease is compatible with the programs of the National Park Service;
>
> (e) The lease is for rent at least equal to the fair market value rent of the leased property as described in § 18.5;
>
> (f) The proposed activities under the lease are not subject to authorization through a concession contract, commercial use authorization or similar instrument; and
>
> (g) If the lease is to include historic property, the lease will adequately insure the preservation of the historic property.[148]

All leases must have as short a term as possible and no lease may have a term of more than sixty years.[149]

Hawai‘i's National Parks

Comprised of land on the islands of Hawai‘i and Maui, Hawai‘i National Park was created by Congress on August 1, 1916.[150] In the early 1960s, the lands located on Maui were renamed Haleakalā National Park and the land located on the island of Hawai‘i was renamed Hawai‘i Volcanoes National Park.[151]

Volcanoes National Park (Volcanoes) is located on the southeastern portion of the island of Hawai‘i and encompasses 333,000 acres ranging from sea level to the summit of one of earth's most massive volcanoes,

Mauna Loa, at 13,677 feet. The Park mission is to "protect, conserve and study volcanic landscapes and the associated natural and cultural resources and processes; facilitate public use and safe access to active volcanism, scenic vistas, diverse geographic settings and wilderness for recreation, education and public enjoyment."[152]

Volcanoes has been designated an International Biosphere Reserve (1980) and a World Heritage Site (1987).[153] Within the park, Kīlauea, one of the world's most active volcanoes, offers scientists insights on the birth of the Hawaiian Islands and gives visitors views of dramatic volcanic landscapes, including lava flows into the ocean. Over half of the park is designated wilderness, providing unique hiking and camping opportunities.[154]

Like many other national parks, Volcanoes allows for private activities within the park lands through the granting of special use permits and concession contracts. Currently, the park issues permits for research, commercial filming, businesses, weddings, and the scattering of ashes. These permits require the permit holder to meet certain conditions and in some cases pay a nonrefundable application fee.[155] Generally, the conditions restrict the permit holder from disturbing park features such as rocks, vegetation, or other natural resources and interfering with other visitors' access, use, or enjoyment of an area.

The purpose of concession contracts is to authorize concessioners to provide visitor services in park areas.[156] The NPS director awards concession contracts through a public solicitation process.[157] A concession contract is generally awarded for a term of ten years or less unless the director determines that the contract terms and conditions warrant a longer term.[158] In no event, however, may the contract have a term of more than twenty years unless extended in accordance with regulations.[159]

All concession contracts contain provisions for suspension and termination of the contract for (1) default, (2) unsatisfactory performance, and (3) when necessary to protect, conserve, and preserve park area resources and providing necessary and appropriate visitor services in park areas.[160] Concessioners may not assign, sell, convey, grant, contract for, or otherwise transfer any concession contract, rights to operate under a contract as a subconcessioner, controlling interest in a concessioner, leasehold surrender, or possessory interest without the prior written approval of the director.[161] Additionally, a concessioner may not encumber, pledge, mortgage, or otherwise provide as a security interest any concession contract, rights to operate under a contract as a subconcessioner, controlling interest in a concessioner, leasehold surrender, or possessory interest for any purpose without prior written approval of the director.[162]

NPS works with concessioners to provide visitor services throughout the park system. Volcano House, the only hotel within the park itself, is one such concessioner.[163] Located on the edge of Kīlauea Crater,[164] the old-style country lodge features shops and three dining areas and offers hiking and tours.

Haleakalā National Park (Haleakalā) consists of 30,183 acres, 24,719 acres of which are designated wilderness.[165] The park ranges from sea level to the summit of Haleakalā, at ten thousand feet.[166] The park also requires special use permits for a number of activities within park boundaries, including scattering ashes, wedding ceremonies, rallies, and other "first amendment activities."[167] In 2007, after several deaths and many injuries, the park banned the once-popular commercial downhill bicycle tours leading tourists at dawn from the summit to the sea.[168] Approximately ninety thousand people a year rode from the summit, bringing in approximately $10 million a year for tour operators.[169]

There is a substantial basis of common law supporting NPS authority to regulate private land adjacent to national parks in order to protect them.[170] Thus for example, in *Kleppe v. New Mexico*,[171] the U.S. Supreme Court held that the appropriate federal agencies may regulate private land and property in order to protect federal interest in federal land.

FISH AND WILDLIFE SERVICE REFUGES IN HAWAI'I

The National Wildlife Refuge System (NWRS) is a collection of public federal lands managed by the Fish and Wildlife Service.[172] The lands are set aside for the purpose of conserving the fish, wildlife, and plants within them.[173] The federal government holds fee, leasehold, or easement interests in refuge land.[174] There are over 540 refuges nationwide, at least one in each of the fifty states. The system provides habitat for "more than 700 species of birds, 220 species of mammals, 250 reptile and amphibian species, and more than 200 species of fish."[175] This includes habitat for more than 250 threatened or endangered plants and animals.[176] Ninety-eight percent of refuges are open to the public; they host more than 40 million visitors each year.[177]

Private uses on FWS land are governed by the National Wildlife Refuge Administration Act (also referred to as the National Wildlife Improvement Act) of 1997 (1997 Act)[178] together with federal regulations. Under the 1997 Act, the secretary of the Department of the Interior (secretary) may permit the use of any area within NWRS for any purpose whenever it is determined that such uses are "compatible with the major purposes for which such areas were established."[179] Such uses may include but are not limited to hunting, fishing, public recreation and accommodation, and access.[180] The secretary may also permit the use of or grant easements in, over, across, upon, through, or under any areas within the system whenever it is determined that such uses are compatible with the purposes for which these areas are established.[181] Such uses may include but are not limited to power lines, telephone lines, canals, ditches, pipelines, and roads, including the construction, operation, and maintenance thereof.[182]

NWRS may open an area to public access and use by regulation, individual permit, or public notice.[183] Compatibility determinations will include only evaluations of how the proposed use would affect the ability of the refuge to meet its mandated purposes.[184] The manager of a refuge is authorized to issue permits unless the regulations require the applicant to obtain the applicable permit from the FWS director or the secretary.[185] The refuge manager may terminate or revoke a permit at any time for noncompliance with the terms of the permit or federal regulations, for nonuse, for violation of any law, regulation, or order applicable to the refuge, or to protect public health, safety, or the resources of the refuge.[186] Public use facilities may also be operated by concessioners or co-operators under contract or legal agreement on national wildlife refuges where there is a demonstrated justified need for services or facilities, such as boat rentals, swimming facilities, conducted tours of special natural attractions, shelters, tables, trailer lots, food, lodging, and related services.[187]

There are several natural refuges in Hawai'i.[188] Among the better known are those at Kīlauea and Hakalau. The Kaua'i National Wildlife Refuge Complex consists of Kīlauea Point, Hanalei, and Hulē'ia National Wildlife Refuges. Kīlauea Point Refuge (Kīlauea) was established in 1985 after its transfer from the U.S. Coast Guard and consists of 203 acres of protected land.[189] It is located on the northernmost tip of the island and is one of the few Hawaiian refuges open daily to the public.[190] One of the most popular spots for visitors and residents of Hawai'i alike, it attracts an average of half a million visitors a year.[191]

The refuge is home to both the endangered Hawaiian nēnē and a number of rare and endangered seabirds, including red-footed boobies, Laysan albatrosses, and wedge-tailed shearwaters.[192] To protect the bird populations, the reserve traps predators within the refuge and maintains a predator-proof fence around it.[193] Native plant species are also planted and maintained within the refuge.[194] The waters surrounding the refuge are home to a number of important species, including Hawaiian monk seals, green sea turtles, and humpback whales.[195]

Current private uses that are permitted in the Hanalei area of the refuge are taro farming and kayak rentals. Taro farming is permitted on the refuge because it provides wetland habitat for birds.[196] Because wildlife management and bird use conflicts with taro water management and production, permit fees are set at an appropriate rate to compensate farmers for losses incurred as a result of the requirement to favor the birds in bird-taro conflicts.[197] The conditions attached to the special use permit (SUP) restrict the use of the land to taro farming.[198] The permit also requires farmers to follow certain farming guidelines and report nests of waterbirds to the refuge manager.[199] The current SUP for kayak rentals requires the permittee to remove all trash resulting from the company's activities and forbids dumping trash in the waters.[200] The permittee must also deliver a five- to ten-minute environmental education talk to the general public on each of the kayak trips.[201]

Hakalau Forest National Wildlife Reserve (Hakalau) was set aside in 1985 to protect and manage endangered forest birds and their rain forest habitat.[202] Located on the windward slope of Mauna Kea on the island of Hawai'i, the 32,733-acre refuge supports a diversity of native birds and plants.[203] Currently, Hakalau issues SUPs for ecotours in the refuge; five permits were issued in 2004 and seven were issued in 2005.[204] The maximum number of individuals covered by a single permit is one hundred.[205] Tour groups are limited to twenty-five or fewer people and may be conducted only in the vicinity of Pua Akala tract and the Pua Akala meadow.[206] Permit conditions require a written report of the total number of visits and individuals for each month that visits occur[207] and prohibit open fires on the refuge and the taking of any animal, vegetable, or mineral matter.[208] The permittee is responsible and can be held liable for any damages or injuries resulting from the permitted activity.

NORTHWESTERN HAWAIIAN ISLANDS MARINE NATIONAL MONUMENT

On June 15, 2006, President Bush announced plans to designate the island chain spanning nearly 1,400 miles of the Pacific northwest of Hawai'i, from Nīhoa to Kure Atoll, as a national monument, creating the largest protected marine reserve in the world.[209] Presidential Proclamation 8031 reserved "all lands and interests in lands owned or controlled by the Government of the U.S. in the Northwestern Hawaiian Islands, including emergent and submerged lands and waters."[210] The area of the monument is nearly 140,000 square miles, more than a hundred times larger than Yosemite National Park. Named the Northwestern Hawaiian Islands Marine National Monument (NWHI Monument), it "encompasses a string of uninhabited islands that support more than 7,000 marine species, at least a fourth of which are [so far] found nowhere else on Earth."[211] The NWHI Monument contains almost 70 percent of the nation's tropical, shallow-water coral reefs, a rookery for 14 million seabirds, and the last refuge for the endangered Hawaiian monk seal and the threatened green sea turtle, as well as many large predatory fish, 90 percent of which have disappeared from the world's oceans.[212]

The federal regulations that govern the NWHI Monument do not explicitly refer to land use regulations. Nevertheless, the federal government affects the use of land by strict regulation of access and activities in the area. The following is a description of the structure of the monument and the provisions that most relate to land use.

Three separate agencies oversee the NWHI Monument: the U.S. Department of Commerce, through the National Oceanic and Atmospheric Administration (NOAA), the Department of the Interior, through the U.S. Fish and Wildlife Service (USFWS), and the State of Hawai'i.[213] NOAA has primary responsibility for managing the marine areas of the monument (in consultation with the secretary). USFWS has responsibility for managing the areas of the monument that cover the Midway Atoll National Wildlife Refuge, the Battle of Midway National Memorial, and the Hawaiian Islands National Wildlife Refuge (in consultation with the Secretary of Commerce). The state has primary responsibility for managing the state waters of the monument.[214]

Entrance is strictly regulated. It is unlawful to enter the NWHI Monument unless (1) for emergency or military purposes; (2) after a permit has been issued to perform a specific activity; or (3) when conducting passage without interruption.[215] Once in the monument, the federal government is explicit concerning the kinds of activities allowed. Prohibited and unlawful are the following:

> (a) Exploring for, developing, or producing oil, gas, or minerals;
> (b) Using or attempting to use poisons, electrical charges, or explosives in the collection or harvest of a Monument resource;

(c) Introducing or otherwise releasing an introduced species from within or into the Monument; and

(d) Anchoring on or having a vessel anchored on any living
or dead coral with an anchor, anchor chain, or anchor rope.[216]

The development of structures, such as offshore oil platforms, refineries, or other facilities used to produce energy, is prohibited. Not even the federal government may explore for, develop, or produce oil, gas, or minerals within the monument. Any regulated activity within the monument requires a valid permit that specifically authorizes that activity from NOAA and USFWS.[217] A permit may be granted if the activity:

(1) Is research designed to further understanding of Monument resources and qualities;

(2) Will further the educational value of the Monument;

(3) Will assist in the conservation and management of the
Monument;

(4) Will allow Native Hawaiian practices (discussed below);

(5) Will allow a special ocean use (discussed below); or

(6) Will allow recreational activities (discussed below).[218]

Moreover, regulations provide that a permit may not be issued unless the agencies find that:

(1) The activity can be conducted with adequate safeguards
for the resources and ecological integrity of the Monument;

(2) The activity will be conducted in a manner compatible
with the purposes of the Proclamation, considering the extent
to which the conduct of the activity may diminish or enhance
Monument resources, qualities, and ecological integrity, any
indirect, secondary or cumulative effects of the activity, and the
duration of such effects;

(3) There is no practicable alternative to conducting the
activity within the Monument;

(4) The end value of the activity outweighs its adverse
impacts on Monument resources, qualities, and ecological
integrity;

(5) The duration of the activity is no longer than necessary
to achieve its stated purpose;

(6) The applicant is qualified to conduct and complete the activity and mitigate any potential impacts resulting from its conduct;

(7) The applicant has adequate financial resources available to conduct and complete the activity and mitigate any potential impacts resulting from its conduct;

(8) The methods and procedures proposed by the applicant are appropriate to achieve the proposed activity's goals in relation to their impacts to Monument resources, qualities, and ecological integrity;

(9) The applicant's vessel has been outfitted with a mobile transceiver unit; and

(10) There are no other factors that would make the issuance of a permit for the activity inappropriate.[219]

Monument regulations also take into account traditional and customary Native Hawaiian practices. A permit to allow Native Hawaiian practices requires five specific findings: (1) the activity is noncommercial and will not involve the sale of any organism or material collected; (2) the purpose and intent of the activity are appropriate and deemed necessary by traditional standards in the Native Hawaiian culture and demonstrate an understanding of and background in the traditional practice and its associated values and protocols; (3) the activity benefits the resources of the Northwestern Hawaiian Islands and the Native Hawaiian community; (4) the activity supports or advances the perpetuation of traditional knowledge and ancestral connections of Native Hawaiians to the Northwestern Hawaiian Islands; and (5) any monument resource harvested from the monument will be consumed in the monument.[220]

A special ocean use permit is also available to qualified applicants. According to the applicable regulation, a special ocean use means "an activity or use of the Monument that is engaged in to generate revenue or profits for one or more of the persons associated with the activity or use, and does not destroy, cause the loss of, or injure Monument resources. This includes ocean-based ecotourism and other activities such as educational and research activities that are engaged in to generate revenue, but does not include commercial fishing for bottomfish or pelagic species conducted pursuant to a valid permit issued by NOAA."[221]

Whenever someone applies for a special ocean use permit, the agencies:

(1) Shall authorize the conduct of an activity only if that activity is compatible with the purposes for which the Monument is designated and with protection of Monument resources;

(2) Shall not authorize the conduct of any activity for a period of more than 5 years unless renewed;

(3) Shall require that activities carried out under the permit be conducted in a manner that does not destroy, cause the loss of, or injure Monument resources; and

(4) Shall require the permittee to purchase and maintain comprehensive general liability insurance, or post an equivalent bond, against claims arising out of activities conducted under the permit and to agree to hold the United States harmless against such claims;

(5) Each person issued a permit for a special ocean use under this section must submit an annual report to the Secretaries not later than December 31 of each year which describes activities conducted under that permit and revenues derived from such activities during the year.[222]

Categories of special ocean use permitted for the first time are restricted in duration and permitted only as a special ocean use pilot project. Subsequent permits for any category of special ocean use may be issued only if a special ocean use pilot project for that category meets the requirements of this section and any terms and conditions placed on the permit for the pilot project.[223] Public notice must be provided prior to requiring a special ocean use permit for any category of activity not previously identified as a special ocean use.[224]

Finally, a recreation permit allows a recreational activity within the Midway Atoll Special Management Area. This area of the NWHI Monument surrounds Midway Atoll out to a distance of twelve nautical miles and was established for the enhanced management, protection, and preservation of monument wildlife and historical resources. Recreational activity is defined as "an activity conducted for personal enjoyment that does not result in the extraction of Monument resources or involve a fee-for-service transaction." Such activities include wildlife viewing, SCUBA diving, snorkeling, and boating.[225] Application for a recreation permit must demonstrate that:

> (1) The activity is for the purpose of recreation as defined in the applicable statute;
> (2) The activity is not associated with any for-hire operation; and
> (3) The activity does not involve any extractive use.[226]

The Northwestern Hawaiian Islands Marine National Monument is still in its infancy. It is apparent, however, that the strict regulations basically prohibit most land use or development. What uses are allowable are tightly controlled and require a significant showing that the monument and its resources will be preserved and unharmed.

The Legacy Land Conservation Program

The first permanent funding source for land conservation in Hawai'i was created in 2005 with the enactment of the Legacy Lands Act and the establishment of the Legacy Land Conservation Program.[227] The program provides grants to state agencies, counties, and nonprofit organizations to facilitate the purchase and protection of lands with "cultural, natural, agricultural, historical [or] recreational resources."[228] Funds can also be used to acquire conservation or agricultural easements.[229] The broad goals of the program allow funding for projects outside the "traditional conservation paradigm," including, for example, the conservation of land with cultural or agricultural value.[230]

Grants may provide up to 75 percent of the purchase price; agencies or nonprofit groups must supply at least 25 percent.[231] The program is funded through the conveyance tax on all property sales: 10 percent of such collections are earmarked for the Legacy Land Conservation Fund.[232] The rationale is that the sale and development of property increases the strain on "natural areas, coastal access, agricultural production, and Hawai'i's water resources and watershed recharge areas."[233]

The Legacy Lands Act also includes a graduated increase in the conveyance tax of 30 cents per $100 for sales from $1–2 million, 50 cents per $100 for sales from $2–4 million, 70 cents per $100 for sales from $4–6 million, 90 cents per $100 for sales in the $6–10 million range, and $1 per $100 for sales over $10 million.[234] In 2008, total conveyance tax collections were approximately $43 million,[235] resulting in approximately $4.3 million deposited to the Legacy Land Fund.

The application process for Legacy Land funds is competitive, requiring: (1) applicant submission of the grant application and preliminary documentation by an annual deadline; (2) commission review of applications and the announcement of nominees, who may be asked to submit additional documents, including appraisals and title reports; and (3) commission recommendation of funding awards to the Board of Land and Natural Resources (BLNR), with final awards subject to a consultation process with members of the State Legislature and the approval of the BLNR, attorney general, and governor.[236]

The Legacy Land Conservation Commission advises the DLNR, through the BLNR, on proposed land acquisitions and grant requests, and also makes recommendations for the acquisition of lands.[237] The nine-member commission must include one member from each county in addition to four members with scientific qualifications evidenced by an academic degree, one member also belonging to an environmental organization, one member also belonging to a conservation organization, one member in a statewide agricultural association, and one member knowledgeable about Native Hawaiian culture.[238]

Statutory guidelines instruct the commission on which lands must be given priority in acquisition recommendation: (1) lands with exceptional value due to unique aesthetic resources, cultural or archaeological resources, or threatened or endangered habitats; (2) lands in imminent danger of development; (3) lands in imminent danger of modification in such a way that would impair the land's value; (4) lands providing critical habitats; (5) lands containing cultural or archaeological sites in danger of theft or destruction; and (6) unique and productive agricultural lands.[239]

The first grant was made in fiscal year 2006, awarding $1.1 million to the Maui Coastal Land Trust for a conservation easement over 168 acres on the southeastern shore of Moloka'i.[240] Six awards totaling $4.7 million were made in fiscal year 2007.[241] Awards in the 2008 fiscal year totaled $4.7 million and included the following: $737,300 for the acquisition of eleven acres in Waianae's Lualualei Valley for agricultural protection; $1.5 million for approximately 551 acres in Kāwā on the island of Hawai'i for watershed, coastal, habitat, cultural, recreational, and open space preservation; $700,000 for approximately twenty-one acres on the north shore of Kaua'i for the protection of watershed, coastal, and habitat values; nearly $1 million for 128 acres in Nu'u Makai, Maui, for the protection of coastal, wetland, habitat, historical, and cultural values; and \$767,976 for nearly 200 acres on Moloka'i for the protection of watershed, cultural, and scenic values.[242] The governor approved five fiscal year 2009 awards: nearly \$1 million for 3,583 acres in Honouliuli Preserve in the Wai'anae Range; \$450,000 for approximately 66 acres in Hāmākua, Kailua; \$7,000 for 7 acres in North Kohala, island of Hawai'i; \$1.25 million for 17.05 acres in Lapakahi, Kohala, island of Hawai'i; and just over \$600,000 for an agricultural conservation easement over 27.44 acres in Pūpūkea, on the north shore of O'ahu.[243]

Kapi'olani Park

Kapi'olani Park was originally conceived of as part of a planned community for Hawai'i's elite in the late 1870s.[244] The shareholder organization that established the park—the Kapi'olani Park Association—had two goals: building residences for shareholders and constructing a horse-racing track.[245] The lands used by the project included three hundred acres of crown land leased from King Kalākaua (a shareholder in the association).[246] By the 1890s, the park included a track, artificial ponds, and winding carriage roads surrounded by shareholder houses.[247]

In 1896, the park was transferred by Act 53 of the Legislature of the Republic of Hawai'i from the association to the Honolulu Park Commission, a public agency comprised of six trustees "charged by legislative mandate with operating the site as a public recreation ground for all citizens of Honolulu."[248] Importantly, the act provided that the park was to be "permanently set apart as a free public park and recreation ground forever," while expressly withholding from the commission the ability to lease or sell any park land.[249] The documents surrounding this transfer established the park as a public charitable trust.[250] Following annexation in 1898, it was used by the U.S. Army as troop campgrounds.[251] It was during this period that concessions were first sold in the park; the trustees allowed refreshments to be sold in exchange for a monthly \$25 fee.[252]

In 1913, the Territory of Hawai'i transferred park authority to the City and County of Honolulu, which continues to manage the park today.[253] The nine members of the Honolulu City Council are the Kapi'olani Park trustees.[254] The Kapi'olani Park Preservation Society (KPPS) was founded in 1986 by citizens concerned that the park was not being managed in compliance with the trust.[255] In 1987, in one of the better-known controversies regarding the park, KPPS challenged the city's plan to lease a portion of the park adjacent to the Honolulu Zoo for construction of a seven-unit fast food complex that included a Burger King.[256] The Supreme Court found the planned lease in breach of the trust,[257] citing Act 53 and conveyance deeds to establish the trust's lack of authority to enter into such leases.[258] Beyond stopping the proposed construction, the ruling made clear the public's standing to challenge actions by the city as park trustee,[259] and it has thus facilitated the KPPS taking on a "watchdog role over Park management."[260]

The park and its usage remains controversial; most recently the society has been involved in disputes regarding art sales in the park and proposed parking fee increases. In 2009, the trust—at the prodding of the society—requested instructions on artwork sales and craft fairs held on and along the Honolulu Zoo fence.[261] Although a hearing has not yet been scheduled, a court-appointed master found that the activities were explicitly allowed as "exhibitions," finding any commercial sales to be merely incidental.[262] The report noted that no admission fees were being charged, no mass-produced items were being sold, and that permits and licenses granted for the activities were temporary and did "not unreasonably interfere with other park uses or users."[263] The society maintains that the art sales and craft fairs are not allowed under the trust and are examples of park commercialization, calling the sellers "special interest groups" using the park for "their own purposes."[264] The society has also been vocal in opposing a proposed increase in nearby metered parking fees from 25 cents to $1.50 per hour, arguing that the increases would deter park usage in a way contradictory to the "intent of the park trust."[265]

The Army Compatible Use Buffer Program

Suburban and rural sprawl have brought civilian populations increasingly close to military installations that were originally placed in isolated locations.[266] This proximity often results in encroachment, broadly defined as "the cumulative result of any and all outside influence that inhibit normal military training, testing, and operations."[267] The main encroachment issues are noise pollution, endangered species and critical habitat, wetlands, water quality and supply, air pollution and quality, cultural resources, maritime competition, competition for airspace, competition for radio frequency spectrum, urban growth around military installations, and unexploded ordnance and munitions constituents.[268]

The military thus has an interest in "buffering" military installations from civilian development through funding for cooperative conservation agreements, thereby cutting off future encroachment issues.

In 2002, Congress amended the Department of Defense Authorization Act to include explicit authorization for such partnership agreements between the military and conservation initiatives of state and local governments and nonprofit groups.[269] The amendment allows "[t]he Secretary of Defense or the Secretary of a military department [to] enter into an agreement with an eligible entity . . . to address the use or development of real property in the vicinity of a military installation for purposes of (1) limiting any development or use of the property that would be incompatible with the mission of the installation; or (2) preserving habitat on the property."[270] In response, the Office of the Secretary of Defense (OSD) created what is now known as the Readiness and Environmental Protection Initiative (REDI) in 2003 to provide an overarching framework and funding to the services in exercising the authority to form partnership agreements granted by Congress in 10 U.S.C. § 2684a.[271]

The military branches have developed distinct programs to exercise the power granted under § 2684a. The army's is called the Army Compatible Use Buffer (ACUB) program. The program allows the army to partner with conservation-minded groups to finance purchases, but the army itself does not hold a property interest,[272] which goes instead to a partner with a land or natural resource conservation goal.[273] The army benefits by limiting development on this land, thus cutting off the potential for encroachment issues to arise in the area. There have been three ACUB projects in Hawai'i: Waimea Valley, Moanalua Valley, and Pūpūkea-Paumalū. A fourth partnership involving the purchase of 3,400 acres at Honouliuli Preserve along the Wai'anae Range is expected to be reached in 2009.[274]

Waimea Valley was Hawai'i's inaugural project using ACUB funds, involving the $14 million sale of 1,875 acres near the army's Kahuku Training Area in 2006.[275] After the valley's owner—a mainland investor—attempted to sell the valley as a private residence, the City and County of Honolulu filed a condemnation lawsuit to preserve the valley from development.[276] Eventually, a settlement was reached involving the conservation purchase through funds contributed by the city and county ($5 million), ACUB ($3.5 million), OHA ($2.9 million), DLNR ($1.6 million), and the National Audubon Society ($1 million).[277] The valley is held and managed by Hi'ilei Aloha, a limited liability company created by OHA,[278] and operated as a "historical, cultural, botanical and ecological" attraction for visitors and kama'āina alike.[279]

In 2007, 3,716 acres in Moanalua Valley—which, as one of the few remaining open spaces in the urban Honolulu area, had been both a potential location for the H-3 freeway and under longtime threat of residential development—were purchased by the Trust for Public Land for $5.5 million.[280] The purchase was funded by state general funds, a grant from the Fish and Wildlife Service, and the ACUB program.[281] The valley, containing five distinct forest types, nine miles of streams, and the habitat of endangered plants and animals, is also home to culturally important sites and petroglyphs.[282] Valley management was placed with the DLNR's Division of Forestry and Wildlife, and the site was added to the State Forest Reserve and Ko'olau Watershed Partnership.[283] It is open to the public for hiking, hunting, cultural resource preservation, and education, with the back of the valley managed for wildlife preservation.[284]

In 2007, another partnership to buffer the Kahuku Training Area purchased for $7.95 million the 1,129 acre Pūpūkea-Paumalū coastal bluff along the north shore.[285] Partners included ACUB (approximately $3.3 million), NOAA (nearly $2 million), the City and County of Honolulu ($1 million), the State of Hawai'i ($1 million), and the North Shore Community Land Trust (approximately $600,000).[286] Twenty-five acres were conveyed to the city as nature preserve, with the remaining land going to the state for addition to the Park Reserve System.[287]

Notes

1. State of Hawai'i, Department of Business, Economic Development & Tourism, *State of Hawai'i Data Book 2008* (2009). Note table 6.08 ("Real Property Owned by or Leased to the Federal Government: 2002 to 2007:"); Table 6.10 ("State Public and Set-Aside Land Inventory, by County: January 10, 1999").

2. Id. at Table 6.10.

3. Id. at Table 6.09 ("Department of Hawaiian Home Lands Acreage, Lessees, and Applicants, by Islands, 2007 and 2008"). Only 203,225 acres, which amounts to roughly .05 percent of the total acreage of the state, were held by the Department of Hawaiian Home Lands as of June 30, 2008. Id.

4. "Public lands" as defined by state statute does not include all lands owned by the state. The list of eleven exceptions can be found at Haw Rev. Stat. § 171-2 (2009). Some of the exceptions are for Hawaiian Homes Commission lands, roads and streets, land set aside for the Aloha Tower development corporation, and the University of Hawai'i. Id.

5. Haw Rev. Stat. § 171-3 (2009).

6. Id. § 171-7.
7. Id. § 171-10.
8. Id. §§ 171-11, -33.
9. Id. § 171-32.
10. Id. § 171-36. Residential leaseholds, however, have an initial term of fifty-five years, with the privilege of extending under certain conditions, provided that the total lease period does not exceed seventy-five years. Id.
11. Id.
12. Id.
13. Id. § 171-41.
14. Id. § 171-42.
15. Id.
16. Id. §§ 171-41, -42. Sale of the land requires the prior approval of the governor and is subject to disapproval by the legislature by two-thirds vote of either the Senate or the House of Representatives or by a majority vote of both. Id.
17. Id. § 171-42.
18. Id. § 171-46.
19. Id. § 171-48.
20. Id. § 171-49.5.
21. Id. § 171-70.
22. Id.
23. Id. §§ 171-72, -73.
24. Id. §§ 171-74, -75.
25. Id. § 171-79.
26. Id. § 171-43.1.
27. Id. § 205-1-52. See chapter 1 for a summary of the Land Use Commission's authority and duties.
28. Id. § 102-1(1).
29. State of Hawai‘i, Department of Land and Natural Resources, Division of State Parks, http://www.hawaiistateparks.org/ (last visited Nov. 22, 2009).
30. Haw Rev. Stat. § 184-5(a) (2009).
31. Haw. Code R. § 13-146-66 (2009).
32. Id. § 13-146-67.
33. Id. § 13-146-50.
34. Id. § 13-146-53.
35. Id.
36. State of Hawai‘i, Department of Land and Natural Resources, Division of State Parks, Hawai‘i State Parks, "A visitor's guide to park resources and recreational activities," http://www.hawaiistateparks.org/pdf/brochures/Hawaii_State_Parks_Guide.pdf (last visited Nov. 22, 2009).
37. Haw Rev. Stat. § 171-43 (2009).
38. Id. § 171-44.
39. Lester Chang, "State may end leases of prized Koke‘e cabins," Garden Isle, Oct. 3, 2003, http://www.kauaiworld.com/articles/2003/10/03/news (follow the "Advanced Search Options" hyperlink and type in keywords from article title) (last visited Nov. 22, 2009).
40. Id.

41. Lester Chang, "Attention focused on state park cabin leases," GARDEN ISLE, Nov. 3, 2001, http://www.kauaiworld.com/articles/2001/11/05/news (follow the "Advanced Search Options" hyperlink and type in keywords from article title) (last visited Nov. 22, 2009).

42. Id.

43. Id.

44. Id.

45. Chang, "State may end leases of prized Koke'e cabins," supra note 39.

46. Chang, "Attention focused on state park cabin leases," supra note 41.

47. Lester Chang, "Land board to move on Koke'e plan today," GARDEN ISLE, Jan. 15, 2005, http://www.kauaiworld.com/articles/2005/01/14/news (follow the "Advanced Search Options" hyperlink and type in keywords from article title) (last visited Nov. 22, 2009).

48. Id.

49. Tom Finnegan, "Bill tackles Kokee cabins flap," HONOLULU STAR-BULLE-TIN, May 5, 2008, http://archives.starbulletin.com/2008/05/05/news/story04. html#cxb (last visited Nov. 22, 2009).

50. Id.

51. H.B. 2872, 24th Leg., Reg. Sess. (Haw. 2008).

52. Diana Leone, "State, Koke'e cabin lessees debate terms," HONOLULU ADVERTISER, July 26, 2008, at B5.

53. H.B. 2872, 24th Leg., Reg. Sess. (Haw. 2008).

54. "Lester Chang, "State reviewing Koke'e-Waimea Canyon park," GARDEN ISLE, Oct. 30, 2001, http://www.kauaiworld.com/articles/2001/10/31/news (follow the "Advanced Search Options" hyperlink and type in keywords from article title) (last visited Nov. 22, 2009).

55. Lester Chang, "Attention focused on state park cabin leases," GARDEN ISLE, Nov. 3, 2001. http://www.kauaiworld.com/articles/2001/11/05/news (follow the "Advanced Search Options" hyperlink and type in keywords from article title) (last visited Nov. 22, 2009).

56. Chang, "State reviewing Koke'e-Waimea Canyon park," supra note 54. The Koke'e State Park Draft Master Plan can be viewed at the Department of Land and Natural Resources State Parks Web site at http://www.hawaiistateparks.org/pdf/plans/Kokee_MP_draft.pdf (last visited Nov. 22, 2009).

57. Id.

58. Id.

59. Betsy A. Cody, "Major federal land management agencies: Management of our nation's lands and resources," Congressional Research Services Report 95-599, May 15, 1995, http://www.ncseonline.org/nle/crsreports/natural/nrgen-3.cfm (last visited Nov. 22, 2009).

60. U.S. General Services Administration, GSA Office of Governmentwide Policy, "Federal real property profile," Table 16 at page 19 (2004), *available at* http://www.gsa.gov/gsa/cm_attachments/GSA_DOCUMENT/Annual Report FY2004 Final_R2M-n11_0Z5RDZ-i34K-pR.pdf (last visited Nov. 22, 2009).

61. U.S. Department of the Interior, U.S. Geological Survey, "Federal lands and Indian reservations: Hawaii," http://nationalatlas.gov/printable/images/pdf/fedlands/hi.pdf (last visited Jan. 5, 2010).

62. *See,* e.g., U.S. Army, 652nd Engineers Battalion, *Hawaii Military Installations Map,* Jan. 1979; State of Hawai'i, *State of Hawaii Coastal Management Program and Final Environmental Impact Statement,* chapter 3; Joseph L. Sax, "Helpless giants: The national parks and the regulation of private lands," 75 MICH. L. REV. 239 (1976); Ann Louise Strong, *Land Banking: European Reality, American Prospect,* Baltimore: Johns Hopkins University Press, 1979.

63. *See,* e.g., Benjamin H. Hibbard, *A History of the Public Land Policies,* Madison: University of Wisconsin Press, 1965; Vernon R. Carstensen, *The Public Lands: Studies in the History of the Public Domain,* Madison: University of Wisconsin Press, 1963; Strong, *Land Banking,* supra note 62, at 9–39.

64. Strong, *Land Banking,* supra note 62.

65. Id. at 14–34.

66. Hawaii Statehood Admission Act, Pub. L. No. 86-3, 73 Stat. 4 (1959) (hereinafter "Admission Act").

67. U.S. CONST., art. IV, § 3, cl. 2: "The Congress shall have the power to dispose of and make all needful rules and regulations respecting the Territory or other property belonging to the United States; and nothing in this Constitution shall be so construed as to prejudice any claims of the United States, or of any particular state."

68. Joint Resolution of Annexation, 30 Stat. 750 (1898); Admission Act, supra note 66; *see* Gavin Daws, *Shoal of Time: A History of the Hawaiian Islands,* New York: Macmillan, 1968, at 391.

69. Admission Act, supra note 66, §§ 5(a), (b).

70. Id.

71. Admission Act, supra note 66.

72. Admission Act, supra note 66, §§ 5(a), (b).

73. Id., §§ 5(c), (d), (e), (g).

74. Hibbard, *History of Public Land Policies,* supra note 63, at 70–71.

75. *See* U.S. Congress, Senate Report 675, Land Conveyance—Hawaii (Dec. 3, 1963).

76. U.S. Congress, An Act to Revise the Procedures Established by the Hawaii Statehood Act for the Conveyance of Certain Lands to the State of Hawaii, Pub. L. No. 88-233, 77 Stat. 472 (1963), § 1(a) (hereinafter "Ceded Lands Act").

77. Id.

78. Id. § 2.

79. In the case of the Admission Act, it is the president; as amended by the Ceded Lands Act, it is the administrator of the General Services Administration (GSA). The president delegated his authority to declare lands surplus. "Providing for the performance of certain functions vested in or subject to approval of the president," Exec. Order No. 10530, 19 Fed. Reg. 2709 (May 10, 1954). *See also* "Providing for the performance of certain functions vested in or subject to approval of the president," Exec. Order No. 10960, 26 Fed. Reg. 7823 (Aug. 21, 1961).

80. Ceded Lands Act, § 1(a).

81. Harold W. Seidman, acting assistant dir. for Mgmt. and Org., Bureau of the Budget, to the Hon. Alan Bibb, chairman, Subcomm. on Public Lands, Comm. on Interior and Insular Affairs, U.S. Senate (Nov. 19, 1963).

82. U.S. Office of Management and Budget, *Procedures for Reports on Federal Property in Hawaii*, Budget Circular No. A-52. Washington, D.C.: OMB.

83. *See* Sheryl L. Nicholson, Comment, "Hawaii's ceded lands," 3 U. Haw. L. Rev. 101, 132–133 (1981).

84. *Hawaii v. Gordon*, 373 U.S. 57, 58 (1963).

85. By then Hawai'i Congressman Hiram Fong. *See* Hibbard, *History of Public Land Policies*, supra note 63, at 91.

86. "Providing for the identification of unneeded federal real property," Exec. Order No. 11508, 35 Fed. Reg. 2855 (Feb. 10, 1970); "Federal property council," Exec. Order No. 11724, 38 Fed. Reg. 16837 (June 25, 1973); "Federal property review," Exec. Order No. 11954, 42 Fed. Reg. 2297 (Jan. 7, 1977); U.S. Department of Defense, *Project FRESH—Facility Requirements Evaluation*, State of Hawai'i.

87. U.S. Department of Defense, *Military Property Requirements in Hawaii Study (MILPRO-HI)*.

88. Id. at E-66, -67.

89. Interview with Jake Ours and Anthony Pace, U.S. Gen. Services Admin., in San Francisco, Cal. (July 30, 1980).

90. Nicholson, "Hawaii's ceded lands," supra note 83, at 137–138.

91. Interview by Jack Kaguni, State of Haw. Dept. of Land and Nat. Res., Land Mgmt. Div., with Sheryl Miyahira Nicholson, in Honolulu (Apr. 2, 1980).

92. Admission Act, § 5(f).

93. *See* Haw.Rev. Stat., ch. 171 (1980), § 26-15 (1976).

94. State of Hawai'i, Legislative Auditor, *Financial Audit of the Department of Land and Natural Resources* (report submitted to the governor), 31–37. In particular, the funds made their way into a special land and development fund, many purposes of which had marginal relevance to the public trust purposes set out in section 5(f) of the Admission Act.

95. Election by means of Native Hawaiian voters only was declared unconstitutional by the U.S. Supreme Court in *Rice v. Cayetano*, 528 U.S. 495 (2000).

96. Haw. Rev. Stat. § 10-13.5 (2009).

97. *OHA v. Housing & Cmty. Dev. Corp. of Haw.*, 117 Haw. 174, 180, 177 P.3d 884, 890 (2008).

98. *OHA v. Bd. of Land & Natural Res.*, No. 95-0330-01 (Haw. Sup. Ct. 1998) (holding that "[t]he State of Hawai'i has the power to dispose of ceded lands").

99. *OHA v. Housing & Cmty. Dev. Corp. of Haw.*, at 195, 177 P.3d at 905.

100. *Hawaii v. OHA*, 129 S.Ct. 1436 (2009).

101. Conservation Foundation Letter, "Federal land sales stir up turf dispute," 3 (May 1982).

102. *Kleppe v. New Mexico*, 426 U.S. 529 (1976).

103. *Ventura County v. Gulf Oil Corp.*, 601 F.2d 1080 (9th Cir. 1979).

104. *Cal. Coastal Comm'n v. Granite Rock Co.*, 480 U.S. 572 (1987).

105. Id. at 575.

106. Id. at 586.

107. Id. at 587.

108. Id. at 589.

109. Id. at 587.

110. Phil Mayer, "Native claim opener set for saturday," HONOLULU STAR-BULLE-TIN, Jan. 6, 1982.

111. 63C AM. JUR. 2D *Public Lands* § 1 (2008).

112. Id.

113. Id. § 40.

114. Id.

115. 43 U.S.C. §§ 2301–2306 (2009).

116. Jan G. Laitos and Thomas A. Carr, "The transformation on public lands," 26 ECOLOGY L.Q. 140, 144 (1999).

117. Id.

118. Id.

119. Jim Carlton, "Hot properties: Private 'inholdings' in federal preserves," WALL ST. J., July 28, 2004, at B1, B4.

120. Matt Tuohy, "Victory in the valleys: At Honolulu's doorstep, Moanalua is forever wild," HAWAIIAN ISLANDS PROGRAM, Issue I (2008), at 1, 5.

121. Laitos and Carr, supra note 116 at 160.

122. Id.

123. Id. at 161.

124. Id.

125. Id.

126. Id. at 162–167.

127. Id. at 163.

128. Id.

129. Id.

130. Id. at 163–164.

131. Id.

132. Id. at 166.

133. National Park Service, "Frequently asked questions," http://www.nps.gov/faqs.htm (last visited Nov. 22, 2009).

134. National Park Service, "The National Park Service System: Caring for the American legacy," http://www.nps.gov/legacy/mission.html (last visited Nov. 22, 2009).

135. 16 U.S.C. 1 (2009).

136. William J. Lockhart, "External threats to our national parks: An argument for substantive protection," 16 STAN. ENVTL. L.J. 3 (1997).

137. Id.

138. Id.

139. Id.

140. Id.

141. Id. at 40.

142. 16 U.S.C. § 3.

143. 36 C.F.R. § 1.6.

144. National Park Service, "Director's Order #53: Special park uses," § 4 (Apr. 4, 2000–Dec. 31, 2006), http://www.nps.gov/policy/DOrders/DOrder53.html (last visited Dec. 21, 2009).

145. Id.; 36 C.F.R. § 1-7 (2009).

146. Id.

147. Id.

148. 36 C.F.R. § 18.4.

149. Id. § 18.10.

150. 39 Stat. 432, 16 U.S.C. § 391.

151. Pub. L. No. 86-744, 74 Stat. 881, 16 U.S.C. § 396b; Pub. L. No. 87-278, 75 Stat. 577, 16 U.S.C. § 391d.

152. National Park Service, "Vision statement" (Centennial strategy for Hawai'i Volcanoes National Park), http://www.nps.gov/havo/parkmgmt/upload/havo_centennial_strategy2.pdf (last visited Dec. 21, 2009).

153. National Park Service, Hawai'i Volcanoes National Park main page, http://www.nps.gov/havo/index.htm (last visited Nov. 22, 2009).

154. Id. (click on desired hyperlinks to the left).

155. National Park Service, Hawai'i Volcanoes National Park, "Doing business with the Park," http://www.nps.gov/havo/parkmgmt/businesswithpark.htm (click on "Permits" hyperlink at top) (last visited Nov. 22, 2009).

156. 36 C.F.R. § 51.1 (2009).

157. Id. § 51.4.

158. Id. § 51.73.

159. Id.

160. Id. § 51.74.

161. Id. § 51.85.

162. Id. § 51.86.

163. Volcano House, main page, http://www.volcanohousehotel.com/ (last visited Nov. 22, 2009).

164. Id.

165. National Park Service, "Haleakalā National Park," http://www.nps.gov/hale/index.htm (last visited Nov. 22, 2009)

166. Id.

167. National Park Service, "Haleakalā National Park, special use permits," http://www.nps.gov/hale/parkmgmt/special-use-permits.htm (last visited Nov. 22, 2009).

168. Alexandre Da Silva, "Park officials put brakes on Haleakala tour rides," Honolulu Star-Bulletin, Oct. 4, 2007, http://archives.starbulletin.com/2007/10/04/news/story03.html (last visited Nov. 22, 2009).

169. Id.

170. Lockhart, supra note 136, at 40.

171. *Kleppe v. New Mexico*, 426 U.S. 529 (1976). *See also United States v. Brown*, 552 F.2d 817 (8th Cir. 1977); *Alexander v. Block*, 660 F.2d 1240 (8th Cir. 1981).

172. U.S. Fish & Wildlife Service, National Wildlife Refuge System, "Welcome to the National Wildlife Refuge System," http://www.fws.gov/refuges/ (last visited Nov. 22, 2009).

173. Id.

174. U.S. Fish & Wildlife Service, National Wildlife Refuge System, "How long has the Federal Government been setting aside lands for wildlife?" http://www.fws.gov/refuges/about/acquisition.html (last visited Dec. 21, 2009).

175. U.S. Department of the Interior, U.S. Fish & Wildlife Service, "America's National Wildlife Refuges" 1 (2007) *available at* http://www.fws.gov/refuges/pdfs/factsheets/FactSheetAmNationalWild.pdf (last visited Nov. 22, 2009).

176. Id.

177. Id.

178. 16 U.S.C. §§ 668dd–668ee (2009).

179. Id. § 668dd(d)(1)(A).

180. Id.

181. Id. § 668dd(d)(1)(B).

182. Id.

183. Id.

184. Id.

185. 50 C.F.R. § 25.41 (2009).

186. Id. § 25.43.

187. Id. § 25.61.

188. U.S. Fish & Wildlife Service, "Refuge list by state: Hawaii," http://www.fws.gov/refuges/profiles/ByState.cfm?state=HI (last visited Jan.5, 2010). The refuges in the state and surrounding area include Baker Island National Wildlife Refuge, Hakalau Forest National Wildlife Refuge, Hanalei National Wildlife Refuge, Hawaiian Islands National Wildlife Refuge, Howland Island National Wildlife Refuge, Hūleʻia National Wildlife Refuge, James Campbell National Wildlife Refuge, Jarvis Island National Wildlife Refuge, Johnston Island National Wildlife Refuge, Kakahaiʻa National Wildlife Refuge, Keālia Pond National Wildlife Refuge, Kīlauea Point National Wildlife Refuge, Kingman Reef National Wildlife Refuge, Midway Atoll National Wildlife Refuge, Oʻahu Forest National Wildlife Refuge, Palmyra Atoll National Wildlife Refuge, Pearl Harbor National Wildlife Refuge, and Rose Atoll National Wildlife Refuge.

189. U.S. Fish & Wildlife Service, "Kīlauea Point National Wildlife Refuge: Aboutus," http://www.fws.gov/kilaueapoint/aboutus.html (last visited Dec. 21, 2009).

190. Id.

191. Id.

192. U.S. Fish and Wildlife Service, "Kilauea Point National Wildlife Refuge," http://www.fws.gov/refuges/profiles/index.cfm?id=12530 (last visited Dec. 21, 2009).

193. Id.

194. Id.

195. Id.

196. U.S. Fish & Wildlife Service, Copy of Special Conditions on Special Use Permit No. 12522-98001, issued on June 15, 1998 (on file with author).

197. Id.

198. Id.

199. Id.

200. U.S. Fish & Wildlife Service, Copy of Special Conditions on Special Use Permit No. HUL-93-55779, issued to Robert Crane, fax received July 26, 2005 (on file with author).

201. Id.

202. U.S. Fish & Wildlife Service, "Hakalau Forest National Wildlife Refuge," http://www.fws.gov/hakalauforest/ (last visited Nov. 22, 2009).

203. Id.

204. Telephone Interview with Richard Waas, refuge manager, Hakalau Forest National Wildlife Refuge (July 26, 2005).

205. U.S. Fish and Wildlife Service, Copy of Special Conditions on Special Use Permit No. 12516-04023, issued to Hawai'i Forest and Trail on May 1, 2004, fax received July 26, 2005.

206. Id.

207. Id.

208. Id.

209. Juliet Eilperin, "Hawaiian marine reserve to be world's largest; Bush to designate national park in Pacific waters," WASH. POST, June 15, 2006, at A01.

210. "Northwestern Hawaiian Islands Marine National Monument," 71 Fed. Reg. 51,134 (Aug. 29, 2006); 50 C.F.R. pt. 404 (2009).

211. Diana Leone, "Largest U.S. coral reef gets vast government protection," HONOLULU STAR-BULLETIN, June 15, 2006, at A1.

212. Eilperin, supra note 209.

213. "Proclamation No. 8031," 71 Fed. Reg. 36,443 (June 26, 2006). These three entities, known collectively as the Co-Trustees, "are working cooperatively and will consult to administer the Monument. The Co-Trustees have established a goal to provide unified management in the spirit of cooperative conservation." Id.

214. Id.

215. Notification of entry must be provided at least seventy-two hours, but no longer than one month, prior to the entry date. Notification of departure from the monument must be provided within twelve hours of leaving. A person providing notice under this paragraph must provide the following information, as applicable: position when making report; vessel name and International Maritime Organization identification number; name, address, and telephone number of owner and operator; USCG documentation, state license, or registration number; home port; intended and actual route through the monument; general categories of any hazardous cargo on board; length of vessel and propulsion type (e.g., motor or sail). Id. at 51,137; 50 C.F.R. § 404.4 (2009).

216. 50 C.F.R. § 404.6 (2009).

217. Id. § 404.11(a).

218. Id. § 404.11(c).

219. Id. § 404.3.

220. Id. § 404.11(a).

221. Id. § 404.3.

222. Id. § 404.11(f).

223. Id. § 404.11(f)(3).

224. Id. § 404.11(f)(4).

225. Id. § 404.3.

226. Id. § 404.11(g).

227. Joshua Stanbro, "Hawai'i state tax fund a reality," TRUST FOR PUBLIC LAND, Dec. 2005, http://www.tpl.org/tier3_print.cfm?folder_id=269&content_item_id= 20300&mod_type=1 (last visited Dec. 21, 2009).

228. State of Hawai'i, Department of Land and Natural Resources, "Legacy Land Conservation Program," http://Hawaii.gov/dlnr/dofaw/llcp (last visited Nov. 22, 2009).

229. HAW. REV. STAT. § 173A-5(h)(1) (2009).

230. "Sprawl vs. farms," HONOLULU WEEKLY, Feb. 13, 2008, http://honolulu weekly.com/cover/2008/02/sprawl-vs-farms/ (last visited Nov. 22, 2009).

231. HAW. REV. STAT. § 173A-5(j) (2009).

232. Id. § 173A-5(d).

233. *Sprawl vs. Farms*, supra note 230.

234. H.B. 1308, 23rd Leg., Reg. Sess. (Haw. 2005).

235. State of Hawai'i, Department of Taxation, "Annual Report 2007–2008," *available at* http://www6.Hawaii.gov/tax/pubs/08annrpt.pdf (last visited Nov. 22, 2009).

236. "Legacy Land Conservation Program," supra note 228.

237. HAW. REV. STAT. § 173A-2.5 (2009).

238. Id. § 173A-2.4.

239. Id. § 173A-2.6.

240. State of Hawai'i, Department of Land and Natural Resources, "Legacy Land Conservation Program projects," http://Hawaii.gov/dlnr/dofaw/llcp/legacy-land-conservation-program-projects-new (last visited Nov. 22, 2009).

241. Id.

242. Id.

243. E-mail from Molly Schmidt, coordinator, Legacy Land Conservation Program, June 22, 2009 (on file with author).

244. Robert R. Weyeneth, *Kapi'olani Park: A History*, Honolulu: Kapi'olani Park Preservation Society, 2002, at 22.

245. Id.

246. Id. at 23.

247. Id. at 41–42.

248. Id. at 45.

249. Id.

250. Kapi'olani Park Preservation Society, "Historical context," http://www.kapiolanipark.org/about/history.html (last visited Dec. 21, 2009).

251. Weyeneth, supra note 244, at 65.

252. Id.

253. Id. at 77.

254. Kapi'olani Park Preservation Society, supra note 250.

255. Id.

256. Weyeneth, supra note 244, at 110.

257. *Kapiolani Park Pres. Soc'y v. City & County of Honolulu*, 69 Haw. 569, 751 P.2d 1022 (1988).

258. Id. at 1026.

259. Id. at 1025.

260. Kapi'olani Park Preservation Society, supra note 250.

261. "Zoo fence art, fairs at Kapiolani allowed," HONOLULU STAR-BULLETIN, May 26, 2009, http://www.starbulletin.com/news/20090526_Zoo_fence_art_fairs_at_Kapiolani_allowed.html (last visited Nov. 22, 2009).

262. Id.

263. Id.

264. Lisa Kubota, "Controversy over Kapi'olani Park activities," KGMB9 News Hawai'i, Nov. 25, 2007.

265. Gary T. Kubota, "Parking fee increase opposed," HONOLULU STAR-BULLETIN, June 2, 2009, http://www.starbulletin.com/news/20090602_Parking_fee_increase_opposed.html (last visited Nov. 22, 2009).

266. Beth E. Lachman, Anny Wong, and Susan A. Resetar, *The Thin Green Line: An Assessment of DoD's Readiness and Environmental Protection Initiative to Buffer Installation Encroachment*, Santa Monica, CA.: RAND Corp., 2007, at 11.

267. J. Douglas Ripley, "Legal and policy background," in *Conserving Biodiversity on Military Lands: A Guide for Natural Resources Managers*, NatureServe, 2008, *available at* http://www.dodbiodiversity.org/Full_Publication_Conserving_Biodiversity_on_Military Lands.pdf (last visited Nov. 22, 2009).

268. Id.

269. Robert Boonstoppel and Adriane Miller, "U.S. military and communities seek ways to share natural resources," 38 MD. B.J. 32 (March/April 2005).

270. 10 U.S.C. § 2684a (2009).

271. Lachman et al., supra note 266, at 1.

272. U.S. Army Environmental Command, "Army compatible use buffer program: Year end summary FY07" 2, http://aec.army.mil/usaec/acub/docs_acub/eoys-fy07.pdf (last visited Dec. 21, 2009).

273. U.S. Army Garrison, "Pupukea-Paumalu protected," June 27, 2007, http://www.25idl.army.mil/pressrelease/20070606.pdf (last visited Dec. 221, 2009).

274. Lea Hong, Mark Fox, and Black McElheny, "Environmentalists, army join forces on preservation," U.S. Army INCOM-Pacific, May 21, 2009, *available at* http://www.imcom.pac.army.mil/news/article.aspx?id=44 (last visited Nov. 22, 2009).

275. Will Hoover, "Waimea Valley preserved," HONOLULU ADVERTISER, Jan. 14, 2006, http://the.honoluluadvertiser.com/article/2006/Jan/14/ln/FP601140338.html (last visited Nov. 22, 2009).

276. Stefanie Gardin, U.S. Army Garrison, Hawaii, "Partnership preserves Hawaii's Waimea Valley," Fall 2006, http://aec.army.mil/usaec/newsroom/update/fall06/fall0602.html (last visited Nov. 20, 2009).

277. Hoover, supra note 275.

278. OHA, "OHA to assume management of Waimea Valley," Sept. 28, 2007, http://www.oha.org/index.php?option=com_content&task=view&id=436&Itemid=224 (last visited Nov. 22, 2009).

279. Waimea Valley, "A living culture: Experience living Hawaiian culture at Waimea Valley," http://www.waimeavalley.net/living_culture.aspx (last visited Dec. 21, 2009).

280. "3716 acres protected," TRUST FOR PUBLIC LAND, Apr. 2, 2008, http://www.tpl.org/tier3_cd.cfm?content_item_id=22107&folder_id=269 (last visited Nov. 16, 2009).

281. Id.

282. Id.
283. Id.
284. Id.
285. "Coastal bluff on Oahu's north shore protected," TRUST FOR PUBLIC LAND, June 27, 2007, http://www.tpl.org/tier3_cd.cfm?content_item_id=21669&folder_id=269 (last visited Nov. 20, 2009).
286. Id.
287. Id.

Chapter 5

Redevelopment and the Role of Public Corporations

The Hawai'i State Legislature has created a number of special-purpose agencies with independent powers to develop or control the use of land within their geographic boundaries. In many instances, that power is exclusive and the county or counties in which such agencies are authorized to act have little or no regulatory authority within such geographic limits. While some—such as the Hawai'i Community Development Authority (HCDA)—are mature and have been more or less active for several decades, some are new, at least since the first edition of this book. To these we now turn.

The HCDA

In 1976, the legislature created the Hawai'i Community Development Authority for the purpose, among other things, of meeting community development needs such as housing, rental, commercial, industrial facilities, parks, and open space.[1] Aside from its extensive planning, land acquisition, and development powers,[2] the HCDA may also establish development rules that supersede all inconsistent county use regulations.[3] This it has done, making it a potentially powerful land development agency.

The legislature established HCDA during an affordable housing crisis, with a particular redevelopment area in mind: the collection of mostly commercial and industrial buildings near downtown Honolulu known as Kaka'ako.[4] It was the intent of the legislature to create an agency to plan and guide the development of Kaka'ako for a mixture of land uses.[5] It was to proceed by means of a "joint development" approach, combining the "strengths of private enterprise" with "public development and regulation."[6]

The reasons given for the creation of the district directly address community development needs:

> (1) The Kakaako district is centrally located in Honolulu proper, in close proximity to the central business district, the government center, commercial industrial and market facilities, major existing and contemplated transportation routes and recreational and service areas;
>
> (2) Due to its present function as a service and light industrial area, the district is relatively underdeveloped and especially in view of its proximity to the urban core where the pressure for all land uses is strong, has the potential for increased growth and development that can alleviate community needs such as low-income housing, parks and open space, and commercial and industrial facilities;
>
> (3) The district, if not redeveloped or renewed, has the potential to become a blighted and deteriorated area. Due to its present economic importance to the State in terms of industry and subsequent employment, there is a need to preserve and enhance its value and potential;
>
> (4) Kakaako has a potential, if properly developed and improved, to become a planned new community in consonance with surrounding urban areas.[7]

The legislature also set out development guidance policies that generally govern the HCDA's action in the Kaka'ako community development district.[8] First, it directed that the Kaka'ako district be developed for mixed land uses, provided its "function as a major economic center" was preserved.[9] The legislature then listed a series of specific "development guidance policies" to govern the authority's Kaka'ako activities:

> (1) Development shall result in a community which permits an appropriate land mixture of residential, commercial, industrial, and other uses. In view of the innovative nature of the mixed use approach, urban design policies should be established to provide guidelines for the public and private sectors in the proper development of this district; while the authority's development responsibilities apply only to the area

within the district, the authority may engage in any studies or coordinative activities permitted in this chapter which affect areas lying outside the district, where the authority in its discretion decides that those activities are necessary to implement the intent of this chapter. The studies or coordinative activities shall be limited to facility systems, resident and industrial relocation, and other activities with the counties and appropriate state agencies. The authority may engage in construction activities outside of the district; provided that such construction relates to infrastructure development or residential or business relocation activities; provided further, notwithstanding section 206E-7, that such construction shall comply with the general plan, development plan, ordinances, and rules of the county in which the district is located;

(2) Existing and future industrial uses shall be permitted and encouraged in appropriate locations within the district. No plan or implementation strategy shall prevent continued activity or redevelopment of industrial and commercial uses which meet reasonable performance standards;

(3) Activities shall be located so as to provide primary reliance on public transportation and pedestrian facilities for internal circulation within the district or designated subareas;

(4) Major view planes, view corridors, and other environmental elements such as natural light and prevailing winds, shall be preserved through necessary regulation and design review;

(5) Redevelopment of the district shall be compatible with plans and special districts established for the Hawai'i Capital District, and other areas surrounding the Kakaako district;

(6) Historic sites and culturally significant facilities, settings, or locations shall be preserved;

(7) Land use activities within the district, where compatible, shall to the greatest possible extent be mixed horizontally, that is, within blocks or other land areas, and vertically, as integral units of multi-purpose structures;

(8) Residential development may require a mixture of densities, building types, and configurations in accordance with appropriate urban design guidelines; integration both vertically and horizontally of residents of varying incomes, ages, and family groups; and an increased supply of housing

for residents of low- or moderate-income may be required as a condition of redevelopment in residential use. Residential development shall provide necessary community facilities, such as open space, parks, community meeting places, child care centers, and other services, within and adjacent to residential development;

(9) Public facilities within the district shall be planned, located, and developed so as to support the redevelopment policies for the district established by this chapter and plans and rules adopted pursuant to it.[10]

"OK, WE'VE STOPPED ANOTHER ATTEMPT TO DEVELOP KAKAAKO ... UH, WHAT'S NEXT ?..."

The HCDA developed a detailed Kakaʻako Community Development District Plan that, when stripped of its artists' renderings and explanatory language, most resembles a zoning ordinance to be administered by HCDA.[11] The present version of the plan envisions four land-use designations and seven neighborhoods.[12] The districts are Mixed-Use Zone (MUZ), Mixed-Use Zone Residential (MUZ-R), Public, and Park.[13] The neighborhoods are Sheridan, Thomas Square, Civic Center, Kapiʻolani, Central Kakaʻako, Auahi, and Pauahi.[14] While a neighborhood may be mostly residential or consist of public facilities, ultimately they are all mixed use.[15] The result is that residential, commercial, and industrial uses would be permitted nearly anywhere in Kakaʻako—subject to the lengthy land use plan and urban design principles contained in the plan.[16] The HCDA has embarked on a major revision of the plan, which will be promulgated after public hearings in 2009 using "Smart Growth" principles to model the housing, transportation, and aesthetic aspects.[17] The entity has drafted another plan particularly directed at approximately thirty "prime" acres—the site of a very public project failure described below—to commence in late 2009.[18]

Apparently reacting to selective community opposition to a proposal to develop high-density residential towers on land to be sold by the state to the developer, the legislature made an important statutory change in 2006: HCDA was prohibited "from approving any plan or proposal for any residential development in that portion of the Kakaʻako community development district makai of Ala Moana Boulevard and between Kewalo basin and the foreign trade zone."[19] HCDA also cannot sell or otherwise assign the fee simple interest in any lands in the Kakaʻako Community Development District to which the authority in its corporate capacity holds title, except for utility easements, remnants, grants to state or county departments or agencies or private entities of any easement, roadway, or infrastructure improvements.[20] The amendment stirred much controversy in the community. Although some criticized it as the result of pressure from a small special interest group and not in the best interest of the environment, economy, or the public, others applauded it, claiming that it would not have added substantially to affordable housing inventories.[21] Furthermore, it allegedly saved the area from being sold to Alexander and Baldwin below market value to be developed into a high-end project that would ultimately harm coastal view planes.[22] In either event, the result is a legislative end run around the carefully drafted, painstakingly crafted plans for the development of

Kakaʻako, effectively gutting the provisions for residential development in the Makai Area Plan.

The Aloha Tower Development Corporation

In 1981, the Hawaiʻi State Legislature found that the area in downtown Honolulu on the water, known as the Aloha Tower complex, needed to be developed, renovated, and improved to "better serve the economic, maritime, and recreational needs of the people of Hawaii."[23] To do this, the legislature created the Aloha Tower Development Corporation (ATDC) "for the purpose of undertaking the redevelopment of the Aloha Tower complex, to strengthen the international economic base of the community in trade activities, to enhance the beautification of the waterfront, and in conjunction with the department of transportation, to better serve modern maritime uses, and to provide for public access and use of the waterfront property. Properly developed, the Aloha Tower complex will further serve as a stimulant to the commercial activities of the downtown business community and help transform the waterfront into a 'people place.'"[24]

POWERS OF THE ATDC: STATUTES, RULES, AND REDEVELOPMENT PLANS

The ATDC is a "public body corporate and politic, public instrumentality, and agency of the State" placed for administrative purposes within the Department of Business, Economic Development & Tourism.[25] ATDC is governed by a board of directors with seven voting members: the director of Business, Economic Development & Tourism, the director of transportation, the chairperson of the Board of Land and Natural Resources, the mayor of the City and County of Honolulu (as ex officio voting members), and three remaining members appointed by the governor from the public at large.[26]

The general powers of the ATDC are extensive, particularly for land use and development:

(a) The development corporation shall have all the powers necessary to carry out its purposes, including the following:

(7) To prepare or cause to be prepared a development plan for the Aloha Tower complex, incorporating the needs of the department of transportation and accommodating the plans,

specifications, designs, or estimates of any project acceptable to
the development corporation;

(8) To own, lease, hold, clear, improve, and rehabilitate
real, personal, or mixed property and to assign, exchange,
transfer, convey, lease, sublease, or encumber any project or
improvement, including easements, constituting part of a
project within the Aloha Tower complex, except that required
for necessary maritime purposes, including leases or other
agreements for the rehabilitation, repair, maintenance, and
operation of the Aloha Tower;

(9) By itself, or in conjunction with qualified persons, to
develop, construct, reconstruct, rehabilitate, improve, alter, or
repair or provide for the development, construction, reconstruction, rehabilitation, improvement, alteration, or repair of
any project, including projects or any portion thereof under
the control or jurisdiction of qualified persons; to own, hold,
assign, transfer, convey, exchange, lease, sublease, or encumber
any project, including projects or any portion thereof under
the control or jurisdiction of qualified persons;

(10) Notwithstanding any other provision of law to the contrary, to arrange or initiate appropriate action for the planning,
replanning, opening, grading, relocating, or closing of streets,
roads, roadways, alleys, easements, piers, or other places, the
furnishing of facilities, the acquisition of property or property
rights, or the furnishing of property, development rights, or
services in connection with a project;

(11) To grant options or renew any lease entered into by it
in connection with any project, on terms and conditions as it
deems advisable;

(12) To prepare or cause to be prepared plans, specifications, designs, and estimates of project cost for the development, construction, reconstruction, rehabilitation, improvement, alteration, or repair of any project, and from time
to time to modify such plans, specifications, designs, or
estimates;

(b) The development corporation shall impose, prescribe,
and collect rates, rentals, fees, or charges for the lease and use
and services of its projects at least sufficient to pay the costs of
operation, maintenance and repair, if any, of its projects and

the required payments of the principal of and interest on all
bonds issued to finance its projects. Notwithstanding anything
to the contrary contained in this section, the development
corporation may take into account any project costs supplied
by qualified persons in calculating such rates, rentals, fees,
or charges, to the extent that if the qualified person selected
by the development corporation is willing to underwrite the
entire or substantially all of the costs of development and
construction of that project, the development corporation is
empowered to negotiate nominal rentals.[27]

ATDC's powers are not without limit, however. First, the legislature
restricted ATDC from selling any submerged lands of the Aloha Tower
complex.[28] Second, ATDC must preserve Aloha Tower as a historical
monument and may not sell, remove, demolish, deface, or alter the
structure "in any reasonable degree to lessen its historical value to the
community."[29] This does not apply to any "essential" reconstruction that
is necessary for the preservation of Aloha Tower as a historical monument.[30] Third, Irwin Memorial Park must be retained as a public park.[31]
Lastly, ATDC or its lessees cannot exercise "any jurisdiction over the
provided replacement facilities located within the Aloha Tower complex required for necessary maritime purposes and activities."[32]

The relevant statutes provide that ATDC adopt administrative
rules to be followed during the course of the development of the Aloha
Tower complex that "are to be known as development rules in connection with health, safety, building, planning, zoning, and land use."[33]
ATDC has in fact adopted such rules, which supersede all other inconsistent ordinances and rules relating to the use, zoning, planning, and
development of land and construction within the Aloha Tower complex. However, the statute requires that "[r]ules adopted under this section . . . shall follow existing law, rules, ordinances, and regulations as
closely as is consistent with standards meeting minimum requirements
of good design, pleasant amenities, health, safety, and coordinated
development."[34]

While it is in the process of developing the Aloha Tower complex,
if ATDC determines that leasing any portion of property constituting
a project will still conform to the development plan, it may do so, as
long as the lease does not exceed a term of sixty-five years.[35] However, it
must first agree upon the terms and conditions of that lease and what
qualifications a person must have to apply for it.[36]

DEVELOPMENT OBJECTIVES: THE ALOHA
TOWER PROJECT AREA PLAN

The ATDC has also completed and promulgated an Aloha Tower Project Area Plan. The plan contains some of the following development objectives:

(1) Ensure the project is capable of integration into any overall development plan, which may be adopted for the Honolulu waterfront.

(4) Provide ease of pedestrian access to the project and waterfront, and generous open spaces for public enjoyment by eliminating visual and physical barriers between the waterfront and downtown, and by creating strong pedestrian links between downtown and Aloha Tower, particularly along Fort and Bishop streets.

(5) Improve view corridors down Fort street, Bishop street and Alakea street.

(8) Feature and enhance the physical, public use and visual characteristics of the historic Aloha Tower.

(9) Minimize unattractive physical facilities (e.g. parking, utilities, service, and back-of-house operation).

(10) Plan buildings and project features to attract people to the waterfront and create a major public gathering place at the Aloha Tower complex by enhancing public access to and along the water's edge and by creating opportunities for a variety of water's-edge experiences appropriate to the downtown waterfront.

(11) Develop uses which would stimulate and be compatible with the commercial activities of the downtown business community, which may include, but need not be limited to, retail, restaurant, office, hotel, condominium, recreational, historical and cultural uses; and create new activities to assist in bringing people to the waterfront.

(12) Provide accessible vehicular ingress and egress, and create a parking strategy which minimizes both the cost and impact of parking on the Aloha Tower complex.

(13) Establish a construction phasing strategy which will minimize disruption of maritime operations and achieve planned development of the Aloha Tower in the earliest practicable time.

(14) Create a financially feasible and aesthetically creative
project which can be initiated at the earliest practicable
time.

(15) Encourage, to the extent possible, development of
the Aloha Tower complex and adjoining areas by a qualified
private sector developer who will provide all or substantially all
of the costs of development.

(16) Utilize the powers of the development corporation to
transcend, as necessary, zoning, density, and height limitations
in an aesthetically pleasing manner to accomplish the goals of
the development corporation and to encourage private sector
developers to undertake development plan solutions which will
satisfy the foregoing development objectives.[37]

The ATDC's development priority is thus the creation of an area that will
become a "people place" by largely aesthetic and commercial endeavors. It currently has the power to override all other applicable land use
requirements, including county zoning.[38]

HAWAI'I ADMINISTRATIVE RULES: LAND USE PROVISIONS

If the enabling legislation laid the foundation for the development
power of the ATDC, the administrative rules define that power:

In harmony with the purpose and intent of chapter 206J, HRS,
these rules are established by the ATDC for the project area
controlling, regulating, and determining the height of buildings; minimum setbacks; required open spaces; the density
of buildings; the location and amount of retail, office, hotel,
residential, maritime, park, cultural, and other appropriate
uses; the location of buildings and other structures; architectural designs; urban design; historic and cultural sites; circulation criteria; and other appropriate regulations relating to land
use, zoning, and planning for buildings and structures for all
properties within the Aloha Tower project area.[39]

Thus for example,

  • A building permit cannot be issued for any development
    within the Aloha Tower complex until the developer has
    obtained a development permit from the ATDC, certifying

that the development complies with the ATDC rules and the development plan.[40]

- The ATDC also hears and determines the necessity for variances by developers, provided: (1) the applicant-developer would be deprived of the reasonable use of land or building if it were used only for the purpose allowed in that zone; (2) the request of the applicant-developer is due to unique circumstances and not the general conditions in the area, so that the reasonableness of the zoning is not drawn into question; and (3) the use sought to be authorized by the variance will not alter the essential character of the area nor be contrary to the intent and purpose of the ATDC development plan or ATDC's administrative rules.[41]

LAND USE ZONES

Within the project area, the ATDC has five different zones (a map of the land use zones can be found on the last page of the ATDC administrative rules attachment):

- maritime (M) zone

- commercial (C) zone

- hotel/office/residential (H/O/R) zone

- park (P) zone

- residential/office (R/O) zone

The rules outline the purpose and intent of each zone, specify permitted uses, and list the development requirements within each zone. For example, the commercial zone (C) is designed to promote an environment where retail commercial uses will coexist compatibly alongside maritime uses, as well as to create a vibrant, attractive, retail commercial "people place" that will attract downtown workers, local residents, and tourists.[42] Some of the uses expressly permitted in the C zone are drugstores, theaters, banks, eating and drinking establishments, sales offices for commercial maritime operations, and plazas and other public open spaces.[43] The development requirements list maximum floor areas (for retail uses, 300,000 gross square feet for the first three floors; for office uses, a maximum of 160,000 gross square feet located on the third and fourth floors), minimum parking spaces (2,000), and maximum building height (ninety feet).[44]

ATDC's attempts to meet the development goals that the legislature created have been fraught with controversy, some of which has landed in the courts. In a long-running controversy over the rights conferred by a development agreement,[45] the State Supreme Court, in a lengthy discussion of contractual rights and theory, found that a controversial letter agreement was the operative development agreement contemplated by the parties.[46] However, due to indefiniteness, the contract was unenforceable. Because the letter development agreement was not specifically enforceable, the Court found that the plaintiff "ha[d] no rights to develop the Aloha Tower complex."[47]

Despite the development agreement's unenforceability, however, the Court found that the developer might be entitled to damages: "Such damages arise from a number of possible grounds, including the apparent repudiation of the letter development agreement calling for further negotiations. ATDC may have breached an obligation to negotiate in good faith" as well.[48] ATDC was again embroiled in litigation over an alleged attempt to rewrite a development agreement months after its mutual execution. In 2009, an arbitrator found that ATDC had negotiated in bad faith and awarded the plaintiff-developer in excess of $1.2 million in damages.[49] Twenty years after its creation, most of the land under its jurisdiction languishes underdeveloped.

Housing and Community Development: HCDCH, HPHA, and HHFDC

In 2004, the legislature passed a resolution requesting the Housing and Community Development Corporation of Hawai'i (HCDCH) "to convene a task force to develop near-term solutions to Hawai'i's affordable housing shortage problem with respect to ownership and real markets."[50] During this time, the HCDCH provided some 200–250 affordable units per year. However, because of the housing development crisis, the legislature wanted to provide "incentives for private developers to build affordable housing projects," as well as to raise more revenue for the rental housing trust fund (discussed below).[51] It accomplished both tasks in 2005 by amending the conveyance tax provision[52] and by passing

Act 196, A Bill for an Act Relating to Housing, which amended the old chapter 201G of the Hawaii Revised Statutes and implements many of the recommendations of the task force. One of the recommendations was to split the corporation "into two organizations to more effectively concentrate on the development of affordable housing."[53] The two roles of maintaining affordable housing have become (1) administering the state's public housing programs and (2) financing and developing affordable housing.[54] Act 196 creates two administrations to accomplish these tasks: the Hawai'i Public Housing Administration (HPHA) and the Hawai'i Housing Finance and Development Corporation (HHFDC).[55]

The HHFDC officially assumed the HCDCH's functions under several former chapter 201G sections. The change became effective on July 1, 2006.[56] The HHFDC was established under the Department of Business, Economic Development & Tourism (DBEDT)[57] and is governed by a board of directors made up of six public members (at least four of whom must have knowledge and expertise of finance and development of affordable housing) appointed by the governor. The DBEDT director, the director of finance, and a representative of the governor's office make up the three ex officio voting members.[58]

Hawai'i Public Housing Authority

Part I, Section 2 of Act 180 creates and defines HPHA, its staff,[59] board,[60] and general powers.[61]

HPHA has the power to acquire, own, hold,[62] develop, clear, improve, and rehabilitate property, along with the power to plan, develop, construct, and finance public housing projects.[63] HPHA may acquire property through a variety of methods, including exercising the power of eminent domain.[64] It may also enter into contracts with the federal government and is authorized to do all things necessary to secure the financial aid and the cooperation of the federal government in the undertaking, construction, maintenance, and operation of any public housing project that HPHA is empowered to undertake.[65]

Hawai'i Housing Finance and Development Corporation

Part II, Section 3, of Act 180, entitled "Housing Development Programs," amends chapter 201H of the Hawaii Revised Statutes by adding a new part that creates and defines the HHFDC.[66] The HHFDC is a corporation administered by DBEDT.[67] This section is the most relevant to land use and development. The powers conferred upon HHFDC in this chapter are additional and supplemental to powers conferred upon it by any other law.[68] The overall focus and intent of this chapter relates to the supply of housing and the assistance in obtaining housing to those most in need of assistance.[69]

HHFDC has the power to develop fee simple or leasehold property and to construct dwelling units on such property.[70] It also has the power to sell, lease or rent, or cause to be leased or rented at the lowest possible price to qualified residents,[71] nonprofit organizations, and government agencies.[72] HHFDC established a system to determine preferences by lottery in the event it receives more qualified applicants than available dwelling units.[73] It has specific authority to adopt rules on health, safety, building, planning, zoning, and land use that relate to the development, subdivision, and construction of dwelling units in housing projects in which the state participates. These rules supersede all other inconsistent laws relating to the use, zoning, planning, and development of the land and the construction of dwelling units thereon, presumably including county zoning, subdivision ordinances, use restrictions, and State Land Use Law classifications.[74]

HHFDC may acquire by exchange, negotiation, or the exercise of the power of eminent domain land or property required in the foreseeable future for the purposes of this act.[75] For example, Act 288[76] preserves Kukui Gardens (an affordable rental housing project built in part with federal funds whose affordability restrictions expire in the year 2011) as an affordable housing project. Since it is irreplaceable in the current housing market, the legislature sought to extend the affordable rent rates at least through 2016. If Kukui Gardens does not comply within a reasonable time, HHFDC may exercise its power of eminent domain to acquire the property. Furthermore, HHFDC is authorized to do "all other things necessary and convenient" to carry out the purposes of the act.[77]

On behalf of the state or in partnership with an eligible developer, HHFDC may develop or assist under a governmental assistance program in the development of housing projects that are exempt from all statutes, ordinances, charter provisions, and rules of any government agency relating to planning, zoning, construction standards for subdivision, development and improvement of land, and the construction of dwelling units thereon. However, these exemptions exist only if the development is consistent with the intent and purpose of the statute, meets minimum safety and health requirements, and does not contravene any safety standards, tariffs, or rates of public utilities. Furthermore, the legislative body of the relevant county must approve the project and the Land Use Commission must approve a boundary change within forty-five days after HHFDC has submitted a petition to the commission.[78] HHFDC may accept and approve housing projects independently initiated by private developers that, in its judgment, are primarily designed for low-income housing.[79]

In connection with the development of any dwelling units under Hawaii Revised Statutes section 201H, HHFDC may also develop commercial, industrial, and other properties if it determines that their uses can be an integral part of the overall project by preserving the lifestyles of the residents of the dwelling units. In doing so, HHFDC again has the power to bypass all statutes, ordinances, charter provisions, and rules of any government agency pursuant to § 201H-38,[80] and it may utilize any of the funds authorized under the act.[81] HHFDC must adopt rules that indicate the manner in which the uses of the properties are designated and provide that any commercial, industrial, or other property so developed is sold or leased at cost to owners of commercial, industrial, or other facilities that were displaced by HHFDC or at economic rents or sale prices regarding all other leases.[82]

Transfer of property developed and sold under this statute is restricted for a period of ten years. During this period, if the purchaser wishes to transfer title, HHFDC has the first option to purchase the property.[83] If HHFDC opts not to purchase the property, then the purchaser may sell to a "qualified resident" as defined in section 201H,[84] but only upon terms that preserve the intent of the act.[85] HHFDC may nevertheless waive or release the aforementioned restrictions under certain circumstances.[86] After ten years, the purchaser may sell or assign the real property free from any restrictions, provided that the purchaser pays HHFDC all amounts owed, interest, and any subsidy or deferred sales price, together with HHFDC's share of any appreciation.[87]

Two chapters of administrative rules are particularly related to land development. Chapter 174[88] is dedicated to the state-assisted land and housing development program and seems to correspond to the Housing Development Program of Part II, Section 3 of Act 180. The rules declare that HHFDC may develop land or housing projects in accordance with the provisions of section 201G[89] on its own behalf or any government landowner or developer or with any eligible developer or contractor. HHFDC may develop housing projects for various groups, including employees, teachers, university students and faculty, and government agencies for special needs housing projects.[90]

Subchapter 2 of chapter 174 governs the development of land and the construction of units thereon.[91] An individual, partnership, firm, or other type of organization that wants to be considered to develop a project, either with the HHFDC or independently, and which will need assistance, such as acquisition of land or developmental rights to land and aid with financial processing matters, submits a developer's application to HHFDC.[92] This form usually will include evidence of the applicant's legal authority, financial status and ability to secure funds, ties to and support from the community, descriptions of existing projects owned by the applicant, a project proposal, and anything else HHFDC deems necessary to determine the qualifications of an applicant.[93] If the HHFDC Board of Directors finds that the applicant has the necessary experience, adequate financial resources or ability to secure such resources, and has demonstrated compliance with all legal and other requirements that HHFDC determines to be appropriate and reasonable, it may certify the applicant as an eligible developer.[94]

Whether the project proposal is submitted by an applicant, an eligible developer, or initiated by HHFDC itself, it must contain certain minimum information to be considered for approval. Hawaii Administrative Rules section 15-174-24(a) presents this extensive list of requirements, which includes a comprehensive master plan of the proposed project, proposed financing of the project, descriptions of how the proposed project shall meet the needs of those targeted, how it will affect the area's scenic and historical value, and applicable provisions of existing state and county general plans.[95]

If a project proposal requires a land use district boundary amendment by the State Land Use Commission (LUC) concurrently with its review of the project proposal, HHFDC may petition the state LUC for the boundary amendment as provided in section 205 of the Hawaii Revised Statutes.[96] HHFDC may also designate portions of the land for commercial, industrial, or other uses, provided that the development is reasonably necessary and primarily for the benefit of the residents of the development.[97]

The Office of Hawaiian Affairs

The Office of Hawaiian Affairs (OHA) has been operating as a public trust for over thirty years.[98] Until 2005, its only land use impacts were the enforcement of the state's obligation to protect Hawaiian rights.[99] Thus, for example, OHA sued the state DLNR for failure to protect Native Hawaiian claims to ceded lands and its revenues. The court found no such failure to protect traditional and cultural rights, culminating in a lengthy unpublished memorandum opinion by the State Supreme Court.[100] The opinion appears to resolve many of the legal issues that the Court later addressed and upon which it appeared to reverse itself in *OHA v. Housing & Community Development Corp.*, which the U.S. Supreme Court in turn unanimously overturned in early 2009.[101]

OHA was created by the 1978 Hawaii Constitutional Convention and subsequent election.[102] OHA's primary mandate is "[t]he betterment of conditions" of Hawaiians and Native Hawaiians.[103] Its other purposes include developing programs, procuring and distributing grants, and advocating for Hawaiians.[104] OHA also advises other agencies on the impact of their policies on Hawaiians.[105] OHA is a public trust and a body corporate that is entirely independent of the Hawai'i State Executive Branch.[106] Its powers include acquiring and using both real and personal property "in such manner and to the extent necessary or appropriate to carry out its purpose," controlling its own bylaws, governing its own finances, contracting, and generally taking "such actions as may be necessary or appropriate to carry out the powers conferred upon it by law."[107] Thus, OHA is not quite a state agency.[108]

An elected board of trustees governs OHA.[109] The board manages the office's income and controls all real and personal property transferred to the office.[110] It generally acts as a trustee, managing the office's resources for the benefit of Hawaiians.[111] OHA is funded in part by revenue from the state public land trust.[112] Upon Hawai'i's admission to the United States as a state in 1959, the federal government returned land ceded to it when Hawai'i was annexed in 1898.[113] The state used that land to establish a public trust for five purposes, one of which was the betterment of Native Hawaiians.[114] When the new constitution created OHA in 1978, it crafted an entitlement by requiring that the state give a 20 percent prorated share of public trust land revenue to OHA.[115] OHA and the state have argued over the details of that payment since OHA's inception, and OHA has repeatedly sued the state for its share of the proceeds.[116] Nevertheless, OHA is hardly impecunious: the 2008 OHA budget was $42 million.[117]

From the outset, OHA has had the power to administer land set aside for the benefit of Hawaiians,[118] but it has only recently come to directly control large amounts of land.[119]

OHA presently holds title to two important tracts of land in Hawai'i: Wao Kele O Puna on the Big Island and Waimea Valley on O'ahu.[120] In a recent State of OHA Address, OHA trustee and chairperson Haunani

Apoliona described how holding title to these lands set aside for conservation coincides with OHA's mission:[121] "Mālama 'āina goes to the core of who we are as a people. Our cultural practices and our values are all about caring for the 'āina, loving our motherland, not just to use, but to conserve and replenish. These traditions and values coincide with the global desire to protect the environment to secure and sustain a certain quality of life for future generations."[122] Together, Wao Kele O Puna and Waimea Valley comprise almost 28,000 acres,[123] title to which makes OHA the thirteenth largest landowner in the state.[124]

Waimea Valley is an 1,875-acre parcel of land on the north shore of O'ahu, 300 acres of which have been developed as a park.[125] The valley shows signs of inhabitation dating back several centuries, and it was used extensively for agriculture and fishing during the nineteenth century.[126] In 1929, Castle & Cooke purchased the valley from the territorial government for use as a cattle ranch.[127] In 1996, after a series of private owners, New York theme-park developer Christian Wolffer bought the state conservation-classified valley for $12 million.[128] Wolffer attempted to sell the valley for private development in 2000.[129] In 2001, he filed for bankruptcy protection, and in 2002 the City and County of Honolulu began the process of acquiring the property through eminent domain.[130] The city offered only $5.1 million in compensation for the valley, so Wolffer challenged the condemnation.[131] In 2005, the city and Wolffer reached a tentative settlement to divide the valley.[132] The 300-acre park would go to the city for the $5.1 million, and Wolffer would keep the remaining 1,575, where he planned a luxury residential development.[133] The settlement sparked substantial public opposition, and eventually the City Council rejected it.[134]

In 2006, the Trust for Public Land, the U.S. Army, OHA, DLNR, the Audubon Society, the city, and the landowner reached an agreement to purchase the property for $14 million.[135] Contributions to the purchase price were as follows: the U.S. Army $3.5 million, OHA $2.9 million, DLNR $1.6 million, the Audubon Society $1 million, and the City and County of Honolulu $5.1 million:[136]

> By agreement of the parties, and with the blessing of the interested contributors toward settlement, title to the property will lodge with OHA. This removes for the City the costs and expenses usually associated with fee ownership of real property, chief among which are the necessary and expensive ones of insuring and maintaining the property.

In exchange, the City, and all other entities involved in this process, will secure, for themselves and for the general public, a far more lavish real property interest. OHA, in exchange for title, will convey an expansive conservation and public access easement, such as would not only preserve the valley in its present state, but would also permit reasonable access to all who desire to experience the splendor of it.

The settlement agreement will also contain one or more negative covenants, which will run with the land, to insure that no future development of the valley will be permitted, and that it will remain as it is for all future generations, forever.[137]

Indeed, OHA has granted the City and County of Honolulu and the State of Hawai'i "a perpetual and irrevocable conservation easement in gross over the Property solely for the purpose of protecting and preserving the Conservation Values of the Property."[138] The "Conservation Values" include "archaeological, historical, cultural, educational, natural, ecological, botanical, scenic, aesthetic, open-space and recreational values and values specific to Hawaiian culture and History, including, without limitation, the exercise of Hawaiian subsistence, cultural and religious practices."[139] The army was involved because it has a forty-foot-wide road running through the valley, and development along it would make it difficult to continue use for training.[140] Preserving the valley for conservation purposes provided the army with a buffer for its training activities on the road, which is currently being improved on neighboring parcels for use by a Stryker brigade.[141]

Although the document granting the conservation easement is titled "Grant of Conservation and Access Easement," and it acknowledges that the city conveyed the valley to OHA on the condition that OHA would convey to the city an "[e]asement for the benefit of the public," no public *access* easement is ever specifically conveyed in the document.[142] The first sentence of the document refers to "THIS GRANT OF CONSERVATION AND ACCESS EASEMENT," but it appears to be referring to the title of the document rather than actually conveying an access easement to the public.[143] OHA's director of land management contends that the public was granted an access easement—but not for unfettered access.[144] He notes that under the document, OHA can never completely exclude the general public but that access must be limited in order to properly protect the valley.[145]

The easement document states that OHA "will afford the general public reasonable managed public access to the Property for passive, noncommercial, recreational purposes."[146] OHA intends to limit the general public's access to the upper valley to guided excursions.[147] The director cites unexploded ordnance as a possible concern.[148] He notes that ordnance in the upper valley is not of particular concern to cultural practitioners because they tend not to go far up enough in the valley to encounter the area where the ordnance may be.[149] OHA's position is that the primary public benefits for which the city paid $5.1 million were preventing the development of the upper valley, inappropriate use of the lower valley, and the privatization of access.[150] Nevertheless, OHA has also reserved the right to—and intends to—charge admission and establish the hours that the valley will be open to the public.[151]

Indeed, under the agreement, OHA reserves full control over the day-to-day operations of the valley.[152] Since granting the easement, OHA has established a limited liability corporation (LLC), Hiʻilei Aloha, to govern operations at Waimea.[153] It is that LLC that will develop the policies governing the valley.[154] OHA's status as a public trust and not a state agency with the power to write regulations that have the force and effect of law makes enforcement of rules in Waimea Valley an issue.[155] OHA claims that enforcement will be partially community based, with members of the community guiding one another on the proper way to use the valley and its resources.[156]

Although Waimea Valley is of considerable cultural significance to Native Hawaiians, it is OHA's acquisition of Wao Kele O Puna that has made it one of the largest landowners in the state. Wao Kele O Puna on the Big Island consists of 25,856 acres of rain forest, the last large intact lowland rain forest in the state.[157] Hawaiians have long used it for traditional hunting, gathering, and religious practices.[158] To preserve the rain forest, the Trust for Public Land worked with Senator Daniel Inouye to fund the acquisition of the property from the Estate of James Campbell.[159] Eventually, it was purchased for $3.4 million dollars from a federal Forest Legacy Grant and $250,000 from OHA.[160] Again, OHA holds title.[161] Land purchased by a state with a U.S. Department of Agriculture Forest Legacy Grant must be "managed and administered for goals consistent with Forest Legacy conservation purposes."[162] These include the "protection of important scenic, cultural, fish, wildlife and recreational resources," and may include "traditional forest uses" such as hunting, fishing, and hiking.[163]

Wao Kele is also the first non–DLNR forest reserve in the state.[164] DLNR and OHA entered into a memorandum of agreement for sharing Wao Kele management responsibilities.[165] The purpose of the agreement is both to "provide proper management" of Wao Kele O Puna and "to develop OHA's own capacity to manage lands independently from DLNR."[166] Under the ten-year agreement, initial management responsibility rests with DLNR and will be gradually turned over to OHA "as OHA acquires capacity, experience, and expertise in land management."[167] DLNR's responsibility for managing Wao Kele O Puna expires after ten years—sooner if DLNR and OHA agree that OHA is capable of managing the reserve as required by a forthcoming Comprehensive Management Plan.[168] For every year that DLNR manages the property, OHA will transfer up to $228,000 to DLNR.[169] Although this amount may vary, "the amount of funds transferred will determine the level of management and protection that is implemented" by DLNR.[170]

The DLNR–OHA agreement for Wao Kele identifies public access, cultural, natural resources, open space and recreational use, preservation of plant and wildlife habitat, traditional hunting and gathering practices, and water extraction as allowable uses of the reserve.[171] Mineral extraction, grading and excavation, subdivision, commercial uses inconsistent with the Forest Legacy Program Guidelines, signage (except as needed for the management of the reserve), storage of waste, and the introduction of exotic plants or animals are prohibited.[172] The agreement also specifically guarantees Hawaiian subsistence and cultural practitioners and their companions access to both the developed and undeveloped portions of Wao Kele.[173]

OHA has also used the courts to protect Hawaiian interests.[174] In particular, the Hawai'i State Constitution requires the state to protect Hawaiian rights "customarily and traditionally exercised for subsistence, cultural and religious purposes,"[175] subject to reasonable regulation by the State Legislature. The Hawai'i Supreme Court reinforced such rights in *Public Access Shoreline Hawaii v. City Planning Commission*,[176] when it held that "the State is obligated to protect the reasonable exercise of customarily and traditionally exercised rights of Hawaiians to the extent feasible."[177] In a later decision, the Court stressed that such rights could only be exercised upon proof that the particular activity was demonstrably traditional and customary and that the land upon which the exercise was taking place was "undeveloped."[178] OHA has acted to enforce this obligation in the courts. For example, when the state Board of Land and Natural Resources (BLNR) issued a conservation district use area permit for the dredging of a marina entrance channel, OHA sued, arguing in part that BLNR failed to protect Native Hawaiian rights.[179] The Hawai'i Supreme Court agreed, holding that in issuing such a permit, BLNR must "make express findings as to the existence and extent of traditional and customary practices in the subject area. If the issuance of the permit will impair these rights, BLNR must determine whether this impairment is justified."[180] Because BLNR failed to do so, the Court vacated the permit and remanded to the board to determine whether Hawaiian rights were exercised in the area and, if so, the extent to which they would be affected by the project and any feasible action that could be taken to mitigate those effects.[181] However, the Court explicitly rejected all of the remaining OHA claims, including those related to the use, sale, and use of sale proceeds of ceded lands, noting that the ceded lands trust expressly permitted their use for five purposes, only one of which was for the benefit of Native Hawaiians. Thus, for its first twenty-five years OHA "focused on monitoring federal and state use of lands and waters" and protecting Hawaiian interests therein.[182] Only recently has the office come to directly control large amounts of land; it has developed a vision to be "the real estate partner of choice" in Hawai'i.[183]

OHA is becoming a major landowner in Hawai'i. Whether this changes its largely supervisory role in land use in Hawai'i or simply adds a new dimension to it remains uncertain. In either event, OHA's participation in conservation and landownership will almost certainly grow in the years to come.

The Department of Hawaiian Home Lands

In 1920, Congress passed the Hawaiian Homes Commission Act (HHCA).[184] The purpose of the act was to "enable native Hawaiians to return to their lands in order to fully support self-sufficiency for native Hawaiians and the self-determination of native Hawaiians in the administration of this Act, and the preservation of the values, traditions, and culture of native Hawaiians."[185] However, as discussed below, the state agency charged with the administration of the Act can and does lease "surplus" homelands for commercial purposes, and it is not at all clear that such leases are subject to otherwise applicable state and county plans and land use controls.

There are five "principal purposes" enumerated in the HHCA, but the language of the act suggests that there may be others.[186] The enumerated principal purposes are as follows:

(1) Establishing a permanent land base for the benefit and use of native Hawaiians, upon which they may live, farm, ranch, and otherwise engage in commercial or industrial or any other activities as authorized in this Act;

(2) Placing native Hawaiians on the lands set aside under this Act in a prompt and efficient manner and assuring long-term tenancy to beneficiaries of this Act and their successors;

(3) Preventing alienation of the fee title to the lands set aside under this Act so that these lands will always be held in trust for continued use by native Hawaiians in perpetuity;

(4) Providing adequate amounts of water and supporting infrastructure, so that homestead lands will always be usable and accessible; and

(5) Providing financial support and technical assistance to native Hawaiian beneficiaries of this Act so that by pursuing strategies to enhance economic self-sufficiency and promote community-based development, the traditions, culture, and quality of life of native Hawaiians shall be forever self-sustaining.[187]

Central to the enforcement of these principal purposes is a "trust relationship" that is created between the federal government and the State of Hawai'i as trustees and Native Hawaiians as the beneficiaries.[188]

THE HAWAIIAN HOMES COMMISSION

While the Department of Hawaiian Home Lands (DHHL) was created by statute in order to administer the land trust created by the HHCA,[189] the HHCA provides for a Hawaiian Homes Commission (HHC) to actually run the department.[190] The HHC consists of nine members. As with most state commissions, the governor nominates and appoints the members, with the consent of the State Senate.[191] The HHCA imposes further restrictions on the eligibility of prospective commissioners:

[T]hree shall be residents of the city and county of Honolulu; two shall be residents of the county of Hawaii one of whom shall be a resident of east Hawaii and the other a resident of west Hawaii; two shall be residents of the county of Maui one of whom shall be a resident from the island of Moloka'i; one shall be a resident of the county of Kaua'i; and the ninth member shall be the chairman of the Hawaiian homes commission. All members shall have been residents of the State at least three years prior to their appointment and at least four of the members shall be descendants of not less than one-fourth part of the blood of the races inhabiting the Hawaiian Islands previous to 1778. . . . The governor shall appoint the chairman of the commission from among the members thereof.[192]

The chairman is required to serve in a full-time capacity and may be delegated by the other commissioners "such duties, powers, and authority or so much thereof, as may be lawful or proper for the performance of the functions vested in the commission." The HHC has promulgated rules vesting the chairperson with the following powers:

> (1) To appoint special committees and prescribe their powers and duties;
> (2) To preside over all meetings of the commission;
> (3) To approve and sign all vouchers, and to approve the assignment of funds to be received;
> (4) To approve leaves of absence;
> (5) To approve plans for construction of homes and improvements;
> (6) To screen matters referred to the chairman by staff and to select those of sufficient importance to place on the agenda for consideration by the commission; and
> (7) To sign commission resolutions, licenses, leases, and contracts approved by the commission.[193]

The chairperson may also, subject to ratification by the commission,

> (1) Grant loans from any loan fund;
> (2) Approve the designation of successors;
> (3) Accept surrenders of homestead leases; and
> (4) Approve, with regard to general leases, plans, assignments, subleases, and mortgages.[194]

These last powers grant the authority to effect the general purpose of the HHCA: returning Native Hawaiians to their lands.[195]

HOMESTEADING

The act authorizes DHHL to allocate its federally granted lands to Native Hawaiians (Homestead Lands). Housing constructed on these lands must be either single-family or multifamily dwellings, with the manner of allocation and the terms of the disposition of Homestead Lands determined by the rules promulgated by the commission.[196] The HHCA does impose limitations on the disposition of Homestead Lands, requiring among other things that allotments not exceed one acre for residential lands, forty acres for agricultural lands, and one hundred acres for irrigated pastoral lands and that all Homestead Lands be leasehold tenures.[197]

Apportionment of Homestead Lands is governed by administrative rules promulgated by the commission. Thus, for example, an applicant for Homestead Lands must be Native Hawaiian. Upon completion of an application for Homestead Lands, an applicant is placed on a waiting list. Waiting lists are divided by island and again by the type of land sought: Each island has lists for residential, agricultural, and pastoral lands, respectively.[198] Generally, lands are allocated by date of application, except that applicants who already have Homestead Land leases or who have spouses with such leases will have their subsequent awards deferred until applicants without Homestead Land leases are accommodated.[199] These standards for the apportionment of Homestead Lands do not apply to all lands held by the DHHL. Where DHHL has determined that lands it controls are not needed for homesteading, the Homestead Land application rules do not apply.[200]

COMMERCIAL LICENSES AND LEASES

There are two avenues for commercial activity on DHHL's federally granted lands: by license and by lease. Commercial activity must take place by license when the desired location is situated within a district where Homestead Lands are leased to Native Hawaiians.[201] Commercial leases are made on Hawaiian Home Lands that are not needed or unsuitable for homestead purposes and which may be disposed of as the HHC sees fit in the course of "managing" such surplus lands.[202] Such leases create millions of dollars of income for DHHL and fund a substantial portion of its annual operating budget.[203] Those interested in leasing DHHL's nonhomestead lands must file an application identifying the land desired and a proposed use.[204] Lease terms and rates are determined by DHHL and approved by the HHC.[205]

Under the HHCA, it is clear that "the department is expressly authorized to negotiate . . . the disposition of a lease of Hawaiian home lands . . . for commercial, industrial, or other business purposes"[206] and with "the approval of the governor, undertake and carry out the development of available lands for homestead, commercial, and multipurpose projects as provided in section 220.5 of this Act."[207] This Section confers upon HHL the ability to enter into contracts and project developer agreements to develop available lands for commercial projects.[208] The act further defines a "commercial project" as one "designed and intended to generate revenues."[209]

However, the authority for the proposition that development on homestead lands is not subject to local or state land use controls is less clear. According to Hawai'i's attorney general, "Where Hawaiian home lands are needed or required for the purposes of the Hawaiian Homes Commission Act, any zoning ordinance purporting to change the land use designation by the department of Hawaiian home lands or to impose restrictions on the use of such Hawaiian home lands would be outside the scope of any power granted to counties."[210] Based on this "Opinion of the Attorney General" and in conjunction with the above sections, the DHHL consensus is that lands on its property are exempt from city zoning laws.[211]

The Urban Redevelopment Act

In 1949, the Hawai'i Territorial Legislature passed the Urban Redevelopment Act in order to establish a method to develop blighted areas in the Territory of Hawai'i.[212] The Territorial Legislature found that the conditions existing in the territory's blighted areas:

> impair property values and tax revenues in the same and
> surrounding areas, cause an increase in and spread of disease,
> infant mortality, juvenile delinquency and crime, and consti-
> tute a menace to the health, safety, morals and welfare of the
> inhabitants of the communities in which they exist and of the
> inhabitants of the Territory generally, and necessitate excessive
> and disproportionate expenditures of public funds for crime
> prevention and punishment, public health and safety, fire and
> accident protection, and other public services and facilities,
> and encourage and hasten decentralization necessitating

additional large expenditures for public services and facilities in outlying areas.[213]

The legislature concluded that it was too costly for individual owners of property in blighted areas to redevelop themselves and that typical land use regulations were insufficient.[214] An urban redevelopment act was thus necessary, and the Territorial Legislature sanctioned the acquisition and redevelopment of blighted areas "in accordance with sound redevelopment plans and principle."[215] Moreover, the Territorial Legislature stated (in language similar to the future U.S. Supreme Court opinion in *Berman v. Parker*[216]) that the acquisition and redevelopment of blighted areas was "necessary for the public health, safety, morals and welfare and are public uses and public purposes for which public moneys may be spent and private property acquired by purchase or by the exercise of eminent domain, and are governmental functions of grave concern to the Territory."[217] With that, it enacted the Urban Redevelopment Act (URA).

The URA does not establish a state agency but instead enables the four counties to create their own redevelopment agencies. A county council may create a local redevelopment agency by passing a resolution. The agency must consist of five members, appointed by the mayor, with the approval of the council, who are "outstanding and public-spirited citizens" and have resided in the county for at least three years immediately preceding their appointment.[218] Once established, the redevelopment agency has certain powers and duties. The agency's mission is to undertake and carry out urban renewal projects within the county.[219] In doing so, the agency may "make and execute contracts and other instruments necessary or convenient to exercise its powers."[220] The agency is also required to promulgate rules and regulations to carry into effect the powers and purposes of its agency.[221]

The agency must make preliminary surveys, studies, and plans to identify redevelopment areas "provided that the studies and initial determination of what areas are blighted . . . are made exclusively by the planning commission."[222] In addition, the redevelopment agency must make redevelopment plans for the areas in conformity with the master plan for the development of the locality. Each plan must show the outline of the area, character of existing development, proposed use of land, general character of new buildings, and other general details of redevelopment, as well as the preliminary estimated cost of the development. "Further, the plans shall give due consideration to the provision of adequate park and recreational areas and facilities that may be desirable for neighborhood improvement, with special consideration for the health, safety and welfare of children residing in the general vicinity of the site covered by the plans."[223]

The agency is also obliged to "prepare a general neighborhood renewal plan for urban renewal areas which may be of such scope that urban renewal activities may have to be carried out in stages over an estimated period of up to ten years."[224] Under Hawaii Revised Statutes Section 53-5(7), the plan may include but is not limited to a preliminary plan that (1) outlines the urban renewal activities proposed for the area involved, (2) provides a framework for the preparation of urban renewal plans, and (3) indicates generally the land uses, population density, building coverage, prospective requirements for rehabilitation and improvement of property, and portions of the area contemplated for clearance and redevelopment. "A general neighborhood renewal plan shall, in the determination of the local governing body, conform to the general plan of the locality as a whole and the workable program of the county."[225]

A redevelopment agency also must accommodate the people it will displace by a redevelopment project. The agency must prepare plans for and assist in the relocation of persons (including individuals, families, business concerns, nonprofit organizations, and others) displaced from an urban renewal area and make relocation payments from funds provided by the federal government.[226] At the same time, the agency must establish and operate a central relocation office that will "perform such functions and activities as may be necessary and proper for the satisfactory relocation of families, individuals, businesses, and nonprofit organizations, incorporated and unincorporated, displaced by any governmental action to decent, safe, and sanitary locations at rents and prices within the financial means of the displaced families, individuals, businesses, and nonprofit organizations."[227]

Once it has satisfied its relocation obligations, the agency then submits the redevelopment plan to the county planning commission for study and approval.[228] Assuming the planning commission approves the redevelopment plan, the agency then submits the plan to the relevant county council. The council then holds a public hearing after affording its citizens published notice. The council may approve or amend and approve the proposal only if it finds that the redevelopment project is a blighted area within the jurisdiction of the county.[229]

The statute contemplates the use of private developers on urban redevelopment projects. If the agency finds that the owners or developers of project lands can "effectively, expeditiously, and economically" undertake the project as well or better than the agency could by itself, the agency must include a provision "for the execution of the project by an alternative method of private development thereof on the basis of an agreement between the agency and the owners or developers and imposing such requirements, restrictions, and sanctions as the agency may deem necessary to effectuate the basic purposes of this chapter and to assure the successful completion of the project by private development."[230]

The agency is authorized to acquire said land "by condemnation or otherwise."[231] The property may be sold or leased to one or more individuals, corporations, or public bodies or to a redevelopment corporation "under such limitations, restrictions, requirements, or covenants as will insure its being developed and continued in use in accordance with the redevelopment plan, and in a manner that will best promote the interests and welfare of the urban area in which the project is situated."[232] If leased, the lessee must be given an option to purchase the leased property during the first twenty years of the lease. During the balance of the lease term, the lessee has the first right of refusal to purchase the leased property, provided that the leased property may not be sold by the agency to any person or corporation except to the lessee during the first twenty years of the lease. In the event the lessee fails to exercise the first right of refusal, the agency may sell the leased property to any person or corporation at fair value, subject to the lease.

Surprisingly, the agency may not actually build new structures on any of its property (except structures that will be held and used by the government for public purposes). However, if it will promote the realization of the redevelopment plan, it may grade, drain, construct streets, and install necessary utilities such as sewers, water, and lights.[233] In other words, the agency is limited to clearing out blighted areas and constructing the basic infrastructure needed to bring new development to the area.[234]

Hawai'i's counties have used the URA many times since its inception. During the late 1950s the Honolulu Redevelopment Agency "determined that the area bounded by Liliha, Queen Emma, and Beretania streets and Vineyard (i.e., Chinatown)[235] was filled with slums that needed to be bulldozed for the greater public good."[236] Buddhist temples, Shinto shrines, Chinese schools, a dozen Chinese societies, and other historic facilities were condemned. The agency apparently planned to buy the entire tract, relocate the inhabitants, and sell the land to private developers.[237] "Proposals included affordable housing, a cultural center, commercial areas, and a park. But for many years the land lay fallow because of delays and disagreements over development. Much of the area was used for parking."[238]

More recently, the Maui Redevelopment Authority is implementing the Department of Planning's Wailuku Redevelopment Plan. According to the Maui Department of Planning, the Wailuku Redevelopment Plan "provides the vision, direction, and plan of action for the revitalization of the Wailuku Redevelopment Area. The Plan also establishes the policy framework and process within which the Maui Redevelopment Agency (MRA) will implement specific projects intended to foster economic revitalization. This plan is not intended to be a regional plan for Central Maui, an urban design plan for Wailuku Town or an economic feasibility study for a specific project. It is a strategic plan for the economic and physical revitalization of the Wailuku Redevelopment Area."[239]

Once the plan is fully implemented, the county will benefit in several ways: (1) new amenities (theater, restaurants, festivals, commercial and residential opportunities); (2) more job opportunities (entrepreneurial start-up, construction, retail, service, office); (3) restoration of pride in Maui's Civic Center; (4) increased tax base to provide greater public safety and services; and (5) rehabilitation and restoration of buildings and public spaces.[240]

The plan provides specific actions to "foster an economic renaissance throughout the Wailuku Development Area."[241] Important objectives for the MRA include streetscape beautification, streamlined regulation, attracting more activities and people to the area, and targeted tax incentives.

Notes

1. HAW. REV. STAT. § 206E-1 (2008).
2. Id. § 206E-4.
3. Id. § 206E-7.
4. Id. §§ 206E-31, -33. This district includes the roughly rectangular area bounded by King Street to the north, Pi'ikoi Street to the east, Ala Moana Boulevard to the south, and Punchbowl Street to the west. Id. § 206E-32. Legislation in 2006 amended the boundaries of Kaka'ako by conveying lots A-1 and A-2, at Pier 1 and Pier 2, to the Department of Land and Natural Resources. The parcels are reserved for the Department of Business, Economic Development & Tourism's Foreign Trade Zone division and the Department of Transportation to ensure continued maritime

and foreign commerce use. Id. The amendment further provided that all existing easements affecting and appurtenant to the parcels be deleted from the Kaka'ako Community Development district boundary will not be affected by this change. Id. The Kaka'ako district also includes the parcel of land located *mauka* of Pier 6 and Pier 7 and *makai* of Nimitz Highway, which is the site for the existing Hawaiian Electric power plant and related facilities. Id.

5. S. Rep. No. 23- 41-76 (Haw. 1976) (Conf. Rep.).

6. HAW. REV. STAT. § 206E-1 (2008). *See*, e.g., David L. Callies, "A hypothetical case: Value capture/joint development techniques to reduce the public costs of public improvements," 16 URB. L. ANN. 155 (1979).

7. HAW. REV. STAT. § 206E-31 (2008).

8. Id. § 206E-33.

9. Id. § 206E-31.

10. Id. § 206E-33.

11. Id. § 206E-5.

12. EDAW, Inc., *Revisions to the Kakaako Community Development District Mauka Area Plan and Rules*, SUPPLEMENTAL ENVIRONMENTAL IMPACT STATEMENT PREPARATION NOTICE 2-1 (Dec. 2007).

13. Id.

14. Id.

15. Id. at 2-2, -3.

16. The original $650 million proposal HCDA selected for the area in 2005 was created by an Alexander & Baldwin subsidiary and included retail, dining, three twenty-story residential towers containing 947 condominium units, and nearly three thousand parking spaces. Allison Schaefers and Stewart Yerton, "A&B subsidiary gets big Kakaako project," HONOLULU STAR-BULLETIN, Sept. 15, 2005, at A1.

17. Hawaii Community Development Authority, *Kaka'ako Mauka Area Plan and Rules Comprehensive Review Seeks Public Input*, KAKA'AKO CONNECTION, Apr. 2006, hcdaweb.org/the-kakaako-connection/newlayout2_a989.pdf/download (last visited Apr. 20, 2010).

18. Andrew Gomes, "A new look for Kaka'ako," HONOLULU ADVERTISER, May 17, 2009, at A5.

19. HAW. REV. STAT. § 206E-31.5 (2008).

20. Id.

21. C. Richard Fassler, "The winners and losers in Kakaako Makai fiasco," HONOLULU STAR-BULLETIN, May 14, 2006, http://archives.starbulletin.com/2006/05/14/editorial/special3.html (last visited Nov. 20, 2009).

22. Nancy Helund, "Kakaako Makai needs protection of HB 2555," HONOLULU STAR-BULLETIN, June 15, 2006, at A12. Nevertheless, the Hawai'i Housing Finance and Development Corporation, discussed in full later in this chapter, is currently moving forward on a partnership with Stanford Carr to develop an affordable rental high-rise in Kaka'ako. Andrew Gomes, "Affordable housing tower will break ground," HONOLULU ADVERTISER, Mar. 13, 2007, at C1. During the strong real estate market in 2005, a number of high-density residential projects in Kaka'ako and the surrounding areas were in the pipeline. Andrew Gomes, "Kaka'ako on the rise," HONOLULU ADVERTISER, Oct. 30, 2005, http://www.oahuexpert.com/articles/articles/New/kakaako%20on%20the%20rise.htm (last visited Apr. 12, 2010).

23. HAW. REV. STAT. § 206J-1 (2007); *see also* Act 127, H.B. 250 HD2 SD2 CD1, 24th Leg., Reg. Sess. (Haw. June 4, 2007) (formalizing ATDC's relationship with the State Department of Transportation and expanding its harbor duties).

24. HAW. REV. STAT. § 206J-1 (2007).

25. Id. § 206J-4(a).

26. Id. § 206J-4(b).

27. Id. § 206J-5.

28. Id. § 206J-6(a).

29. Id. § 206J-6(b).

30. This might include repairs, maintenance, or relocation of pier platforms, etc. Id.

31. Id. § 206J-6(c). An interesting limitation, since Irwin Park presently serves as a parking lot.

32. Id. § 206J-6(d). The statute goes on to say that "Jurisdiction over any such replacement facilities shall be in the department of transportation. Facilities functionally related to maritime purposes and the purposes outlined in the development plan for the Aloha Tower complex, such as hotel facilities for maritime passengers and waterfront visitors, concession facilities adjacent to maritime terminal facilities, public parking facilities which are situated on property not currently under the jurisdiction of the department of transportation, and commercial, retail, residential, and office facilities may be under the jurisdiction of the development corporation or its lessees."

33. Id. § 206J-7.

34. Id.

35. Id. § 206J-11.

36. Id.

37. Aloha Tower Development Corporation, "Aloha Tower Project Area Plan," 26-3 to 26-4 (2006), http://www.alohatower.org/areaplan.pdf (last visited Dec. 22, 2009).

38. HAW. REV. STAT. § 206J-7 (2007).

39. HAW. CODE R. § 15-26-58(a) (Weil 2007).

40. Id. § 15-26-60.

41. Id. § 15-26-63.

42. Id. § 15-26-84.

43. Id. § 15-26-85.

44. Id. § 15-26-86.

45. *Honolulu Waterfront Ltd. v. Aloha Tower Dev. Corp.*, 692 F. Supp. 1230 (D. Haw. 1988), *aff'd mem.*, 891 F.2d 295 (9th Cir. 1989).

46. Id. at 1234.

47. Id. at 1238–1239.

48. Id. at 1236.

49. *Kenneth H. Hughes, Inc. v. Aloha Tower Dev. Corp.*, DPR No. 07-0459-A (Apr. 29, 2009) (Arbitrator's Partial Final Decision and Award); *see also* Nina Wu, "Developer awarded $1.2M," HONOLULU STAR-BULLETIN, May 12, 2009 at 20.

50. S.C. Res. 135, 22nd Leg., Reg. Sess. (Haw. 2004).

51. S.B. 179 SD3 HD2 CD1, 23rd Leg., Reg. Sess., Act 196 (Haw. July 6, 2005).

52. According to HAW. REV. STAT. § 247-1 (2008), the conveyance tax levies

a tax "on all transfers or conveyances of realty or any interest therein, by way of deeds, leases, subleases, assignments of lease, agreements of sale, assignments of agreement of sale, instruments, writings, and any other document, whereby any lands, interests in land, tenements, or other realty sold shall be granted, assigned, transferred, or otherwise conveyed to, or vested in the purchaser or purchasers, lessee or lessees, sublessee or sublessees, assignee or assignees, or any other person or persons, by the persons or their direction."

    53. S.B. 179 SD3 HD2 CD1, 23rd Leg., Reg. Sess., § 19 (Haw. July 6, 2005).
    54. Id.
    55. Id.
    56. *See* id. § 41.
    57. HAW. REV. STAT. § 201H-2 (2007).
    58. Id. § 201H-3(a).
    59. Id. § 356D-2.
    60. Id. § 356D-3.
    61. Id. § 356D-4.
    62. Id. § 356D-8.
    63. Id. § 356D-11.
    64. Id. § 356D-15.
    65. Id. § 356D-16 .
    66. Id. §§ 201H-1 to H-220 .
    67. Id. § 201H-2.
    68. Id. § 201H-70.
    69. Currently, there are nearly five thousand units slated for delivery by 2011. The units are distributed through projects in Kapolei, Waipahu, Wahiawā, and Kaka'ako. Andrew Gomes, "Affordable housing in Hawaii back on the map," HONO-LULU ADVERTISER, Feb. 25, 2007, at F1. Additionally, there is a high-rise with 269 affordable units being developed in Salt Lake. Andrew Gomes, "Affordable condo going up in Salt Lake," HONOLULU ADVERTISER, Sept. 21, 2007, http://the.hono luluadvertiser.com/article/2007/Sep/21/bz/hawaii709210323.html (last visited Nov. 20, 2009). Of the five thousand units being developed, an $11.6 million dollar, forty-eight-unit affordable rental housing project has already opened in Mililani Mauka. Those units are available to households with incomes at or below 60 per-cent of the O'ahu median income, and affordable rental rates are locked in for the next thirty years. Lynda Arakawa, "New affordable housing finished," HONOLULU ADVERTISER, Sept. 21, 2007, http://the.honoluluadvertiser.com/article/2007/Sep/21/ln/hawaii709210344.html (last visited Nov. 20, 2009). Another project, to be completed in 2009, will deliver 472 townhouses, 244 for rental units, and 228 for fee-simple sale. The project combines private financing with state tax credits and a general excise tax exemption. The state also contributed the land and major infra-structure improvements for the project. Andrew Gomes, "Affordable townhouses on tap down-home prices," HONOLULU ADVERTISER, Aug. 25, 2006, http://the. honoluluadvertiser.com/article/2006/Aug/25/bz/FP608250330.html (last visited Nov. 20, 2009).
    70. HAW. REV. STAT. § 201H-33(a) (2007). For purposes of this section, "dwell-ing units" include condominiums, planned units, or cluster developments.
    71. Id. § 201H-45.

72. Id. § 201H-52.
73. Id. § 201H-33(b).
74. Id. § 201H-33(c).
75. Id. § 201H-33(d).
76. H.B. 2239 HD1 SD2 CD1, 23rd Leg., Reg. Sess. (Haw. July 7, 2006).
77. HAW. REV. STAT. § 201H-33(f) (2007).
78. Id. § 201H-38(a).
79. Id. § 201H-41.
80. Id. § 201H-38.
81. Id. § 201H-44(a).
82. Id. § 201H-47(a)(1). "At cost" is a price that shall not exceed the sum of the original cost to the purchaser, the cost of any improvements added by the purchaser, and simple interest on the original cost and capital improvements at the rate of 1 percent per year.
83. Id. § 201H-47(a)(1).
84. Id. § 201H-32. "Qualified resident" means a U.S. citizen or resident alien at least eighteen years old, domiciled in Hawai'i, and actually residing in the subject residence who is able to pay the rent or mortgage and does not own a majority interest or more in another habitable dwelling.
85. Id. § 201H-47(b).
86. Id. § 201H-47(c)-(d).
87. Id. § 201H-47(a)(4).
88. HAW. CODE R. §§ 15-174-1 through 15-174-241 (2007).
89. HAW. REV. STAT. § 201G (repealed 2006).
90. HAW. CODE R. § 15-174-4(b) (2007).
91. Id. § 15-174-23(a) (2009).
92. Id.
93. Id. §§ 15-174-23(a)(1)-(16).
94. Id. § 15-174-23(b).
95. Id. § 15-174-24(a).
96. Id. § 15-174-29.
97. Id. § 15-174-30.
98. *See infra* Part II.
99. *See infra* Part III.
100. *Trustees of OHA v. Bd. of Land & Nat. Res.*, 87 Haw. 471, 959 P.2d 841 (Haw. 1998) (mem).
101. *OHA v. Hous. & Cmty. Dev. Corp. of Haw.*, 117 Haw. 174, 177 P.3d 884 (2008), *rev'd and remanded sub nom. Hawaii v. OHA*, 129 S. Ct. 1436 (2009). As near as anyone can tell, the only difference in facts between the State Supreme Court's 1998 and 2008 opinions was the passage of an "apology resolution" by Congress during the Clinton administration, which is just what its name implies: an apology resolution, nothing more or less. As the U.S. Supreme Court unanimously held, that resolution cannot form the basis for any claims on the so-called ceded lands.
102. HAW. CONST. art. XII, §§ 5, 6; Curt Sanburn, "OHA: The beginning—part one," KA WAI OLA O OHA, Apr. 1991, at 13, http://www.oha.org/pdf/OHA10yrHistory/KWO0491YR10PRT1.pdf (last visited Dec. 22, 2009).
103. HAW. REV. STAT. § 10-3(1)-(2) (2007). The distinction between "Hawaiian"

and "Native Hawaiian" is based on blood quantum. Id. § 10-2. "'Hawaiian' means any descendant of the aboriginal peoples inhabiting the Hawaiian Islands which exercised sovereignty and subsisted in the Hawaiian Islands in 1778, and which peoples thereafter have continued to reside in Hawaii" and "'Native Hawaiian' means any descendant of not less than one-half part of the races inhabiting the Hawaiian Islands previous to 1778, as defined by the Hawaiian Homes Commission Act, 1920." Id. These definitions were upheld in *Hoohuli v. Ariyoshi*, 631 F. Supp. 1153 (D. Haw. 1986). Except where the distinction is material, the term "Hawaiians" will be used in this chapter to refer to Native Hawaiians and Hawaiians inclusively.

104. HAW. REV. STAT. § 10-3(3)-(6) (2007). The list of its purposes specifically excludes the responsibilities already held by the Department of Hawaiian Home Lands, which is a government-sponsored homesteading program for Native Hawaiians. Id. § 10-3(3); HAW. CONST. art. XII, § 1.

105. HAW. REV. STAT. § 10-3(4) (2007).

106. Id. § 10-4; *Ako v. OHA*, 87-1 Haw. Legal Rep. 87-537, -555, -556 (1st Cir. Ct. 1987); *see* HAW. CONST. art. XII, § 5.

107. HAW. REV. STAT. § 10-4(1)-(9) (2007).

108. *Ako v. OHA*, 87-1 Haw. Legal Rep. at 87-555 to -556.

109. HAW. CONST. art. XII, § 5; HAW. REV. STAT. § 10-4 (2007). Initially, the board members were required to be Hawaiians, and only Hawaiians could vote in the OHA trustee elections. Id. This voting scheme was overturned as violative of the Fifteenth amendment by the United States Supreme Court in *Rice v. Cayetano*, 528 U.S. 495 (2000).

110. HAW. REV. STAT. § 10-5(2) (2007).

111. Id. § 10-5(1),(2),(5); *see* id. § 10-3(1); *Ako v. OHA*, 87-1 Haw. Legal Rep. at 87-555, -556.

112. HAW. CONST. art. XII, § 6.

113. HAW. REV. STAT. § 10-3 (2007); *Pele Def. Fund v. Paty*, 73 Haw. 578, 585, 837 P.2d 1247, 1251 (1992).

114. HAW. REV. STAT. § 10-1 (2007).

115. HAW. CONST. art. XII, § 6.

116. *See generally OHA v. State*, 96 Haw. 388, 31 P.3d 901 (2001); *Trustees of OHA v. Yamasaki*, 69 Haw. 154, 737 P.2d 446 (1987). Although a settlement was reached in 1990 and written into state law, Curt Sanburn, "*I luna a'e:* OHA at the end of a decade," KA WAI OLA O OHA, Sept. 1991, at 14, http://www.oha.org/pdf/OHA10yrHistory/KWO0991YR10PRT5.pdf (last visited Nov. 20, 2009), it was later overturned for conflicting with federal law. *OHA v. State*, 96 Haw. at 388, 31 P.3d at 901. Recently, OHA and the state reached a settlement agreement fixing OHA's yearly payment from the state at $15.1 million dollars in lieu of the 20 percent entitlement. Settlement Agreement between OHA and the State of Hawai'i, Exhibit A at 5, 9, Jan. 17, 2008, http://www.oha.org/pdf/080117_settlement_signed.pdf (last visited Apr. 20, 2010); accord id. at 1. In addition, the 2008 settlement will give OHA title to another approximately two hundred acres in Kaka'ako Makai, Kalaeloa, Makai, and Hilo Banyan Drive, estimated to be worth approximately $186.8 million. Settlement Agreement, supra at Exhibit B. The settlement will not become official unless it is approved by the State Legislature. Id. at 1. However, OHA chose to sue the state over its disposal policies, successfully before

the Hawai'i Supreme Court, which was subsequently unanimously reversed by the U.S. Supreme Court in 2009. OHA then negotiated a settlement with the state, but as of mid-2009, one of the parties to the litigation has refused to accept that settlement, and so the matter is still pending before the Hawai'i Supreme Court.

117. Haunani Apoliona, chairperson, OHA, "2007 State of OHA address," (Dec. 17, 2007), *in* KA WAI OLA, Jan. 2008, at 8.

118. HAW. CONST. art. XII, § 5.

119. Jonathan Scheuer, land mgmt. dir., OHA, "Presentation to Lambda Alpha International Hawai'i Chapter" (Nov. 16, 2007).

120. Apoliona, "State of OHA address," supra note 117 at 7.

121. Id.

122. Id.

123. Press Release, City and County of Honolulu, "Mayor approves Waimea Valley resolution" (April 3, 2006), http://www.honolulu.gov/refs/csd/publiccom/honnews06/mayorapproveswaimeavalley resolution.htm (last visited Nov. 20, 2009).

124. Scheuer, "Presentation," supra note 119.

125. Gregg K. Kakesako, "People wonder . . . Why Waimea?" HONOLULU STAR-BULLETIN, Oct. 6, 2000, http://starbulletin.com/2000/10/06/news/story4.html (last visited Dec. 22, 2009).

126. Id.

127. Id.

128. Id.; Rosemarie Bernardo, "Under new management," HONOLULU STAR-BULLETIN, Sept. 29, 2007, http://starbulletin.com/2007/09/29/news/story03.html (last visited Nov. 20, 2009); Joseph Kennedy, OHA, "Valley of the priests: Highlights of Waimea Valley's extraordinary history," http://www.oha.org/index.php?Itemid=225&id=180&option=com_content&task=view (scroll down to the "Valley of the Priests" article) (last visited Nov. 20, 2009).

129. Press Release, supra note 123.

130. Id.; Bernardo, supra note 128.

131. Press Release, supra note 123; *see* U.S. CONST. amend V.

132. Bernardo, supra note 128; Press Release, supra note 123.

133. Id. Such a development would have been contingent on getting land use permission to build in the extremely prohibitive conservation zone; however, Wolffer did already have a permit from the 1970s, allowing him to build an "eco camp." Nevertheless, depending on the specifics of the development plan, other potentially problematic discretionary permits may have been needed, as well as an environmental assessment or environmental impact statement. Catharine Lo, "Waimea indivisible: Who will save the valley?" HONOLULU WEEKLY, Nov. 30–Dec. 6, 2005, at 6.

134. Bernardo, supra note 128; Press Release, supra note 123. Rejection of the settlement exposed the city to a possible forfeiture of the valley, the entire $5.1 million in escrow, plus possible additional damages or payment of a court-determined price for the condemned land. Lo, supra note 133, at 6.

135. *City & County of Honolulu v. Attractions Haw.*, Civ. No. 01-1-03622-12 (D. Haw. Jan. 13, 2006).

136. Id.; Press Release, supra note 123.

137. *City & County of Honolulu v. Attractions Haw.*, Civ. No. 01-1-03622-12, at 7.

138. OHA, *Grant of Conservation and Access Easement* 3 (Jun. 30, 2006).

139. Id. at 1.

140. Telephone interview with Jonathan Scheuer, land mgmt. dir., OHA, in Honolulu (Jan. 28, 2008).

141. Id.

142. OHA, *Grant*, supra note 138, at 1.

143. Id.

144. Telephone interview with Jonathan Scheuer, supra note 140.

145. Id.

146. OHA, *Grant*, supra note 138, at 4.

147. Telephone interview with Jonathan Scheuer, supra note 140.

148. Id.

149. Id.

150. Id.

151. Id.; OHA, *Grant*, supra note 138, at 4.

152. OHA, *Grant*, supra note 138, at 5.

153. Bernardo, supra note 128; Scheuer, "Presentation," supra note 119.

154. Telephone interview with Jonathan Scheuer, supra note 140.

155. *See* infra Part II.

156. Telephone interview with Jonathan Scheuer, supra note 140.

157. Trust for Public Land, "Wao Kele O Puna now protected," http://www.tpl.org/tier3_cd.cfm?content_item_id=21822&folder_id=269 (last visited Dec. 22, 2009); OHA Public Information Office, "Protection of Wao Kele O Puna celebrated," Aug. 27, 2007, http://www.oha.org/index.php?Itemid=224&id=398&option=com_content&task=view (last visited Apr. 20, 2010).

158. Id.

159. Id.; OHA, Public Information Office, "Wao Kele O Puna fact sheet," http://www.oha.org/index.php?Itemid=224&id=398&option=com_content&task=view (scroll down to "Wao Kele O Puna fact sheet" section) (last visited Nov. 20, 2009).

160. Id.

161. Trust for Public Land, "Wao Kele O Puna now protected," supra note 157; OHA, "Wao Kele O Puna fact sheet," supra note 159.

162. U.S. Department of Agriculture, State and Private Forestry, Coop. Forestry, "Forest Legacy Program implementation guidelines" 24 (2003), http://www.fs.fed.us/spf/coop/library/fpl_guidelines.pdf (last visited Dec. 22, 2009).

163. Id. at 3.

164. Telephone interview with Sheri Mann, coop. res. mgmt. forester, Div. of Forestry & Wildlife, Dept. of Land & Nat. Res., in Honolulu (Jan. 14, 2008).

165. State of Hawai'i Department of Land and Natural Resources, *Memorandum of Agreement between the Department of Natural Resources, State of Hawaii and the Office of Hawaiian Affairs* 1 (June 27, 2006) (hereinafter "OHA Agreement June 2006").

166. Id.

167. Id.

168. Id. at 3.

169. Id. at 9. In addition, DLNR will contribute up to $100,000 in funds or work. Id. With the current OHA contribution, Wao Kele O Puna is receiving approximately ten times the funding typically provided for a DLNR forest reserve. Telephone interview with Sheri Mann, supra note 164.

170. OHA Agreement June 2006, supra note 165, at 10.

171. Id. at 6–7.

172. Id. at 7–8.

173. Id. at 3. This access for Hawaiian cultural practitioners was mandated of the former landowner in *Pele Def. Fund v. Estate of James Campbell*, Civ. No. 89-089, slip op. at 2 (D. Haw. Aug. 26, 2002). This includes access for blood relatives, spouses, and adopted children of cultural practitioners. Id.; OHA Agreement June 2006, supra note 165, at 3.

174. *OHA v. State*, 96 Haw. 388, 31 P.3d 901 (2001) (OHA suing the State of Hawai'i for ceded land revenue); *Trustees of OHA v. Bd. of Land & Natural Res.*, Civ. No. 95-0330-01, slip op. (Haw. 1995) (mem.) (OHA arguing that the BLNR failed to protect the traditional and customary rights of Hawaiians); *Trustees of OHA v. Yamasaki*, 69 Haw. 154, 737 P.2d 446 (1987) (OHA suing the State of Hawai'i for ceded land revenue); *OHA v. O'Keefe*, Civ. No. 02-00227 SOM/BMK, slip op (D. Haw. Jul. 15, 2003) (OHA arguing that the National Aeronautics and Space Administration should complete a full environmental impact statement before participating in development of ceded land on Mauna Kea).

175. HAW. CONST. art XII, § 7.

176. *Public Access Shoreline Haw. v. City Planning Comm'n*, 79 Haw. 425, 903 P.2d 1246 (1995).

177. Id.; *Trustees of OHA v. Bd. of Land & Natural. Res.*, Civ. No. 95-0330-01 (D. Haw. 1995).

178. *State v. Hanapi*, 89 Haw. 177, 970 P.2d 485 (Haw. 1998) (specifically holding that a sixteen-acre parcel zoned residential and improved with a single-family home was "developed" and so not subject to the exercise of traditional and customary rights). For an extended discussion, see Peter Orebech et al., *The Role of Customary Law in Sustainable Development*, Cambridge: Cambridge University Press, 2005, at ch. 2; Paul M. Sullivan, "Customary revolutions: The law of custom and the conflict of traditions in Hawaii," 20 U. HAW. L. REV. 99 (1998); D. Kapua Sproat, "The backlash against PASH: Legislative attempts to restrict Native Hawaiian rights," 20 U. HAW. L. REV. 321 (1998).

179. *Trustees of OHA v. Bd. of Land & Natural Res.*, Civ. No. 95-0330-01, slip op. at 29.

180. Id. at 30.

181. Id. at 31.

182. Scheuer, "Presentation," supra note 119.

183. Id.

184. Hawaiian Homes Commission Act, 1920, Pub. L. No. 67-34, 42 Stat. 108 (1921) (hereinafter "HCCA").

185. Id. § 101(a).

186. Id. § 101(b).

187. Id.

188. Id. § 101(c).

189. Id. § 202(a).

190. Id.

191. HAW. REV. STAT. § 26-34 (2009).

192. HHCA § 202(a).

193. HAW. CODE R. § 10-2-16(b) (Weil 2007).

194. Id. § 10-2-16(c).
195. HHCA § 101(a).
196. Id. § 207.5.
197. Id. § 207.
198. Haw. Code R. § 10-3-6 (Weil 2007).
199. Id. § 10-3-7.
200. Id. § 10-4-1.
201. HHCA § 207(c)(1).
202. Id. § 204(a)(2).
203. Andrew Walden, "Big Island superstore ban rejected," Hawai'i Free Press, Oct. 19, 2007, http://www.hawaiireporter.com/story.aspx?36a593b3-efee-4f28-9084-7b4d108a559a (last visited Nov. 20, 2009).
204. Haw. Code R. § 10-4-21 (Weil 2007).
205. Id. § 10-4-21(b).
206. HHCA § 204(a)(2).
207. Id. § 204.5(2).
208. Id. § 220.5.
209. Id. § 220.5(g).
210. Id. § 204, Opinion of the Attorney General No. 72-21 (1972).
211. Gordon Y. K. Pang, "Huge Kapolei mall project on track despite Hawai'i's economy," Honolulu Advertiser, Mar. 12, 2009, http://the.honoluluadvertiser.com/palm/2009/Mar/12/ln/hawaii903120339.html (last visited Jan. 5, 2010).
212. Urban Redevelopment Act, 1949 Haw. Sess. Laws 329.
213. Id.
214. Id.
215. Id.
216. *Berman v. Parker*, 348 U.S. 26 (1954).
217. Urban Redevelopment Act, supra note 212.
218. Haw. Rev. Stat. § 53-2 (2007).
219. Id. § 53-5(1).
220. Id.
221. Id. § 53-5(2)).
222. Id. § 53-5(4).
223. Id.
224. Id. § 53-5(7).
225. Id. § 53-5(4).
226. Id. § 53-5(6).
227. Id.
228. Id. § 53-6(b).
229. Id.
230. Id. § 53-6(d).
231. Id. § 53-8.
232. Id. § 53-12.
233. Id.
234. Id.
235. Michael Tsai, "Saving Chinatown," Honolulu Advertiser, Dec. 14, 2005, at 1E.

236. Editorial, "Car dealership not ideal urban renewal," Honolulu Adver-tiser, Jan. 26, 2004, at 6A.

237. Id.

238. Id.

239. Maui County Department of Planning, "Wailuku Redevelopment Plan frequently asked questions," http://www.mauicounty.gov/faq.aspx (scroll down to "Wailuku Redevelopment Plan" section) (last visited Nov. 20, 2009).

240. Id.

241. Maui County Planning Department, *Wailuku Redevelopment Plan*, at xi (Feb. 2000).

Chapter 6

Managing the Coastal Zone

Coastal zone management has been the subject of state and local regulation through much of the last five decades in the United States. This is not particularly surprising since fully three-quarters of the population of the United States lives in the coastal zone.[1] However, it was not until the mid-1970s that a national program of coastal zone management commenced under the federal Coastal Zone Management Act (CZMA).[2] Designed largely to encourage states in coastal areas to plan, manage, and regulate the use of land therein, the CZMA provides funds for the creation and implementation of state coastal zone management plans, on the condition that they follow various coastal land regulatory and management guidelines. In 1975, the State of Hawai'i responded to this federal coastal zone initiative, first with a Shoreland Protection Act, then with a Coastal Zone Management Act of its own. The Hawai'i Coastal Zone Management Act (HCZMA) is applicable to Hawai'i's vast coastal areas, in which much intensive development has occurred in the past and which continue to be subject to intense development pressures.[3]

What follows is a summary of the federal program of which Hawai'i is a part, Hawai'i's state and local response to the federal coastal zone program, and a brief look at what judicial comment there is on both.

The Federal Framework and the Hawaiian Response

The CZMA of 1972 was passed during the heady days of national land use and environmental activism in response to competing development and preservation demands on the nation's coastal areas. Congress found that population growth and development in coastal areas resulted in the destruction of marine resources, wildlife, open space, and other important ecological, cultural, historic, and esthetic values.[4] In response, Congress created a management and regulatory framework and appropriated money for the development and implementation of state-run coastal zone management programs. The framework is imposed if, but only if, a state chooses to accept the money. Most of the thirty-five eligible coastal states and territories have so chosen.[5] The program consists of three parts: a management plan/program, implementation regulations, and consistency regulations.

THE PLAN/PROGRAM

The CZMA requires a state's coastal zone management program to include nine planning elements, the most important plan themes of which are a definition of the boundaries of that part of a coastal zone that is subject to the program, objectives and policies for coastal area protection, a statement of permissible land and water uses, and the identification of special management areas.[6]

The program's coastal zone boundaries are defined as coastal waters and adjacent shorelands that are strongly influenced by each other.[7] While it is not particularly difficult to define the seaward boundary, the trick is to identify the vaguely defined inland boundary. The zone extends seaward to the outer limit of the U.S. territorial sea, but the inland boundary of the zone is based on the extent of area necessary to control shorelands, the use of which has a direct and significant impact on coastal waters, and to control those geographical areas which are likely to be affected by or vulnerable to sea level rise.[8] According to federal regulations, areas that might be included are "areas of particular concern" (discussed below), salt marshes and wetlands, beaches, state-determined floodplains, islands, and watersheds. However vague the regulations, a state must define its inland boundary with sufficient precision so that "interested parties" can determine whether the management program controls their activities.[9] CZMA regulations also set out criteria for determining permissible uses subject to the management program.[10]

The process of defining the Hawai'i coastal zone boundary in the late 1970s provoked one of the more spirited disputes in recent Hawai'i state-county history. The seaward boundary was easy: the seaward limit of the state's jurisdiction, except those areas owned, leased, held in trust, or otherwise subject to the power and authority of the federal government.[11] But except for some state forest preserve lands and federal lands, the inland boundary stretches across the entire land area of the state.[12] This is not so extensive for regulatory purposes as it first appears. The whole of the coastal zone boundary area is subject to the HCZMA objectives and policies, but the control and management of areas requiring special management attention, where special permits from county agencies are required, cover a far smaller area.

The objectives and policies mandated by the CZMA are set out in detail in HCZMA. Covering recreational, historic, scenic, and open space resources, coastal ecosystems and hazards, economic uses, and development management, they are enforced through a complicated networking process discussed later in this chapter. They apply to the entire coastal zone management area. For example, the objective of protecting scenic and open space resources reads, "protect, preserve, and where desirable, restore or improve the quality of coastal scenic and open space resources."[13] This leads to the following policies:

(1) Identify valued scenic resources in the coastal zone management area;

(2) Insure that new developments are compatible with their visual environment by designing and locating such developments to minimize the alteration of natural landforms and existing public views to and along the shoreline;

(3) Preserve, maintain, and where desirable, improve and restore shoreline open space and scenic resources; and

(4) Encourage those developments that are not coastal dependent to locate in inland areas.[14]

Areas requiring special management attention because of unique coastal values or characteristics or because the area faces pressure that requires detailed attention beyond the general planning and regulatory systems of a typical management program must be designated by a management plan. These are called "areas of particular concern" (APCs) and "special management areas" (SMAs) and are the linchpin of the Hawaiian response to the CZMA's requirements. Their boundaries are established in accordance with the following criteria:

(1) Areas of unique, scarce, fragile or vulnerable natural habitat; unique or fragile, physical figuration (as, for example

Niagara Falls); historical significance, cultural value or scenic
importance (including resources on or determined to be
eligible for the National Register of Historic Places);

(2) Areas of high natural productivity or essential habitat
for living resources, including fish, wildlife, and endangered
species and the various trophic levels in the food web critical to
their well-being;

(3) Areas of substantial recreational value and/or
opportunity;

(4) Areas where developments and facilities are dependent
upon the utilization of, or access to, coastal waters;

(5) Areas of unique hydrologic, geologic or topographic
significance for industrial or commercial development or for
dredge disposal;

(6) Areas or urban concentration where shoreline utilization and water uses are highly competitive;

(7) Areas where, if development were permitted, it might
be subject to significant hazard due to storms, slides, floods,
erosion, settlement, salt water intrusion, and sea level rise;

(8) Areas needed to protect, maintain or replenish coastal
lands or resources including coastal flood plains, aquifers
and their recharge areas, estuaries, sand dunes, coral and
other reefs, beaches, offshore sand deposits and mangrove
stands.[15]

Special procedures for assessing public beach areas and other
coastal areas (especially erosion) requiring access or protection are
also required.[16] The most critical special management area in Hawai'i
extends inland from the shoreline and is defined as "the upper reaches
of the wash of the waves, other than storms and seismic waves, at high
tide during the season of the year in which the highest wash of the
waves occurs, usually evidenced by the edge of vegetation growth, or
the upper limit of debris left by the wash of the waves."[17] The purposes
of implementing controls in this special management area are to "avoid
permanent losses of valuable resources" and to preserve public access to
beaches and natural reserves.[18] Maps showing the boundaries of the area
are required by statute to be filed with the county permitting authority.[19]
The mapping of areas of particular concern is primarily controlled by
the state directly rather than by the counties, which have only administrative responsibilities for some.

IMPLEMENTATION: WHAT THE LAW REQUIRES

The key to any land use planning system is implementation. Courts seem increasingly inclined to accept coastal zone management and preservation rationales as the bases for upholding coastal land use controls.[20] Participating states must have the authority to implement the management plan in order for it to be approved by the secretary of the U.S. Department of Commerce.[21] There are three permissible options for implementation:

> (1) State establishment of criteria and standards for local implementation, subject to administrative review and enforcement of compliance; or
> (2) Direct state land and water use planning and regulation; or
> (3) State administrative review for consistency with the management program of all development plans, projects, or land and water use regulations, including exceptions and variances thereto, proposed by any state or local authority or private developer, with power to approve or disapprove after public notice and an opportunity for hearings.[22]

Option 2, direct state control, is the one that Hawai'i chose. While seemingly the most onerous, it is not, primarily due to a concept called "networking."[23] For a state to utilize networking in meeting the state control implementation option, it must:

> (1) Demonstrate that, taken together, existing authorities can and will be used to implement the full range of policies and management techniques identified as necessary for coastal management purposes; and
> (2) Bind each party that exercises statutory authority which is part of the management program to conformance with relevant enforceable policies and management techniques. Parties may be bound to conformance through an executive order, administrative directive or a memorandum of understanding provided that:
> > (i) The management program authorities provide grounds for taking action to ensure compliance of networked agencies with the program. It will be sufficient if

any of the following can act to ensure compliance: The
State agency designated pursuant to subsection 306(d)
(6) of the Act, the State's Attorney General, another
State agency, a local government, or a citizen.

(ii) The executive order, administrative directive or
memorandum of understanding establishes conformance requirements of other State agency activities or
authorities to management program policies. A guber-
natorial executive order will be acceptable if networked
State agency heads are directly responsible to the
Governor.

Where networked State agencies can enforce the management program policies at the time of section 306 approval
without first having to revise their operating rules and regulations, then any proposed revisions to such rules and regulations which would enhance or facilitate implementation need
not be accomplished prior to program approval. Where State
agencies cannot enforce coastal policies without first revis-
ing their rules and regulations, then these revisions must be
made prior to approval of the State's program by the Assistant
Administrator.[24]

Hawai'i has managed to accomplish networking—and so obtain
federal approval of the implementation section of its management
plan—in several ways. First, the HCZMA itself states that its objectives
and policies are binding on both state and county agencies. In the
event that regulations of state and county agencies fail to so comply, the
HCZMA requires that they be amended. Second, a governor's directive
requires all state departments and agencies to act—within the scope of
their respective statutory authority—in accordance with the objectives
and policies of the HCZMA.[25] Finally, any person or agency may challenge any state or county agency's lack of compliance with the approved
management program's objectives, policies, and guidelines within the
waters of the coastal zone boundaries and the land within a special
management area or its failure to perform an act or duty required by
HCZMA. Courts may provide "any relief as may be appropriate, including a temporary restraining order or preliminary injunction."[26]

The state and county laws thus networked number at least fifty-
eight. They are generally directed at fulfilling the recreational, historic,

scenic, and open space, as well as the coastal economic and development management objectives of the program.[27] The most noticeable
and potentially effective element of the network is that which deals with
the special management areas and areas of particular concern. While
the state perforce retains overall power and responsibility for assuring
that the regulations guiding management and development in these
areas accord with the state programs, the counties define the special
management areas and pass appropriate ordinances and regulations
governing the use of land within their boundaries.[28] After state designation, they also permit certain land uses by way of variances for areas of
particular concern.[29] These systems are partly responsible for the promi-
nent position Hawai'i holds in those U.S. jurisdictions experiencing a
"permit explosion."[30]

Special Management Areas

In Hawai'i, no development may proceed in an SMA unless an
applicant obtains a permit from a county permit granting authority,
which is either the county planning commission or, if it is only advisory,
the council or its designated agency.[31] Development is defined as any of
the uses, activities, or operations on land in or underwater within the
SMA that includes the following:

(1) Placement or erection of any solid material or any
gaseous, liquid, solid, or thermal waste;
(2) Grading, removing, dredging, mining, or extraction of
any materials;
(3) Change in the density or intensity of use of land, including but not limited to the division or subdivision of land;
(4) Change in the intensity of use of water, ecology related
thereto, or of access thereto; and
(5) Construction, reconstruction, demolition, or alteration
of the size of any structure.[32]

The following uses, activities, or operations are not "development"
(and therefore need no SMA permit) unless the county permit granting authority finds they are or may become part of a larger project,
the cumulative impact of which may have a significant environmental
or ecological effect on the SMA, in which case it slides back into the
regulated "development" category:

(1) Construction of a single-family residence that is not part of a larger development;

(2) Repair or maintenance of roads and highways within existing rights-of-way;

(3) Routine maintenance dredging of existing streams, channels, and drainage ways;

(4) Repair and maintenance of underground utility lines, including but not limited to water, sewer, power, and telephone and minor appurtenant structures such as pad mounted transformers and sewer pump stations;

(5) Zoning variances, except for height, density, parking, and shoreline setback;

(6) Repair, maintenance, or interior alterations to existing structures;

(7) Demolition or removal of structures, except those structures located on any historic site as designated in national or state registers;

(8) Use of any land for the purpose of cultivating, planting, growing, and harvesting plants, crops, trees, and other agricultural, horticultural, or forestry products or animal husbandry, or aquaculture or mariculture of plants or animals, or other agricultural purposes;

(9) Transfer of title to land;

(10) Creation or termination of easements, covenants, or other rights in structures or land;

(11) Subdivision of land into lots greater than twenty acres in size;

(12) Subdivision of a parcel of land into four or fewer parcels when no associated construction activities are proposed; provided that any land which is so subdivided shall not thereafter qualify for this exception with respect to any subsequent subdivision of any of the resulting parcels;

(13) Installation of underground utility lines and appurtenant aboveground fixtures less than four feet in height along existing corridors;

(14) Structural and nonstructural improvements to existing single-family residences, where otherwise permissible;

(15) Nonstructural improvements to existing commercial structures; and

(16) Construction, installation, maintenance, repair, and

replacement of civil defense warning or signal devices and
sirens; provided that whenever the authority finds that any
excluded use, activity, or operation may have a cumulative
impact, or a significant environmental or ecological effect on a
special management area, that use, activity, or operation shall
be defined as "development" for the purpose of this part.[33]

County permitting authorities may issue three types of permits:

(1) "Special management area emergency permit"—an
action by the authority authorizing development in cases of
emergency requiring immediate action to prevent substantial
physical harm to persons or property or to allow the reconstruction of structures damaged by natural hazards to their
original form; provided that such structures were previously
found to be in compliance with requirements of the Federal
Flood Insurance Program.

(2) "Special management area minor permit"—an action by
the authority authorizing development the valuation of which
is *not in excess* of $125,000 and which has no substantial adverse
environmental or ecological effect, taking into account potential cumulative effects.

(3) "Special management area use permit"—an action by
the authority authorizing development the valuation of which
exceeds $125,000 or which may have a substantial adverse envi-
ronmental or ecological effect, taking into account potential
cumulative effects.[34]

In issuing these permits, the county permitting authority also considers whether the development complies with SMA guidelines designed
to ensure access to public beaches and recreation areas, control sewage
disposal, regulate site clearing for construction, and generally prohibit
adverse environmental effects.[35] Maui, Hawai'i, and Kaua'i Counties
have designated their plan commissions as their permitting authority,
while Honolulu has made it a council function.[36]

In Honolulu the administration of the SMA permit system (filing
for permits, hearings, and so on) is the responsibility of its director of
the Department of Planning and Permitting (DPP).[37] It is the Honolulu
City Council, however, that decides whether the permit will be granted.[38]
Honolulu also requires that the DPP conduct an environmental impact

assessment using the procedural guidelines in the Hawai'i Environmental Impact Statement law (HEIS).[39] However, if an environmental impact statement has been prepared under either the HEIS or the National Environmental Policy Act (NEPA), an applicant is excused from that requirement.[40]

Maui's SMA provisions are set out in the Rules and Regulations of the Planning Commission.[41] As in Honolulu, a key part of the SMA permitting process is the making of an assessment, here by the planning director, of the "proposed action" to determine the extent and scope of the permit review process. In instances of clearly significant (fair market value over $125,000) or potentially environmentally adverse developments, the applicant may waive assessment and go directly to a hearing and review. As the assessment process requires the filing of a fairly detailed application and review by the planning director, waiver could result in the saving of both time and expense. If he finds no significant effect or a less-than-$125,000 development, the planning director issues a "minor" SMA permit, with or without conditions. If the applicant has waived the assessment process or if the planning director finds a potentially significant adverse effect, then the applicant must submit to an extensive review process involving, among other things, a "Central Coordinating Agency" of the Planning Commission and an "Urban Design Review Board."[42]

Where a county planning commission has delegated authority to its director, the Hawai'i Supreme Court has held that the director's decision is considered a final administrative decision.[43] The "final decision" designation is significant because it allows a permit applicant to appeal to the state's courts, bypassing further administrative appeals. In Maui and Kaua'i, this means that the Planning Commission has no direct authority over the processing of minor SMA permits.

Ultimately, it is the Planning Commission that issues the permit, but only if it finds that "the development will not have any substantial adverse environmental or ecological effect, except as such adverse effect is minimized to the extent practicable and clearly outweighed by public health, safety, or compelling public interests" that "the development is consistent with the objectives, policies, and special management area guidelines of [HRS chapter 205A] and any guidelines enacted by the [State] legislature" and that "the development is consistent with the [Maui] county general plan and zoning."[44] The wording of the final requirement is especially important, as it represents two tiers of analysis before SMA permits are issued on Maui or any other county in Hawai'i—one for general plan consistency and another for zoning consistency. In *GATRI v. Blane*, the Hawai'i Supreme Court enforced this double consistency requirement.[45] There, the Court rejected the developer's argument that zoning consistency alone was sufficient. The Court further stated that, for the purposes of SMA permits, county general plans have the force and effect of law. The rules also provide for the expansion of the SMA boundaries on Maui.[46] This Maui has done, primarily for wetland (1,400 acres) and stream (7,600 acres) protection and development control (1,850 acres).[47]

As with Maui, Kaua'i has promulgated rules that give the Planning Commission the authority to grant or deny most SMA permits. Kaua'i has also adopted an initial assessment process similar to the one used on O'ahu and in Maui County, except that the standards for assessing the significance of potential environmental effects are more extensive. If the effects are found to be significantly adverse, a formal SMA permit application and hearing are required. The commission holds a public hearing and makes a decision on the application, which is deemed approved if not decided within the time periods described in the rules.[48] The extent to which the Hawai'i courts will strictly enforce the "findings" requirements is clear from a 1982 decision of the Hawai'i Supreme Court in *Mahuiki v. Planning Comm'n of Kauai*.[49] There, the Court struck down an SMA permit granted by the Kaua'i Planning Commission solely on the ground that the commission failed to make the required finding of no substantial adverse environmental or ecological effects.

Kaua'i also deals extensively with the amendment of SMA boundaries. A change in boundaries may be initiated only by the director of planning. Even a request addressed to the director may come only from a state or county department (or agency) head, the Kaua'i County Council, or any owner or lessee (not merely an "interested person") of the affected land.[50]

As in Maui and Kaua'i, Hawai'i County vests its SMA authority in its Planning Commission by Planning Commission rules. As in the Kaua'i rules, the objectives and policies of the HCZMA are recited word for word, followed by the usual list of SMA guidelines dealing with issues such as access, dredging, ocean views, and water quality. An assessment is required of most projects proposed in the SMA, unless the applicant determines "on his own" that his project will cost or be valued over $125,000 or will have a significant adverse effect, in which case he goes directly to the SMA permit process. The SMA permit is heard and decided by the Planning Commission much the way it is on Maui and

Kauaʻi. Unlike Kauaʻi, however, if a decision is not forthcoming within the time limits prescribed by the rules, it is deemed denied. Hawaiʻi also authorizes the appointment of a hearing officer by the commission to conduct the hearings required by its SMA rules, although the commission is, of course, free to decide the SMA permit application any way it chooses.[51] SMA boundary applicants in Hawaiʻi County may also petition the Planning Commission (through the director) for boundary amendments.[52]

The Hawaiʻi Intermediate Court of Appeals set out a textbook guide to precisely how counties may define the regulatory coastal zone in *Topliss v. Planning Commission.* In a well-structured two-part decision, the court first upheld Hawaiʻi County's inclusion of land hundreds of yards inland and steeply elevated from the beach because it was visible to anyone looking *along* the coast (but not away and upland from the coast). Second, the court held that the county improperly denied the permit because the adverse effects—traffic—of the development were not related to any effect on the coastal zone itself or any of its statutory values.

Areas of Particular Concern

APCs, like SMAs, are regulated by the networked laws controlling the broadly defined coastal zone subject to the State Management Plan's general objectives and policies. An APC is created by means of a number of statutory schemes, some of which provide for state regulation, others of which provide for local (county) regulation. Most of these programs were both authorized and operating well before the federal CZMA made their networking a part of Hawaiʻi's Coastal Zone Management Program. Among them are the Natural Area Reserve System, the Marine Life Conservation District Program, the National Estuarine Research Reserve System, the Shoreline Setback Law, and the Hawaiʻi Community Development Authority.

The legislature established the Natural Area Reserve System to protect unique geological, volcanic, and other natural areas with distinctive marine, animal, and terrestrial features from loss due to human population and technology growth.[53] The Natural Area Reserve System Commission recommends areas for inclusion. Rules specifying use, control, and protection of the areas recommended by the commission are promulgated by the Board of the State Department of Land and Natural Resources (BLNR), also referred to as the Land Board.[54] For example, chapter 13 of the Hawaiʻi Administrative Rules, promulgated by BLNR, provides for a range of prohibited activities in all natural reserves, among them disruptive vehicle use, camping, construction of any kind, and the removal or injury of wildlife.[55] The regulations make some allowances for hiking and hunting.[56]

The Marine Life Conservation District (MLCD) was established to preserve unique areas of Hawai'i's marine environment, such as bays, shoals, and estuaries that are vulnerable to loss.[57] These districts, designated by BLNR, are protected by regulations that prohibit certain activities, control allowable uses, and regulate scientifically related permits.[58] A separate regulation is issued for each district. Thus, for example, BLNR's regulations governing the Waikīkī MLCD on O'ahu prohibit fishing and possession, in the water, of any device that can be used to take marine or geological specimens.[59] Additions to this variety of APC include the Wai'ōpae Tidepools MLCD on Hawai'i in June of 1983.

The National Estuarine Research Reserve System was established by section 315 of the CZMA to provide long-term protection for natural areas so that they may be used for research, scientific, and educational purposes.[60] The permitted uses of a sanctuary (which may include low-intensity uses such as recreation, fishing, hunting, and wildlife observation) are determined on a case-by-case basis. Hawai'i's only reserve, the Waimanu Valley Estuarine Reserve, located in Waimanu Valley on the island of Hawai'i, was withdrawn from the National Estuarine Research Reserve System in 1996.[61]

The establishment of shoreline setback areas, also APCs, is left largely to the counties, in accordance with statutory guidelines. Thus, while the State Land Use Commission has the initial authority to establish a setback (of not less than twenty nor more than forty feet inland from the upper reaches of the wash of the waves), it is the counties that are specifically empowered to regulate, administer, and enlarge (by ordinance) the land in such areas. This is subject to statutory prohibitions against permitting the construction of any structure, including seawalls unless they are necessary for the safety of a preexisting structure, or the removal of any sand, coral, rocks, or other beach material for commercial purposes.[62] Setbacks may also be established by private agreement. In *Brescia v. North Shore Ohana*, the Hawai'i Supreme Court held that a developer's more restrictive, self-imposed setbacks would be treated as the effective shoreline setback for that subdivision.[63] Further, the Court held that setbacks imposed by restrictive covenant are not diminished by zoning ordinances or other statutory or administrative laws that are more permissive.[64]

Recall from Chapter 5 that the Hawaiʻi Community Development
Authority (HCDA) is responsible for developing and implementing
community development plans and programs in underdeveloped or
blighted areas designated by the legislature.[65] This is significant for
Hawaiʻi's CZ program because many urban developments are coastal
related and because the authority has the power to override county controls and regulations if necessary to better serve the public interest of the
state. The program is treated as an area of particular concern because of
its treatment of concentrated urban activities in areas where shoreline
utilization and water uses are highly competitive. The Kakaʻako area
near downtown Honolulu was designated as the first area subject to the
program because of its proximity to the coast and its potential impact in
coastal development activities.

Consideration, Consultation, Coordination,
and the Siting of Facilities
Federal approval of any state coastal zone management program
depends on a series of consultation, coordination, and participation
efforts on the part of the state, not only with federal and local officials
but with the general public as well. One element of management program approval is the requirement that the state "adequately" consider
the national interest when planning and siting facilities that "are of
greater than local significance," such as energy facilities.[66] For energy
facilities, the state must have considered any applicable national or
interstate energy plan or program.[67]

Of equal importance in the process of approval for state management programs is the requirement that an environmental impact statement be prepared under the National Environmental Policy Act, in
which the state program must be explained in detail. Hawaiʻi's runs to
several hundred pages.[68]

Finally, the CZMA requires that states provide for participation by
other state agencies, local governments, regional organizations, port
authorities, and other "interested" public and private parties during the
development of a management program. In addition, certain elements
of the program must be coordinated with local, area-wide, and interstate plans applicable to the coastal zone. These include housing and
land use plans, wastewater treatment facilities plans, highway plans, and
flood insurance program plans.[69] The process of coordination continues after program approval, especially where the state management program decisions may conflict with a local zoning ordinance decision.[70]

In response to these requirements, the HCZMA declared the following matters to be in the national interest: (1) national defense, (2) mineral extraction, (3) energy facilities, energy research and energy reserves, and (4) resource conservation.[71] However, as Hawai'i has a local government structure consisting of but four counties, each of which has islandwide jurisdiction, the concept of "regional" benefit beyond local benefit is nearly impossible to apply, so the management program interprets the concept as applying to land and water uses of statewide benefit or of benefit to more than one county. The program declares the following uses to have regional benefit: (1) scientific field research, (2) marine-related research facilities, (3) energy research and development facilities, (4) mineral extraction, (5) intrastate or international communication and transportation facilities, (6) mineral or fuel processing or transshipment facilities, and (7) national defense and coastal protection facilities.[72]

Compliance

The extent to which the CZMA as a voluntary program results in the achievement of federal statutory objectives depends on evaluation and compliance review. This the CZMA provides by requiring the Office of Coastal Zone Management (OCZM) to "conduct a continuing review of the performance of coastal states with respect to coastal management."[73] Usually, evaluation takes place on an annual basis. The state prepares a response to an OCZM "information request," OCZM representatives visit the state, and the OCZM prepares "findings" based on both. If a state deviates without justification from its approved program, the OCZM has the authority to withdraw that program's federal funds. As experience with evaluations increases, the techniques for evaluation have become more sophisticated in theory, but they are frequently chaotic and highly subjective in practice. This may be due to the relatively broad goals to be accomplished by the review—program justification, information gathering, accountability—and the different perspectives state program managers and federal evaluators bring to the process.[74] Congress asks the OCZM, not the states, to account for money spent on coastal zone management programs. Nevertheless, it is at the state and local level that coastal zone management actually occurs.

CONSISTENCY

A major incentive (besides federal money) for states to participate in the coastal zone management program is the federal consistency requirement in all states with approved coastal zone management programs. "Consistency" means that federal agencies must operate "to the maximum extent practicable"—that is, act, license, subsidize, and so forth—in a manner consistent with the objectives and policies of an approved state coastal zone management program.[75] Because federal lands (which may, at the option of the federal government, be exempt from state and local zoning and subdivision laws) are excluded from the boundaries of state-defined coastal zone management areas, state and local coastal zone land use regulations do not apply to them.[76] Thus, for any state with substantial federal coastal lands, like Hawai'i, the consistency provisions of the CZMA represent the principal method of reviewing federal activities on these lands.

The CZMA subjects five categories of federal actions to some consistency with state management programs:

(1) Federal activities (initial determination by federal agency).

(2) Federal development projects (initial determination by federal agency).

(3) Activities requiring a federal license or permit (initial determination by state agency).

(4) Outer Continental Shelf (OCS) exploration, development, and production activities (initial determination by U.S. Secretary of the Interior).

(5) Federal assistance activities to state and local governments (initial determination made by the state).[77]

In none of these categories is the federal government ultimately foreclosed from acting. Rather, the CZMA creates a hierarchy of reviews, findings, and high-level approvals before any action found to be inconsistent with an approved state coastal zone management plan may proceed.

In Hawai'i, DBEDT's Office of Planning has primary responsibility for reviewing federal programs, activities, permits, licenses, and development proposals for consistency with the state's approved management program.[78] The federal guidelines, discussed below, guide the Office of Planning in making consistency determinations on activities and development projects. All other federal actions in the coastal zone are reviewed by the appropriate federal agency for an initial consistency decision before the Office of Planning's consistency determination.[79]

Federal Agency Activities and Development Projects

Federal agency activities and development projects affecting the coastal zone must be consistent with state management plans to the maximum extent practicable. A "federal agency activity" is any function performed by or on behalf of a federal agency in the exercise of its statutory responsibilities.[80] A "federal development project" is an activity involving the planning, construction, modification, or removal of public works, facilities, or other structures and the acquisition, utilization, or disposal of land or water resources.[81] The phrase "affecting the coastal zone" is defined as an activity that has "reasonably foreseeable direct [or] indirect effects on any coastal use or resource."[82] Federal development projects within the coastal zone are to be considered as affecting it, while all other types of federal activity either in or outside that zone may be "determined" to affect it after review by the acting federal agency.[83] In borderline cases, "affecting the coastal zone" is supposed to be "broadly construed."

The phrase "consistent to the maximum extent practicable" means that activities and development projects must be consistent with approved state management programs unless another law defining the acting federal agency's activities prohibits such consistency. Then, the federal agency must point out to the state the law that prohibits consistency. However, consistency with an approved management plan is required of a federal agency only "to the maximum extent practicable."[84]

Finally, it is only the so-called enforceable policies of the state management program with which federal activities and projects *must* be consistent. Provisions that are in the nature of recommendations require mere "consideration." What consistency requirements there are therefore depend to a large extent upon the level and sophistication of the approved state coastal zone management program.[85]

Conflict over consistency does arise. An example is the disagreement between DBEDT (then the Department of Planning and Economic Development) and the National Marine Fisheries Service (NMFS) over proposed federal regulations (an "activity") for the harvesting of precious coral. The state gave the Land Board jurisdiction over coral, and the board has issued regulations that heavily restricted where coral could be harvested and by what means. The proposed federal regulations allowed harvesting in more areas and by nonselective (nets, dredges, and so on) means. DBEDT had notified NMFS that it disagreed with the NMFS determination that the proposed regulations were consistent with Hawai'i's Coastal Zone Management Program to the maximum extent practicable.[86]

Activities Requiring a Federal License

Any applicant for a federal license or permit to conduct an activity affecting the coastal zone must show that the activity complies with and will be conducted in a manner consistent with a state's approved management program, without which the permit or license may not be issued.[87] A federal license or permit is an authorization, certification, approval, or other form of permission that any federal agency is authorized to issue to an applicant, except for projects that involve outer continental shelf exploration and development.[88] An applicant is virtually anyone who files an application for a federal license or permit to conduct an activity in the coastal zone. This could be an individual, a public or private corporation, partnership, association, or any other entity organized or existing under state and local government.[89]

The phrase "affecting the coastal zone," like "directly affecting the coastal zone," is not defined. Presumably the difference in language signals a difference in thresholds, with a federal license held to a higher standard in applying consistency regulations. In the same vein, "in a manner consistent" (also undefined) differs from the phrase "consistent to the maximum extent practicable," which is applied to federal activities and development projects.

In contrast to federal activities and projects where the federal agency makes the initial determination, whether or not a federal license or permit activity affects the coastal zone is initially determined by the state, which lists the permits and licenses that will be subject to consistency review in their management programs. Once it is determined that a permit or license activity is subject to consistency requirements, the applicant must prepare and furnish to the state and the issuing federal agency a certificate indicating that the proposed activity will be consistent with the state's approved management program. If the state objects to the certification, the federal agency may not issue the license or permit until the applicant successfully appeals to the secretary of Commerce, who may permit the activity either because it is in the interests of national security or it is consistent with the CZMA. In so finding, the secretary must determine that there is no reasonable alternative available.[90]

OCS Exploration, Development, and Production
Leases for OCS projects require the approval of the secretary of the Interior.[91] An applicant submits a plan for the required license or permit, describing federal license and permit activities in detail, which must be conducted in a manner consistent with an approved state management plan.[92] The procedure for consistency determination is virtually identical to the aforementioned federal license and permit activities procedure. Any OCS activities for which the secretary failed to require a description in the OCS plan were theoretically caught up in the consistency requirements for federal permits and licenses generally,[93] and the federal courts upheld stringent state and local permit programs based upon such consistency determinations, despite industrial complaints about both the programs and their enforcement to regulate OCS exploration and development.[94] However, in *Secretary of the Interior v. California*,[95] the U.S. Supreme Court held that the lease and sale of OCS resources by the secretary of the Interior in 1982 did not directly affect California's coastal zone under the California-approved coastal zone management plan. Therefore the secretary could ignore the federal CZMA by selling oil and gas leases without making a consistency determination under section 307(c)(1) of that act. Essentially, the Court held that the sale of OCS oil and gas leases is not an activity "directly affecting" the coastal zone, thus obviating the need for a consistency review. It based that decision on an interpretation of congressional intent not to subject such lease sales to consistency review. In response, Congress amended the federal CZMA to make clear that oil and gas leases constituted federal activities subject to consistency review.[96] By doing so, Congress protected the only form of control coastal states may exert over federal activities affecting the coastal zone.

Preemption
Federal laws supersede state laws where Congress intends to be the sole authority on a particular issue or where state law directly conflicts with federal law. In states that participate in CZMA regulation, does the federal CZMA represent the extent to which the participating state may regulate its coastal lands? This question arose in *California Coastal Commission v. Granite Rock Co.*[97] In *Granite Rock*, a mining company objected to California's imposition of permitting requirements on the mining

company's operations on federal lands. The mining company raised three arguments: first, that the federal government's environmental regulations over mining claims demonstrated an intent to preempt any state regulations; second, that as state land use regulations were pre- empted by federal regulations, the same should follow for the state's permit requirement; and finally, that because the CZMA had excluded federal lands from its definition of the "coastal zone," it follows that there was a legislative intent to exclude all federal lands from state coastal zone regulation.[98]

Writing for the Court, Justice O'Connor held that Congress explic- itly expressed its intent not to preempt state regulation through the CZMA and that, even if federal lands were excluded from the CZMA definition of "coastal zone," the CZMA does not prevent a state from regulating activity on federal lands.[99] First, examination of applicable federal laws revealed an intent to comply with, not preempt, state laws. For example, federal laws required that all operators comply with state air and waste disposal regulations and that all plans of operations must be approved by *both* federal and state laws.[100] Second, while the Court appeared to concede that a state land use regulation would be preempted by a federal land use regulation, it held that the permit requirement in this case was merely an environmental regulation. The Court drew a sharp distinction between "land-use planning" and "environmental regulation." While the former "in essence choose particular uses for the land," the latter "does not mandate particular uses of the land but requires only that, however the land is used, damage to the environ- ment is kept within prescribed limits."[101] Accordingly, the Court did not address whether state land use planning was preempted by the federal land use plan but held that the permit requirement was not preempted, as it did not seek to prohibit the mining company's activities, just regu- late it. Finally, the Court found that the statutory language of the CZMA itself expressly indicated that it was not intended to be "an independent cause of preemption except in cases of actual conflict."[102] The CZMA explicitly declared that it was not intended to diminish federal or state authority or "change interstate agreements"; accordingly, the Court found that the CZMA could not be used as a source to preempt all state regulation of activities on federal lands.[103]

Federal Assistance to State and Local Government
Federal funds for state and local activities affecting the coastal zone (highways, sewage treatment, urban renewal) may be granted

only when consistent with an approved state management program, as determined by review.[104] Assistance is broadly defined as grants or contractual arrangements, loans, subsidies, guarantees, insurance, or other forms of financial aid. There are two steps to state and local assistance consistency review. First, the state must decide on what assistance programs are subject to consistency review. Normally, the state will list these assistance programs in its management program. Should the affected federal agency disagree, either the state or the federal agency may seek a determination either by the Secretary of Commerce or by judicial review. Once the state and federal agency are agreed that the assistance program is subject to consistency review, local or state agencies applying for that assistance must notify the state reviewing agency. If that agency determines the assistance activity is inconsistent with the approved state coastal zone management plan, the federal agency is prohibited from making that assistance available unless the state or local applicant successfully appeals to the Secretary of Commerce, who may override the state review agency in the interests of national security or consistency with the goals of the CZMA.[105]

In sum, the coastal zone program in Hawaiʻi consists primarily of a state-local regulatory partnership that owes much but not by any means all to the federal guidelines and standards framework that accompanied the federal funds used to develop the program. Key to its implementation are county SMA permit procedures and state APC management programs. A growing issue, if not a problem in Hawaiʻi, is the way in which the CZMA program regulatory scheme—especially where networking is involved—intersects, overlaps, and conflicts with other federal or federally mandated programs, especially as those programs are carried out at the local level. In a way, some of these problems are at least examined under the so-called 312 Evaluation Process, under which state CZM programs are regularly reviewed and rated.[106] Others have been the subject of report and concern at the federal level, especially the potential conflict between federally suggested rules and statutes for the location of transportation facilities and various flood hazard and coastal zone regulatory programs. It is at least probable since the *Texas Landowners Rights Assoc. v. Harris* case in 1978 that the federal government will continue to duck behind the nonrequirement shield when such conflicts surface.[107] Briefly, the argument is that since most federal programs are voluntary, and the regulatory programs that may come with the federal program (and federal money, the key inducement usually for state and local governments to "volunteer") therefore avoidable, the conflicts, if any, are state-local problems and represent no legal federal involvement. While this may be legally correct, it is hardly defensible in terms of actual conflict resolution, programmatic coordination, and efficiency.

Notes

1. Daniel R. Mandelker and Thea A. Sherry, "The national Coastal Zone Management Act of 1972," 119 URB. L. ANN. 7 (1974).
2. Coastal Zone Management Act of 1972, 16 U.S.C § 1451 et seq. (2000) (hereinafter "CZMA"). For general description and comments, see Sarah Chassis, "The Coastal Zone Management Act," 46 J. OF THE AM. PLAN. ASS'N 145 (April 1980); Gilbert L. Finnell Jr., "Coastal Zone Management: An introduction," 1978 AM. B. FOUND. J. 153 (1978); Fred P. Bosselman, Duane A. Feuer, and Tobin M. Richter, *Federal Land Use Regulation*, New York: Practicing Law Institute, 1977 at ch. 5; Elaine Moss, ed., *Land Use Controls in the United States: A Handbook on the Legal Rights of Citizens*, Natural Resources Defense Council, New York: Dial, 1977 at ch. 6; Daniel R. Mandelker, *Environmental and Land Control Legislation*, Indianapolis: Bobbs-Merrill, 1976 at ch. 6.
3. HAW. REV. STAT. § 205A-1 et seq. (1993 and Supp. 2007).
4. CZMA, § 302(c), (e), 16 U.S.C. § 1451(c), (e) (2000).
5. National Oceanic and Atmospheric Association, "Coastal programs: Partnering with states to manage our coastline," http://coastalmanagement.noaa.gov/programs/czm.html (last visited Nov. 17, 2009).
6. CZMA, § 306(d)(2), 16 U.S.C. §1455(d)(2) (2000).
7. Id. § 304(1).
8. Id. § 304(1).
9. 15 C.F.R. §§ 923.31(a), (a)(8), (b) (2009).
10. Id. §§ 923.11(b), (c); CZMA, § 306(d)(2), 16 U.S.C. §1455 (2000).
11. HAW. REV. STAT. § 205A-1 (1993).
12. State of Hawai'i, *State of Hawaii Coastal Zone Management and Final Environmental Impact Statement.*
13. HAW. REV. STAT. § 205A-2(b) (1993).
14. Id. § 205A-2(c)(3).
15. 15 C.F.R. § 923.21(b) (2009).
16. Id. §§ 923.24, .25.
17. HAW. REV. STAT. § 205A-1 (1993).
18. Id. § 205A-21.
19. Id. §§ 205A-23(a), (b). The county permit granting authority for Kaua'i, Maui, and Hawai'i is their respective planning commission. The county permit granting authority for the City and County of Honolulu is the City Council.
20. See *Just v. Marinette County*, 201 N.W.2d 761 (Wis. 1972) (upholding Wisconsin's shoreland protection, zoning); *Candlestick Properties v. San Francisco BCDC*, 89 Cal. Rptr. 897 (1970) (upholding California's Bay Area Conservation and Development Commission); *In the Matter of Stoeco Dev., Ltd.*, 621 A.2d 29 (N.J. Super.

1993) (holding that even though defendant had exemption from requirements for Coastal Area Facility Review Act, this did not automatically qualify it for a Section 404 permit, as the state's Coastal Zone Management Program covered much broader environmental policies beyond those addressed in the CAFRA); *Morgan v. Planning Dep't, County of Kauai*, 104 Haw. 173, 86 P.3d 982 (2004) (holding that the Planning Department has the authority to modify an existing SMA permit in order to give effect to the policies and objectives of the Coastal Zone Management Act); *California v. Norton*, 150 F. Supp. 2d 1046 (N.D. Cal. 2001) (holding that in order for the mining service to extend a mining lease, due to potentially significant environmental concerns the mining service cannot merely rely on categorical exclusions but must submit a reasoned explanation for its reliance); *United States v. Irizarry*, 98 F. Supp. 2d 160 (D.P.R. 2000) (holding that even though defendant's house enjoyed a "grandfather" exception to Puerto Rico's Coastal Zone Management Plan, upon expansive renovation it became necessary to obtain the necessary CZM certification); *DuRant v. S.C. Dep't of Health and Envtl. Control*, 604 S.E.2d 704 (S.C. 2004) (upholding department's denial of defendant's dock permit because it extended into a Geographical Area of Particular Concern under the CZMA and was therefore entitled to heightened protection). See also cases collected in Fred P. Bosselman, David L. Callies, and John Banta, *The Taking Issue: An Analysis of the Constitutional Limits of Land Use Control*, Prepared for the Council on Environmental Quality, Washington, D.C.: U.S. Government Printing Office, 1973 at ch. 1–4, 9–11.

21. CZMA, §§ 306(d)(2)(D), 306(d)(7), 306(d)(10), 16 U.S.C §§ 1455(d)(2)(D), (d)(7), (d)(10) (2008). The secretary acts upon recommendation of the administrator of the National Oceanic and Atmospheric Administration, which is responsible to the secretary for CZMA programs and policy.

22. Id. §306(d)(11).

23. The 1979 Code of Federal Regulations contained a comment describing the concept of networking: "Networking in this context is the coordination of state and local land and water use regulatory programs with a primary state coastal zone regulatory statute, so that a comprehensive scheme emerges for the planning and regulation of such areas in the coastal zone." 15 C.F.R. § 923.43(b)(2) (Comment 1979). However, all comments were dropped from this section in the 1980 publication.

24. Id. § 923.43(c).

25. State of Hawai'i, Governor's Administrative Directive No. 78-3 (1978).

26. HAW. REV. STAT. §§ 205A-4(b), -3(8), -6(a), -6(c) (1993).

27. State of Hawai'i, "Inventory of existing control mechanisms related to coastal zone management," *Hawaii Coastal Zone Management Program Document Six: Legal Aspects of Hawaii's Coastal Zone Management Program* 2 (1976); State of Hawai'i, *State of Hawaii Coastal Zone Management Program and Final Environmental Impact Statement*, 86–92.

28. HAW. REV. STAT. §§ 205A-21 through -30 (1993 and Supp 2007).

29. *See* State of Hawai'i, *Hawaii Coastal Zone Management Program Document Six: Legal Aspects of Hawaii's Coastal Zone Management Program*; State of Hawai'i, *State of Hawaii Coastal Zone Management Program and Final Environmental Impact Statement*.

30. Fred P. Bosselman, Duane A. Feuer, and Charles L. Siemon, *The Permit Explosion*, Washington, D.C.: Urban Land Institute, 1976. "Permit explosion" refers

to the proliferation of land development permits required by increased state and federal land regulatory activities during the 1970s.

31. HAW. REV. STAT. § 205A-28 (1993).
32. Id. § 205A-22; see *Leslie v. Board of Appeals of County of Hawaii*, 109 Haw. 385, 126 P.3d 1071 (Haw. 2006) for Hawai'i court interpretation of this requirement.
33. Id.
34. Id.
35. Id. §205A-26.
36. County of Kaua'i, *Special Management Area Rules and Regulations*; County of Maui, *Special Management Area Procedures*, subchapter 2; County of Hawai'i, *Rules and Regulations Relating to Environmental Shoreline Protection*, Rules and Protection 9; HONOLULU, HAW., REV. ORDINANCES § 25.
37. HONOLULU, HAW., REV. ORDINANCES § 25-1.3 (1983 and Supp. 1987).
38. Id. § 25-5.5.
39. Id. § 25-3.3(c)(1).
40. Id. § 25-3.3(c)(2).
41. County of Maui, *Planning Commission Rules*, art. II, § 12-200 et seq. (2004).
42. Id. §§ 12-202-14, -15.
43. *GATRI v. Blane*, 88 Haw. 108, 962 P.2d 367 (1988).
44. Maui, *Planning Commission Rules*, art. II, § 12-202-15(g).
45. *GATRI v. Blane*, 88 Haw. 108, 962 P.2d 367. The Court later expanded this consistency requirement to all local land use regulations, whether or not in the coastal zone. *Save Sunset Beach Coal. v. City & County of Honolulu*, 102 Haw. 465, 78 P.3d 1 (2003).
46. County of Maui, *Planning Commission Rules*, art. II, § 12-202-22 (2004).
47. Hawai'i 312 Evaluation Response (1980), at I-A.
48. County of Kaua'i, *Planning Commission Rules*, §§ 1.4-A, 1.4-C, 1.4-I, 5.0, 8-10 (1984).
49. *Mahuiki v. Planning Comm'n of Kauai*, 65 Haw. 506, 654 P.2d 874 (1982).
50. County of Kaua'i, *Planning Commission Rules*, § 18 (1984).
51. County of Hawai'i, *Planning Commission Rules*, §§ 9-6, -7, -10, -11, -19 (updated Jan. 2006).
52. Id. § 9-21.
53. HAW REV. STAT. § 195-1 (1993).
54. Id. § 195-5.
55. HAW. CODE R. § 13-209-4 (2007).
56. Id. § 13-209-3.
57. HAW. REV. STAT. § 190-1 (1993).
58. Id. at ch. 190.
59. HAW. CODE R. § 13-36-2 (1988).
60. CZMA, § 315, 16 U.S.C. § 1461 (2000).
61. "Ocean and coastal resource management," 61 Fed. Reg. 32774 (June 25, 1996).
62. HAW. REV. STAT. § 205A-41 through -49 (1993).
63. *Brescia v. N. Shore Ohana*, 115 Haw. 477, 168 P.3d 929 (2007).
64. Id. at 494, 168 P.3d at 946.
65. HAW. REV. STAT. ch. 206E (1993).

66. CZMA, §306(d)(8), 16 U.S.C. § 1455(d)(8) (2000); 15 C.F.R. § 923.52 (2009).

67. In the March 28, 1979, *Federal Register,* publication of § 923.52 was accompanied by a table listing facilities that would trigger the "national interest" inquiry. These facilities included those connected with national defense and aerospace programs; with energy production and transmission; with recreation, including national seashores, parks, and forests; and with transportation, including interstate highways, railroads, airports, and so forth. "National Oceanic and Atmospheric Administration," 44 Fed. Reg. 18608 (Mar. 28, 1979). The agencies listed as requiring consultation before a state could plan any such "extra-local" facilities included the Department of Defense and NASA; the Departments of Energy and the Interior; the National Oceanic and Atmospheric Administration; the Federal Energy Regulatory Commission and Nuclear Regulatory Commission; the Departments of Agriculture and Housing and Urban Development; the Departments of Transportation and Commerce; and the Corps of Engineers. This table appeared for only one year and was absent from the 1980 edition of the Code of Federal Regulations.

68. State of Hawai'i, *State of Hawaii Coastal Zone Management and Final Environmental Impact Statement,* 129.

69. 15 C.F.R. § 923.56(b) (2009).

70. 15 C.F.R. §§ 923.57(b)(1), .57(b)(3) (2009).

71. State of Hawai'i, *State of Hawaii Coastal Zone Management and Final Environmental Impact Statement,* 139–140.

72. Id. at 80.

73. 16 U.S.C. § 1458 (2000).

74. *See also* Kem G. Lowry, "Policy-relevant assessment of coastal zone management programs," 7 COASTAL ZONE MGMT. J. 2 (1980).

75. CZMA, §§ 307(c) and 307(d), 16 U.S.C. §§ 1456(c), (d) (2000 and Supp. 2005).

76. *See Kleppe v. New Mexico,* 426 U.S. 529 (1976); *Ventura County v. Gulf Oil Corp.,* 601 F.2d 1080 (9th Cir. 1979).

77. CZMA, §§ 307(c), (d), 16 U.S.C. §§ 1456(c), (d). (2000 and Supp. 2005).

78. HAW. REV. STAT. § 205A-3(3) (1993).

79. State of Hawai'i, *State of Hawaii Coastal Zone Management and Final Environmental Impact Statement,* 128.

80. 15 C.F.R. § 930.31(a) (2009).

81. Id. § 930.31(b).

82. Id. § 930.33(a)(1).

83. Id. § 930.33(b), (c).

84. Id. §§ 930.32, .39(a), .39(b).

85. *See* id. § 930.39(c).

86. *See Hawaii Coastal Zone News* 5 (1981): 3 and 7. Sea Grant Marine Advisory Program, University of Hawai'i.

87. CZMA, § 307(c)(3)(A), 16 U.S.C. § 1456 (c)(3)(A) (2000).

88. 15 C.F.R. § 930.51(a) (2009).

89. Id. § 930.52.

90. Id. §§ 930.11(d), .53(b). States were also urged by the regulations to monitor unlisted license and permit activities as well; *see* id. §§ 930.54(a), .57(a), .64, .65, .120; CZMA, § 307(c)(3)(A), 16 U.S.C. § 1456(c)(3)(A) (2000).

91. Outer Continental Shelf Lands Act, 43 U.S.C. § 1331 et seq. (2007).

92. CZMA, § 307(c)(3)(A), 16 U.S.C. § 1456(c)(3)(A) (2000).

93. 15 C.F.R. § 930.71 (2009).

94. For example, *see Am. Petroleum Inst. v. Knecht*, 609 F.2d 1306 (9th Cir. 1979).

95. *Sec'y of the Interior v. California*, 464 U.S. 312 (1984).

96. 16 U.S.C. § 1456 (2008).

97. *Cal. Coastal Comm'n v. Granite Rock Co.*, 480 U.S. 572 (1987).

98. Id. at 581–582.

99. Id. at 593.

100. Id. at 583.

101. Id. at 587.

102. Id. at 591.

103. Id. at 592.

104. CZMA, § 307(d), 16 U.S.C. § 1456(d) (2000 and Supp. 2005).

105. 15 C.F.R. §§ 930.91(a), .95, .97, .99, .116, .120 (2009).

106. *See* G. Kem Lowry Jr. and Norman H. Okamura, "Evaluation and inter-governmental relations in CZM: The case of coastal zone management," 13 PUBLIUS 4 (1983).

107. *Texas Landowners Rights Ass'n v. Harris*, 453 F. Supp. 1025 (D.D.C. 1978), *aff'd mem.*, 598 F.2d 311 (D.C. Cir. 1979), *cert. denied*, 444 U.S. 927 (1979).

Chapter 7

Floodplains and FEMA

Disaster protection as a policy goal sounds unassailable. In practice, it is a barely mitigated catastrophe. This is in part due to the tendency to build houses in floodplains and coastal hazard areas, despite the virtually certain knowledge that a flood will one day destroy whatever is built there. Living in flood-prone areas, whether riverine or coastal, will eventually be costly, if not disastrous. In August 2005, Hurricane Katrina ravaged the Gulf Coast region of the United States, causing over $80 billion in damages and over 1,300 direct fatalities.[1] Less cataclysmic but no less devastating, Tropical Storm Ike swept through southeastern Texas, causing severe damage, injuries, and deaths in Galveston and Houston.[2] After the storm, however, citizens and officials of the devastated areas commenced rebuilding on the same land.[3]

In Hawai'i, the flood hazard is both riverine and coastal. Heavy rainfall causes riverine flooding, resulting in the temporary rise of the water level of streams and other natural watercourses. When the carrying capacity of watercourses is exceeded, the adjacent lands, or the floodplain, are inundated. One example of riverine flooding is the Halloween Eve 2004 flood in Mānoa Valley on the island of O'ahu. On Saturday, October 30, nine inches of rain fell in Mānoa Valley within a six-hour period. The storm washed trees and debris into Mānoa Stream, forming a dam. A four-foot-high wall of water flowed down the valley, through the Institute for Astronomy, several schools, and eventually made its way to the University of Hawai'i at Mānoa, "damaging 200 homes and businesses and causing an estimated $80 million in damage to the University and to the Mānoa community."[4]

In contrast, coastal flooding occurs when unusual surf conditions or tsunamis generate waves that inundate shoreline areas. Damage from tsunamis is due not only to flooding but also results from the velocity of onrushing water. Tsunamis also cause extensive beach and shoreline erosion. There is no more graphic an example of the destructive power of a tsunami than the December 2004 tsunami that struck Southeast Asia. An earthquake with a magnitude of 9.15 on the Richter scale generated a wave that killed some 150,000 people[5] and displaced at least another 500,000.[6] Hawai'i experienced a major tsunami in 1960. That tsunami, which reached a height of thirty-five feet, killed sixty-one people and caused an estimated $155 million (in present value) of damage to the Hilo community.[7]

The U.S. mainland shares many characteristics with coastal areas of Hawai'i in terms of coastal flooding. Likewise, the disastrous 2004 stream overflow floods on the island of O'ahu near Mānoa were similar to riverine floods that occur on the mainland. Relatively speaking, however, coastal flooding has more potential for damage in Hawai'i because of the intense development of Hawai'i's coastal zone.

The floodplain is the land area on either side of a river that is likely to be inundated in the event of a hundred-year flood, so named because of the 1 percent statistical likelihood of its occurring in any one year or, conversely, the likelihood of its occurring but once every hundred years.[8] However, such floods have occurred with alarming frequency on the U.S. mainland in the past two decades.[9] The floodway is that portion of the floodplain adjacent to and including the river channel that is expected to carry the greatest volume and flow (velocity) of floodwaters, including those of lesser frequency than a hundred-year flood.[10] Common sense dictates that no structures should be built in the latter and as few as possible in the former, not only to decrease the likelihood of personal and property injury, but also to preserve the capacity of the floodway to carry water and the floodplain to absorb it. Development in either simply causes more water to flow both laterally and downstream, thus enlarging the area of both floodplain and floodway and increasing the velocity of floodwaters and the likelihood of both downstream and upstream damage to any structures.[11]

This brief sketch of the hazards of flooding may help to explain and justify, in legal terms, floodplain zoning: the exercise of police power to prevent damage to life and property from floodwaters. Indeed, many courts have precious little difficulty in sustaining local regulation of both coastal and riverine flood-prone lands in principle, although other courts have held that if the prohibition of use goes too far, a "taking" of property results for which compensation is due.[12] This is particularly true when the protective rationale appears to be tainted by other public purposes such as the need for open space or the preservation of views.[13]

Nevertheless, the theoretical public purpose behind the local regulation of flood-prone lands—the protection of life and property—is well established. This is particularly critical because the Flood Disaster Protection Act (FDPA) and its predecessors require nothing unless and until a community chooses to become part of a federal program, which it does largely because of various financial inducements.[14] Thus, the issue of federal power to enact floodplain/flood disaster protection laws never arises; it is always the local ordinance that does the regulating. One of the key issues in discussing the regulatory aspects of the federal flood laws is thus local court attitude toward floodplain zoning. In Hawai'i, this issue has yet to be decided by the state's highest court.

The Flood Disaster Protection Act

The federal government has been in the flood control business for over three-quarters of a century since the Mississippi River Valley flooded in 1927.[15] Acknowledging "the considerable risk to life and property arising out of the continued development of the floodplain," Congress enacted the Omnibus Flood Control Act of 1936.[16] Essentially, federal flood control programs have approached flood hazard by (1) attempting to control floods by various preventive measures—dams, levees, reservoirs, as in New Orleans, with obviously limited results—and (2) regulating the use of land within the floodplain. It was the insurance aspect of flood hazard mitigation that involved the government in flood control through the promulgation of land use regulations. As a condition of providing flood hazard insurance—in order to minimize the extent of claims thereon—early programs directed first that the state or local government with jurisdiction over an insurance applicant's property must first adopt floodplain zoning restrictions sufficient to reduce flood damages, and second that the property proposed to be insured had not been declared by an appropriate public body to be in violation of those floodplain zoning laws.

For a variety of reasons—including lack of congressional funding—the first attempt to promote floodplain regulation at the state and local level failed.[17] Nevertheless, the insurance aspect of flood hazard mitigation became firmly engrafted onto the federal flood hazard program.

Hurricane Betsy gave it considerable impetus in 1965. Betsy, destroyed 1,500 homes, damaged 150,000, damaged or destroyed 1,400 farms and small businesses, and adversely affected close to a million people in Florida, Louisiana, and Mississippi.[18] As a result, the federal government developed the first comprehensive disaster protection act: the National Flood Insurance Act of 1968 (FIA).[19]

FIA set out clearly the dichotomy between individual and community participation in a federally sponsored flood hazard mitigation disaster relief program. Under the terms of the act, eligibility for federally backed private flood insurance for primarily residential properties depended upon state and local community participation in the program. A condition for participation for the community was the formal adoption of a land management system based upon permanent land use controls, such as zoning, subdivision, a hazard mitigation plan, building requirements, flood control projects, floodproofing of buildings, flood warning systems, and emergency preparedness plans.[20] A condition of eligibility for private individuals was compliance with these state or local controls. No federally subsidized insurance—and therefore usually no flood hazard insurance—was available in areas in which the state and local government chose not to participate. There was nothing the private individual could do to become eligible. Nor was there any sanction against nonparticipation by state and local government beyond the penalty that ultimately fell on the private landowner—no subsidized flood insurance. The number of policies in force in the United States has increased from about 95,000 before the Flood Disaster Protection Act of 1973 to 2.2 million in 1989 and to over 4.3 million in 2002.[21]

When flood insurance first became available under the National Flood Insurance Act of 1968, the City and County of Honolulu and the Hilo area of the County of Hawai'i were among the first communities in the nation to become eligible.[22] Under the program, it is the local governmental units, not the states, that are the primary implementing agencies. The role of the states is limited to assisting and coordinating local government efforts.[23] The State of Hawai'i specifically authorized the mayor or executive officer and the councils of its four counties to participate in and to pass the flood zoning ordinances required by the program. The State Department of Land and Natural Resources (DLNR) was designated to coordinate the program.[24]

A major defect of the FIA was its failure to "equate federal assistance with the purchase of flood insurance."[25] As a result, Congress enacted the FDPA of 1973 (as amended) with the purpose of discouraging the building of structures on floodplains as well as providing relief to victims of floods.[26] It is supposed to do this by making available federally subsidized insurance to those who have suffered flood damage on the condition that the local government in whose jurisdiction they reside passes certain restrictive land development and flood-proofing regulations. It increased considerably the penalty that flood-prone communities—and their residents—would suffer for choosing not to participate in the program and its accompanying land use and flood-proofing regulations. Collectively, the National Flood Insurance Act and the Flood Disaster Protection Act are known as the National Flood Insurance Program (NFIP).

A principal sanction against communities that opt not to participate in NFIP is that no federal aid is available for the building of structures in flood hazard areas subject to the jurisdiction of nonparticipating local governments. This includes urban renewal aid, Clean Water Act assistance, wastewater treatment grants, and a host of other federal aid programs.[27] Individuals in nonparticipating communities are not eligible for federal disaster assistance of any kind. Individuals living in flood-prone areas in participating communities that fail to obtain flood insurance are not only excluded from receiving federal disaster aid, but they are also ineligible for mortgage loans from any federally insured lending institution. The latter can be very effective, since federally insured lending institutions control more than 80 percent of the available funds for residential purchase-money mortgages.[28]

The Sequence of Federal Actions under the NFIP

The number of communities having flood-proofed and regulated flood hazard areas as a result of participation in NFIP was at first fairly small. This was so because of the relatively onerous and time-consuming tasks that NFIP imposes on the federal government before it can make flood-proofing and development regulation demands of participating communities. Basically, these tasks are to identify the flood-prone areas of a community and to determine flood elevations so as to ascertain the level at which habitable dwellings must be constructed in these areas. These tasks are carried out by the Federal Insurance and Mitigation Administration (FIMA), which is a part of the Federal Emergency Management Agency (FEMA).

First, FIMA prepares maps for the community showing the general flood hazard areas, beginning with a Flood Hazard Boundary Map (FHBM), defined as "an official map of a community issued by the

Federal Insurance Administrator, where the boundaries of the flood, mudslide (i.e., mudflow) related erosion areas having special hazards have been designated as Zone A, M, and/or E."[29] Zone A is the area of special flood hazard in the community in which land in the floodplain is subject to a 1 percent or greater chance of flooding in any given year. Zone M is the area of special mudslide hazard in the community in which land is most likely to be subject to severe mudslides. Zone E is the area of special flood-related erosion hazard in the community in which land is most likely to be subject to severe flood-related erosion losses.

After issuing the FHBM, the administrator must then notify the chief executive officer of the relevant community of any flood hazards identified by the FHBM.[30] At this point, the community must either (1) promptly apply to participate in the program or (2) within twelve months submit technical data to show that the community is not flood prone.[31] In order to qualify for federally subsidized flood insurance, a community must adopt and enforce floodplain management regulations addressing the flood hazards within its jurisdiction.[32]

In practice, when a disaster occurs, FEMA will "coordinate federal assistance efforts and designate specific areas eligible for such assistance."[33] An example of FEMA in action occurred during the February and March 2006 flooding on O'ahu and Kaua'i. During this period, the state experienced heavy rainfall that resulted in severe flooding, landslides, mudslides, and the failure of the Kaloko Reservoir dam on Kaua'i, resulting in the deaths of seven people. Damage from the flooding was estimated at $50 million. President Bush declared a major disaster, which qualified the Islands for federal disaster relief. The governor's office stated that the U.S. Department of Agriculture, Small Business Administration, and FEMA would make an announcement on how residents could apply for disaster assistance.[34] Furthermore, a federal disaster assistance coordinating officer was appointed to meet with the state vice director of Civil Defense.[35]

If the community fails to become a participant in the program within one year of notification and fails to show it is not flood prone, it is subject to the sanctions imposed on nonparticipating communities. FIMA can suspend communities from the program for failure to adopt (once the community is notified of being flood prone) or to maintain a floodplain management ordinance that meets or exceeds the minimum requirements of the NFIP.[36] Since 1968, just over 2,300 communities have been suspended for failure to adopt a floodplain management ordinance.[37]

If the community decides to participate in the program, it must satisfy certain eligibility requirements discussed later in this chapter. It will then be allowed to enter the "emergency" phase of the program. Under this phase, the community is eligible for lower level "first layer" insurance at subsidized rates,[38] but it must utilize data from any federal, state, or other source to establish minimum land use and construction standards in flood-prone areas.[39] At this stage of the program, the local government must require permits for all proposed development; it must review permits for a determination of reasonable safety from flooding and for compliance with federal and state laws; and it must enforce certain design, construction, and placement standards for all new construction and for substantial improvements.[40]

Communities are not eligible to enter the regular phase of the program until they adopt and approve strict floodplain regulation. Maximum insurance coverage is available to homeowners in communities participating under the regular phase of the program. The City and County of Honolulu and the County of Hawaiʻi entered the emergency phase of the NFIP and became eligible to provide subsidized flood insurance on June 5, 1970, when preliminary FHBMs were issued. The Hilo area became eligible under the regular phase of the program on June 4, 1971. Other areas of the county have been participating in the emergency portion of the program since March 5, 1971. Maui County entered the emergency phase and became eligible to provide subsidized flood insurance on September 18, 1970. Its preliminary FHBM was not issued until December 6, 1977. The County of Kauaʻi entered the emergency phase of the program and became eligible to provide subsidized flood insurance on April 2, 1971. Its FHBM was issued on December 20, 1974.[41]

After filing a detailed environmental impact statement, the administrator must next publish the more detailed Flood Insurance Rate Map (FIRM), which is established by a community's Flood Insurance Study (FIS). The FIRM sets out for each area identified as flood prone (by the FHBM) a refined identification of special flood hazard and flood elevation areas.[42] It is "an official map of a community, on which the Federal Insurance Administrator has delineated both the special hazard areas and the risk premium zones applicable to the community."[43] The FIRM is prepared after an FIS for the community has been completed and general risk insurance premium rates have been established.[44] The risk premium zones are considerable both in number and detail.[45]

FIMA determines the 1 percent annual-chance flood, shown on the

FIRMs as A Zones or V Zones, from information obtained through consultation with the community, floodplain topographic surveys, detailed
hydrologic and hydraulic analyses, and historic records. FIMA uses commonly accepted computer models and engineering methods that estimate hydrologic and hydraulic conditions to determine the 1 percent
annual-chance flood, to determine flood elevations, and to designate
flood-risk zones.[46] These flood elevations are shown on the FIRM and
are the minimum building levels for new construction.[47]

Concerned that FIMA was not adequately considering local community views, Congress added a consultation and appeal procedure for
flood elevation determinations as part of the NFIP. Whenever FIMA
determines or modifies flood elevations, it is required to inform the
community of the nature and purposes of the study, the areas involved,
the manner in which the study is to be undertaken, the general principles and methods employed, and the use to be made of the data
obtained.[48]

There follows a host of publication, notice, and hearing requirements, the upshot of which is that until the process is completed and
FIMA makes a proposed final determination of flood elevations and
so notifies the community, the community remains eligible under the
emergency phase for federally subsidized flood insurance (and, therefore, the land use impacts of the program may be minimal). Moreover,
the determination of elevations also signals the earliest date from which
a participating community can be required to adopt local land use control measures.

Honolulu received its detailed FIRM from the FIMA on March 3,
1980, and it took effect on September 3, 1980. There has been considerable activity statewide under the NFIP because FIRMs have been
approved in all areas of the state. This means that detailed flood hazard
regulations must be enacted in all counties.[49] Some already have been,
as discussed below.

Land Use Controls

Assuming a local community desires to participate in the NFIP—in
order for its citizens to permanently receive maximum subsidized flood
insurance and for the community to become eligible for other federal
programs—it must meet a number of eligibility requirements.[50] Many of
these are largely administrative, directing the community to outline the
manner in which it is (or is proposed to be) complying with the land use

control and flood protection requirements described below. These are the heart of the land use control aspects of the NFIP, for they virtually dictate what kinds of regulatory programs must be locally enacted once FIMA has issued FHBMs and FIRMs as described above.

The NFIP provides that flood insurance may not be sold or renewed under the program in a community unless the community has adopted adequate floodplain management regulations consistent with federal criteria.[51] Such regulations must be enforceable, applied uniformly throughout the community to all privately and publicly owned land within flood-prone, mudslide, or flood-related erosion areas and must take precedence over any less restrictive conflicting local laws, ordinances, or codes. The type of land use regulations required depends on the amount of the information that FIMA has provided to the community.[52] A community is considered to be participating as soon as it has begun the emergency phase.

A participating community's land use regulation obligations start when the community has identified a floodway or coastal high-hazard area within its boundaries in an application to participate in NFIP, even though the FIMA has provided no information—certainly no FHBM— whatsoever on flood data at that point. The community's land use obligations are thus negligible, amounting to little more than requiring permits for developments and identifying those developments that will be newly constructed or substantially improved in flood-prone areas and seeing that they are constructed in a reasonable flood-proof manner.[53]

Upon FIMA's publication of a participating community's FHBM but before identification of either water surface elevation or floodway/coastal high-hazard area, the level of required regulation increases modestly. Large subdivisions must provide the community with flood elevation data, and the community must seek out and use whatever other flood elevation data is available. Utilizing that flood elevation data, the community must require all new residential constructions to have the lowest floor (including basement) elevated to or above the base flood level and all new nonresidential structures to be either so raised or flood-proofed. The community must also assure that the flood carrying capacity of any related or relocated portion of any watercourse is maintained.[54]

When FIMA locates final base flood elevations in certain zones on a participating community's FIRM, the land use requirements become more complicated, even though FIMA has not yet identified either a regulatory floodway or coastal high-hazard area. The zones in which flood-proofing or construction above base flood levels must be required (unless exceptions or variances are granted) are expanded. Moreover, until the regulatory floodway is defined, no new construction, substantial improvements, or other developments are to be permitted within certain zones unless it can be demonstrated that the cumulative effect thereof, when combined with all other existing and anticipated development, will not increase the water surface elevation of the base flood more than one foot at any point within the community.[55]

Once FIMA has provided additional flood elevation data on a participating community's FIRM, including data from which the community "shall" designate its regulatory floodway, the community must "select and adopt" such a floodway and prohibit encroachments (including fill) that would result in any increase in flood levels in the community during a flood.[56] Finally, when FIMA has provided similar flood elevation data to coastal participating communities (such as Hawai'i) and has identified in their FIRMs a coastal high-hazard area, the community must see that all new construction within that zone is located landward of the reach of the mean high tide and is elevated so the lowest floor is above the flood level and the lower levels of buildings have breakaway walls.[57]

As NFIP reached its twenty-fifth anniversary, Congress realized that the program had failed to achieve its original goals of providing affordable flood insurance to property owners and encouraging state and local governments to make land use adjustments to minimize damage caused by flood losses.[58] In response, Congress enacted reforms to NFIP that sought to increase compliance with insurance purchase requirements by lenders and secondary market purchasers, reduce the number of properties in the program that do not comply with flood protection standards, strengthen the Community Rating System (CRS) program that provides incentives in the form of reduced premiums to communities that voluntarily adopted and enforced stricter measures to reduce the risk of flood damage, and provide grants to states and communities that engage in activities mitigating the risk of flooding.[59]

In response to long-standing criticism of NFIP,[60] the legislation also authorized studies of possible future reforms.[61] The most important of these are several related studies that respond to criticism that insurance rates for coastal properties are based solely on the risk posed by flooding and do not reflect the significant risks represented by the effects of erosion. As a result, the argument is that owners of coastal properties pay flood insurance premiums that do not reflect the true scope of the risk of damage to their properties.[62]

1994 Amendments

The 1994 amendments to NFIP provide for a voluntary community rating system program to provide incentives in the form of credits on premium rates for flood insurance for measures that reduce the risk of flood or erosion damage.[63] Such credits are available for flood insurance coverage in communities the director of FEMA determines have adopted and enforced measures that reduce the risk of flooding and erosion damage exceeding specified criteria.[64] In addition, the 1994 amendments to the NFIP created the Mitigation Assistance Program.[65] This program provides grants to states and communities for planning and carrying out activities designed to reduce the risk of flood damage to structures covered by flood insurance under the NFIP.[66] To be eligible for financial assistance under this program, a state or community must develop a flood risk mitigation plan to be approved by the director of FEMA.[67]

The 1994 amendments also made several changes in the insurance purchase requirements in an effort to increase compliance by lenders and secondary market purchasers.[68] The 1994 act requires federal agencies regulating financial institutions[69] to issue "any regulations necessary" to direct lending institutions to meet the requirement that they not make, increase, extend, or renew any loan secured by improved real estate or a mobile home located in an identified flood hazard area in which flood insurance was available, unless the building or mobile home and any personal property securing the loan was covered for the term of the loan by flood insurance in an amount at least equal to the lesser of the outstanding principal balance of the loan or the maximum limit of coverage available under the act with respect to the particular type of property.[70]

The act also addresses the problem caused by borrowers who, having experienced an insured flood loss and not expecting another flood, cease payment of their insurance flood premiums during the term of their loan. The act now requires that financial institutions that put aside taxes, insurance premiums, or any other fees or charges for applicable noncommercial loans do the same for all premiums and fees for flood insurance.[71]

Other provisions of the 1994 act imposing new obligations on lenders include the following: (1) increasing the requirement that lenders and servicers that determine that a building or mobile home and any personal property securing an applicable loan is not covered by flood insurance—or is covered in an inadequate amount—must purchase flood insurance on behalf of a borrower and may charge the borrower for the cost of premiums and fees incurred when a borrower fails to purchase such flood insurance within forty-five days of being notified of the lack or inadequacy of such flood insurance;[72] (2) obligating federal agencies to publish regulations requiring financial institutions to notify FEMA of the servicer of any loan covered by flood insurance and also requiring them to notify FEMA of any change in the servicer of any loan covered by flood insurance no later than sixty days after the effective date of the change;[73] and (3) subjecting financial institutions to civil penalties if found to have a pattern or practice of committing violations of the insurance requirements, escrow provisions, flood insurance notice requirements, or the "forced placing" of flood insurance provisions.[74] The penalties may increase to $350 for each violation, up to an aggregate of $100,000 in a single calendar year.[75] Despite the importance of the 1994 amendments to NFIP, however, the core of the program itself has basically not changed since the 1970s.

Hawai'i Participation in the Flood Insurance Program

Since Honolulu's FIRM includes base flood elevations, floodways, and coastal high-hazard areas, the city was required to adopt the strictest federal land use requirements by the effective date of the FIRM in order to comply with the program. On August 20, 1980, the mayor approved amendments to the Comprehensive Zoning Code (CZC), Building Code, Electrical Code, and Plumbing Code to satisfy federal requirements.[76] FIMA reviewed these amendments and stated that they meet the federal land use requirements of the program.[77]

The former flood districts section of the CZC was amended in its entirety and replaced by a new ordinance in 1999, which takes precedence over any less restrictive or conflicting law or regulation of the city.[78] The flood hazard districts ordinance establishes four districts: floodway, flood fringe, coastal high hazard, and general floodplain. The flood hazard districts cover all areas so designated on the FHBMs and FIRMs prepared by FIMA.[79] They are overlay districts, and all land uses within these districts must comply with their regulations as well as with the applicable restrictions of the underlying zoning district. The new ordinance then sets out permitted uses and provides general construction standards for each district. It also contains sections dealing with variances, exemptions, and nonconforming uses, all as required by the federal program. The director of the Department of Planning and Permitting (DPP), with the assistance of the chief engineer of the Department of Public Works and the building superintendent, is responsible for the ordinance's administration.

The ordinance begins by setting forth a series of broad and general construction, water, and drainage standards applicable to developments in all four districts. Individual standards for each district follow, with the degree of restriction dependent upon the likelihood of and proximity to a flooded area. Since it comprises the areas required to carry or discharge the flood without increasing the flood elevation of the floodplain more than one foot at any point, the floodway district is the most heavily restricted district. Only a few uses having low flood damage potential, such as agricultural uses and drainage improvements, are permitted, and then only if they do not adversely affect the carrying capacity of the floodway.[80] The flood fringe district, the portion of the floodplain outside the floodway, is considerably more permissive. Uses otherwise allowable in the underlying zoning district are permitted, provided that the lowest habitable floor is elevated to the regulatory flood level (the hundred-year flood) as shown on the FIRM.[81] The restrictions in the coastal high hazard district, the area subject to high-velocity waters including tsunamis, are similar to those in the flood fringe district.[82]

Finally, the regulations in the general floodplain district—consisting of the approximate floodplain area as delineated on the flood maps where detailed engineering studies have not been conducted to designate flood fringe and floodway areas—subject all developments on a project-by-project basis to review/approval by the DPP director to determine if the proposed development is within a flood fringe or floodway.[83] This is to accommodate those areas where base flood elevations have not yet been determined by the federal government, making further mapping impossible. Until a floodway or flood fringe district is designated, no development is allowed if it increases the water surface elevation more than one foot at any point. Nearly identical provisions apply to proposed developments adjacent to a stream, river, or drainage facility outside one of the four zones.[84]

In the County of Hawai'i, flood hazard regulations are contained in Chapter 27 of the Hawai'i County Code. The Hawai'i County Code provides for floodplain regulation in five distinct areas based on the FIRM of the island. The floodway area is watercourse reserved to discharge the base flood without cumulatively increasing the water surface elevation more than one foot.[85] Development in this area is prohibited unless a registered professional engineer can certify that the encroachment will not cause any increase in the base flood elevation.[86] The flood fringe area is the area of a floodplain on either side of the designated floodway where encroachment may be permitted.[87] The coastal high hazard area, also known as the tsunami inundation area, is the special flood hazard area extending from offshore inland that is subject to high-velocity wave action from storms or seismic sources.[88] Any new construction or substantial improvements are required to follow a number of provisions, including using materials and utility equipment resistant to flood damage and using methods that minimize flood damage.[89] The next area is known as the general floodplain. These areas of special flood hazards have not been studied to determine the base flood elevation or to identify floodways. Any construction or improvement is subject to an application and review process conducted by the director of Public Works.[90] The final area is known as land adjacent to drainage facilities (in other words, a watercourse). Any new construction or substantial improvement is also subject to the review and approval of the director of Public Works.

As a condition of obtaining a building permit and an eventual certificate of occupancy in any special flood hazard area, a developer must follow three guidelines: First, a number of documents (such as the building plans, elevation certification, and flood-proofing certification) must be submitted to the director of Public Works. This is known as preconstruction certification.[91] Second, a set of standards must be followed during the construction phase. Examples of these standards include anchoring improvements to resist flotation, preventing the collapse or lateral movement of the structure, and using materials and equipment resistant to flood damage.[92] Finally, a postconstruction certification must be satisfied in order for the director to approve the certificate of occupancy.[93]

Maui received final notice of proposed base flood elevations on July 9, 1980, and then entered the regular phase of the NFIP.[94] The flood hazard regulation is found in Chapter 19.62 (Zoning) of the Maui County Code, which is entitled "Flood Hazard Areas.[95] It provides for the establishment of special flood hazard areas, uses within those areas, standards for development, the granting of variances, and the appeals process. The practical effect is the establishment of overlay zones in which uses are regulated in addition to the regulations in the county's comprehensive zoning ordinance. Any floodway district is adopted by ordinance and designated on the official zoning maps of the county. Prior to the mapping, the ordinance is effective only for those areas found by the director of Public Works and the County Council to be subject to recurrent flooding or tsunami inundation.

As might be anticipated, the floodway district is the most restrictive. No encroachment—including fill, new construction, substantial improvement, or other new development—is allowed within floodways without certification by a civil engineer and provided to the director of Public Works demonstrating that the encroachment will not result in any increases in base flood levels.[96] Uses are less restrictive in the coastal high hazard area, where as long as a number of requirements are followed, any new construction or substantial improvement will be allowed.[97] Some of these requirements include the prevention of flotation, collapse or lateral movement of the structure, locating the development on the "landward side of the reach of the mean high tide," and certification by an engineer that the construction abides by these requirements.[98] The final area, known as developments adjacent to drainage facilities, applies to developments encompassing or adjoining any stream, river, or drainage facilities and is subject to review by the director of Public Works. The director will grant such application only when the modification, construction, lining, or alteration does not reduce the capacity of the drainage facility, a river or stream, or adversely affect any downstream property.[99]

Kaua'i is also in the regular phase of the NFIP. As discussed in more detail in chapter 2, Kaua'i has enacted development restriction zones called constraint districts, which operate as overlay zones, as part of its Comprehensive Zoning Ordinance. The constraint districts are divided into six subdistricts: tsunami districts (S-TS), flood districts (S-FL), drainage districts (S-DR), soils districts (S-SO), slope districts (S-SL), and shore districts (S-SH). With the exception of the shore districts, all of the subdistricts regulate uses to prevent flood, tsunami, erosion, or mudslide damage and therefore are related to floodplain management. Only the first three, however, are directed toward the mitigation of flood hazards.

The purpose of the tsunami district is "to minimize the threat to the public health and safety, and damage to property due to extraordinary ocean wave action."[100] No zoning, building, or use permit can be issued for development of any portion of the tsunami district unless the applicant establishes conformity with certain requirements, including a prohibition against constructing schools, hospitals, and nursing homes.

In addition, the applicant must delineate the boundaries of the tsunami district as shown on the flood maps, designate the base flood elevations for the site, and follow additional construction and development standards relating to floodplain management.[101]

Flood districts are established in order "(1) to minimize the threat to public health and safety due to periodic inundation by storm water," and "(2) to maintain the characteristics of floodplain areas which contribute to ground water recharge, storm water storage, silt retention and marine water quality."[102] The flood district includes all lands subject to flooding and identified as flood fringe, floodway, and general flood plain areas by FIMA in its FIS engineering report.[103] Uses requiring the development, grading, or alteration of any portion of the flood district are permitted if the applicant satisfies such requirements as the filing of detailed development plans, an environmental impact statement, hydrologic and geologic reports (when required by the Department of Public Works or the planning director), and a series of flood and structural showings.[104]

Drainage districts are established for three purposes: "(1) to protect the function of natural and existing water courses as a part of the system for surface water collection and dispersal; (2) to maintain the quality of surface and marine water as a valuable public resource;" and "(3) to regulate the modification of water."[105] The drainage district includes all rivers, streams, storm water channels, and outfall areas indicated in the development restriction zones of the county general plan and in other areas of similar physical characteristics and conditions.[106]

Variances and Exemptions

As local zoning and subdivision controls are the primary method of enforcing NFIP land use requirements, the various techniques and tools of local zoning assume critical importance. Two of the mechanisms used to provide relief from general ordinance provisions in unusual cases are treated in the NFIP: variances and exceptions. Theoretically, the variance is granted in cases of unusual individual hardship and should represent the least tinkering as possible with the ordinance as applied, consonant with affording the applicant some relief.[107] An example is the varying of an eight-foot side yard requirement by a few inches to permit the construction of a house addition in a residential zone. In practice, however, local zoning boards have often converted the variance process into a mini-rezoning process, granting so-called use variances by which uses inconsistent with a zone classification are often permitted after an applicant has unsuccessfully sought to have the subject property reclassified from a zone prohibiting such use to one permitting it. In other words, the variance process became a zoning appeals process. Permitting such variances to flood hazard regulations would result in the undermining of the NFIP. Therefore, NFIP regulations permit the granting of variances only upon the showing of good and sufficient cause, a determination of exceptional hardship, and a finding that granting the variance "will not result in increased flood heights, additional threats to public safety, extraordinary public expense, create nuisances, cause fraud on or victimization of the public, or conflict with existing local laws or ordinances."[108]

In Honolulu, subject to the review and approval of the DPP director, the following may be permitted as a flood hazard variance: "new structures except in the Floodway District which are to be erected on a lot of one-half acre or less in area, contiguous to and surrounded by lots with existing structures below the regulatory flood elevation" and "uses, structures and standards in the Floodway District as permitted under the underlying zoning district, which do not result in any adverse increase in the regulatory flood elevation."[109]

The director must consider a series of factors in the grant or denial of the variance:

(a) The danger to life and property including surrounding properties due to increased flood elevations or velocities caused by the variance.

(b) The danger that materials may be swept on to other lands or downstream to the injury of others.

(c) The proposed water supply and sanitation systems and the ability of these systems to prevent disease, contamination, and unsanitary conditions.

(d) The susceptibility of the proposed facility and its contents to flood damage and the effect of such damage on the individual owners.

(e) The importance of the services provided by the proposed facility to the community.

(f) The availability of alternative locations not subject to flooding for the proposed use.

(g) The compatibility of the proposed use with existing development anticipated in the foreseeable future.

(h) The relationship of the proposed use to the floodplain management program for the area.

(i) The safety of access to the property in times of flood for ordinary and emergency vehicles.

(j) The expected elevations and velocity of the regulatory flood expected at the site due to the variance.

(k) The failure to grant the variance would result in exceptional hardship to the applicant.

(l) The variance will not result in adverse increase to the regulatory flood elevations, additional threat to surrounding properties and to public safety, extraordinary public expenses or conflict with other laws or regulations.[110]

The director may also attach conditions to the variance, should he choose to grant it. If a variance is granted, the applicant must agree to insert a covenant in deeds and other conveyancing documents filed with the Bureau of Conveyances, stating that the property is located in a flood area, is subject to flooding and flood damage, that increased flood insurance premiums will result from the variance, and that he will not sue the city for loss or damage as a result of being permitted to build.[111]

The granting of variances is reviewable by FIMA. If a pattern inconsistent with the objectives of sound floodplain management emerges, FIMA may suspend a community from the flood insurance program. However, applicable regulations specifically permit the reconstruction, rehabilitation, or restoration of structures listed on either the National Register of Historic Places or the Hawaiʻi Register of Historic Places.[112]

While a variance represents personal relief for an individual from a zoning regulation, an exception is a waiver from federal land use standards directed to a community that relieves it from the requirements of a rule, regulation, order, or other determination. FIMA permits certain exceptions from federal land use standards because of extraordinary circumstances and local conditions that make their application the cause of severe hardship and gross inequity for a particular community. A community seeking an exception must justify the request by showing supporting economic, environmental, topographic, hydrologic, and other scientific and technical data.[113] None of Hawaiʻi's four county ordinances allow for exceptions to flood hazard regulations.[114]

The Takings Clause and the National
Flood Insurance Program

Local floodplain regulations can severely restrict the use of private property.[115] Despite these limitations, flood hazard regulations are often upheld because courts recognize the need to protect the health and safety of the public,[116] and they realize that they serve a legitimate state interest in reducing flood hazards.[117] This suggests that a developer challenging a local floodplain regulation scheme would most likely fail.[118] Most courts have taken a favorable view of floodplain regulation under the takings clause. *Turnpike Realty Co. v. Town of Dedham* is a typical case.[119] The court upheld a floodplain ordinance that allowed only passive uses and prohibited any building or structure, even though these restrictions allegedly reduced the value of the subject property from $431,000 to $53,000. The court noted that floodplain regulation protects individuals who might choose to build there despite the flood danger, protects other landowners from floodplain development, and protects the "entire community from individual choices of land use which require subsequent public expenditures for public works and disaster relief." It held that these regulatory purposes satisfy the usual substantive due process tests. The court also held that the ordinance did not deprive the landowner of all of the use of its land because it allowed a number of passive uses. The court balanced the restrictions the ordinance imposed on the property "against the potential harm to the community from overdevelopment of a flood plain area." It applied standard regulatory taking law to hold that a taking had not occurred even though the ordinance substantially diminished the value of the property.[120]

A number of cases that have rejected regulatory taking objections to floodplain regulations emphasized the dangers that flooding creates.[121] In *Krahl v. Nine Mile Creek Watershed District*,[122] a landowner who was denied a permit to construct a building in a floodplain challenged the floodplain regulation as a regulatory taking.[123] The court observed and agreed with the watershed district that the proposed development would increase the likelihood of flooding downstream.[124] Moreover, the court stated that a number of nonstructural uses of the land were allowed.[125] In addition, restrictions on the land were not permanent and would be modified once permanent flood control facilities were constructed. The court cited *Penn Central Transportation Co. v. City of New York*[126] for the proposition that "this is not a case where a property owner is burdened with a restriction without receiving a reciprocal benefit in his favor."[127]

Lower courts have also upheld the NFIP. In *Texas Landowners Rights Ass'n. v Harris*,[128] the district court held that the National Flood Insurance Program did not constitute a taking of land without payment of just compensation as required by the Fifth and Fourteenth Amendments. The court utilized a balancing test of social policy and public interest versus the rights of a landowner to be unencumbered in the use of his property.[129] The scale tipped in favor of the public interest since the public safety, health, and general welfare favor the program.[130]

In *Adolph v. Federal Emergency Management Agency*,[131] the court held that when NFIP was operating precisely as intended by Congress, it resulted in no unconstitutional taking of property, regardless of state law, even if elevation requirements actually deprived the landowner of all use without compensation.[132] In any event, FEMA could not be charged with the unconstitutional taking of property, since it did not compel the state to participate in NFIP. The regulations were local, even if federal in nature.

Coordination with other Federal Programs

Pursuant to Executive Order 11988, all federal agencies are required to conduct their activities in a manner consistent with the objectives of NFIP.[133] The problem of coordination has been particularly acute with respect to the U.S. Department of Transportation's Federal Highway Administration, whose design standards and approved routes for federally funded highways often traverse or follow floodplains—which are flat and even-graded—for considerable distances. Indeed, some federal officials have wondered aloud whether they may not be promoting (if not requiring) some contradictory local activities. It would not be the first time.[134]

Conclusion

Hawai'i's four counties are full participants in the National Flood Insurance Program. The extent to which the various ordinance amendments, passed pursuant to federal guidelines and standards, will begin to affect development is therefore unclear—for the moment. Unfortunately—and obviously—the subsidizing of structures in a flood hazard zone by means of insuring against losses tends to encourage building in that zone, despite the onerous land use regulations the FDPA requires of local governments as a condition for insurance. Moreover, it has taken so long for the various government agencies to produce the maps and data and issue the regulations that are necessary before the flood-proofing and development regulations can be required that little has happened in the decade since FDPA was passed.

The extent to which the granting of exceptions and variances may tend to soften the effect of these ordinances also remains to be seen. Given Hawai'i's substantial coastal areas and the tendency so far to develop such areas, the coastal hazard program responses of the counties and their implementation will bear watching. Enforce they must, however. The federal government has taken an increasingly hard line with communities that have failed to enforce their floodplain regulations; it has sued several local governments in Louisiana to recover nearly $100 million in national flood insurance claims paid by the U.S. government for flood damage to structures either built in areas that should have been development free or built improperly in flood-prone areas, contrary to local regulations that the local governments allegedly failed to enforce.[135] If the United States is successful in persuading the federal court that the fault—and the liability—lies with local government for the flood damage because they failed to enforce their own ordinances, this will be a powerful incentive for stringent enforcement nationally.

Notes

1. U.S. Department of Congress, Service Assessment: Hurricane Katrina August 23–31, 2005 1 (2005), http://www.weather.gov/om/assessments/pdfs/Katrina.pdf (last visited Nov. 20, 2009).

2. James C. McKinley Jr., "Three weeks after storm, a grim task of recovery," N.Y. TIMES, Oct. 5, 2008, at A20.

3. See, e.g., "New Orleans mayor backs building plan," WASH. POST, Mar. 20, 2006, at A03.

4. Beverly Creamer, "Manoa flood may cost $80M," HONOLULU ADVERTISER, Dec. 7, 2004, http://the.honoluluadvertiser.com/article/2004/Dec/07/ln/ln03p.html (last visited Nov. 8, 2009).

5. Glen Kessler, "Powell pledges long-term aid; confirmed death toll from tsunami rises to 147,000," WASH. POST, Jan. 8, 2005, at A14.

6. Denise Grady, "Even good health system is overwhelmed by tsunami," N.Y. TIMES, Jan. 9, 2005, at 10.

7. "Tsunamis and the United States: The past . . . ," WASH. POST, Jan. 9, 2005, at B02.

8. Federal Emergency Management Agency, "National Flood Insurance Program: Program description" 3 (2002) (hereinafter "FEMA NFIP description")

http://www.fema.gov/library/viewRecord.do?id=1480 (follow the "View / Download / Print" hyperlink) (last visited Nov. 20, 2009).

9. *See* Jim E. O'Connor and John E. Costa, U.S. Geological Survey, "Large floods in the United States: Where they happen and why," Circular 1245 (2003), http://pubs.usgs.gov/circ/2003/circ1245/pdf/circ1245.pdf (last visited Nov. 16, 2009).

10. FEMA NFIP Description, supra note 8, at 5.

11. *See* Alan L. Marcus and George H. Abrams, "Flood insurance and flood plain zoning as compatible components: A multi-alternative approach to flood damage reduction," 7 NAT. RESOURCES LAW. 581 (1974); Note, "Various aspects of flood plain zoning," 55 N.D. L. Rev. 429 (1979).

12. *See*, e.g., *McCarthy v. City of Manhattan Beach*, 264 P.2d 932 (Cal. 1953); *Turnpike Realty, Co. v. Town of Dedham*, 284 N.E.2d 891 (Mass. 1972); *Morris County Land Improvement Co. v. Parsippany-Troy Hills*, 193 A.2d 232 (N.J. 1963); *MacGibbon v. Bd. of Appeals of Duxbury*, 255 N.E.2d 347 (Mass. 1970). Other cases are collected in Robert Meltz, Dwight H. Merriam, and Richard M. Frank, *The Takings Issue: Constitutional Limits on Land Use Control and Environmental Regulation*, Washington, D.C.: Island Press, 1998 at 227–229.

13. For an extensive analysis, see the seminal article on this subject by Allison Dunham, "Flood control via the police power," 107 U. PA. L. REV. 1098 (1959); *see also* Wm. David Taylor III, Comment, "He who calls the tune must pay the piper: Compensation for regulatory takings of property after *First English Evangelical Lutheran Church v. County of Los Angeles*," 53 Mo. L. REV. 69 (1988); William K. Jones, Confiscation: A rationale of the law of takings," 24 HOFSTRA L. REV. 1 (1995); *Lucas v. S.C. Coastal Council*, 505 U.S. 1003, 1024–1025 n.11 (1992) (expressing skepticism that the hazard purposes of the statute were the primary goal since owners of existing homes were allowed to remain in the hazard area and rebuild after a disaster if their homes were not destroyed and finding a taking for which compensation was required).

14. And "choose" it does, even if the "choice" is not to join up—as in NFIP, which often provides the only insurance available for flood-prone lands; lack of participation strips communities' eligibility for a host of other federal programs, according to the federal courts in *Texas Landowners Rights Ass'n v. Harris*, 453 F. Supp. 1025 (D.D.C. 1978), *aff'd mem.*, 598 F.2d 311 (D.C. Cir. 1979), *cert. denied*, 444 U.S. 927 (1979). *See also Adolph v. FEMA*, 854 F.2d 732 (5th Cir. 1988).

15. *See* Charles T. Griffith, "The National Flood Insurance Program: Unattained purposes, liability in contract, and takings," 35 WM. & MARY L. REV. 727, 728–729 (1994); *see also* Oliver A. Houck, Rising water: The national flood program and Louisiana, 60 TUL. L. REV. 61, 65 (1985).

16. Saul Jay Singer, "Flooding the Fifth Amendment: The National Flood Insurance Program and the 'takings' clause," 17 B.C. ENVTL. AFF. L. REV. 323, 334 (1990); Flood Control Act of 1936, 33 U.S.C. § 701 et seq. (2006).

17. Frank E. Maloney and Dennis C. Dambly, "The National Flood Insurance Program: A model ordinance for implantation of its land management criteria," 16 NAT. RESOURCES J. 665 (1976).

18. Id. at 674.

19. 42 U.S.C. § 4001 et seq. (2006).

20. Singer, supra note 16, at 336.
21. FEMA NFIP description, supra note 8, at 16.
22. Honolulu Star-Bulletin, Apr. 8, 1970, at A20.
23. *See* 44 C.F.R. § 60.2; Section IID2d, infra at 48.
24. Haw. Rev. Stat. § 46-11, 179 et seq. (2005). Authority to enact floodplain regulations for the counties of Honolulu, Hawai'i, Kaua'i, and Maui comes from Haw. Rev. Stat. § 46-1.5 (2005), which provides that "Each county shall have the power to . . . enact zoning ordinances providing that lands deemed subject to seasonable, periodic, or occasional flooding shall not be used for residence or other purposes in a manner as to endanger the health or safety of the occupants thereof, as required by the Federal Flood Insurance Act of 1956."
25. Singer, supra note 16, at 336.
26. 42 U.S.C. § 4001 (2006).
27. Id. § 4106 (2006); Rutherford H. Platt, "The National Flood Insurance Program: Some midstream perspectives," 42 J. Amn. Inst. Planners 304–305 (1976).
28. *See* Barry Lee Myers and Jeffery K. Rubin, "Complying with the Federal Disaster Protection Act," 7 Real Est. L. J. 116, 123 (1978).
29. 44 C.F.R. § 59.1 (2007): "After detailed ratemaking has been completed in preparation for publication of the [FIRM], Zone A usually is refined into Zones A, AO, AH, A1-30, AE, A99, AR, AR/A1-30, AR/AE, AR/AO, AR/AH, AR/A, VO, or V1-30, VE, or V."
30. 42 U.S.C. § 4105(a) (2006).
31. Id. § 4105(b).
32. *See* id. § 4022; 44 C.F.R. § 60.1(a) (2006).
33. Jan TenBruggencate, "Federal disaster relief on way," Honolulu Advertiser, May 3, 2006, at B1.
34. Id.
35. Id.
36. 44 C.F.R. § 59.24(a),(d) (2007).
37. FEMA NFIP description, supra note 8, at 12.
38. Applicable amounts of coverage are contained in 44 C.F.R. § 61.6 (2007).
39. Minimum criteria for flood-prone areas are contained in 44 C.F.R.§ 60.2-.3 (2007).
40. Patrick J. Rohan, *Zoning and Land Use Controls*, Matthew Bender & Co. (Eric Damian Kelly, ed., 2006) § 18.02(2)(c)(i) (citing 44 C.F.R. § 60.3[a]).
41. Dept. of Land Utilization, City and County of Honolulu, *Summary of Flood Hazard Ordinances of the City and County of Honolulu.*
42. FEMA NFIP description, supra note 8, at 5.
43. 44 C.F.R. § 59.1 (2007).
44. FEMA NFIP description, supra note 8, at 5.
45. *See* 44 C.F.R. § 59.1 (2007); FEMA NFIP description, supra note 8, at 6.

Zones B, C, and X
Areas with less than a 1% chance of flooding each year; areas that have less than a 1% chance of sheet flow flooding with an average depth of less than 1 foot; areas that have less than a 1% chance of stream flooding where the contributing drainage area is less than 1

square mile; or areas protected from floods by levees. No base flood
elevations or depths are shown within these zones.

Zone A
Areas with a 1% annual chance of flooding and a 26% chance of
flooding over the life of a 30-year mortgage. Because detailed analyses
are not performed for such areas, no depths or base flood elevations
are shown within these zones.

Zone AE and A1–A30
Areas with a 1% annual chance of flooding and a 26% chance of
flooding over the life of a 30-year mortgage. In most instances, base
flood elevations derived from detailed analyses are shown at selected
intervals within these zones.

Zone AH
Areas with a 1% annual chance of shallow flooding, usually in the
form of a pond, with an average depth ranging from 1 to 3 feet. These
areas have a 26% chance of flooding over the life of a 30-year mortgage. Base flood elevations derived from detailed analyses are shown
at selected intervals within these zones.

Zone AO
River or stream flood hazard areas, and areas with a 1% or greater
chance of shallow flooding each year, usually in the form of sheet flow,
with an average depth ranging from 1 to 3 feet. These areas have a
26% chance of flooding over the life of a 30-year mortgage. Average
flood depths derived from detailed analyses are shown within these
zones.

Zone AR
Areas with a temporarily increased flood risk due to the building or
restoration of a flood control system (such as a levee or a dam). Mandatory flood insurance purchase requirements will apply, but rates
will not exceed the rates for unnumbered A zones if the structure is
built or restored in compliance with Zone AR floodplain management
regulations.

Zone A99
Areas with a 1% annual chance of flooding that will be protected by a
Federal flood control system where construction has reached specified
legal requirements. No depths or base flood elevations are shown
within these zones.

Zone V
Coastal areas with a 1% or greater chance of flooding and an additional hazard associated with storm waves. These areas have a 26%
chance of flooding over the life of a 30-year mortgage. No base flood
elevations are shown within these zones.

Zone VE and V1 - 30
Coastal areas with a 1% or greater chance of flooding and an additional hazard associated with storm waves. These areas have a 26% chance of flooding over the life of a 30-year mortgage. Base flood elevations derived from detailed analyses are shown at selected intervals within these zones.

Zone D
Areas with possible but undetermined flood hazards. No flood hazard analysis has been conducted. Flood insurance rates are commensurate with the uncertainty of the flood risk.

46. FEMA NFIP description, supra note 8, at 5.
47. Id. at 10.
48. 42 U.S.C. § 4107 (2006); 44 C.F.R. §§ 66.1–66.5 and 67.5–67.12 (2006).
49. FEMA NFIP description, supra note 8, at 12–13.
50. 44 C.F.R. § 59.22 (2007).
51. 42 U.S.C. § 4022 (2006).
52. 44 C.F.R. §§ 60.1–60.5 (2007). *See also* Rohan, supra note 40, § 18.02(2)(c) (ii).
53. 44 C.F.R. § 60.3(a) (2007).
54. Id. § 60.3(b).
55. Id. § 60.3(c).
56. Id. §§ 59.1, 60.3(d). "Regulatory floodway" is defined as "the channel of a river or other watercourse and the adjacent land areas that must be reserved in order to discharge the base flood without cumulatively increasing the water surface elevation more than a designated height."
57. Id. § 60.3(e).
58. Rohan, supra note 40, § 18.02(2)(b)(ii).
59. Id. (citing H.R. REP. No. 103-865, at 195–196 [1994] [Conf. Rep.]).
60. *See generally* Charles T. Griffith, Note, "The National Flood Insurance Program: Unattained purposes, liability in contract and takings," 35 WM. & MARY L. REV. 727 (1994); John Herke, Note, "Teething pains at 25: Developing meaningful enforcement of the National Flood Insurance Program," 7 TUL. ENVTL. L.J. 165 (1993); Oliver A. Houck, "Rising water: The National Flood Insurance Program and Louisiana," 60 TUL. L. REV. 61, 73–78 (1985); Bryant J. Spann, Note, "Going down for the third time: Senator Kerry's reform bill could save the drowning National Flood Insurance Program," 28 GA. L. REV. 593 (1994).
61. H.R. Rep. No. 103-865, at 196 (1994) (Conf. Rep.).
62. Id.; *see also* Spann, supra note 60, at 603–604.
63. 42 U.S.C. § 4022(b) (2006).
64. Id. § 4022(b)(2). The specified criteria are those referred to in 42 U.S.C. § 4102.
65. 42 U.S.C. § 4104c (2006).
66. Id. § 4104c(a).
67. Id. § 4104c(c).
68. *See generally* Leonard A. Bernstein, Philip H. Myers, and Daniel Steen, "Flood Insurance Reform Act engulfs mortgage lenders," 112 BANKING L.J. 238 (1995).

69. The Federal Reserve Board, Federal Deposit Insurance Corporation, Comptroller of the Currency, National Credit Union Administration, Office of Thrift Supervision, and Farm Credit Administration. Rohan, supra note 40, § 18.02(2)(i) n.114.

70. 42 U.S.C. § 4012a(b)(1) (2006).

71. Id. § 4012a(d).

72. Id. § 4012a(e).

73. Id. § 4104a.

74. Id. § 4012a(f)(2).

75. Id. § 4012a(f)(5).

76. HONOLULU, HAW., Ordinance No. 80-62, An Ordinance to Amend Article 11 of the Comprehensive Zoning Code Relating to Flood Hazard Districts; Ordinance no. 80-63, An Ordinance to Amend Chapter 16, Relating to the Building Code; Ordinance No. 64, An Ordinance to Amend Chapter 17, Relating to the Electrical Code; Ordinance no. 64, An Ordinance to Amend Chapter 17, Relating to the Electrical Code; Ordinance no. 65, An Ordinance to Amend Chapter 19, Relating to the Plumbing Code.

77. *See* 44 C.F.R. § 60.1(b).

78. HONOLULU, HAW., LAND USE ORDINANCE No. 99-12 (1999) (hereinafter "Honolulu LUO").

79. HONOLULU, HAW., REV. ORDINANCES, § 21-9.10-2 (2005) (hereinafter "Honolulu Ord.").

80. Id. § 21-9.10-5.

81. Id. § 21-9.10-6.

82. Id. § 21-9.10-7.

83. Id. § 21-9.10-8.

84. Id. § 21-9.10-9.

85. County of Hawai'i, *Hawaii County Code,* § §§ 27-12(a)(28) and 27-22 (2005).

86. Id. § 27-22(a).

87. Id. § 27-12(a)(29).

88. Id. §§ 27-12(a)(69), (70), 27-23.

89. Id. § 27-23.

90. Id. § 27-24.

91. Id. § 27-17(a).

92. Id. § 27-18.

93. Id. § 27-17(b).

94. *Honolulu Advertiser,* July 9, 1980, E-9; HAW. REV. STAT. § 46-11 (1976).

95. County of Maui, *Maui County Code,* § 19.62 (2006).

96. Id. § 19.62.060(F).

97. Id. § 19.62.060(G).

98. Id.

99. Id. § 19.62.100.

100. County of Kaua'i, *Kauai County Code,* ch. 8, art. 16, § 8-16.1 (2006).

101. Id. § 8-16.3.

102. Id. § 8-12.1.

103. Id. § 8-12.2.

104. Id. § 8-12.3.

105. Id. § 8-11.2

106. Id.

107. *See* David W. Owens, "The zoning variance: Reappraisal and recommendations for reform of a much-maligned tool," 29 Colum. J. Envtl. L. 279 (2004); Osborne M. Reynolds, Jr., "Self-induced hardship in zoning variances: Does a purchaser have no one but himself to blame?" 20 Urb. Law. 1 (1988); David L. Callies and J. F. Garner, "Planning law in England and Wales and in the United States," 1 Anglo-Am. L. Rev. 292 (1972).

108. 44 C.F.R. § 60.6(a)(3).

109. Honolulu Ord. § 21-9.10-11(a).

110. Id. § 21-9.10-11(b).

111. Id. § 21-9.10-11(b)(6).

112. 44 C.F.R. § 60.6(a) (2007).

113. Id. §§ 59.1, 60.6(b).

114. *See, e.g.,* Honolulu Ord. 04-09, Ordinance to Amend Chapter 21 (April 7, 2005).

115. Meltz, Merriam, and Frank, *The Takings Issue,* supra note 12, at 227.

116. Id.

117. Id. (citing *Dolan v. City of Tigard,* 512 U.S. 374, 385–386 (1994)).

118. While *Lucas v. South Carolina Coastal Council* usually forbids government from depriving a landowner of "all economically beneficial use" through regulation, forbidding building in a floodplain is one of the "nuisance exceptions" to this rule that the court expressly recognized. 505 U.S. 1003 (1992).

119. 284 N.E.2d 891 (Mass. 1972).

120. *See also S. Kemble Fischer Realty Trust v. Bd. of Appeals of Concord,* 402 N.E.2d 100 (Mass. App. 1980); *Dur-Bar Realty Co. v. City of Utica,* 394 N.Y.S.2d 913 (App. Div. 1977).

121. *Turner v. County of Del Norte,* 101 Cal. Rptr. 93 (Ct. App. 1972); *Foreman v. State,* 387 N.E.2d 455 (Ind. Ct. App. 1979); *Subaru of New England v. Bd. of Appeals of Canton,* 395 N.E.2d 880 (Mass. App. Ct. 1979). *See also Fortier v. City of Spearfish,* 433 N.W.2d 228 (S.D. 1988) (upholding purpose of ordinance).

122. 283 N.W.2d 538 (Minn. 1979).

123. Id. at 542.

124. Id. at 543.

125. Id.; *see also* Meltz, Merriam, and Frank, *The Takings Issue,* supra note 12, at 228 (citing to a number of relevant cases and stating that "[n]umerous low-density land uses have been accepted as reasonable uses left to land subject to floodplain regulations.")

126. 438 U.S. 104 (1978).

127. *Krahl,* 238 N.W.2d at 543.

128. 453 F. Supp. 1025, 1032–1033 (D.D.C. 1978), *aff'd mem.,* 598 F.2d 311 (D.C. Cir. 1979), *cert. denied,* 444 U.S. 927 (1979).

129. Id. at 1032.

130. Id.

131. 854 F.2d 732 (5th Cir. 1988).

132. Id. at 737 (citing *Texas Landowners Rights Ass'n v. Harris,* 453 F. Supp. 1025, 1032–1033 (D.D.C. 1978)).

133. "Floodplain management," Exec. Order No. 11988, 42 Fed. Reg. 26951 (May 25, 1977).

134. *See* Daniel R. Mandelker et al., *State and Local Government in a Federal System,* 5th ed., New York: LexisNexis, 2004 at ch. 1.

135. *United States v. Parish of St. Bernard,* Civ. No.'s 81-1808 and 81-1810 (E.D. La. 1981).

Chapter 8

Historic Preservation

Recapturing the Past

The preservation of historic buildings and archaeological sites has been something of a national crusade, especially since the mid-1960s. In 1966, Congress passed the National Historic Preservation Act (NHPA), which accomplished four major things: "First, it created the National Register of Historic Places [National Register], the federal government's official list of properties worthy of preservation. Second, it led to the appointment, in every state and territory, of a State Historic Preservation Officer (SHPO) with responsibility for encouraging and assisting preservation efforts at the state level."[1] Third, the legislation established the Historic Preservation Fund, which helps "the states carry out the preservation responsibilities mandated to them."[2] Finally, the NHPA created the President's Advisory Council on Historic Preservation (Advisory Council), an independent federal agency given the authority to review and comment on any proposed project involving the use of federal resources and affecting sites listed on the National Register.

The reasons for promoting preservation range from the desire to preserve links with the past to the retention of tourist attractions. There are essentially three major elements in modern historic preservation programs: (1) regulation to prevent damage or destruction of private sites, (2) rehabilitation to encourage reuse of private sites, and (3) the protection of sites from federally funded redevelopment or public works projects through "listing" and the associated mandatory consulting process. While some sites are also saved through outright public acquisition, historic properties are expensive to purchase and maintain. Therefore, in times of tight budgets and increasing demand upon government at all levels, reliance on such acquisitions to save a substantial share of historic sites is misplaced.

The Basic Program: What is Possible

The essential issue in any regulatory program is the extent to which the regulation may permissibly restrict private action. So it is with historic preservation. The issue of private restriction is particularly acute because health and safety, traditional bases for regulation, are not affected by the damage or destruction of a historic site. This leaves public welfare, a vaguely defined concept that is often used to justify regulatory systems when all else fails. It is the basis for most historic preservation laws, which prevent the alteration (and sometimes require the maintenance) of a historic structure or site whether in public or private hands.

Courts have been and continue to be sympathetic in supporting the designation and regulation of historic sites by qualified public bodies.[3] But the full extent to which the police power could be invoked to prevent an owner from altering or demolishing such sites was vastly enlarged in 1978 by the U.S. Supreme Court in the landmark *Penn Central Transportation Co. v. City of N.Y.* case.[4] There, the Court upheld a New York City ordinance that heavily restricted the development potential of Grand Central Station solely because of its historic significance. The Court recounted those aspects of the regulatory scheme that made it defensible: expertise and due process in both the selection of historic sites and the granting (or refusal) of a "certificate of appropriateness" for exterior modifications or demolition; economic viability of the site in its present condition; availability of tax relief for designated properties; and ability of the private owner to transfer air development rights to nearby properties.[5] State courts were quick to seize upon *Penn Central* as a precedent for other similar historic preservation schemes, with the result that most programs that (1) use defensible criteria (or experts) in identifying historic sites, (2) provide fair procedures for landowners to seek permits for alteration, and (3) leave some economic *use* of the site have been upheld.[6]

Regardless of the regulatory framework, a usable building is more likely to be preserved than one that depends solely on the force of the law for its maintenance. Thus, the historic preservation movement increasingly shifted to incentives for commercial rehabilitation and reuse of old buildings, relying primarily on tax incentives, especially with the passage of the Economic Recovery Act of 1981. The incentive programs provided financial benefits to owners otherwise burdened by preservation laws and countered private and public land use policies favoring demolition and new construction.[7] For a time, the programs— jointly administered by the National Park Service (NPS), SHPOs, and the Internal Revenue Service (IRS)—proved successful, revitalizing communities and preserving the special character of rural areas and towns.

However, significant changes in the law have limited the act's applicability and utility. Gone are the days when accelerated depreciation and five-year amortization periods were allowed.[8] What remains are straight-line depreciation methods over 27.5 or 39 years, depending upon whether the property is residential.[9] The two main tax incentive programs presently are the tax credits of 10 or 20 percent for qualified rehabilitation expenditures, based on whether the building is a "certified historic structure," and income tax deductions for charitable contributions of interests in historic property.[10] A certified historic structure is one listed on the National Register or one located in a registered historic district and certified as such by the NPS or the secretary of the Interior.[11]

To qualify for a 20 percent credit, the structure not only has to be a building (as opposed to a bridge, dam, or railroad car), but also it must be depreciable: It can be an office or any commercial enterprise used for the production of income as long as it does not serve as the taxpayer's personal residence.[12] In addition, the rehabilitation of the building must be substantial. The "expenditures must exceed the greater of $5,000 or the adjusted basis of the building and its structural components" during a twenty-four-month period selected by the taxpayer.[13] Finally, the building must have been "a certified historic structure when it is placed in service."[14] Otherwise, "the owner must have requested on or before the date that the building was placed in service a determination from the NPS that the building is a certified historic structure, and have a reasonable expectation that the determination will be granted."[15]

The qualifications for a 10 percent tax credit are similar to those of the 20 percent, with certain exceptions. For example, the buildings must be nonhistoric, nonresidential, and placed into service before 1936. So while a building can be old, it need not be historic to be eligible for a credit. There are other specific requirements mandated in the rehabilitation process, including making sure that "75 percent or more of the existing external walls of such building are retained in place as internal or external walls."[16] Determining which tax incentive applies is a function of the building, not owner preference. Furthermore, the two credits are mutually exclusive; one or the other applies. Even compliance with all these provisions may be for naught if one disposes of the building within five years. The full tax credit is recaptured if the building "ceases to be investment credit property" during the first year, and that amount is reduced by 20 percent a year.[17]

Finally, for the qualified conservation contributions, an individual may take income tax deductions on any donated structure (not just a building), including land, whether or not depreciable.[18] For example, easements on private residences qualify. The structures, however, must still conform to the IRS' definition of a "historically important land area."[19] With all these different criteria, standards, and definitions, not to mention the reduced tax benefits compared to the mid-1970s and early 1980s legislation, it is no surprise that many "states have created their own historic rehabilitation tax credit programs, to fill the incentive gap created by the downsizing of the federal program."[20]

The aforementioned NHPA, coupled with the National Environmental Policy Act (NEPA) passed in 1969, provide some measure of temporary protection for historic sites.[21] NHPA is the latest in a series of federal laws directed toward the survey and preservation of historic sites.[22] One of its more salient features, under Section 106, is the requirement that federal agencies "take into account the effects of their undertakings, on historic properties and afford the Council a reasonable opportunity to comment on such undertakings."[23] Indeed, the Advisory Council must be permitted to comment on the proposed action.[24] Native Hawaiian organizations are explicitly listed as consulting parties regarding any historic properties for which they attach any cultural or religious importance.[25]

Though Section 106 review does not mandate preservation or prevent construction, it does "ensure that preservation values are factored into [f]ederal agency planning and decisions" and that "[f]ederal agencies must assume responsibility for the consequences of their actions on historic properties."[26] Thus, Section 106 applies only to those historic sites listed or eligible to be listed on the National Register *and* where the proposed project or development utilizes federal funds or otherwise "involves" a federal agency, including the issuance of federal permits, licenses, or approvals.[27] Thanks to the pervasiveness of the federal government in much of Hawai'i's development activity, this temporary protection is likely to be invoked often.[28] Even a less obvious action, such as a Federal Communications Commission license for construction of a cellular tower, may compromise view planes, landscapes, or properties valued for traditional, cultural, or religious practices.

A listing on the National Register could be just as broad and comprehensive. The register includes those historic resources, districts, sites, buildings, structures, and objects significant in American history, architecture, archaeology, engineering, and culture. National Register listings thus are those:

> [t]hat possess integrity of location, design, setting, materials, workmanship, feeling and association, and: (a) that are associated with events that have made a significant contribution to the broad patterns of our history; or (b) that are associated with the lives of persons significant in our past; or (c) that embody the distinctive characteristics of a type, period, or method of construction, or that represent the work of a master, or that possess high artistic values, or that represent a significant and distinguishable entity whose components may lack individual distinction, or (d) that have yielded, or may be likely to yield, information important in prehistory or history.[29]

The secretary of the U.S. Department of the Interior maintains the database from sites nominated by anyone, but this is usually in conjunction with review by SHPO. The benefits of a National Register listing are fourfold: (1) It is an honorific designation; (2) it meets the basic eligibility criteria for any available preservation funding; (3) it qualifies for the higher (i.e., 20 percent) property rehabilitation tax credit; and (4) it enjoys some protection through the mandatory Section 106 review process. If the property owner objects to the nomination, however, then the site is simply not listed. Reasons for declining a nomination include concerns that listing will severely restrict private property rights. However, "[l]isting in the National Register imposes no restrictions on an owner's right to do anything to his or her property that local law allows."[30] Hence, state or county laws regarding nationally registered properties, if any, will more likely affect the use of the listed property.

Because there is no legal requirement that a project must be abandoned, even if the Advisory Council strenuously objects, what the NHPA does is buy time. For example, a Department of Transportation policy forbids the use of either public or private land from a historic site for a transportation program or project unless (1) there is no "prudent and feasible" alternative and (2) all "possible" planning to minimize harm to the site is undertaken.[31]

Such consideration of historic sites is not confined to the NHPA. Before undertaking a federal action that significantly affects the human environment, NEPA requires an environmental impact statement (EIS) of the proposed action to be prepared.[32] An environmental assessment must be made for virtually every federal action to determine its significance and the probable effect on the environment; it is then used to determine whether a full EIS is warranted.[33] NEPA is of considerable help in buttressing the protection of historic sites because it states that one of the environmental policies to be effectuated is to "preserve important historic . . . aspects of our national heritage."[34]

Indeed, a federal court held in 1979 that the U.S. Department of Housing and Urban Development had to prepare an EIS on proposed destruction of register-eligible properties in an urban renewal project so long as it has any discretion over it.[35] The *Stop H-3 Association v. Dole* case in Hawai'i is another example of the interplay between NHPA and NEPA.[36] At issue was the legality of a federally funded highway route passing within a few feet of a petroglyph in Moanalua Valley on O'ahu. In holding that both NHPA and NEPA were triggered, the court held that before the transportation secretary may authorize the construction of a highway through a site eligible for listing on the National Register, he must first find that there is no prudent and feasible alternative. The state and federal governments then switched the route to the nearby Hālawa Valley, only to find that the original injunction banning construction in Moanalua Valley was also applicable there.[37]

More complicated was the status of the island of Kaho'olawe in Maui County. Literally awash in *heiaus* (places of worship), adze quarries, and petroglyphs, the small island had been a U.S. Navy bombing target since World War II.[38] After protracted litigation concerning the need for a federal EIS to continue bombing the island, the navy conducted a four-year, $600,000 survey, nominated 171 sites to the National Register, and restricted bombing to those parts of Kaho'olawe that were free of such sites.[39] This failed to satisfy the Protect Kaho'olawe Ohana (PKO), an organization seeking to end the bombing, which observed that the number of sites so chosen was far fewer than those that had been uncovered and that minimally every site should be listed. In fact, the keeper of the National Register listed the entire island as an archaeological district in early 1981.[40] As a result of PKO actions and litigation, President George Bush Sr. ordered a halt to the bombing of Kaho'olawe in 1990.[41] The navy transferred ownership of the island back to Hawai'i in 1994.[42]

Historic Preservation in Hawai'i

That Hawai'i has many historic sites worth preserving is beyond question. Approximately 713 sites are currently listed on local and national registers of historic places.[43] But while procedural irregularities have resulted in some delisting of these sites, such listing has only marginal protective significance. Listing requires virtually no state or local regulation of a site. At best, private owners of a listed site must merely provide the state with notice of an intended alteration or demolition and under certain circumstances file an EIS. Either or both merely delay the action. Only when such sites also fall within the boundaries of either county-enacted special zoning districts or state conservation districts is there any regulatory protection.

Hawai'i's Constitution specifically links the police power with historic site preservation under the public health and welfare rubric: "The State shall have the power to conserve and develop objects and places of historic or cultural interest and provide for public sightliness and physical good order. For these purposes private property shall be subject to reasonable regulation."[44] Pursuant to this broad constitutional mandate, the State of Hawai'i enacted a historic preservation program dealing with historic sites that are (1) publicly owned and (2) privately owned. While it is the latter in which issues of public control and the limits of police power arise, the number of sites on public lands makes the first category an important element in surveying the manner and effectiveness of historic preservation in Hawai'i.

ON PUBLIC LANDS

Hawai'i has always recognized "the value of conserving and developing historic and cultural property within the State for the public good."[45] Consequently, several state statutes deal with the classification and regulation of historic sites on state lands, much of which falls under the auspices of the Department of Land and Natural Resources (DLNR). The department is responsible for administering a "historic preservation program" designed to protect and preserve Hawai'i's historical, architectural, archaeological, and cultural resources.[46] DLNR must approve any proposed project or transfer of historic property, whether on land or underwater.[47] Indeed, the statute defines "project" to encompass almost any real property-related activity undertaken or even partially supported by the state, including contracts, grants, subsidies, loans, leases, permits, and licenses.[48]

While a historic preservation officer appointed by the governor is responsible for the program and serves as a liaison with the public and other government agencies, much authority also rests with the Historic Places Review Board, statutorily created to administer the Hawai'i Register as well as to recommend sites for inclusion on the National Register.[49] The board is comprised of ten members, appointed and removed by the governor, who must have professional qualifications in fields such as archaeology, architecture, history, sociology, and knowledge of traditional Hawaiian society and culture among its membership.[50]

One method of regulating or restricting development of historic sites is to simply acquire the lands. DLNR has authority to preserve lands with "historic value."[51] It may also promulgate and administer rules concerning permissible uses based upon recommendations of the Natural Reserve System Commission, composed of thirteen members who possess scientific qualifications in forestry or wildlife biology and memberships in hiking and hunting organizations.[52] With the DLNR's recommendation, the governor is empowered to classify landmarks, historic and prehistoric structures, and other objects of historic interest on state land to be state monuments.[53] Similar to the "project" definition, almost anything may be deemed "historic" as long as it is at least fifty years old. Thus, "aviation artifacts," burial sites, and *heiaus* are all within DLNR's jurisdiction.[54] Any entity may appeal the department's determination, however.[55] Even after a "historic site" designation, the preservation of these locations remains paramount. As a result, the state cannot dispose of the properties without DLNR's approval.[56] Further, any disposition is subject to the restrictions and covenants intended to protect the sites, including rights of access and public visits.[57]

ON PRIVATE LANDS

The Historic Places Review Board also exercises limited authority over privately held lands by ordering "and enter[ing] historic properties into the Hawai'i Register on the basis of their value to Hawai'i's heritage."[58] Nominating considerations include the quality of the site's significance to Hawaiian history and culture, taking into account the "location, design, setting, materials, workmanship, feeling, and association . . . with events that have made a significant contribution to the

broad patterns" of the state's history.[59] The Review Board also evaluates
the environmental impact and takes into account other "social, cultural,
educational, and recreational" values of the potentially listed structures
or sites.[60] Though nominations for listing are customarily made by the
SHPO, anyone may nominate a site.[61]

While hardly a paragon of strength, a Hawai'i Register listing does
provide for a measure of temporary site protection. An owner of a listed
site must notify and secure the concurrence of DLNR for any proposed
construction, alteration, transfer, or improvement that will affect a historic property.[62] In the event DLNR approval is not secured, however,
the owner need only wait ninety days before altering or demolishing a
site.[63] During that time, DLNR may commence condemnation proceedings or undertake investigation, recordation, preservation, and salvage
of "any historical information deemed necessary to preserve Hawaiian
history."[64] Violation of these regulations results in a fine of up to $1,000
per offense, and "each day of continued violation shall constitute a distinct and separate offense."[65]

Though infrequent, properties listed on either register of historic
places can be removed. But they are usually not delisted unless there
was an error in judgment, the qualities for which they were listed in the
first place are no longer present, or statutory procedures were not cor-
rectly followed.[66] For example, a cause célèbre in both local and national
historic preservation circles had been the listing of the Royal Hawaiian
Hotel on the Hawai'i Register in 1980. Though itself subject to critical historic preservation comment during construction because several
structures deemed to be historic were demolished to make way for it,
the Royal Hawaiian was also nominated to the National Register. However, the owner of the property, Kyo-Ya Co., Ltd., was able to remove this
"Pink Palace of the Pacific" from the Hawai'i Register because of alleged
noncompliance with the notice provisions under the statutes. Presently,
the hotel is now on neither the Hawai'i nor the National Registers of
Historic Places.

The opposite is also possible. A building that no longer exists could
remain on the National Register. Not so famous outside of Hawai'i,
the Alexander Young Building in Honolulu was also something of a
cause in the historic preservation community before its demolition.
Once a luxurious downtown hotel with architecture borrowed from
both the Renaissance and classical Rome, the structure even had a
roof garden for dancing. Although listed on both the Hawai'i and the
National Registers of Historic Places, there was considerable division

in the community over its historic value. It was described both as a "nostalgic grey giant" and as a "renaissance monstrosity." DLNR opted not to purchase the building, and its owner demolished it to make way for the currently existing twenty-nine-story Pauahi Tower of the Pacific Trade Center office building and the three-quarter-acre Tamarind Park. However, because there is no regular review or update of a site's status, a listing remains on the database unless the National Park Service, the official keeper of the register, is notified. Thus, a thirty-year-old vestige of the Alexander Young building still exists on the National Register.

One statute does provide incentives to private owners of sites to help preserve them. While not particularly generous, it will probably account for as much state-fostered historic preservation as the process of listing described above. Under a section of the state's tax code, owners of listed sites are exempt from real property taxes, except for a $100 minimum tax, for that part of the site dedicated to public use.[67] The state director of Taxation must additionally find that the benefit to the public from said dedication is equal to the foregone property taxes. The initial period of dedication is ten years, renewable indefinitely but "subject to cancellation by either the owner or the director upon five years' notice at any time after the end of the fifth year."[68] Furthermore, if the owner fails to maintain the dedicated land, then the special tax exemption is lost and all prior foregone real property taxes must be repaid, with interest.[69] Given the narrowness of the exemption, it is not surprising that little use has so far been made of it.

The state also affects the use that the owner of a listed site can make of his land by virtue of certain classification criteria under Act 187, Hawai'i's landmark statewide "zoning" act, described in detail in chapter 2. The land in one of the four classifications into which all state land is classified, the conservation district, is regulated by DLNR's Land Board. The uses listed for this district are restrictive. Among the lands that are required to be classified into this conservation district by the State Land Use Commission are "[l]ands and waters necessary for the preservation and enhancement of designated historic or archaeological sites."[70]

Under certain circumstances or conditions, a historic site may also be subject to review under Hawai'i's environmental impact statement law.[71] The environmentally significant actions that can trigger an impact assessment requirement include proposing "any use within any historic site as designated in the National Register or Hawai'i Register."[72] In the assessment, the "historic perspective" must be addressed as part of the project description.[73] The environment in the vicinity of the proposed action must also be described, including "natural or human-made resources of historical, archaeological, or aesthetic significance."[74] Once such an assessment is made and there is no significant environmental impact, then the project may proceed. However, if the proposed action "may have a significant impact, a more detailed environmental impact statement (EIS) [must] be prepared."[75] The EIS is subject to various reviews and legal challenges by both the public and government agencies. Only the governor, mayor, or relevant agency may determine the acceptability of the final EIS, upon which an appeal may be taken directly to the Environmental Council. "A final EIS must be accepted by a government entity before a[ny] project can proceed."[76]

The State's Coastal Zone Management Act (described in detail in chapter 6)—surprisingly—also deals with the preservation of historic sites.[77] Each county administers extensive coastal zone special management areas (SMA)s under state statutory standards through the requirement of an SMA permit for most developments. One of those standards requires a proposed development to be consistent with the state's statutory objectives, policies, and SMA guidelines.[78] One of the county objectives is to "protect, preserve, and, where desirable, restore those natural and manmade historic and prehistoric resources in the coastal zone management area that are significant in Hawaiian and American history and culture."[79] This gives counties the right to deny a permit for any development that threatens a significant resource as defined in the act. Presumably, listing on either the Hawai'i or National Register raises a presumption in favor of "significance" sufficient to trigger this part of the CZM program's regulatory regime. On the other hand, lack of such listing may raise a contrary presumption against significance.

Yet one more state statute affects the preservation of historic sites: the Hawai'i State Planning Act (HSPA), enacted in 1978 and since amended.[80] This act contains a number of broad policies, objectives, and goals, such as the following that address historic preservation:

Objectives:
1. Planning for the state's physical environment shall be directed towards achievement of the objective of enhancement of Hawaii's . . . historical resources.

Policies:
   1. Promote the preservation and restoration of significant
natural and historic resources.
   2. Provide incentives to maintain and enhance historic,
cultural, and scenic amenities.
   3. Protect those special areas, structures, and elements that
are an integral and functional part of Hawaii's ethnic and
cultural heritage.[81]

These criteria are binding on both state agencies and on the
counties' development planning and implementation processes, all as
explained in chapter 2. As there described, all state government agencies are bound by HSPA in making land use decisions, and counties must
take its provisions into account. Certain words and phrases are therefore
critical: What does "promote" preservation of historic resources mean?
What are "historic resources"? Is there any significance to the absence
of the word "historic" from the third policy quoted above, the only one
that appears to guarantee protection, or are historic sites included in
the phrase "special areas, structures, and elements that are an integral
function of Hawaii's ethnic and cultural heritage"?
   Answers to these and other questions should have been answered
by the implementation of the State Functional Plan on Historic Preservation, which the legislature approved in 1984. The plan, however,
added little regulatory muscle with respect to historic sites on either
public or private land. "[B]oth the State Plans and the Functional Plans
fell into disuse" in the early 1990s due to fiscal constraints.[82] Moreover,
according to our State Supreme Court, "the state functional plans are
broad policy guidelines providing a framework for state and county
planning and do not constitute legal mandates, nor legal standards of
performance."[83] The most recent iteration of the State Historic Preservation Plan addresses historic preservation at a broad level "and as
such does not become immersed in place-specific or decision-making
specific levels of activity."[84] It "has been developed to provide a vision
for historic preservation, . . . to serve as a guide for effective decision
making on a general level, . . . and for communicating statewide historic preservation goals, policies and objectives."[85] Ultimately, lack of
the prior definitions may be moot because other explicit but broadly
defined synonyms (e.g., "historic property") have been employed in
the name of "historic preservation," to which an entire statutory chapter is dedicated.[86]

The Legislative Options

While not specific in its statutory language, the state has given its counties discretion to preserve historic sites through their zoning power.[87] Thus, while "historic sites" are not specifically mentioned, ordinances "establishing historical, cultural, and scenic districts" are.[88] Each of Hawai'i's four counties has passed historic preservation zoning schemes offering various degrees of protection to historic sites within a historic or scenic district. What follows is a summary of the pertinent local regulations in each county.

HONOLULU

The City and County of Honolulu essentially has a three-tier system of "objectives, policies, planning principles, guidelines and regulations" with regard to land use and growth.[89] The General Plan forms the first tier of the system and provides six policy statements in support of "Objective B": "To protect O'ahu's cultural, historical, architectural, and archaeological resources."[90] Development and sustainable community plans form the second tier and elaborate further on the island's significant cultural and natural resources but do not add any specific regulatory material. For example, the north shore plan stresses the importance of its historical and cultural sites as representative of the area's precontact and plantation eras and includes an inventory of those sites listed on the National and State Registers of Historic Places, but it implements nothing further.[91] Honolulu's zoning for historic preservation lies in the third tier, in the City and County's Land Use Ordinance (LUO), and more specifically in the special design district (SDD).

In addition to creating an O'ahu Historic Preservation Commission, the County Code also allowed for an SDD in its LUO, whose purpose is to conserve "the city's natural, historic and scenic resources."[92] SDD would "provide a means by which certain areas in the community in need of restoration, preservation, redevelopment or rejuvenation may be designated . . . to guide development to protect and/or enhance the physical and visual aspects of an area for the benefit of the community as a whole."[93] SDD is a zoning district that is approved and mapped by the City Council.[94] Once mapped, it takes precedence over any previous zone district regulations and classifications.[95] Procedurally initiated by the City Council, the Department of Permit and Planning (DPP), or the landowner, the proposal to establish an SDD is first reviewed informally by DPP in conjunction with the applicant. After consultation with affected and interested citizens and organizations such as the relevant neighborhood board, the DPP director sends the SDD application to a design advisory committee for comment and review.[96] The design committee consists of DLNR's SHPO as well as architects and urban planners.[97] After the committee makes its comments and recommendations, the director then prepares a report and the proposed ordinance for the Planning Commission, which holds a hearing and submits its findings and recommendations to the council.[98] The council then conducts another public hearing and may approve the ordinance as submitted, with modifications, or deny it.[99]

A good example of the detailed regulations placed on both existing and potential structures is the Chinatown Special District because of "a concern that architectural and historic elements of the district may . . . be lost."[100] The LUO sets the objectives and the boundaries of the special district and then provides an inventory of significant structures, both listed and unlisted on the dual registers.[101] It then promulgates design controls and development standards within the precinct, including landscaping and use regulations, density, architectural review, and sign size limitations.[102] New structures, for example, "shall not exceed 40 feet."[103] Street furnishings, such as benches, lampposts, and planters, are not to be of a style and "detailing inappropriate to Chinatown's period of significance, which is from the 1880s to the 1940s."[104] These types of controls exist for the other six special districts within the county: Diamond Head, Punchbowl, Waikīkī, Hale'iwa, Thomas Square/Honolulu Academy of Arts, and the Hawai'i Capital.

Kaua'i

Historic preservation in Kaua'i County consists of a robust General Plan augmented by a blend of zoning ordinance and development plans. Almost every single one of the plan's nine chapters mentions historic preservation.[105] Indeed, the very first policy item sets the theme. "The General Plan establishes . . . the . . . preservation of natural, cultural and scenic resources."[106] The plan then depicts the locations of these important resources on Heritage Resource Maps, including both registered historic buildings and unregistered but otherwise important structures.[107] The pertinent provisions of Kaua'i's zoning ordinance, which set out special districts created in part to preserve historic places, may be supplemented by area-specific development plans, the provisions of which supersede any conflicting provision of that zoning ordinance.[108]

The county zoning ordinance deals with historic preservation in two special zoning districts: special treatment districts and special planning areas. The former is explicitly considered an overlay district, whereas the latter is implied.[109]

Special treatment districts, drafted to designate and guide development in areas with "unique or critical cultural, physical or locational characteristics," are specifically authorized for those areas with "significant historic background, structures, or land forms."[110] The district is created by the County Council and recorded on the county's zoning map.[111] All "uses, structures, or development" require a use permit, "except repairs or modifications of land and existing structures that do not substantially change exterior form or appearance."[112]

In contrast, the special planning area is a creation of the Planning Commission, which "may" formulate development plans for it.[113] Such development plans "shall include, wherever appropriate and practical," among other things, "a review of the . . . historic characteristics of the area."[114] The critical tool is the Development Plan, which, by incorporation into the county zoning ordinance, nominally supersedes any conflicting district regulations: "After the Council adopts a Development Plan for a Special Planning Area, no development, use or activity may be undertaken in the area that is contrary to the Development Plan."[115] Through a series of Development Plans passed by the County Council, Kaua'i has designated a number of historic sites and districts, including locations in Hanalei, Wailua, Līhu'e, Waimea, and Kōloa.[116]

Other ordinances support historic preservation through both regulatory and incentive provisions. These include relief from building code compliance, broader permitted use of a historic structure, and tax exemptions for commercial historic properties.[117] One of the more important enactments is the creation of the Kaua'i Historic Preservation Review Commission, whose purpose is to protect, preserve, perpetuate, promote, enhance, and develop "the historic resources of the County of Kaua'i."[118] The commission's establishment, plus a requirement for "adequate public participation," permits Kaua'i County to take advantage of a sometimes overlooked proviso in the National Historic Preservation Act.[119] That is, the "certified local government" designation provides Kaua'i with federal funds equal to a "minimum of 10 per centum of the annual apportionment distributed by the Secretary [of the Department of the Interior] to each State for the purposes of" historic preservation.[120] It is the state—and in particular, the SHPO— along with the secretary that certify such a designation, providing an example of how all three levels of government legislation—national, state, and local—can work together to promote the preservation of historic sites.[121]

HAWAIʻI

Historic preservation in Hawaiʻi County, as in Kauaʻi and Maui, depends on what the county's General Plan contains. The county-adopted (by ordinance) General Plan is comprehensive with respect to historic preservation, devoting an entire chapter to historic sites.[122] Fourteen pages delineate the goals, policies, and standards for evaluating a particular site and include a listing of historical sites and districts placed on the Hawaiʻi or National Registers, along with an islandwide map depicting these locations.[123] Indeed, the plan mandates that any new listing on the registers must be included in future general plans.[124] The Hawaiʻi Heritage Corridor Program, currently unique to the Big Island, seeks "to preserve historic sites by enabling non-profit organizations in the various County districts [to] preserve historic sites and buildings along a transportation corridor."[125] The county charter also makes it clear that "[n]o public improvement or project, or subdivision or zoning ordinance, shall be initiated or adopted unless the same conforms to and implements the general plan."[126] Such plan provisions as applied to historic preservation therefore have the force of law not only in addition to, but also in case of conflict, superior to any land development ordinance to the contrary.

The Hawaiʻi General Plan has much to say about historic preservation, most of which—as indicated by the aforementioned charter language—is binding upon the council, Planning Commission, and other land use decision makers. Probably the most significant provisions are the goal to "[p]rotect, restore, and enhance the sites, buildings, and objects of significant historical and cultural importance to Hawaiʻi" and the policies that specifically address historic preservation:

> Amend appropriate ordinances to incorporate the stewardship and protection of historic sites, buildings and objects.

> Require both public and private developers of land to provide historical and archaeological surveys and cultural assessments, where appropriate, prior to the clearing or development of land when there are indications that the land under construction has historical significance.

Public access to significant historic sites and objects shall be acquired.

Embark on a program of restoring significant historic sites on County lands. Assure the protection and restoration of sites on other public lands through a joint effort with the State.[127]

These goals and policies of the General Plan are buttressed by action plans specific to the historic site or district. For example, a "course of action" for the North Kona District is to "[e]stablish suitable visual buffers for the Keakealaniwahine and Keolanahihi complexes as a condition of rezoning or Special Management Area permits, for nearby properties."[128]

Recognizing that the plan is intended only to generally set forth objectives, goals, and policies, Hawai'i County has left it to the community development plans to "translate the broad General Plan statements to specific actions as they apply to specific geographical areas."[129] The development plans, in conjunction with the county code and ordinances, provide for various regulatory schemes and incentives related to the preservation of historic sites. Thus, the Zoning Code creates a Design Commission for the Kailua Village Special District to review any proposed architectural and design changes that will affect the physical appearance of the village.[130] Other "carrots and sticks" include the creation of a fund and commission for the "[p]reservation of historic or culturally important land areas and sites," subdivision restrictions (e.g., "historical sites and structures shall be preserved"), real property tax exemption for dedications of historic residential real property, except for a minimum tax, and exemptions of historic sites from compliance with the applicable building code.[131]

MAUI

The Maui County Charter provides for a General Plan, a "cultural resource management program," and a fund to preserve "historic or culturally important land areas."[132] One of the General Plan's policies is to "[i]dentify and preserve significant historic and cultural sites," and this policy is bolstered by some of the strongest ordinance language relating to historic preservation.[133] Indeed, besides Kaua'i, Maui is currently the only other county in the state to receive a "certified local government" designation.

Maui has adopted a full-blown historic district ordinance complete with a historic district commission, historic districts (three), and detailed design and use standards. The ordinance creates the nine-member Maui County Cultural Resources Commission, whose members are appointed by the mayor and approved by the City Council.[134] The commission must also include at least one representative from each island in Maui County (i.e., Lāna'i and Moloka'i).[135] One of the commission's duties is to review all plans for the construction, reconstruction, alteration, repair, moving, or demolition of structures in the historic districts.[136] Unless the commission issues a "certificate of approval," the county superintendent of building inspection cannot issue a building permit for the requested change to the structure.[137] The ordinance also creates three historic districts: two in Lahaina and one in Wailuku.[138] The boundaries of each district are extensively and explicitly described. While Historic District no. 2 differs from no. 1 because there are no historic structures or sites within the district to be preserved or restored, it is intended "to preserve the charm of Lahaina by preserving the architectural styles" unique to it.[139]

Finally, there are regulations for the architectural styles and uses for the commission to use as standards for granting certificates of approval. They require the exterior of all new buildings to keep with the architectural style of the district so as not to impair the value of other buildings in the immediate vicinity.[140] For Historic District no. 1 and Historic District no. 2, the preferred styles of architecture are "Native Hawaiian," nineteenth-century New England, "Monterey" or Western; and for single-family dwellings, "any architectural style prevalent during the nineteenth century in Lahaina or which evolved from 1900 to the present in Lahaina, being unpretentious in style and painted in muted tones."[141] For Historic District no. 3, the restrictions are largely stated in the negative. European, Asian, excessively decorated, flat-roofed, modernistic, and gaudy styles are prohibited.[142] The regulations list specific criteria for use, such as height (two stories, thirty-five feet for Lahaina) and off-street parking ("one canopy tree shall be planted for every eight parking stalls").[143]

Burials

A study of historical and cultural land use and regulation in Hawai'i cannot be complete without a review of those governing Native Hawaiian *iwi* (bones) and burials that are found throughout the Islands. Indeed, between 1991 and 2000, nearly three thousand sets of Native Hawaiian

remains have been discovered and reinterred.[144] Any land development must stop when such sites are discovered.[145] Failure to comply with the relevant statutory provisions may result in civil, administrative, and criminal penalties.[146] Furthermore, if such finds occur on federal or tribal lands, then the 1990 federal Native American Graves Protection and Repatriation Act (NAGPRA) also applies.[147]

According to Native Hawaiian tradition, the bones of family members possess "mana," or spiritual power.[148] Unlike human flesh, which decays, the bones of the dead allegedly contain the spirit of the deceased and transfer their power to their living Hawaiian descendants.[149] This belief is reflected in Hawaiian proverbs:

ʻAʻohe e nalo ka iwi o ke aliʻi ʻino, o ko ke aliʻi maikaʻi ke nalo.

The bones of an evil chief will not be concealed, but the bones of a good chief will.

When an evil chief died, the people did not take the trouble to conceal his bones.[150]

While Native Hawaiians once buried their dead in graveyards, "wicked, traitorous, and desecrating chiefs" regularly exhumed fresh corpses to use the flesh as food and shark bait and to fashion the bones into arrows and fishhooks.[151] Thereafter, Hawaiians concealed their dead without identifying the sites.

Sand was the preferred location for burials because it better preserved remains than higher, wetter elevations.[152] Therefore, coastal areas with subsurface beach sand are likely to contain *iwi*.[153] "[T]he confidentiality of description and location information, especially for burial and other cultural sites, is a highly sensitive issue [in] the Hawaiian community. The final resting place of the ancestors of Native Hawaiians has always been sacred and consequently, hidden to protect its sanctity."[154]

Hence, burial secrecy lies at the heart of the state's burial statutes. The watershed event that resulted in legislative language to protect ancestral bones occurred in 1988, during the construction of the Ritz-Carlton at Honokōhau in Kapalua, Maui. The unearthing of approximately one thousand sets of remains caused an uproar in the Native Hawaiian community. Activists immediately protested the development, and—after a $6 million settlement that included the relocation of the hotel to another parcel—the State Legislature amended Chapter 6E of the Hawaiʻi Revised Statutes to include burial sites as part of its historical and cultural preservation provisions.[155]

Central to the enforcement of burial site regulation is the DLNR's State Historic Preservation Division (SHPD). One may not so much as photograph remains without SHPD's approval.[156] Indeed, SHPD is involved even if the private owner or developer is not, at least directly. "Before any agency or officer *of the State* or its *political subdivisions* approves any project involving a permit, license, certificate, land use change, subdivision, or other entitlement for use, which may affect . . .

a burial site, the agency or office shall advise the department and prior to any approval allow the department an opportunity for review and comment on the effect of the proposed project."[157]

SHPD responds primarily to "inadvertently discovered" burial remains, defined as "the unanticipated finding of human skeletal remains and any burial goods resulting from unintentional disturbance, erosion, or other ground disturbing activity."[158] Upon discovery of a potentially historic burial site, SHPD requires that it, the medical examiner, and the appropriate police department be notified as soon as possible.[159] A qualified archaeologist and a medical examiner must examine the remains to determine whether the remains are over fifty years old.[160] Once SHPD is contacted, administrative procedures require a response time of twenty-four hours on Oʻahu, forty-eight hours on other islands, and an additional twenty-four hours if multiple sets of remains are reported to determine if the burial is historic.[161] If the bones are of animal origin, then no statutory obligations are incurred. However, if the remains are over fifty years old and of Native Hawaiian ancestry, then SHPD must begin gathering information about the history of the burial and determine whether the remains will be preserved in place or relocated.[162] If the remains were discovered with no relation to a planned development project, SHPD must prepare a mitigation plan requiring "appropriate treatment . . . of burial sites or human skeletal remains."[163] However, if the discovery of remains was related to a planned development project, the landowner must prepare the mitigation plan with the concurrence of SHPD.[164] The process often raises concerns in the Hawaiian community because "developers may conduct cursory archaeological inventory surveys, claim that burials are 'inadvertently discovered,' and then attempt to force SHPD to agree to removal/relocation."[165] When it comes to land development in Hawaiʻi, inadvertent discoveries of Native Hawaiian burial sites usually lead to controversy and consequent delays in a project.[166]

The determination to preserve a burial site in place or relocate remains may be based upon the advice of an Island Burial Council (IBC), which DLNR establishes to advise both the department and SHPD regarding burial matters.[167] IBCs exist for the following five districts: Hawaiʻi, Oʻahu, Kauaʻi/Niʻihau, Molokaʻi, and Maui/Lānaʻi.[168] Comprised of between nine and fifteen members appointed by the governor, each council is charged with making an inventory of burial sites in Hawaiʻi.[169] The councils have jurisdiction over all requests to preserve or relocate "previously identified" Native Hawaiian burial sites, while SPHD has jurisdiction over those burial sites that are determined to hold remains of non-Native Hawaiian origin.[170] "Previously identified" burial sites are those "containing human skeletal remains and any burial goods identified during archaeological inventory survey and data recovery of possible burial sites, or known through oral or written testimony."[171] IBCs often hold regular public meetings where they may collect information from Hawaiians; this information serves to "previously identify" burial sites.[172] The archaeological inventory survey identifies and documents the historic sites in the project area, including subsurface excavations, to determine the location of buried sites.[173] Because of the nature and sensitivity, IBCs often keep locations confidential, unrecorded in the public records of DLNR.[174]

If Native Hawaiian remains are discovered in an area where burials have been previously identified, whoever finds the remains may not move them without SHPD's approval.[175] SHPD refers the matter to the appropriate IBC, which will determine whether the remains will be either undisturbed or reinterred at a different location.[176] The councils are more likely to recommend preservation in place for the following burials: "areas with a concentration of skeletal remains, or prehistoric or historic burials associated with important individuals and events, or areas that are within a context of historic properties, or have known lineal descendants."[177] The relevant IBC has forty-five days, commencing with the date that SHPD makes a referral to it, to render a determination about the disposition of the remains.[178] It must also make a good-faith effort to give notice to possible lineal or cultural descendants of any proposed burial treatment plan.[179]

If the IBC determines that the burial site should be preserved in place, the applicant must then develop a preservation plan providing for both short- and long-term preservation of the burial site.[180] When the IBC determines to relocate the burial site, the landowner must complete an archaeological data recovery plan outlining the reasons for relocation, the methods for disinterment, and the location and manner of reinterment.[181] SHPD must approve within ninety days; however, before approving the plans, SHPD must first consult with the applicant, any known lineal descendants, the IBC, and any appropriate Hawaiian organizations.[182] Even after approval of the final plans to preserve or reinter, the SHPD must record the determination of the IBC with the Bureau of Conveyances to ensure that the burial sites are protected in perpetuity.[183]

There are several locations in Hawai'i in which the state's burial laws have delayed development projects, including the site of a Wal-Mart and a Whole Foods Market on O'ahu, a luxury golf-residential development on the Big Island of Hawai'i, and private residences on Maui. Most recently, sixty-nine Hawaiian remains discovered during earthmoving for the construction of a $17.5-million multipurpose center on the grounds of Honolulu's famous and largely Native Hawaiian–attended Kawaiaha'o Church has resulted in a temporary halt in construction due to "one of the largest graveyard intrusions on O'ahu."[184] An archaeologist hired by an interested third party found that the excavation is also encroaching on the burial plot of one of Hawai'i's prominent figures, Queen Kapi'olani.[185] The project halted while the church supplied the state with "documentation on past burials, conduct[ed] hand excavations of newly discovered remains and develop[ed] a detailed reburial plan for bodies that [have been] unearthed."[186] The church was also required to use ground-penetrating radar to examine the property for additional burials that might not yet have been disturbed.[187]

Earlier, a huge controversy erupted on Kaua'i over remains on a single residential lot. On December 11, 2007, the Kaua'i County Planning Commission approved the construction of a single-family home on a lot in Ha'ena, conditioned on an archaeological survey of the land and a subsequent approval by the SHPD.[188] The archaeological survey uncovered thirty sets of Native Hawaiian remains on the half-acre lot. SHPD then required the landowner to draw up a burial treatment plan for protecting the remains.[189] The plan proposed preservation in place of twenty-four sets of remains that would not be impacted by the construction and on-site relocation of the six others that would be under the footprint of the proposed house.[190]

Upon receiving the burial treatment plan, however, the Kaua'i/Ni'ihau IBC recommended that all thirty sets of remains, together with those that may be found on the property in the future, should be preserved in place.[191] The landowner then revised the burial treatment plan to preserve all thirty remains in place, by capping the graves with cement blocks and adding vertical buffers to protect the human remains.[192] After consulting with Native Hawaiian organizations and the Kaua'i/Ni'ihau IBC, SHPD approved the plan,[193] though it apparently approved the vertical buffers and concrete cappings as a means of preservation of the remains without the approval of the Kaua'i/Ni'ihau IBC.[194] As the burial statute presently provides, although the IBCs have the authority to determine the preservation or relocation of previously identified Native Hawaiian burials, the councils may only make recommendations regarding the appropriate management treatment and protection of the Native Hawaiian burial sites after making their initial determination.[195]

For burials "excavated intentionally or discovered inadvertently" on federal lands in Hawai'i and Hawaiian Home Lands, NAGPRA applies. NAGPRA mainly deals with three issues: (1) the custodial priority of the cultural items excavated or discovered to the organizations or descendants who lay claim to them; (2) the process by which intentional removal of cultural items are allowed; and (3) "inadvertent discoveries" of native remains and objects.[196] Regulations promulgated by the Department of the Interior then govern the process by which "human remains, funerary objects, sacred objects, or objects of cultural patrimony are excavated or removed."[197] For the latter two, and for any event in which a Native Hawaiian organization is likely a consulting party, the rules require that "the responsible Federal agency official must" notify said organizations in writing in addition to any other communication that may have occurred.[198]

In general, the federal mandates are similar to those of the state, requiring the immediate cessation of activity in the case of inadvertent discoveries and the consent of Native Hawaiian organizations in the case of intentional excavations.[199] There is at least one difference, however. Whereas an IBC can require the preservation of bones as-is and where-is on state and private lands, site activity *may* resume within thirty days on federal lands "after certification by the notified Federal agency of receipt of the written confirmation of notification of inadvertent discovery if the resumption of the activity is otherwise lawful."[200] The presumption is that state burial regulations do not apply to federal lands. Instances of removals or excavations are not an issue because these are explicitly covered in the NAGPRA regulations.[201] Federal agencies are encouraged to come to an agreement with local organizations with respect to human remains and other sacred objects.[202]

Sacred Sites

Sacred sites, or *wahi pana*, are also important to the Native Hawaiian community. According to Native Hawaiian belief, sacred places, like human remains, possess mana or spiritual power in connection with the gods or important chiefs that may have resided there, the events or natural phenomena that occurred there, or the usefulness or aesthetic value of the location.[203] "[Hawaiian sacred places] are more than remnants of a distant past; they are enduring reminders of Hawaiian identity, a rich heritage left by kapuna."[204] Native Hawaiians are spiritually connected to these sacred places, linking them to their past, present, and future.[205]

Native Hawaiians believe that such sites can be irreparably harmed physically as well as spiritually; the mere visitation of certain locations or touching of certain objects could cause the sacred spirits to be destroyed or to leave the site.[206] The destruction or departure of spirits from *wahi pana* is said to be detrimental to the Native Hawaiian culture. There are many examples in Hawai'i where the Native Hawaiian community has tried to protect their sacred sites. In 2007, challenges by environmental and Hawaiian groups temporarily halted plans for the Outriggers Project, a $50 million addition to the W. M. Keck Observatory on Mauna Kea's summit.[207] Mauna Kea is allegedly sacred to the Hawaiian people not only as a place of worship and prayer, but also because Hawaiian legend suggests it was here that the first ancestors of the Hawaiian people, Papa and Wakea, met.[208]

A court reversed a decision by DLNR that granted a conservation district permit allowing the University of Hawai'i Institute for Astronomy to proceed with the Outriggers Project.[209] It ordered the completion of a comprehensive management plan before any project could proceed, stating "the resource that needs to be conserved, protected and preserved is the summit area of Mauna Kea, not just the area of the Project."[210]

While not perfect, historic preservation is alive and well in Hawai'i. The state's legislative protection has been strengthened over the years, and there are some linkages to other laws that are variously triggered when a historic site is listed and that provide a measure of protection to certain sites. But the state could do more, especially given the constitutional mandate that other states with stronger preservation laws lack. Indeed, Hawai'i is in the minority of states that fail to provide rehabilitation tax credits for historic buildings.[211] It is the counties that play a major role in enacting ordinances with the most promise for preserving Hawai'i's historic heritage. Witness two of the four counties' "certified local government" status and the Big Island's Hawai'i Heritage Corridor program. Given the strong language of the *Penn Central* decision from our nation's highest court upholding historic preservation restrictions prohibiting demolition altogether, it is clear that there would be no legal barriers to more forceful implementation of our state constitutional mandate that "private property *shall* be subject to reasonable regulation" in order to "conserve and develop objects and places of historic or cultural interest."[212]

Notes

1. Robert Saarnio, *Legal Framework for Historic Preservation in Hawaii: National Historic Preservation Act / Preservation 101*, Historic Preservation: Easements, Tax Incentives and Litigation, Lorman Education Services, June 18, 2008 at 6–7.
2. Id. at 7.
3. *Rebman v. City of Springfield*, 250 N.E.2d 282 (Ill. App. Ct. 1969*); A-S-P Associates v. City of Raleigh*, 258 S.E.2d 444 (N.C. 1979); *Sills v. Walworth County Land Mgmt. Comm.*, 648 N.W.2d 878 (Wis. Ct. App. 2002).
4. *Penn Cent. Transp. Co. v. City of New York*, 438 U.S. 104 (1978).
5. Id.; see David L. Callies, "Grand Central Station: Landmark preservation law," HAW. ARCHITECT, Oct. 1978 at 11; John J. Costonis, "The disparity issue: A context for the Grand Central Terminal decision," 91 HARV. L. REV. 402 (1977).
6. *See Embassy Real Estate Holdings, LLC v. D.C. Mayor's Agent for Historic Preservation*, 944 A.2d 1036 (D.C. 2008); *Casey v. Mayor of Rockville*, 929 A.2d 74 (Md. 2007); *Kalorama Heights Ltd. v. D.C. Dep't of Consumer & Regulatory Affairs*, 655 A.2d 865 (D.C. 1995).
7. Saarnio, supra note 1, at 15.
8. 26 U.S.C. §§191(a), (e) (repealed 1981).
9. Michael J. Auer, *Preservation Tax Incentives for Historic Buildings*, Washington D.C.: U.S. Dept. of the Interior, National Park Service, Heritage Preservation Services, 2004.
10. 26 U.S.C. § 47(a) (2008); 26 C.F.R. § 1.170A-14 (2008).
11. 26 U.S.C. § 47(c)(3); 26 C.F.R. § 1.48-12(d) (2008).
12. 26 C.F.R. § 1.48-12(c)(4) (2008).
13. Auer, supra note 9, at 8; *see* 26 U.S.C. § 47(c)(1)(C) (2008).
14. Auer, supra note 9, at 9.
15. Id.
16. 26 U.S.C. § 47(c)(1)(A)(iii) (2008).
17. Id. § 50(a)(1)(B) (2008).
18. *See* 26 C.F.R. § 1.170A-14(d)(5) (2008).
19. Id.
20. Saarnio, supra note 1, at 12.
21. 16 U.S.C. § 470 (2008); 42 U.S.C § 4321 (2008).
22. The Antiquities Act of 1906, 16 U.S.C. § 431 (1906); The Historic Sites Act of 1935, 16 U.S.C. § 461 (1935).
23. 36 C.F.R. § 800.1(a) (2008).
24. 16 U.S.C. § 470(f) (2008).
25. Id. § 800.2(c)(2)(ii).

26. Advisory Council on Historic Preservation, *Protecting Historic Properties: A Citizen's Guide to Section 106 Review* (2002) at 4.

27. Id. at 6–8.

28. *See Stop H-3 Ass'n v. Dole*, 870 F.2d 1419 (9th Cir. 1989). This "pervasiveness" is due primarily to the large number of projects— highways, housing, wastewater treatment plants, and programs such as coastal zone, flood hazard—that are partially or completely funded by the federal government in Hawai'i.

29. 36 C.F.R. § 60.4 (2008).

30. Saarnio, supra note 1, at 10; *see also* "National Register of Historic Places: Owner information," http://www.nps.gov/history/nr/owners.htm (last visited Nov. 26, 2009): "Under Federal law, private property owners can do anything they wish with their National Register-listed property, provided that no Federal license, permit, or funding is involved. Owners have no obligation to open their properties to the public, to restore them, or even to maintain them, if they choose not to do so."

31. 49 U.S.C. § 303(c) (2008).

32. 42 U.S.C. § 4332(2)(c) (2008).

33. 40 C.F.R. §§ 1501.4, 1508.9, 1508.4, 1508.14 (2008); *see Aluli v. Brown*, 602 F.2d 876 (9th Cir. 1979). *See Sierra Club v. DOT*, 167 P.3d 292 (Haw. 2007), involving Hawai'i's version of NEPA, the Hawai'i Environmental Protection Act (HEPA).

34. 42 U.S.C. § 4331(b)(4) (2008).

35. *WATCH v. Harris*, 603 F.2d 310 (2d Cir. 1979).

36. *Stop H-3 Ass'n*, 870 F.2d 1419.

37. Id. at 1425.

38. County of Maui, *Kaho'olawe Community Plan* 5 (1992).

39. *See Aluli*, supra note 28.

40. Maui, *Kaho'olawe Community Plan*, supra note 38, at 7.

41. Kaho'olawe History, "Hanau hou he 'ula 'o Kaho'olawe—Rebirth of a sacred island," http://www.kahoolawe.Hawaii.gov/history.shtml (last visited Dec. 29, 2009).

42. Id.

43. Telephone interview with Katie J. Kastner, Architectural Historian, State Historic Pres. Div. of Forestry & Wildlife, Dept. of Land & Nat. Res., in Kapolei, Haw. (July 9, 2008).

44. Haw. Const. art. IX, § 7 (2008).

45. Haw. Rev. Stat. § 6E-1 (2008).

46. Id. § 6E-3.

47. Id. § 6E-7.

48. Id. § 6E-2.

49. Id. §§ 6E-5, -5.5.

50. Id.

51. Id. §§ 173A-1, -2.

52. Id. §§ 195-5, -6.

53. Id. § 6E-31.

54. Id. § 6E-8.

55. Id. § 6E-5.5.

56. Id. § 6E-7(d).

57. Id. § 6E-7(b).

58. Id. § 6E-5.5(b)(1).

59. HAW. CODE R. § 13-198-8(1) (Weil 2005).

60. Id. § 13-198-8(2)-(3).

61. Id. § 13-198-3.

62. HAW. REV. STAT. § 6E-10(a) (2008).

63. Id.

64. Id.

65. Id. § 6E-10(c).

66. HAW. CODE R. § 13-198-10.

67. HAW. REV. STAT. § 246-34.

68. Id. § 246-34(c).

69. Id. § 246-34(d).

70. HAW. CODE R. § 13-5-11(b)(2) (Weil 2005).

71. HAW. REV. STAT. § 343.

72. Id. § 343-5(a)(5).

73. HAW. CODE R. § 11-200-17(e)(7).

74. Id. § 11-200-17(g).

75. Office of Environmental Quality Control, *A Guidebook for the Environmental Review Process*, 6 (April 2004).

76. Id. at 9; *see also* HAW. CODE R. § 11-200-2.

77. HAW. REV. STAT. § 205A (2008).

78. Id. § 205A-29.

79. Id. § 205A-2(b)(2).

80. Id. § 226.

81. Id. §§ 226-12(a), (b).

82. The Hawai'i Community Services Council & the Hawai'i Institute for Public Affairs, *Hawaii State Policy & the Nonprofit Sector: Optimizing the Relationship between Nonprofits and Government*, 17 (Dec. 2002).

83. *Lum Yip Kee, Ltd. v. Honolulu*, 767 P.2d 815 (Haw. 1989).

84. State Historic Preservation Division, *Statewide Historic Preservation Plan for the State of Hawaii* 2 (Nov. 2001).

85. Id.

86. HAW. REV. STAT. §§ 6E-2, 6E (2008).

87. Id. § 46-4.

88. Id. § 46-4.5.

89. City and County of Honolulu Department of Planning and Permitting, *Primary Urban Center Development Plan* P-1 (May 2004).

90. City and County of Honolulu Department of Planning and Permitting, *General Plan* § X (Oct. 2006).

91. City and County of Honolulu Department of Planning and Permitting, *North Shore Sustainable Communities Plan* 3-41, Table 3-2 (Apr. 2000).

92. HONOLULU, HAW., REV. ORDINANCES §§ 3-10.3, 21-1.20(a)(2).

93. Id. § 21-9.20.

94. *See* id. §§ 21-2.20(a), -2.70.

95. Id. § 21-3.30(a).

96. Id. §§ 21-2.40-2(b), -2(c)(5).

97. Id. § 21-9.20-5.

98. Id. §§ 21-2.40-2(c)(8), 21-2.70(a).

99. Id. § 21-2.70(b).

100. Id. § 21-9.60(b).

101. Id. §§ 21-9.60-1 through -9.60-4.

102. Id. § 21-9.60-5.

103. Id. § 21-9.60-9(a).

104. Id. § 21-9.60-12(c).

105. *See* County of Kaua'i Planning Department, *Kauai General Plan* (Nov. 2000).

106. Id. § 1.4.1(a)(1).

107. Id. § 3.1.1.

108. County of Kaua'i, Comprehensive Zoning Ordinance, § 8-9.6(e) (1972 & Supp. 2004).

109. Id. §§ 8-1.3(j), (l), (m):

> Overlaying the regulation of development or use in any or all of the Use Districts are additional special regulations which relate more specifically to the land and the existing community structure. These special regulations have been defined in the . . . Special Treatment District and may modify the manner in which uses regulated under the Use Districts may be developed or may require special performance in the development. The Special Treatment District specifies the additional performance required when critical or valuable social or aesthetic characteristics of the environment or community exist in the same area as a parcel where particular functions or uses may be developed. Any or all of these districts may overlap any Use Districts, creating accumulated regulations which more nearly relate to the conditions of the specific location where the development or use may occur.

Id. §§ 8-9.6(c)(7), (e).

110. Id. §§ 8-9.1(a), -9.2(a)(2).

111. Id. § 8-1.3(a); *see* id. § 8.2.2(c).

112. Id. § 8-9.3.

113. Id. § 8-9.6(a).

114. Id. § 8-9.6(c)(2).

115. Id. § 8-9.6(f).

116. Id. at Heritage Resource Maps.

117. Id. § 3.3.4.1.

118. Id. §§ 8-25.1 through 8-25.3.

119. 16 U.S.C. § 470a(c) (2008).

120. Id. §§ 470c(c), 470w(15).

121. Id. § 470a(c)(1).

122. County of Hawai'i, *General Plan* at ii (Feb. 2005).

123. Id. at 6-1 through 6-14; Facilities-2 (Fig. 27).

124. Id. at 6-3.

125. Id. at 6-2.

126. Hawai'i, *Charter* § 3-15(b) (2000).
127. Hawai'i, *General Plan*, supra note 122, at 6-2, -3.
128. Id. at 6-11.
129. Id. at 15-1.
130. County of Hawai'i, *Hawaii County Code*, §§ 25-7-2, 25-7-4(b)-(c) (1975).
131. Id. §§ 2-214, -215; 23-26; 19-89.1; 5-2.2.4.
132. Maui, *Charter*, 20, 36, (Jan. 2003).
133. Maui, *General Plan*, § I.B.1.a (1990).
134. Maui, *County Code*, § 2.88.030(B) (Dec. 2007).
135. Id. § 2.88.030(C).
136. Id. § 19.52.020 (Ord. 757 § 1(b), 1973).
137. Id.
138. Id. §§ 19.50.010 - .030.
139. Id. § 19.50.020.
140. Id. § 19.52.010(A).
141. Id. § 19.52.010(B).
142. Id. § 19.52.010(C).
143. Id. §§ 19.52.090(C), 19.52.100(D).
144. Lisa Woods Munger, *Hawaii Environmental Law Handbook*, 3rd ed., Honolulu: Government Institutes, 2000 at 400.
145. HAW. REV. STAT. § 6E-43.6(g).
146. Id. §§ 6E-11, -73.
147. 25 U.S.C. 3001 (2008); 43 C.F.R. §§ 10.3-10.7 (2008).
148. Melody Kapilialoha MacKenzie, *Native Hawaiian Handbook*, Honolulu: University of Hawai'i Press, 1991 at 246–249.
149. Id.
150. Mary Kawena Pukui, *'Ōlelo No'eau: Hawaiian Proverbs & Poetical Sayings*, Honolulu: Bishop Museum Press, 1983.
151. *See* Samuel Manaiakalani Kamakau, *Ka Po'e Kahiko: The People of Old*, Honolulu: Bishop Museum Press, 1991.
152. *See* Sean Hao, "Ancient burials likely in transit path," HONOLULU ADVERTISER, June 22, 2008, at A13 (quoting Thomas Dye).
153. Id.
154. Comm. on Water, Land, and Haw. Affairs, Standing Comm. Rep. 2868, 20th Leg., Reg. Sess., at 1 (2000) (re: H.B. 2762).
155. *See* HAW. REV. STAT., §§ 6E-3(3), (10), (11).
156. HAW. CODE R. § 13-300-32.
157. HAW. REV. STAT. § 6E-42(a) (emphasis added).
158. HAW. CODE R. § 13-300-2.
159. HAW. REV. STAT. § 6E-43.6(b).
160. Id. § 6E-43.6(c). If the remains are not over fifty years old, the medical examiner must investigate, and SHPD's involvement at the burial site ends.
161. Id.
162. Id. § 6E-43.6(c)(2).
163. Id. §6E-43.6(e)(3).
164. Id. §6E-43.6(e)(1).
165. Lisa A. Bail, Maren Calver, Robert D. Harris, Lea Hong, Naomi U. Kuwaye,

and Paul J. Schwind, "Emerging environmental and land use issues," HAWAI'I BAR JOURNAL (June 2005).
166. Id.
167. HAW. REV. STAT. § 6E-43.5(d).
168. Id. § 6E-43.5(a).
169. Id. §§ 6E-43.5(b), (f).
170. HAW. CODE. R. §§ 13-300-33 to 34.
171. Id. § 13-300-2.
172. Id. § 13-300-31(a).
173. Id. §§ 13-276-3 to 5.
174. HAW. REV. STAT. § 6E-43.5(e).
175. Id. § 6E-43(a).
176. Id. § 6E-43(b).
177. Id.
178. Id.
179. HAW. CODE R. § 13-300-33(b)(1).
180. Id. § 13-300-38(e).
181. Id. § 13-300-38(f).
182. Id. §§ 13-300-38(e)-(f).
183. Id. § 13-300-38(g).
184. Rick Daysog, "Kawaiaha'o church center's fundraising costs questioned," HONOLULU ADVERTISER, May 29, 2009, at A1-A2.
185. Rick Daysog, "OHA asks for study of burials," HONOLULU ADVERTISER, June 9, 2009, at B1.
186. Rick Daysog, "Church project in need of disinterment permit," HONOLULU ADVERTISER, June 13, 2009, at B1.
187. Id.
188. *Brescia v. Edends-Huff,* No. 08-1-0107 (D. Haw. 5th Cir. Oct. 2, 2008) (Order Granting in Part and Denying in Part Defendant's Motion for Preliminary Injunction) at 2.
189. Id. at 2–3.
190. Id. at 3.
191. Id.
192. Id.
193. Id.
194. Indigenous Mapping Network, "Kānaka Maoli scholars against desecration—Second statement on Naue," March 24, 2009, http://indigenousmapping.net/newitem.html?start=25 (scroll down to "Kānaka Maoli Scholars Against Desecration") (last visited Dec. 29, 2009)
195. HAW. REV. STAT. § 6E-43.5(f).
196. 25 U.S.C. §§ 3002(a)-(d).
197. 43 C.F.R. § 10.3(c)(4)(i).
198. Id. §§ 10.3(c)(1), 10.4(d)(1)(iii), 10.5(b)(1).
199. Id. §§ 10.4(c), 10.3(b)(2).
200. Id. § 10.4(d)(2).
201. Id.
202. Id. at § 10.5(f).

203. Edward L. H. Kanahele, *Ancient Sites of Oahu.* Honolulu: Bishop Museum Press, 1991, at ix, xi.

204. J. Mikilani Ho, *Pana Oʻahu: Sacred Stones, Sacred Lands,* Honolulu: University of Hawaiʻi Press, 1999, at xxvi, xxvii.

205. Kanahele, supra note 203, at ix.

206. Ho, supra note 204, at xxvii.

207. Kevin Dayton, "Big push to erect telescope in Isles," HONOLULU ADVER-TISER, Aug. 10, 2008 at 1A.

208. Id.

209. *Mauna Kea Anaina Hou v. DLNR,* Civ. No. 04-1-397 (D. Haw. Aug. 3, 2006).

210. Id. at 7.

211. National Trust for Historic Preservation, *State Tax Credits for Historic Preservation: A State-by-State Summary* (Aug. 2007).

212. HAW. CONST. art. IX, § 7.

Chapter 9

Federalization of Land Use Control in Hawai'i

Clean Air, Clean Water, Species Protection, and Environmental Impacts

The federal government injected itself into environmental law in a series of statutes passed in the 1970s. The late Don Hagman called the new environmental laws with their significant land use implications "The Federalization of land use controls."[1] The complex array of federal environmental statutes spawned a cottage industry of lawyers devoted to keeping businesses in compliance with the laws. From a land use perspective, the most important of these laws are the Clean Air Act, the Clean Water Act, and the Endangered Species Act.[2] In some instances, Hawai'i's state environmental laws go even further. For example, as interpreted in a series of Hawai'i Supreme Court decisions, the Hawai'i Environmental Impact Statement (EIS) law has been so broadly construed that any land use project that so much as touches state land, however minimal the effect, triggers a time-consuming, expensive EIS review.

Clean Air

What began as a set of guidelines for the states in the Air Quality Act of 1967 became a comprehensive, multilevel regulatory scheme to control air pollution through amendments in 1972, 1977, and 1990. Designed by the federal government and implemented largely by the states to protect and maintain healthy air, the act has achieved many of its goals. The amount of pollution released into the environment in the United States has declined since 1970, even as the size of the economy doubled.[3] The Clean Air Act is a command-and-control environmental scheme. The Environmental Protection Agency (EPA) and the states

CORKY

ACTUALLY THE DAMAGE TO THE ENVIRONMENT
HAS ALREADY BEEN DONE.

set emission limits for specific pollutants, issue permits, and punish the noncompliant.[4]

In spite of its success, the Clean Air Act faces criticism for its emphasis on legal compliance, which deters businesses from misbehavior but offers no incentive to exceed minimum standards.[5] The costs of compliance can be high. Nevertheless, Hawai'i has a relatively easy time of it. The geography and composition of the Hawai'i economy together bless Hawai'i with some of the best air quality in the country. There are few major stationary sources of pollution, and trade winds normally disperse pollutants from automobiles.

The purpose of the Clean Air Act is "to protect and enhance the quality of the Nation's air resources so as to promote the public health and welfare and the productive capacity of its population."[6] It achieves this by directing the EPA to develop National Ambient Air Quality Standards (NAAQS) for certain named pollutants that are deemed hazardous to public health and welfare.[7] Primary ambient air standards are those designed to protect public health (plus an extra margin). Secondary ambient air standards safeguard "public welfare,"[8] which includes ecological concerns such as healthy vegetation, wildlife, damage to property, and general prevention of environmental degradation.[9]

NAAQS are enforced through state-created State Implementation Plans (SIPs) that provide for the implementation, maintenance, and enforcement of standards in an air quality control region.[10] SIPs are mandatory, on pain of revocation of highway funds, and the EPA will draw up a Federal Implementation Plan. The EPA must approve an SIP to ensure that it conforms to the requirements of the Clean Air Act before the SIP becomes enforceable. Nevertheless, SIPs are a source of some autonomy for the states in implementing the Clean Air Act. Through the development of SIPs, state officials are responsible for the localization of the Clean Air Act to suit the particular needs of their state. Though the act is a federal mandate imposed on the states, in practice it relies on the states' cooperation; approximately 80 percent of enforcement actions for federal environmental laws are brought by state authorities.[11]

A state implementation program must follow a number of statutory requirements to be approved by the EPA.[12] The requirements with the most significance for land use are the following:

> (1) enforceable emission limitations and other techniques permitted by the state (including economic incentives such as fees, marketable permits, and auctions of emissions rights), as well as schedules and timetables for compliance;
>
> (2) a program to enforce those emission limitations and regulate the modification and construction of any stationary source within the areas covered by the plan, including a permit program in which applicants pay the cost;
>
> (3) prohibitions of stationary sources or other emissions that would interfere with the prevention of significant deterioration of air quality or to protect visibility.[13]

The impact of these requirements on land use can be significant. Development opportunities are limited in areas at or near emission limits of the SIP due to the prohibition of new sources of pollution that might push pollutants over the limit, while areas that are under the limit are more attractive.[14] In practice, this is not a huge concern in Hawai'i. Emissions are about half the federal limits.[15] Even in areas with good air, compliance with the prevention of significant deterioration requirement can distort urban growth patterns. Land use controls as a requirement for SIPs were removed from the 1972 Clean Air Amendment, but the legislative history indicates that land use controls are not out of bounds.[16]

Hawai'i has not revised its SIP since 1994. With some of the best air in the country, it is not surprising that the EPA has paid relatively little attention to the state's delay, but the Hawai'i State Department of Health's Clean Air Branch is planning to update the SIP in the near future.

PRECONSTRUCTION REVIEW

Amendments to the Clean Air Act require preconstruction review of every new[17] major stationary source or modification of an existing stationary source of air pollution in order to assure the attainment or maintenance of national primary and secondary ambient air quality.[18] Consequently, major new developments often must undergo a federally mandated review. Negative reviews can delay a project even further—a potentially ruinous delay amid other local permitting requirements. If state and local officials are not up to the task of performing the review, the EPA has the power to perform the review for them.

The act established review of proposed sites of stationary sources of pollution as a natural counterpart to the stationary source emission limitations (new-source performance standards). The performance standards place a ceiling on maximum emissions; however, to rely on that measure alone would be to ignore the effects of geography in channeling and concentrating emissions. A factory located in a valley is a recipe for bad air quality no matter how seriously emissions limits are taken and enforced, because dispersion cannot have its usual beneficial effect of improving air quality.[19] The preconstruction review is an opportunity to confront rank unsuitability of a particular project to a particular area. Unhappily for those projects that would benefit from easier compliance with the Clean Air Act, a facility located on the coast encounters two more federal programs, the Coastal Hazards Protection

"LET'S STAY AWAY FROM THE ALA WAI
UNTIL IT'S REALLY POLLUTION-FREE."

and the Coastal Zone Management Acts, which present their own challenges.[20] As a result of the preconstruction review amendments, the SIP contains enforceable measures to review whether the proposed entity would complicate the maintenance or attainment of ambient air quality standards, either through direct emissions or the likely result of a new building: increased traffic. The amendments set out further submissions state agencies may require from developers to fully inform their decisions.[21]

Hawai‘i requires both a permit and registration for the preconstruction review process.[22] Construction of major new stationary sources of air pollution triggers tougher levels of control. The involvement

of regulatory agencies in the permitting process before construction
begins gives the agencies a degree of control over where new sources
are located and how they are designed in order to minimize harmful
effects on air quality. The New Source Performance Standards (NSPS)
program compiles a list of non–NAAQS pollutants designated by the
EPA through regulations. The EPA requires that emissions standards
be the lowest achievable emission, through the best technology available, given the "non-air-quality health and environmental impacts and
energy requirements." Standards may be based on design, equipment,
work practice, or operational standards where it is not feasible to require
adherence to a specific emissions limit.[23]

PREVENTION OF SIGNIFICANT DETERIORATION (PSD)

In attainment areas like Hawai'i, PSD permits are required before
construction begins on any new stationary source of pollution or any
major modification to an existing source in order to prevent air quality deterioration and maintain air quality above the federally mandated
minimum.[24] PSD areas cover all of Hawai'i. There are three classes of
PSD areas.[25] Class I areas are national parks, national memorials, and
national wilderness areas of greater than five thousand acres in size that
are deemed to deserve special protection. Class II areas are attainment
areas not otherwise classified where some deterioration in air quality
accompanying growth is permissible. Class III areas are those in which
air quality is allowed to degrade to reach national secondary ambient
air qualities. So far, no area in Hawai'i has been designated a growth-
friendly Class III. Except for the two national parks that are required to
be Class I, every area in Hawai'i is Class II. The EPA faults the Hawai'i
SIP for not including "approvable procedures for preventing the significant deterioration of air quality."[26] Nevertheless, the implications of the
Clean Air Act for land use in Hawai'i are likely to remain minimal.

Clean Water

The Clean Water Act (CWA) is the philosophical and regulatory frater-
nal twin of the Clean Air Act. The CWA is a federal statutory scheme
that mixes ambient water standards and technology-based controls to
regulate pollution. The two schemes are not identical, however; the
outlook on the CWA is less rosy for all concerned, whether concerned
about regulatory burdens on property or polluted water. While the
characteristics of geography and economy in Hawai'i combine to ease

the impact of the Clean Air Act and enable the state to easily achieve attainment, the Clean Water Act grapples less successfully to balance the regulatory burden placed on land use with the need to obtain high water quality standards.[27]

The objective of the Clean Water Act is to "restore and maintain the chemical, physical, and biological integrity of the Nation's waters."[28] Under the CWA, the EPA must develop programs aimed at "preventing, reducing, or eliminating the pollution of the navigable waters and ground waters and improving the sanitary condition of surface and underground waters."[29] The CWA was born from the frustration of federal legislators with the ineffectiveness of state water quality control measures. The federal government stepped forcefully into the water pollution control business with the 1972 amendments to the CWA. The state programs that preceded the CWA focused on ambient water quality. Congress was well aware of the problems with state-led ambient water quality programs and focused their efforts instead on controlling polluting industrial and sewage treatment facilities through technology-based controls.[30] Federal regulations mandate that every discharger adopt the best practicable technology to minimize the pollution of the waters of the United States. Overall, the CWA has been successful. Waters that were once so polluted they were not safe to swim in are on their way to recovery.[31] But the CWA's success in regulating the traditional factory pipe may just have been picking the low-hanging fruit. Probably most of the remaining pollutants in the water are due to nonpoint sources such as agricultural runoff. Nonpoint sources are estimated to be responsible for 99 percent of suspended solids and 50–90 percent of other pollutants.[32] Revisions to the CWA since the mid-1980s are designed to give federal and state regulators more muscle and more options in handling other significant sources of pollution, most notably storm water discharges and the polluted runoff from dirty city streets; the 1987 CWA amendments and subsequent rules have increased regulatory hurdles for most land use and development. Overall, the impact of attempts to control runoff has been anemic.

Clean water is particularly important to Hawai'i. Tourists are the consumers of the major state industry, and they flock to Hawai'i for the beaches, the waterfalls, the marine wildlife, and the diving and snorkeling. Hawai'i regulators are aware of the importance of maintaining that experience for visitors.[33]

The relative lack of heavy industry makes regulating point sources unproblematic. Of more concern are the nonpoint sources—pollutants that cannot be defined as emanating from a discrete source like a pipe but which are responsible for most of the pollution in Hawai'i's streams and nearshore marine areas. Nonpoint pollution comes from herbicides, fertilizers, insecticides, and soil from eroded cliffs being washed by storms into bodies of water. Hawai'i's geography offers unusual challenges to controlling nonpoint source pollution. Streams flow short and steep down the mountain, and most are intermittent. Moreover, as in other states, Hawai'i's enthusiasm for regulatory controls falls short of meaningful (i.e., mandatory) runoff control of agricultural interests. As regulators struggle with plans for dealing with the water runoff, the state may contemplate greater restrictions imposed on land use.

NPDES PERMITS AND POINT SOURCES

Anyone who discharges pollutants into "waters of the United States" from a "point source" must get a permit to do so.[34] Section 402 National Pollutant Discharge Elimination System (NPDES) permits,[35] along with Section 404 "dredge and fill permits,"[36] are the centerpiece of regulated water pollution under the CWA.[37] The "discharge of a pollutant" is defined as the "addition of any pollutant to navigable waters from any point source."[38] What constitutes an "addition" can sometimes be a subtle thing. The Ninth Circuit Court of Appeals, of which Hawai'i is a part, has tended to interpret "addition" more broadly than some other circuits, including soil, sand, and rocks taken from a streambed, sifted for gold, and returned to the water.[39] The Ninth Circuit similarly decided that spraying aquatic herbicide into canals to destroy vegetative growth in the water was a discharge.[40] What constitutes a "point source" requiring a permit is also the subject of litigation. A point source is "any discernable, confined and discrete conveyance, including but not limited to any pipe, ditch, channel, conduit, well, discrete fissure, container, rolling stock, concentrated animal feeding operation," and so on.[41] "Point sources" include "surface runoff which is collected or channeled by man."[42] Courts have taken the definition even further.[43] Navy planes and cattle feedlots during a storm have both been held to be point sources.[44] A dairy farm, in aggregate, has been found to be a point source, or—as the court found in the alternative—so are the manure-spreading vehicles that spread manure onto fields. The manure subsequently flows to streams.[45] The CWA is lenient toward farmers, however, leaving them largely unregulated: Agricultural storm water discharges and flows from irrigated agriculture are not "point sources."[46]

The definition of "waters of the United States" has also undergone some revision by the courts since the first expansive constructions by the Army Corps of Engineers. Regulations promulgated by the agency cast a very broad net to bring virtually all surface waters (and many surfaces without waters) into the ambit of federal regulation. These regulations were narrowed by the Supreme Court in *Rapanos v. United States.*[47] The Court determined that although a body of water need not be constantly flowing to be regulated under the Clean Water Act, there must be at least a "significant nexus" to waters that were actually navigable.[48] Due to the interconnectedness of the waters and terrain in Hawaiʻi, the impact of this ruling is likely to be slight for the state's land use. NPDES permits are not required for nonpoint agricultural or silvicultural (tree farming) projects.[49] Dredged or fill materials are regulated with the separate 404 permit elsewhere in the CWA. NPDES permits are also not required for sewage from vessels and the discharge of pollutants to a treatment works.[50] The CWA does not normally require NPDES permits for discharges to groundwater or wells either,[51] although some courts have found them to be necessary when discharges into groundwater resulted in contamination of connected surface waters.[52] The EPA is less demanding in protecting groundwater and usually allows state programs to take the lead in such programs; action under the CWA is limited to a reporting requirement.[53] Hawaiʻi has been active in promoting voluntary guidelines to limit the harm caused to groundwater from golf courses.[54]

The federal government delegates the NPDES permitting system to the states in accordance with federal statutes and regulations, but state NPDES permits must still comply with applicable federal requirements.[55] The most significant of these are technology-based limitations. Technology-based limits do not mandate the use of a particular technology or design; instead, they hold permittees to an achievable level of pollution control based on technology available in the industry.

The CWA has inconsistent standards for facilities of different ages and for those discharging different types of pollution.[56] Discharges of conventional pollutants by existing sources to surface waters require the "best practicable control technology currently available" (BPT) or the "best conventional pollutant control technology" (BCT).[57] BPT standards are created by surveying what the best in the industry achieve with a model technology and holding dirtier dischargers to that standard, though "the best" is no specific percentage and in one case was based on a model technology used by over 70 percent of the industry.[58] Congress enacted BCT as a fuzzy intermediate stage between the "best available technology economically achievable" (BAT), which could be unreasonably costly, and BPT. BCT is applied if it is deemed to be cost effective based on two arbitrary benchmarks created by the EPA.[59]

New sources are subject to still higher technological standards: new source performance standards (NSPS). A "new source" is a "building, structure or facility" that was built after the promulgation of an applicable NSPS,[60] which was constructed at a site without a preexisting source, totally replaces the process or production equipment, or is separate and independent of sources already in place at the same site.[61] In Hawai'i, new sources or increased sources of pollution must "provide the highest and best degree of waste treatment practicable under existing technology."[62] Under federal regulations, NSPS standards are at least as tough as BAT; the theory is that it is most practical to require new facilities to design their facilities with the best technology from the start rather than require existing facilities designed with old technology in mind to undergo costly renovations and thereby phase in higher water quality technologies over time as old facilities are replaced.

NPDES permits come in two forms: a general permit or an individual permit. An individual permit is a site-specific permit for one facility. A general permit is for a group of similar facilities not expected to greatly impact waters, but it is desirable that they adhere to BPT standards. General permits are usually instigated by the permitting organization, and the organization cannot rely on site-specific information.[63] They are used for sources of pollutants that are conveniently managed together, such as storm water associated with industrial activity, storm water associated with construction activities, and treated effluents leaking from underground storage tanks. An application for a permit (or notice of intent to be covered by a general permit) must be filed at least 180 days prior to the first discharge,[64] with the exception of storm water construction discharge permits, which may be applied for at least ninety days before the beginning of construction.[65] An NPDES permit application must contain substantive information on the proposed activity.[66]

The Hawai'i Department of Health (DOH) may require additional information from the applicant. If the NPDES application is deficient in some fashion, it will not be processed until the deficiency is cured.[67] The applicant is also required to send a copy of the permit application to the State Historic Preservation Division when review is required.[68]

Before the public has a chance to comment on the application and tentative issuance or denial, the DOH must make tentative determinations as to the ground rules of the permit, including proposed effluent

limitations, a proposed schedule of compliance with dates and requirements, monitoring requirements, and any other proposed special
conditions to granting the permit.[69] The DOH must then give notice
"designed to inform interested and potentially interested persons of the
proposed discharge."[70] Notice must be circulated within the geographical area—potentially including post offices near the entrance of the
premises of the proposed discharge and to newspapers—paid for by the
applicant.[71] A public hearing will be held if a request is submitted within
thirty days and there is "significant public interest," with instances of
doubt resolved in favor of holding a hearing.[72] Once a final determination is made, the DOH must send a final decision to the applicant and
those who submitted written comments.[73]

An NPDES permit may not be granted for a duration longer than
five years. It may be terminated by natural expiration, noncompliance
with any condition of the permit, failure by the permittee to "disclose
fully all relevant facts" or "misrepresentation of any relevant facts at any
time," a determination that the permitted activity endangers human
health, or a change in conditions requiring a temporary or permanent
reduction or elimination of a discharge.[74] Once an NPDES is acquired,
compliance with the effluent limitations listed in the NPDES permit
satisfies the CWA. The permittee is shielded from new regulations and
requirements promulgated by the EPA for the duration of the permit.[75]
During the duration of the permit, permittees are subject to monitoring to ensure compliance. All records and samples taken of water quality must be retained and included in the mean tests reported to the
DOH.[76]

In addition to an NPDES permit, a water quality certification is
required stating that a proposed activity will not violate water quality
standards for any application for a federal license or permit that may
cause a discharge into navigable waters.[77] Navigable waters are defined
by Hawai'i regulations to include all waters that could be used by foreign or interstate travelers for recreation, from which fish could be
taken and sold in interstate commerce, or that could be used by industries engaged in interstate commerce. As a practical matter, navigable
waters encompass most surface waters in Hawai'i.[78] The application for
a water quality certification must make a "reasonable assurance" that
the proposed activity will not violate water quality standards. The water
quality certification should include any conditions that DOH deems
necessary or desirable to meet water quality assurances. DOH will issue
the certification if there is "reasonable assurance" water quality stan-

dards will be maintained and "best practicable methods of control" will be applied to a discharge. Permits and water quality certifications relating to the construction or rehabilitation of Hawaiian fishponds have priority.[79] If for some reason a project or activity requiring a federal permit or license neglects to acquire a water quality certification and the project is begun, an "After the Fact" water quality certification may be obtained, but this certification does not retroactively cover the previous violation.

CONTROLLING STORM WATER POLLUTION

Storm water discharges fall somewhere between point and nonpoint sources. Unlike other runoff, storm water discharges are legally classified as "point" sources because they are often collected and discharged through drains, culverts, and other conveyances and thus meet the definition of a "point source."[80] NPDES permits are required for storm water discharges already permitted, discharges associated with industrial activity, discharges from municipal storm sewer systems serving more than one hundred thousand people, and discharges determined to contribute to "a violation of a water quality standard or is a significant contributor of pollutants."[81] Storm water is "storm water runoff, snow melt runoff, and surface runoff and drainage."[82] Agricultural runoff is pointedly excluded.[83]

In 1999, storm water regulations were extended to cover small construction sites and small, separate municipal storm sewer systems. Permits are now required for construction sites that would disturb one acre or more.[84] Most such sites should fall within general permits and are required to submit a notice of intent for coverage.[85]

WATER QUALITY STANDARDS

Hawaiʻi water quality regulations remain substantially as they were since they were established in 1979, in spite of the more accurate science that has emerged since then.[86] Hawaiʻi State water quality standards seek to maintain current water quality and existing uses.[87] Water degradation may sometimes be allowed when water quality is higher than necessary to support swimming and wildlife, if "allowing lower water quality is necessary to accommodate important economic or social development in the area in which the waters are located," provided that existing uses remain protected and other statutory and regulatory requirements are met for point sources, and all "cost effective and reasonable best management practices" for nonpoint sources are met.[88]

Hawai'i's numeric water quality standards are based on the national effluent limits. National standards were not designed for a tropical environment, however, and some commentators have suggested that as applied to Hawai'i (and areas such as Florida), such standards might be unduly strict, and lack of attainment may not accurately reflect attainment of high-quality water. For instance, the standards issued for certain bacteria that are used as indicators for fecal matter do not recognize that the bacteria flourishes in Hawai'i's soil, while it does not in more temperate areas of the United States, leading to misleadingly high levels not necessarily indicative of sewage problems.[89]

Basic water quality standards set a water quality floor below which water is not allowed to degrade.[90] Standards are both numeric and narrative. All state waters are monitored for toxic or harmful pollutants. Water is to be free of material that settles to become sludge, floating debris, or substances that discolor or "produce taste" in the water or alter the flavor of fish. Water is also to be free of substances in concentrations that would "produce undesirable aquatic life" and toxic or otherwise harmful substances in concentrations that are harmful to humans or wildlife or that "interfere with any beneficial use of the water."[91] State waters must be free at all times from pollutants that would rapidly harm fish life. Standards are somewhat looser for levels of discharges that are harmful only over the long term.[92]

The requirement that water be free of soil from agriculture and erosion is deemed to have been met if the land on which the erosion occurred is managed according to "the best degree of management or control" or a soil conservation program is "actively pursued" *and* the impact on the waters is "acceptable."[93] Unsurprisingly, the waters of national and state parks and wildlife refuges and waters of "exceptional recreational or ecological significance" enjoy higher levels of protection. Water quality in such areas may not be degraded.[94]

Hawai'i divides its waters into a series of classes of higher and lower degrees of protection. "Inland" waters include wetlands, reservoirs, ditches and flumes that discharge into other waters, lakes, and streams (intermittent and perennial).[95] "Intermittent" streams include gulches in which a sudden rainstorm sometimes creates flowing waters.[96] "Marine" waters are embayments (an indentation of a coastline), open coastal waters, and oceanic waters. Coastal waters and embayments are further subdivided into things such as sand beaches and reef flats.[97] Both types of waters contain a hierarchy of protection under Hawai'i water quality standards.

The most protected inland waters are "class 1" waters to be preserved "in their natural state as nearly as possible with an absolute minimum of pollution." Waste discharge is prohibited, and "any conduct which results in a demonstrable increase in levels of point or nonpoint source contamination in class 1 waters is prohibited." There are separate subclasses for waters that warrant this level of protection because of their importance to an ecosystem, and sources for drinking water are separated out in a special subclass to which the public may be prevented access.[98] Waters that are a "unique or critical habitat" for listed threatened or endangered species are class 1, as are waters within conservation areas and refuges and national and state parks.[99]

Class 2 designates less protected waters that protect uses for recreational purposes, aquatic life, shipping, and agricultural and industrial water supplies. Discharges into class 2 waters must receive "the best degree of treatment or control." These are the default waters not listed as class 1. The "basic" water quality standards apply to class 2 waters such as springs and seeps, ditches, and flumes.

Discharges into estuaries and embayments are particularly limited. New treated sewage discharges are prohibited from estuaries and embayments. Industrial discharges are likewise prohibited, with the exception of storm water discharges associated with industrial activity, discharges allowed by a general NPDES permit, and a few specific harbors.[100]

Marine waters likewise have highly protected class AA waters to be preserved in a "natural pristine state."[101] No zones of mixing—where discharges that otherwise would violate water quality standards may be dispersed into the waters to achieve attainment—are permitted in shallow, defined reef areas or within a thousand feet of shore. Class AA waters are to be protected for research, marine life, recreation, and conservation. Hōnaunau, Waialua Bay, Hanauma Bay, and some open coastal waters are all class AA.[102] The primary uses of the less-protected class A waters are recreational and aesthetic. Other uses are permitted if compatible with this objective and the existence of marine life.[103] Class A waters are predominately harbors.[104]

In class I marine bottom ecosystems, only "passive human uses without intervention or alteration" are permitted. In class II marine bottom ecosystems, wildlife and recreational purposes are protected, but actions altering or modifying the seafloor, including the construction of harbors, dams, seawalls, wastewater effluent outfall structures, and landfills are allowed with regulatory approval after weighing the environmental impact against the public interest.

TMDLs: The Seeds of Mandatory Nonpoint Source Regulation?

Generally, the CWA does not directly prohibit nonpoint source discharges,[105] even though nonpoint pollution contributes more to water pollution in the United States than point sources.[106] However, the administrator of the EPA approves the management plans developed by the state and certified by the governor.[107] As part of their plans, the states must develop Total Maximum Daily Loads (TMDLs) to allocate allowable pollutant levels to different sources and implement abatement measures. For many years, the mandate was entirely ignored by the EPA and all but a handful of states, as they devoted energy and resources to implementing the technology-based controls of the recent CWA amendments. Inattention continued until a series of citizen lawsuits in the 1980s forced implementation. The EPA finally began to promulgate guidelines and requirements in the early 1990s.[108] As the pace of listing impaired waters increased, TMDLs became an irresistibly potent mechanism for nonpoint source regulation. Recall that nonpoint sources now account for the majority of impairment in polluted waters. Indeed, according to at least one TMDL developed for Hawai'i, nonpoint sources account for the *entirety* of the impairment.[109]

Here is how it works. Section 303(d) requires that states identify receiving waters that have failed to meet water quality standards for their designated uses after the implementation of technology-based pollution controls. Waters that fail to meet state standards are "impaired"; failure to meet a single water quality criterion, numeric or narrative, results in the designation. States are required to establish a priority ranking of these impaired water bodies and create TMDLs for the waters based on identification of the numeric targets to reach designated beneficial uses of the water and a source analysis to locate the sources contributing to pollution. The TMDL establishes a numerical limit to the pollutant load and allocates those limits to point and nonpoint sources. States are required to have continuing planning processes and mechanisms to implement TMDLs, though in practice they have wide latitude in how they choose to go about it; the EPA is disinclined to pick quarrels in the face of passive defiance or outright resistance.[110] Point source pollution must be consistent with the TMDL, and new discharges are permitted only if there remains capacity in current loads that would not exceed the TMDL allocated to point sources.[111]

Hawai'i has listed 93 stream segments and 209 marine segments as impaired.[112] It has also begun the arduous and expensive process of developing TMDLs for impaired waters according to a priority list. There is a wide variety of potential TMDLs. For example, broad, dry gulches that flow with water in heavy rain are listed as "impaired waters," as they carry pollutants into coastal waters.[113] Several have been approved by the EPA. The most common source of impairment is turbidity resulting from polluted runoff. Excessive amounts of nitrite/nitrates, total nitrogen, and total phosphorous are also common.[114] Some streams are listed as impaired for "turbidity" on the strength of a visual assessment alone (i.e., they looked muddy).[115] The DOH lacks the resources for extensive testing and argues that in cases where it established water impairment visually, later scientific sampling confirmed the visual assessment. Problematically for landowners, it is easier to get on the list of impaired waters than off it: While visual data suffices for a listing, waters may be removed from the "impaired" list only by a showing of "good cause"— and "good cause" requires sampling.

Now that TMDLs have been established for some waters, the big question is what they may mean for previously unregulated nonpoint sources—particularly agricultural runoff. The CWA is ambiguous about whether the TMDL–mandating section of the Clean Water Act, 303(d), reaches nonpoint sources at all. Nevertheless, the EPA has interpreted Section 303(d) to include nonpoint sources since the 1970s, and states have complied by listing nonpoint source allocations in their TMDLs.[116] Because EPA lacks specific authority to regulate nonpoint sources directly, implementation of the nonpoint source TMDL load allocations was left in the hands of the states.[117] However, in *Prosolino v. American Forest & Paper Association*,[118] the Ninth Circuit Court of Appeals ruled that the EPA must step in and set TMDLs for waterways that are polluted by nonpoint sources if a state fails to do so.[119] It reasoned that this did not interfere with the state's traditional control over land use because the TMDLs do "not specify the load of pollutants that may be received from particular parcels of land or describe what measures the state should take to implement the TMDL."[120] Indeed, both the court and the TMDL emphasized that "implementation and monitoring are state responsibilities."[121] Hawai'i has its water quality standards and its TMDLs; now, can it enforce them?

While Hawai'i has adequate authority to regulate nonpoint pollution through TMDLs, it lacks effective enforcement mechanisms.[122] In the words of one TMDL, "Participation in the Polluted Runoff Control program is voluntary, and there are no DOH-imposed regulatory consequences of non-participation."[123] The Polluted Runoff Control Program, the state agency created to apply for and distribute grants for (voluntary) runoff pollution control from Section 319 of the Clean Water Act, is hampered by lack of funding and lack of personnel. In the year 2007, there were two vacancies in a very small department.[124] In one TMDL, the DOH claimed it had authority under Section 342D-11 of the Hawaii Revised Statutes to enforce nonpoint sources violating water quality standards, even absent permitting authority, by filing civil lawsuits. According to the statute, "The [DOH] may institute a civil action in any court of competent jurisdiction for injunctive and other relief to prevent any violation of [the water pollution chapter], any rule adopted pursuant to this chapter . . . to impose and collect civil penalties, to collect administrative penalties, or to obtain other relief."[125] It is unclear whether this vague directive would be sufficient to compel nonpoint source polluters to adopt best management practices or otherwise be liable for the runoff that contributed (but probably did not solely cause) violations of state water quality standards. Such a litigation would no doubt consume legal resources better used elsewhere; no attempts to use 342D-11 in such a manner have yet been attempted on the basis of a TMDL.

What can be expected of TMDLs in Hawai'i? According to one gloomy commentator, "The largest loss leaders of the federal air and water quality acts are the science-based total maximum daily load (TMDL) and state implementation plan (SIP) programs, which absorb large amounts of money, remain information-starved, feature shameless manipulation of the data, face crippling political pressure, and produce little abatement."[126] Another commentator, equally pessimistic, questioned the applicability of the TMDL regulatory scheme to Hawai'i: "The TMDL program was not designed to accomplish water quality improvement in streams in small Hawaiian watersheds impaired mainly by nonpoint source pollutants, habitat destruction, dewatering of streams, and growth of dense stands of introduced vegetation in stream channels. Without changes at the federal level, monies spent on TMDL preparation in Hawai'i will accomplish little beyond satisfying federal paperwork requirements."[127] Regulating nonpoint sources of pollution is not impossible. Relatively simple best management practices are capable of reducing pollutants, at a cost that is relatively cheap compared to requiring BPT or BAT from point sources.[128] The state of Florida decreased nutrient loading into the Everglades from sugar crops by 40 percent.[129] Thus far, however, Hawai'i has not shown much inclination to push for more regulation of the most responsible industries.

DREDGE AND FILL

Historically, the conversion of wetlands into usable land was regarded as a valuable and desirable improvement. It is only in the past few decades that the importance of wetlands to preserving ecosystems and the maintenance of clean water has been recognized and embraced. Section 404 of the CWA is designed to protect wetlands by requiring permits for the discharge of "dredged or fill material" into "waters of the United States."[130] The Army Corps of Engineers is responsible for issuing permits "for the discharge of dredged or fill material into the navigable waters at specified disposal sites."[131] The Corps exercises wide discretion in implementing Section 404, which does not have the same scientific benchmarks as the NPDES program.[132] Though the statute authorizes delegation of the implementation plans, Hawai'i has not adopted one. This section therefore deals entirely with federal statutes and regulations.

"Dredged material" and "fill material" represent different concepts. "Fill material" is "material placed in waters of the United States where the material has the effect of . . . [r]eplacing any portion of a water of the United States with dry land; or [c]hanging the bottom elevation of any portion of a water of the United States."[133] Fill material is brought in from outside the wetland: Excavation debris, sand, rocks, and soil are all fill material. Garbage is not fill material. Fill material might be added to the waters of the United States for the purpose of constructing structures or infrastructure in a waterway, to create causeways or road fills, seawalls, breakwaters, levees, intake and outfall pipes associated with power plants, utility lines placed beneath the water, and artificial reefs.[134]

"Dredged material" is "material that is excavated or dredged from waters of the United States."[135] This refers to substances that come from the wetland itself. "Discharge of dredged material" is "any addition of dredged material into, including redeposit of dredged material other than incidental fallback within, waters of the United States." A 404 permit is not required for "incidental addition" of dredged material if it is not associated with an activity that would degrade or destroy waters of the United States, unless it involves mechanized land-clearing and excavation activity, absent a showing that such activities would not degrade the waters of the United States.[136] The distinction matters because de minimis discharges of dredged material are permitted without a permit as "incidental fallback": "Incidental fall back is the redeposit of small volumes of dredged material that is incidental to excavation activity . . . [s]oil that is disturbed when dirt is shoveled . . . when such small volume of soil . . . falls into substantially the same place from which it was initially removed."[137]

The regulatory burden on the 404 permitting process is huge. The average decision time following an application for a 404 permit is 405 days. However, including the time spent in "preapplication consultation" and the application itself, it takes an average of 788 days to obtain an individual permit. Even very small impacts involving less than one-tenth of an acre take 270 days to go through the permitting process. It costs the Corps about $5,000 to review a permit requesting dredging or filling of one acre of wetland.[138] Predictably, more applications are withdrawn than actually decided by the Corps.

Happily for farmers and road builders, a number of exceptions to the requirement for a 404 permit exist. Exemptions for agriculture are generous. "Normal farming" and ranching, "plowing, seeding, cultivating, minor drainage, and harvesting . . . or upland soil and water conservation practices" are exempt. The farming must already be "established" to fall under this exemption. Other activities associated with agriculture, such as the construction or maintenance of ponds or irrigation ditches and the maintenance of drainage ditches, are likewise exempt. So also are roads "sufficiently far" from water bodies, farm roads, forest roads, and temporary mining, if in accordance with "best management practices." The "[c]onstruction of temporary sedimentation basins on a construction site" not filling in wetlands is also exempt. But if these exempted activities are part of a larger project to "convert an area of the waters of the United States" to a new use that would reduce or impair the circulation of waters, a 404 permit is still required.[139]

There are several types of permits available under Section 404. Nationwide permits (or "general permits") are available for discharges that would "cause only minimal adverse environmental effects when performed separately, and will have only minimal cumulative adverse effect on the environment."[140] Like NPDES general permits, nationwide permits are issued to cover routine activities in order to reduce the delay and expense of the individual permitting process. Examples of activities covered under general permits are agricultural activities, environmental protection actions such as oil spill cleanup and emergency watershed protection, boat ramps, and discharges in ditches.[141] If the conditions attached to the nationwide permit are satisfied, the permittee usually does not need to notify the Corps before proceeding with the activity.[142] Regional permits are similar to nationwide permits but are issued on a case-by-case basis.

The other major permit from the Corps is an "individual permit," which, like the NPDES individual permit, is for a specific proposal at a specific site. The Corps typically requires individual permits for uses that may cause a severe impact on the environment.[143] It will issue a permit if there is no practicable alternative, there will be no significant adverse impacts on aquatic resources, the applicant takes all reasonable mitigation efforts, and the project otherwise complies with applicable law.[144] Applications filed with the Corps district engineer are on a standard form, accompanied by drawings and sketches sufficient to give notice to the proposed project. The engineer must issue a public notice that must provide sufficient information about the scope of the project.[145] The public has thirty days to make comments for the district engineer to consider.[146] For the Corps to reach a decision on a Section 404 permit, the applicant may need to demonstrate compliance with other laws: (1) Unless the proposed activity is exempted, a decision requires compliance and approval pursuant to the National Environmental Policy Act of 1969, which may require an environmental impact statement or environmental assessment; (2) a certification of compliance with state implementation of Coastal Zone Management Act; (3) compliance with applicable regulations of the National Historic Preservation Act; (4) review of the impact on threatened or endangered species under the Endangered Species Act; (5) and compliance with Section 401(a) of the Clean Water Act, which requires a water quality certification.[147]

Ultimately, the Corps decides whether to issue a dredge and fill permit by evaluating the potential benefits and harm of the project and, generally, "the needs and welfare of the people." Federal regulations contain an exhaustive list of specific factors that the Corps considers. There is, for example, a general presumption that the alteration or destruction of wetlands is against the public interest.[148] If conditions necessary to make the proposed activity accord with the public interest are not "reasonably implementable or enforceable," the permit must be denied.[149]

The Endangered Species Act

The Endangered Species Act of 1973[150] (ESA) restricts land use activities on federal, state, and private land by prohibiting activities that may affect endangered or threatened species. In the early 1970s, Congress found that "various species of fish, wildlife, and plants in the U.S. have been rendered extinct as a consequence of economic growth and development untempered by adequate concern and conservation[.]"[151] The ESA was passed in order to (1) "provide a means whereby the ecosystems upon which endangered species and threatened species depend may be conserved," (2) "to provide a program for the conservation of such endangered species and threatened species," and (3) "to take such steps as may be appropriate to achieve the purposes of the treaties and conventions set forth in [the act]."[152] Under certain conditions, the ESA has the potential to halt land development, and it has thus drawn criticism and a reputation as one of the most powerful environmental laws in the world.[153]

There are approximately 1,880 species listed under the ESA.[154] Of these species, approximately 1,310 are found in part or entirely in the United States and its waters; the remainder are foreign species.[155] The National Oceanic and Atmospheric Administration's National Marine Fisheries Service (NMFS) and the U.S. Fish and Wildlife Service (FWS) share responsibility for implementing the ESA.[156] Generally, FWS manages land and freshwater species, while NMFS manages marine and "anadromous" species.[157] NMFS has jurisdiction over approximately sixty listed species.[158]

The ESA directs the secretary of the Interior to list species as threatened or endangered.[159] An "endangered species" is "any species which is in danger of extinction throughout all or a significant portion of its range other than a species of the Class Insecta determined by the Secretary to constitute a pest whose protection under the provisions of this Act would present an overwhelming and overriding risk to man."[160] A "threatened species" is "any species which is likely to become an endangered species within the foreseeable future throughout all or a significant portion of its range."[161]

The secretary may designate any species as endangered or threatened because of any of the following factors: (1) "the present or threatened destruction, modification, or curtailment of its habitat or range"; (2) "overutilization for commercial, recreational, scientific, or educational purposes"; (3) "disease or predation"; (4) "the inadequacy of existing regulatory mechanisms; or" (5) "other natural or manmade factors affecting its continued existence."[162] When determining the status of any species, however, the secretary must base a decision "solely on the basis of the best scientific and commercial data available[.]"[163]

Pursuant to Section 4 of the ESA, the secretary must also designate "critical habitat" for threatened and endangered species.[164] The term "critical habitat" is defined as "(i) the specific areas within the geographical area occupied by the species, at the time it is listed . . . , on which are found those physical or biological features (I) essential to the conservation of the species and (II) which may require special management considerations or protection; and (ii) specific areas outside the geographical area occupied by the species at the time it is listed . . . , upon a determination by the Secretary that such areas are essential for the conservation of the species."[165] The secretary must designate critical habitat on the basis of "the best scientific data available *and after taking into consideration the economic impact,* the impact on national security, and any other relevant impact, of specifying any particular area as critical habitat."[166]

The critical habitat designation (CHD) of the ESA has the most potential for affecting the private use of land, and what is meant by "economic impact" is crucial in determining the area of a CHD. Although the U.S. Supreme Court has not decided this issue, lower federal courts have made it clear that economic impacts of a CHD include those impacts that are attributable coextensively to other causes. In *New Mexico Cattle Growers Ass'n v. U.S. Fish & Wildlife Service,*[167] the court concluded that "Congress intended that the FWS conduct a full analysis of all of the economic impacts of a critical habitat designation, regardless of whether those impacts are attributable co-extensively to other causes."[168]

Section 7 of the act directs federal agencies to consider the impact proposed actions may have on protected species.[169] Once critical habitat is designated, federal agencies must consult with the Fish and Wildlife Service to "insure that any action authorized, funded, or carried out by such agency . . . is not likely to jeopardize the continued existence of any endangered species or threatened species or result in the destruction or adverse modification of [the designated critical] habitat of such species[.]"[170] With respect to any agency action, each federal agency must request from the secretary information on whether any species that is listed or proposed to be listed may be present in the area of such proposed action.[171] "If the Secretary advises, based on the best scientific and commercial data available, that such species may be present, such agency shall conduct a biological assessment for the purpose of identifying any endangered species or threatened species which is likely to be affected by such action."[172]

Section 9 affects private individuals by its prohibition against the "taking" of endangered species.[173] To "take" means to "harass, harm, pursue, hunt, shoot, wound, kill, trap, capture, or collect, or to attempt to engage in any such conduct."[174] Among these proscribed actions, the most significant is "harm," which is defined not in the ESA but in the Code of Federal Regulations (CFR) as "an act which actually kills or injures wildlife. Such act may include significant habitat modification or degradation where it actually kills or injures wildlife by significantly impairing essential behavioral patterns, including breeding, feeding or sheltering."[175] The CFR also defines "harass" as "an intentional or negligent act or omission which creates the likelihood of injury to wildlife by annoying it to such an extent as to significantly disrupt normal behavioral patterns which include, but are not limited to, breeding, feeding, or sheltering."[176]

The U.S. Supreme Court upheld the Department of Interior's definition of "harm" against a facial challenge to its validity in *Babbit v. Sweet Home Chapter of Communities for a Great Oregon*.[177] There, small landowners, logging companies, families dependent on the forest products industries, and organizations that represent their interests brought a declaratory judgment action challenging the statutory validity of the definition of "harm."[178] They alleged that the application of the "harm" regulation to the red-cockaded woodpecker, an endangered species, and the northern spotted owl, a threatened species, had injured them economically.[179]

The Court upheld the definition of "harm," reasoning that the text of the ESA provided three reasons for concluding that their definition of "harm" is reasonable.[180] "First, an ordinary understanding of the word 'harm' supports it. The dictionary definition of the verb form of 'harm' is 'to cause hurt or damage to: injure.' In the context of the ESA, that definition naturally encompasses habitat modification that results in actual injury or death to members of an endangered or threatened species."[181] "Second, the broad purpose of the ESA supports the Secretary's decision to extend protection against activities that cause the precise harms Congress enacted the statute to avoid."[182] "Third, the fact that Congress in 1982 authorized the Secretary to issue permits for [incidental takings], strongly suggests that Congress understood [Section 9] to prohibit indirect as well as deliberate takings. . . . Congress' addition of the [Section 10] permit provision supports the Secretary's conclusion that activities not intended to harm an endangered species, such as habitat modification, may constitute unlawful takings under the ESA unless the Secretary permits them."[183]

Courts have also considered what constitutes a "taking." In *Palila v. Hawaii Department of Land & Natural Resources,*[184] a lower court held that habitat destruction constituted a taking in violation of the ESA. The court found that the state's action in maintaining feral sheep and goats in a critical habitat was a violation of the ESA since it was shown that a listed bird was endangered by the activity.[185] It explained that its conclusion was "consistent with the Act's legislative history showing that Congress was informed that the greatest threat to endangered species is the destruction of their natural habitat."[186]

More than a decade later, another court held that limited development within critical habitat is not necessarily a taking. In *Defenders of Wildlife v. Bernal,*[187] citizen groups sought an injunction to prevent the Amphitheater School District in Tucson, Arizona, from building a "critically-needed" high school, claiming that the proposed construction would result in a "take" of the endangered pygmy-owl.[188] The court held that the citizen groups had not shown that the "proposed construction would harm a pygmy-owl by killing or injuring it, or would more likely than not harass a pygmy-owl by annoying it to such an extent as to disrupt its normal behavioral patterns."[189] The court considered the trial judge's factual findings that (1) "no pygmy-owl had been detected anywhere within the school site itself"[190] and (2) "pygmy-owls can tolerate a fairly high degree of human presence."[191]

Although Section 9 creates a strict ban on actions that affect protected species, the ESA provides some flexibility through its allowance of "Section 10 incidental takings." "Incidental taking" means "any taking otherwise prohibited, if such taking is incidental to, and not the purpose of, the carrying out of an otherwise lawful activity."[192] Section 10 allows for the secretary to permit, under such terms and conditions as he shall prescribe, "any act otherwise prohibited by section 9 for scientific purposes or to enhance the propagation or survival of the affected species, including, but not limited to, acts necessary for the establishment and maintenance of experimental populations[.]"[193] Section 10 incidental taking permits also issue for the taking of any endangered species within the United States or its territorial sea "if such taking is incidental to, and not the purpose of, the carrying out of an otherwise lawful activity."[194] No permit can be issued for the latter reason unless the applicant submits to the secretary a conservation plan that specifies "(1) the impact which will likely result from such taking; (2) what steps the applicant will take to minimize and mitigate such impacts, and the funding that will be available to implement such steps; (3) what alternative actions to such taking the applicant considered and the reasons why such alternatives are not being utilized; and (4) such other measures that the Secretary may require as being necessary or appropriate for purposes of the plan."[195]

After opportunity for public comment, with respect to a permit application and the related conservation plan, the secretary must issue the permit if he finds that: "(1) the taking will be incidental; (2) the applicant will, to the maximum extent practicable, minimize and mitigate the impacts of such taking; (3) the applicant will ensure that adequate funding for the plan will be provided; (4) the taking will not appreciably reduce the likelihood of the survival and recovery of the species in the wild; and (5) the measures, if any, required under [the act] will be met; and he has received such other assurances as he may require that the plan will be implemented[.]"[196] The permit will contain such terms and conditions as the secretary deems necessary or appropriate, including but not limited to reporting requirements for determining whether the permittee is complying with such terms and conditions.[197] If not, the secretary can revoke a Section 10 permit.[198]

INTERPLAY BETWEEN THE ESA AND HAWAI'I LAND USE LAW[199]

Pursuant to this statutory authority and mandate, in early 2003 the FWS proposed to designate several thousand acres in the County of Kaua'i, including thousands of acres of private land, in order to protect two listed species: the cave wolf spider and the cave amphipod. While the FWS has repeatedly claimed that such designation only affects federal activities on federal lands in areas so designated as critical area, such designation will almost certainly trigger further designation and regulation under certain Hawai'i statutes, resulting in severe restrictions on the use of private land with dire economic consequences for affected landowners.

Recall that Hawai'i's State Land Use Law, essentially embodied in Act 187 and Act 100, creates a dual zoning system whereby land is zoned by both the state and county (see chapter 1).[200] Pursuant to the ESA, the FWS is required to designate critical habitat for all listed endangered species, whether on private or public land. The purpose of the designation is to designate specific areas within the geographical area occupied by such listed species essential to its conservation.[201] Conservation is further defined to include not only survival but recovery, if necessary, of the listed endangered species.[202]

The State Land Use Law defines uses in each district, requiring for the conservation district that "[c]onservation districts *shall* include areas necessary for . . . conserving indigenous or endemic plants, fish, and wildlife, including those which are threatened or *endangered*."[203] Given further language in the State Plan,[204] which requires that the state's physical environment planning "[e]ncourage the protection of rare or *endangered plant and animal species and habitats* native to Hawai'i," it is difficult to avoid the conclusion that the State Land Use Commission will be required to reclassify into the State Conservation District all endangered species habitat land that is not already so classified.[205] Further increasing the likelihood of such redistricting, the State Department of Land and Natural Resources is required by statute to "initiate amendments to the conservation district boundaries consistent with section 205-4 in order to include high quality native forests *and the habitat of rare native species of flora and fauna* within the Conservation District."[206] It is difficult to see how the commission can thus avoid classifying land that the FWS designates as critical habitat for listed endangered species immediately into the State Conservation District.

Moreover, it will be extremely difficult to persuade the commission to reclassify designated endangered species habitat lands from the conservation district to any of the other three state land use districts (all of which permit economically beneficial land use, from agriculture to urban development) and equally difficult to persuade the commission to reclassify any such lands in any of the other districts (say, agriculture to rural or urban) to any district but conservation. This is so because the Land Use Law further provides that "[i]n its review of any petition for reclassification of district boundaries pursuant to this chapter, the commission shall specifically consider . . . the impact of the proposed reclassification on . . . areas of state concern [such as the] [p]reservation or maintenance of important natural systems *or habitats*."[207] The Land Use Law also requires that any such boundary amendments (reclassifications) conform to the State Plan, which encourages the protection of endangered plant and animal habitats.[208]

Once the commission classifies lands—private and public alike—in the State Conservation District, control of such lands for regulatory purposes passes to the DLNR, which has exclusive jurisdiction over their use.[209] The DLNR is further required by statute to establish subzones within the conservation district.[210] Finally, except for uses established in 1964 and the rare variance, only those uses permitted in these subzones are permitted uses in the conservation district.[211] The DLNR has by regulation established five such subzones. Very little is permitted in any of them. The most restrictive of these is the protective subzone. The protective subzone "shall encompass . . . [a]reas necessary for preserving natural ecosystems of native plants, fish, and wildlife, *particularly those which are endangered.*"[212] The only uses permitted are "[b]asic data collection, research, education and resource evaluation."[213]

It is thus nearly certain that the DLNR will reclassify any conservation district lands under its jurisdiction that the FWS designates as critical endangered species habitat into the most restrictive—protective—subzone, which permits virtually no economic use of such land. Its value would accordingly plummet. Indeed, should either the commission or DLNR fail to so classify FWS–designated endangered species critical habitat lands, they may well be forced to do so under the rules of *Loggerhead Turtle v. Volusia County*,[214] holding that a county may be charged with violation of the ESA for harmfully inadequate regulation of activity that endangers a listed species.

Hawai'i's Environmental Impact Statement (EIS) Law, which applies to a broader range of activities than the National Environmental Policy Act (NEPA), would almost certainly be triggered by the ESA.[215] This is because any proposed use would now be in a State Conservation District; even in the unlikely event that land in which a use is contemplated is not in a State Conservation District this would be true, because the use would "[s]ubstantially [affect] a rare, threatened, or endangered species, *or its habitat.*"[216] Any use of commission-classified conservation lands (or for that matter any state or county lands, even if that use consists only of intersecting such lands through an underground pipe or overhead wire) triggers at least an environmental assessment, if not a full-blown EIS, as described elsewhere in this chapter.[217]

Recall (from chapter 6) that Hawai'i's CZMA[218] requires a Special Management Area permit (SMAP) from the appropriate county for any development in the designated coastal zone special management area, which extends around each of the state's islands and inland for a mile or more in some instances. The statute provides that the counties must minimize any development that would "adversely affect . . . wildlife habitats,"[219] and it requires that the counties may not approve any development unless they find that it is "consistent with the objectives, policies and . . . guidelines" of the CZMA.[220] The list of CZMA policies in the statute includes ensuring "that the use and development of marine and coastal resources are ecologically and environmentally sound."[221] It will be difficult to obtain an SMAP in ESA–designated critical habitats because it is more than arguable that after designation, development will adversely affect the habitat of an endangered species.

HAWAI'I'S ENDANGERED SPECIES ACT

Hawai'i has the highest number of listed threatened and endangered species in the nation, with 385 threatened and endangered plant and animal species listed under the ESA.[222] Of these 385 species, 285 are plants and 100 are animals.[223] Given the state's abundance of endangered species, Hawai'i has adopted its own version of the ESA to further protect its unique wildlife.[224]

The Hawai'i State Legislature has declared that "[a]ll indigenous species of aquatic life, wildlife, and land plants are integral parts of Hawai'i's native ecosystems and comprise the living heritage of Hawai'i, for they represent a natural resource of scientific, cultural, educational, environmental, and economic value to future generations of Hawai'i's people."[225] Therefore, "[t]o insure the continued perpetuation of indigenous aquatic life, wildlife, and land plants, and their habitats for human enjoyment, for scientific purposes, and as members of ecosystems, it is necessary that the State take positive actions to enhance their prospects for survival."[226] Chapter 195D of the Hawaii Revised Statutes (hereinafter "Hawai'i's Conservation Law") authorizes the DLNR "to conduct investigations on any species of aquatic life, wildlife, and land plants in order to develop information relating to their biology, ecology, population, status, distribution, habitat needs, and other limiting factors to determine conservation measures necessary for their continued ability to sustain themselves successfully."[227] The Hawai'i law is more restrictive than the ESA because it protects both threatened and endangered species and provides for the protection of species that are not listed as endangered or threatened pursuant to the ESA.

Under Hawai'i's statute, "endangered species" means "any species whose continued existence as a viable component of Hawaii's indigenous fauna or flora is determined to be in jeopardy[.]"[228] "Threatened species" means "any species of aquatic life, wildlife, or land plant which appears likely, within the foreseeable future, to become endangered[.]"[229] Although any species that is deemed endangered pursuant to the ESA is deemed to be an endangered species under Hawai'i's statute, the DLNR may determine that any threatened species is an endangered species within the State of Hawai'i. The factors used to determine whether a species is endangered or threatened under the state law are similar to those used in the ESA.

Hawai'i's statute makes it "unlawful for any person to take, possess, transport, transplant, export, process, sell, offer for sale, or ship any species of aquatic life, wildlife, or land plants deemed by the department to be in need of conservation[.]"[230] It is unlawful for any person to "take" any threatened or endangered species within the State of Hawai'i.[231] "Person" means "an individual, corporation, partnership, trust, association, or any other private entity, or any officer, employee, agent, department, or instrumentality of the federal government, of any state or political subdivision thereof, or of any foreign government[.]"[232] The definition of "take" under the state law is similar to, although slightly more expansive than, the definition under the ESA.[233] The Hawai'i statute also provides exceptions similar to the Section 10 incidental taking provisions of the ESA.[234]

Given the interplay between the ESA and Hawai'i's Land Use Law, the designation of a species as endangered under Hawai'i's statute may also trigger a boundary amendment for the lands upon which the endangered species is found.

Hawai'i Environmental Impact and Assessment Law

The Hawai'i Environmental Impact Statements (HEIS) law requires an environmental assessment for actions (projects or proposals) in order that "environmental policies of the legislature are given appropriate consideration in decision-making along with economic and technological considerations."[235] The agency from which approval is sought for a project or proposal must prepare an environmental assessment (EA). If a finding of "no significant impact" is anticipated, a draft environmental assessment is made available for public comment for thirty days. The agency is required to respond to comments in writing and may then prepare a final environmental assessment to determine whether an EIS is required. An EIS is required when the environmental assessment determines that a proposed action will "likely" have a significant effect on the environment.[236] A draft EIS is made available for public review for forty-five days. The applicant or agency must respond in writing to comments received during the review period and prepare a final statement to submit for acceptance.

Acceptance is a formal determination that the EIS adequately describes identifiable environmental impacts and satisfactorily responds to comments received during the review of the statement.[237] It requires no action to mitigate, only to note and record alternatives. Acceptance of

CORKY

"YOU WANT ME TO SUBMIT AN ENVIRONMENT-AL IMPACT STUDY AND STATEMENT ??,,,"

a final statement is a condition precedent for approval of the requested action.[238] Chapter 343 requires disclosure of the environmental effects of the proposed action as well as the effects on the economic welfare, social welfare, and cultural practices of the community, measures proposed to minimize adverse effects, and alternatives to the action and their environmental effects.

The Hawai'i Supreme Court has consistently read chapter 343 to maximize opportunities for public comment and participation in accordance with its reading of the intent of the legislature and consequently has required environmental assessments in close cases. In *Kahana Sunset Owners Ass'n v. County of Maui*,[239] the Court held that a new thirty-six-inch drainage line beneath a public roadway connecting to an existing twenty-four-inch culvert below a state highway was a use of state lands and triggered an environmental assessment.[240] The Court determined the drainage line did not qualify for an exemption for "installation of drains within streets and highways" because it was not in the category of "minor structures accessory to existing facilities." Most importantly, the Court determined that the requirement for an environmental assessment was not confined to the drainage line on state land, but that it must address the environmental effects of the entire proposed development—a 312-unit multifamily residential development that the HEIS process would not otherwise reach. The drainage pipe was a "necessary precedent" for the development and had no independent utility. Thus, "[i]solating only that particular component of the development for environmental assessment would be improper segmentation of the project."[241]

A decision two years later reached a similar result. The developer of a resort with a hotel and golf course was required to file an EIS for the entire resort early in the planning phase because it proposed to construct two underpasses under a state highway so that golf carts and maintenance vehicles could access three golf holes and the golf course maintenance facility.[242]

Finally, a proposed reclassification of property from agricultural district to urban district constituted an "action" proposing the use of state lands, because the proposed development would eventually require sewage and water transmission lines under state highways.[243] Reclassification of land requiring an EA was considered and rejected by the legislature in 1974.[244] Nevertheless, the Court held that although not every reclassification triggered an EA, if the reclassification was the initial step of a project that proposed the use of state lands, an EA was required.[245]

The result is a judicial backdoor into the EIS process at a very early stage for private landowners. Though HEIS does not require any action to be taken as a result of the findings of an EIS, it is a potent tool for those seeking to delay or derail a project. The legislature rejected a proposal in 1974 to apply the HEIS law to all major developments that would likely have significant environmental affects, choosing instead to limit the application of the law to actions proposing the use of state lands and state funds and certain "areas of critical concern," such as the Waikīkī–Diamond Head area, lands classified in the State Conservation District, and the shoreline.[246] But under the Hawai'i Supreme Court's interpretation of the law, every large project that in some minor way touches upon state lands (as a practical matter, almost every such project) is required to undergo the expense, delay, and possible litigation of the EIS process in order to obtain the necessary state and county permits. The Court confirmed its apparent policy of subjecting all property development to the state HEIS process by unanimously deciding in April 2010 that an EIS completed too long ago must be supplemented or redone to take into consideration potential impacts arising outside the boundaries of the subject project, despite the lack of statutory authority for such a requirement.[247]

Environmental regulation in Hawai'i presents significant challenges to land developers, and compliance with various regulatory schemes and inevitable litigation are major costs of financing development. The future may hold even more aggressive land use regulation, since the state-sponsored Hawai'i 2050 Sustainability Plan calls for increased enforcement of habitat management, more "compact patterns of urban development," and generally recommends "building up, rather than out."[248]

Notes

1. Donald G. Hagman and Dean Misczynski, "The quiet federalization of land-use controls: Disquietude in the land markets," REAL ESTATE APPRAISER (Sept./Oct. 1974).

2. Although this section focuses on the CAA, CWA, and ESA, there are a number of other federal statutes relevant to land use. These include the Resource Conservation and Recovery Act (RCRA), the Comprehensive Environmental Response, Compensation and Liability Act (CERCLA), and the Federal Insecticide, Fungicide, and Rodenticide Act (FIFRA). RCRA regulates hazardous waste very strictly at all stages of its generation and disposal, while leaving other types of waste virtually unregulated. John S. Applegate and Jan G. Laitos, *Environmental Law: RCRA, CERCLA and the Management of Hazardous Waste*, New York: Foundation Press, 2005, at 11–12; *see generally* id. at 11–127. CERCLA regulates sites that have already been contaminated with hazardous waste by providing for their identification and remediation and also by determining who is liable for the cost of cleanup. Id. at 128; *see generally* id. at 128–286. FIFRA requires that all pesticides be registered with the EPA before they are sold or distributed. Lynn L. Bergeson, *FIFRA: Federal Insecticide, Fungicide, and Rodenticide Act*, Chicago: American Bar Association, 2000. Additionally, FIFRA notwithstanding, states are free to impose certain types of additional restrictions on pesticide use. Id. at 105.

3. Daniel Fiorino, *The New Environmental Regulation*, Boston: MIT Press, 2006 at 61.

4. For a further summary of the act, *see* Lisa Woods Munger, *Hawaii Environmental Law Handbook*, 3d ed., Honolulu: Government Institutes, 2000 at 12 et seq.

5. Fiorino, supra note 3.

6. 42 U.S.C. § 7401(b)(1) (2006); *see generally* James Salzman and Barton H. Thompson Jr., *Environmental Law and Policy*, 2d ed., Washington, D.C.: Foundation Press, 2007.

7. (1) Particulate matter, (2) sulfur oxides, (3) carbon monoxides, (4) nitrogen dioxide, (5) ozone, (6) hydrocarbons, and (7) lead. 40 C.F.R. pt. 50 (2009).

8. Id. § 50.2(b).

9. Although the EPA does consider new standards every five years, it has been reluctant to add new NAAQS because of their high political and economic cost. Salzman and Thompson, supra note 6.

10. 42 U.S.C. § 7410(a)(1).

11. Environmental Law Practice, 77.

12. 42 U.S.C. § 7410(a)(2) (2006).

13. Id.

14. *See* Daniel R. Mandelker, *Environmental and Land Control Legislation*, Indianapolis: Bobbs-Merrill, 1976.

15. *Hawai'i Environmental Council Annual Report 2006*.

16. "[P]reconstruction reviews of *direct* sources are to include consideration of energy, environmental and economic impacts and that the only land-use regulations which may result from implementation of this act are those which are needed to assure attainment and maintenance of ambient air quality standards and prevent significant deterioration of air quality." U.S. Congress, House Conference Committee, *Congressional Report* 95-564 to accompany H.R. 6161 (Clean Air Act amendments of 1977), reprinted in *United States Code Congressional and Administrative News* (1977): 1502 and 1508.

17. Preconstruction review may also be required if a source is "modified" in such a way that may create a new source of emission. 40 C.F.R. § 51.166(b)(2)(ii) (2009). Although industry challenged the EPA's broad interpretation of the term "modified," the U.S. Supreme Court ultimately upheld it. *Envtl. Def. v. Duke Energy Corp.*, 549 U.S. 561 (2007). The broad interpretation, requiring preconstruction review and associated permits before a modification, has been criticized as "forc[ing] extra pollution reductions from existing sources." David B. Rivkin Jr., Lee A. Kasey, and Mark DeLaquil, *EPA's NSR Enforcement Policy: An Improvident Regulatory Endeavor?* Washington, D.C.: The Federalist Society, 2006.

18. Clean Air Act, 110(a)(2)(D), 42 U.S.C. § 7410(a)(2) (2006).

19. Elaine Moss, ed., *Land Use Controls in the United States: A Handbook on the Legal Rights of Citizens*, Natural Resources Defense Council, New York: Dial, 1977 at 43, 44.

20. *See* discussion of these laws in chapters 6 and 7 infra.

21. 42 U.S.C. § 7410(k) (2006).

22. EPA REPORT, PACIFIC SOUTHWEST/REGION 9 (spring 2003), vol. 2, no. 1, at 2.

23. Id.

24. 40 C.F.R. 52.21(a)(2) (2009).

25. Id. § 52.21(e).

26. 40 C.F.R. 52.632 (2009).

27. Lisa Woods Munger, *Hawaii Environmental Law Handbook*, 3rd ed., Honolulu: Government Institutes, 2000 at 73 et seq.

28. 33 U.S.C. § 1251(a); *see generally* Joel M. Gross and Lynn Dodge, *Clean Water Act: Basic Practice Series*, Washington, D.C.: American Bar Association, 2005.

29. 33 U.S.C. § 1252(a).

30. Drew Caputo, "A job half finished: The Clean Water Act after 25 years," 27 ENVTL. L. REP. 10 (1997).

31. *The Quality of Our Nation's Waters*, 2000 Report to Congress, USEPA, 2002.

32. William H. Rodgers Jr., *Environmental Law*, 2d ed., St. Paul, Minn.: West Publishing, 1994.

33. *2006 Water Quality Report.*

34. *Report*—Circular 1239 13.

35. Clean Water Act § 402, 33 U.S.C. § 1342 (2006).

36. Id. § 404, 33 U.S.C. § 1344.

37. *See* Gross and Dodge, supra note 28.

38. 33 U.S.C. § 1362(12) (2000).

39. *Rybachek v. EPA*, 904 F.2d 1276 (9th Cir. 1990).

40. *Headwaters, Inc. v. Talent Irrigation Dist.*, 243 F.3d 526 (9th Cir. 2001); *see also* Gross and Dodge, supra note 28 ("'[A]ddition' element is met if polluted water from one water body is diverted and discharged into another water body").

41. 33 U.S.C. § 1362(14) (2000).

42. 40 C.F.R. 122.2.

43. *See* Gross and Dodge, supra note 28 (noting point source is "defined broadly as 'any discernable, confined, and discrete conveyance' from which pollutants are or may be discharged").

44. *Weinberger v. Romero-Barcelo*, 456 U.S. 305 (1982); *Carr v. Alta Verde Indus., Inc.*, 931 F.2d 1055 (5th Cir. 1991).

45. *Concerned Area Residents for the Env't v. Southview Farm*, 34 F.3d 114 (2d Cir. 1994).

46. 33 U.S.C. § 1362(14) (2000); Gross and Dodge, supra note 28 (giving examples of point sources exempted from MPDES coverage, such as dredged or fill material, on-site discharges under CERCLA, and some return flows from irrigated agriculture).

47. *Rapanos v. United States*, 547 U.S. 715 (2006).

48. Id. *See also N. Cal. River Watch v. City of Healdsburg*, 496 F.3d 993, 995 (9th Cir. 2007) (determining that a rock quarry pit filled with water possessed a "significant nexus" to waters that were navigable in fact because waters from the pond seeped into a navigable river and significantly affected the "physical, biological, and chemical integrity of the river").

49. The exemption of farms from CWA, and environmental regulations generally, have been criticized. J. B. Ruhl, "Farms, their environmental harms, and environmental law" 27 ECOL. L.Q. 263 (2000) (detailing the adverse environmental effects of agriculture and the exemptions that farming receives from environmental law). The EPA has justified the farm exemption by arguing that it is infeasible to apply exact numerical effluent limits on agricultural operations. Salzman, supra note 6 at 155.

50. 40 C.F.R. 122.3(a), (c).

51. *Exxon Corp. v. Train*, 554 F.2d 1310 (5th Cir. 1977).

52. *See, e.g., Rural Council v. Bosma*, 143 F. Supp. 2d 1169, 1180 (D. Idaho 2001).

53. 40 C.F.R. 123.28.
54. State of Hawai'i Department of Health, "Guidelines applicable to golf courses in Hawai'i" (2002), http://Hawaii.gov/health/environmental/water/sdwb/conmaps/pdf/golfguide.pdf (last visited Nov. 17, 2009).
55. 33 U.S.C. § 1342 (a), (b); Salzman, supra note 6 ("States can qualify to issue the NPDES permits if they can show that they have the needed administrative and engineering capability, and about three quarters of the states currently are qualified to issue them").
56. Salzman, supra note 6 at 147 (attributing the inconsistency to Congress' initial aggressive regulation and subsequent backpedaling under industry influence); see id. at 148 (table of technological standards).
57. For a list of conventional pollutants, see Clean Water Act § 304(a)(4); 40 C.F.R. 401.16 (2009).
58. Karen McGaffrey, "Water pollution control under the national pollutant discharge elimination system," in Mark A. Ryan, The Clean Water Act Handbook, 2d ed., Chicago: Section of Environment, Energy, and Resources, ABA, 2003, at 20. In contrast, the Clean Air Act bases its BPT technology standards rigidly on the top 12 percent. 42 U.S.C. § 7412(d)(3)(A).
59. "Best conventional pollutant control technology," 51 Fed. Reg. 24,974 (July 9, 1986).
60. 40 C.F.R. 122.2.
61. 40 C.F.R. 122.29(b)(1).
62. HAW. CODE R. § 11-55-02(b) (Weil 2005).
63. Randy Hill, "NPDES permit application and issuance procedures," in Mark A. Ryan, ed., The Clean Water Act Handbook, 2d ed., Chicago: Section of Environment, Energy, and Resources, ABA, 2003 at 42.
64. 40 C.F.R. 122.21(c)(1).
65. Id.
66. 40 C.F.R. 122.22(d).
67. HAW. CODE R. § 11-55-04(c) (Weil 2005).
68. Id. § 11-55-04(f).
69. Id. § 11-55-07.
70. Id. § 11-55-09.
71. Id. § 11-55-09(b).
72. Id. § 11-55-13.
73. Id. § 11-54-09(b); 40 C.F.R. 124.17(a).
74. HAW. CODE R. § 11-55-17(c).
75. 33 U.S.C. § 1342(k) (2000). There is an exception for toxic pollutants that are harmful to human health.
76. HAW. CODE R. § 11-55-23 (Weil 2005).
77. Id. § 11-54.9.1.
78. Id. This definition may be somewhat in question since the Rapanos decision.
79. Id. § 11-54-9.1.01.
80. See Gross and Dodge, supra note 28.
81. 33 U.S.C. § 1342(p)(2) (2000).
82. 40 C.F.R. 122.26(b)(14).

83. 33 U.S.C. § 1362(14) (2000).

84. HAW. CODE R. § 11-55-04(a) (Weil 2005).

85. "National pollutant discharge elimination system," 64 Fed. Reg. 68,751 (Dec. 8, 1999).

86. State of Hawai'i Department of Health, "Draft water quality standards revision rationale document" (2005), http://Hawaii.gov/health/environmental/env-planning/wqm/wqm.html/pdf/revrationale.pdf (last visited Nov. 28, 2009).

87. HAW. CODE R. § 1154-1.1(a) (Weil 2005).

88. Id. § 11-54-1.1(b)

89. Roger S. Fujioka, "Microbial pathogens in tropical coastal waters: An ecosystem approach to determine risk and prevent water-borne diseases" (2005), http://www.prcmb.Hawaii.edu/p2.asp (last visited Nov. 17, 2009).

90. Gross and Dodge, supra note 28.

91. HAW. CODE R. § 11-54-4 (Weil 2005).

92. State waters must only meet the standards on average during a twenty-four hour period. Waters must meet standards for "fish consumption" over the course of thirty days (for noncarcinogens) or twelve months (for carcinogens). HAW. CODE R. § 11-54-4(b) (Weil 2005).

93. Id. § 11-54-4(c).

94. Id. § 11-65-1.1(c).

95. Id. § 11-54-2(b).

96. See id. § 11-54-1.

97. HAW. CODE R. § 11-54-2(c) (Weil 2005).

98. Id. § 11-54-3(b)(1)(B).

99. Id. § 11-54-5.

100. Id. § 11-54-3.

101. Id. § 11-54-3(c).

102. Id. § 11-54-6(a)(2)(A).

103. Id. § 11-54-3.

104. Id. § 11-54-6(2)(b).

105. Gross and Dodge, supra note 28.

106. Salzman, supra note 6, at 153.

107. Gross and Dodge, supra note 28, at 116. As of 2001, all states and territories participate in the program. Id.

108. See generally Oliver A. Houck, The Clean Water Act TMDL Program: Law, Policy, and Implementation, Washington, D.C.: Environmental Law Institute, 2002 at 11–34.

109. See Tetra Tech., Inc., "Total maximum daily loads and load targets for the Hanalei Bay watershed" 47 (2007), http://Hawaii.gov/health/environmental/env-planning/index.html/wqm/wqm/hanaleitmdl.pdf (last visited Nov. 17, 2009).

110. Houck, supra note 108.

111. 40 C.F.R. § 122.4(i)(1).

112. Per island breakdown (number of listed impaired waters per island and percentage of total number of listed waters): Kaua'i 28 (13% of total); O'ahu 71 (34% of total); Moloka'i 3 (1% of total); Lāna'i 6 (3% of total); Maui 72 (34% of total); and Hawai'i 31 (15% of total). Thirty-nine additions were made to the list (reflecting increased monitoring rather than increased pollution) and four were removed. 2006 State of Hawai'i Water Quality Monitoring and Assessment Report.

113. *State of Hawai'i Water Quality Monitoring and Assessment Report Response to Public Comments* (2006).

114. *State of Hawai'i Water Quality Monitoring and Assessment Report, Executive Summary* (2006).

115. *State of Hawai'i Water Quality Monitoring and Assessment Report Response to Public Comments* (2006).

116. *See*, e.g., U.S. Environmental Protection Agency, "Guidance for water quality-based decisions: The TMDL process" (1991), http://www.epa.gov/owow/tmdl/decisions/dec1.html (last visited Nov. 17, 2009).

117. Laurie K. Beale and Karin Sheldon, "TMDLs: Section 303(d)," *in* Mark A. Ryan, ed., *The Clean Water Act Handbook*, 2d ed., Chicago: Section of Environment, Energy, and Resources, ABA, 2003 at 216.

118. *Pronsolino v. Nastri*, 291 F.3d 1123 (9th Cir. 2002).

119. Id. at 1132–1133.

120. Id. at 1140.

121. Id. (internal quotation marks omitted).

122. 40 C.F.R. 122.44(d)(1)(vii)(B). Effluent limitations to control the discharge of pollutants are in numerical form. But considering 33 U.S.C. § 1342(p)(3)(B)(iii) (2000), EPA recommends that for NPDES–regulated municipal and small construction storm water discharges, effluent limits be expressed as best management practices (BMPs) or similar requirements, not numeric effluent limits. *See* "Interim permitting approach for water quality-based effluent limitations in storm water permits," 61 Fed. Reg. 43,761 (Aug. 26, 1996).

123. State of Hawai'i Department of Health, "Total maximum daily loads (TDMLs) for total suspended solids nitrogen and phosphorus in Kapa'a Stream" 7-11 (2007), http://Hawaii.gov/health/environmental/env-planning/index.html/wqm/2007_finalkapaastreamreport.pdf (last visited Nov. 17, 2009).

124. State of Hawai'i Department of Health, "End of year report" (2007), http://Hawaii.gov/health/environmental/water/cleanwater/prc/pdf/EndOfYear Report2007.pdf (last visited Nov. 23, 2009).

125. HAW. REV. STAT. § 342D-11 (2008); *see also* TDMLs for Kapa'a Stream, supra note 123.

126. Oliver A. Houck, "Tales from a troubled marriage: Science and law in environmental policy," 17 TUL. ENVTL. L.J. 163, 171-176 (2003).

127. June F. Harrigan-Lum and Arnold L. Lum, "Hawaii's TMDL program: Legal requirements and environmental realities," 15 NAT. RESOURCES & ENV'T 12 (2000).

128. Houck, supra note 108, at 143, 159.

129. Id.

130. 33 U.S.C. § 1344(a) (2000); *see generally* Salzman, supra note 6, at 261–276.

131. 33 U.S.C. § 1362(7) (2000).

132. Gross and Dodge, supra note 28, at 77.

133. 33 U.S.C. § 323.2(e) (repealed 1980); 40 C.F.R. 232.2 (2009).

134. Id.

135. Id.

136. Id.

137. Id.

138. Virginia S. Albrecht, "Role of environmental regulation," *in* Eran Ben-Joseph and Terry S. Szold, *Regulating Place: Standards and the Shaping of Urban America,* New York: Routledge, 2004 at 276–277.

139. 40 C.F.R. 232.3 (2009).

140. 33 U.S.C. § 1344(e)(1).

141. "Reissuance of nationwide permits," 72 Fed. Reg. 11,092, 11,180–11,181 (Mar. 12, 2007).

142. 33 C.F.R. 330.1(e) (2009).

143. Gross and Dodge, supra note 28, at 83.

144. Id. (citing 40 C.F.R. 230.10(a)-(d)).

145. 33 C.F.R. 325.3(a) (2009).

146. Id. § 325.2(a)(2).

147. Id. § 325.5.

148. Id. § 320.4.

149. Id. § 325.4.

150. 16 U.S.C. §§ 1531–1544 (2006); *see generally* Salzman, supra note 6, at 277–295.

151. 16 U.S.C. § 1531(a)(1) (2006).

152. Id. § 1531(b).

153. Salzman, supra note 6, at 278.

154. NOAA Fisheries, Office of Protected Resources, "Endangered Species Act (ESA)," http://www.nmfs.noaa.gov/pr/laws/esa/ (last visited Jan. 1, 2010).

155. Id.

156. Id.

157. Id.

158. Id.

159. 16 U.S.C. § 1533.

160. Id. § 1532(6).

161. Id. § 1532(20).

162. Id. § 1533(a)(1).

163. Id. § 1533(b)(1).

164. Id. § 1533(b)(2).

165. Id. § 1532(5).

166. Id. § 1533(b)(2) (emphasis added).

167. *N.M. Cattle Growers Ass'n v U.S. Fish & Wildlife Serv.*, 248 F.3d 1277 (10th Cir. 2001).

168. Id. at 1285.

169. 16 U.S.C. § 1536.

170. Id. § 1536(a)(2).

171. Id. § 1536(c)(1).

172. Id. In Arkansas, a federal judge halted a $320 million irrigation project over the possibility that the project could harm the habitat of an endangered woodpecker. John Bacon, "Elusive woodpecker halts $320M project," USA TODAY, July 21, 2006, at 3A. Scientists had considered the bird extinct until a 2004 video captured a bird some scientists claimed to be the woodpecker. Id.

173. 16 U.S.C. § 1538(a)(1) (2006).

174. Id. § 1532(19).
175. 50 C.F.R. 17.3 (2006).
176. Id.
177. *Babbitt v. Sweet Home Chapter of Cmtys. for a Great Or.*, 515 U.S. 687 (1995).
178. Id. at 692.
179. Id.
180. Id. at 697.
181. Id. (citations omitted).
182. Id. at 698.
183. Id. at 701.
184. *Palila v. Hawaii Dep't of Land & Natural Res.*, 639 F.2d 495 (9th Cir. 1981).
185. Id. at 497–498.
186. Id. at 498.
187. *Defenders of Wildlife v. Bernal*, 204 F.3d 920 (9th Cir. 2000).
188. Id. at 922.
189. Id. at 925.
190. Id.
191. Id. at 926.
192. Id.
193. 16 U.S.C. § 1539(a)(1)(A) (2006).
194. Id. § 1539(a)(1)(B).
195. Id. § 1539(a)(2)(A).
196. Id. § 1539(a)(2)(B).
197. Id.
198. Id. § 1539(a)(2)(C).
199. This section was first published as an article in the *Pace Environmental Law Review.* David L. Callies, "The interplay between land use and environmental law," 23 PACE ENV'TL L. REV. 685 (2006).
200. Discussed earlier in chapter 1; *see* David L. Callies, *Regulating Paradise: Land Use Controls in Hawaii*, Honolulu: University Press of Hawai'i, 1984, at 7.
201. *See* 16 U.S.C. § 1532(5)(A) (2000).
202. *See* id. § 1532(3).
203. HAW. REV. STAT. § 205-2(e) (1993) (emphasis added).
204. Id. §§ 226-1 to -107.
205. Id. § 226-11(6) (emphasis added).
206. Id. § 195D-5.1 (emphasis added).
207. Id. § 205-17 (emphasis added).
208. Id. § 205-16.
209. *See* id. § 183C-4(b).
210. *See* id. § 183C-4(d).
211. *See* id. § 183C-4(b), (c).
212. HAW. CODE R. § 13-5-11(b) (Weil 2005) (emphasis added).
213. Id. § 13-5-22(A-1).
214. *Loggerhead Turtle v. County Council of Volusia County*, 148 F.3d 1231 (11th Cir. 1998), *cert. denied*, 526 U.S. 1081 (1999).
215. *See* HAW. REV. STAT. § 343-5 (1993).

216. Haw. Code. R. § 11-200-12(B)(9) (Weil 2005) (emphasis added).

217. *See Kahana Sunset Owners Ass'n v. County of Maui*, 86 Haw. 66, 947 P.2d 378 (1997); *Sierra Club v. Office of Planning*, 109 Haw. 411, 126 P.3d 1098 (2006).

218. Haw. Rev. Stat. §§ 205A-1 to -71.

219. Id. § 205A-26(3)(E) (1993).

220. Id. § 205A-26(2)(B).

221. Id. § 205A-2(c)(10)(A).

222. U.S. Fish and Wildlife Service, "Hawaiian islands animals," http://www.fws.gov/pacificislands/publications/listinganimals.pdf; U.S. Fish and Wildlife Service, "Hawaiian islands plants," http://fws.gov/pacificislands/publications/listingplants.pdf (last visited Jan. 20, 2010).

223. Id. The 100 threatened and endangered animals include 4 mammals (the Hawaiian hoary bat, Hawaiian monk seal, humpback whale, and sperm whale), 34 species of birds, 5 sea turtle species, 42 species of snails, and 15 types of anthropods (including the Kaua'i cave wolf spider and its prey the Kaua'i cave amphipod, Blackburn's sphinx moth, and 12 Hawaiian picture-wing flies). Id.

224. For a useful summary, see Munger, supra note 4, at 274 et seq.

225. Haw. Rev. Stat. § 195D-1 (2008).

226. Id.

227. Id. § 195D-3(a).

228. Id. § 195D-2.

229. Id.

230. Id. § 195D-3(b).

231. Id. § 195D-4(3)(2).

232. Id. § 195D-2.

233. Id. "Take" means "to harass, harm, pursue, hunt, shoot, wound, kill, trap, capture, or collect endangered or threatened species of aquatic life or wildlife, or to cut, collect, uproot, destroy, injure, or possess endangered or threatened species of aquatic life or land plants, or to attempt to engage in any such conduct[.]" Id.

234. Id. §§ 195D-4(g), D-21.

235. H. S.C Rep. No. 127-74 House Journal at 612.

236. *Kepoo v. Kane*, 106 Haw. 270, 103 P.3d 939 (2005).

237. Haw. Rev. Stat. § 343-2 (2008).

238. Id. § 343-45.

239. *Kahana Sunset Owners*, supra note 217.

240. Id.

241. Id. at 74, 947 P.2d at 386.

242. *Citizens for Prot. of N. Kohala Coastline v. County of Hawaii*, 91 Haw. 94, 979 P.2d 1120 (1999). In 2008, the Hawai'i State Legislature considered a bill that would have exempted developments that crossed state or county right-of-ways from § 343 environmental assessment requirements. Lynda Arakawa, "EIS exemption bill moves on," Honolulu Advertiser, Mar. 9, 2008, at A33. The language granting the exemption was removed before the bill passed the final reading. S.B. 2808, Twenty-fifth Leg., Reg. Sess. (Haw. 2008); *compare* id. at Senate Draft Two, Feb. 29, 2008 *with* id. at House Draft One, Mar. 28, 2008, available at http://www.capitol.Hawaii.gov/site1/docs/docs.asp (search 2008 Regular Session for S.B. 2808) (last visited Jan. 20, 2010).

243. *Sierra Club*, supra note 217.
244. See H.B. 2067-74, H.D. 1; Comm. Rep. 566-74 in HOUSE JOURNAL at 768.
245. *Sierra Club*, supra note 217.
246. H. S.C. Rep. No. 566-74; S.C. Rep No. 956-74.
247. *Unite Here! v. City and County of Honolulu*, ___P. 3d___(2010).
248. Sustainability Task Force, "Hawai'i 2050 Sustainability Plan: Charting a course for Hawai'i's sustainable future" 39–40 (2008), http://www.hawaii2050.org/images/uploads/Hawaii2050_Plan_FINAL.pdf (last visited Nov. 17, 2009); see also S.B. 1592, 23rd Leg. (Haw. 2005) (enabling legislation for the task force); H.B. 2805, 23rd Leg. (Haw. 2006) (extending plan deadline from 2007 to 2008); H.B. 2806, 23rd Leg. (Haw. 2006) (appropriating funds for task force activities, including research and community outreach). The Hawai'i 2050 Sustainability Plan is not the first such plan in the state's history; a similar plan, Hawai'i 2000, was created in the 1970s. George R. Ariyoshi, "Leadership lessons: Hawai'i 2050," HAW. BUS. (May 2006), http://www.hawaiibusiness.com/Hawaii-Business/May-2006/Hawaii-2050 (last visited Nov. 17, 2009); Jim Dator et al., *Hawai'i 2000: Past, Present and Future*, prepared for the Hawai'i Office of Planning, Department of Business, Economic Development, and Tourism, Dec. 1999. That plan advocated a precautionary approach to land use and encouraged government to create a downward pressure on population until the full environmental effects of development could be ascertained. Id. at 10–11. Unfortunately, the plan did little to help environmental resources; between 1970 and 1999, "over 90% of lowland dry forests have been lost to fire, development, agriculture, or weed invasions"; overall, "most of the loss has occurred along the coasts and in the lowlands, where the majority of habitation exists today." Id. at 35. These losses could be attributed to lack of funding for state environmental and fish and wildlife funding. Id. at 36. In the meantime, development has surged on O'ahu, and the number of units on the island is expected to increase over 25 percent by 2030. Kevin Dayton, "How much is too much?" HONOLULU ADVERTISER, June 23, 2006, at 1A. Even with that increase, because of the growing population, the current shortage of affordable housing will almost certainly continue. "Housing: Development cap, 'enough' affordable homes look unlikely," HONOLULU ADVERTISER, June 23, 2006, at 12A. The 2050 Sustainability Plan was created in part to ensure that quality of life does not decline as population increases. Dayton, supra.

Bibliography

Primary Authorities

FEDERAL STATUTES/RULES AND REGULATIONS

Act of July 7, 1898. 30 Stat. 750 (1898) (Joint Resolution of Annexation).

Act to Revise the Procedures Established by the Hawaii Statehood Act for the Conveyance of Certain Lands to the State of Hawaii. 77 Stat. 472 (1963).

Hawaii Statehood Admission Act. Pub. L. No. 86-3, 73 Stat. 4 (1959).

Hawaiian Homes Commission Act. 1920, Pub. L. No. 67-34, 42 Stat. 108 (1921).

U.S. Advisory Council on Historic Preservation. Protection of Historic Properties. 36 C.F.R. pt. 800 (2008).

U.S. Congress. Agreements to Limit Encroachments and Other Constraints on Military Training, Testing, and Operations. 10 U.S.C. § 2684a.

———. Air Pollution Prevention and Control. 42 U.S.C. § 7602(h).

———. The Clean Air Act. 42 U.S.C. §§ 7401 et seq.

———. Coastal Zone Management Act of 1972. 16 U.S.C. §§ 1451 et seq.

———. Credits Against Tax. 26 U.S.C. § 47 et seq.

———. Endangered Species. 16 U.S.C. §§ 1531-44.

———. Federal Land Transaction Facilitation. 43 U.S.C. § 2301.

———. Flood Control Act of 1936. 33 U.S.C. § 701 et seq.

———. General Duties and Powers. 49 U.S.C. § 303.

———. Hawaii National Park. 16 U.S.C. § 391 et seq.

———. Historic Sites, Buildings, Objects, and Antiquities. General Provisions. 16 U.S.C. § 461 et seq.

———. Historic Sites, Buildings, Objects, and Antiquities. National Historic Preservation. 16 U.S.C. § 470 et seq.

———. National Environmental Policy. 42 U.S.C. § 4321 et seq.

———. National Flood Insurance Act of 1968. 42 U.S.C. § 4001 et seq.

———. National Parks, Military Parks, Monuments, and Seashores. 16 U.S.C § 431.

———. National Wildlife Refuge System. 16 U.S.C. § 668dd, ee.

———. Native American Graves Protection and Repatriation. 25 U.S.C. § 3001 et seq.

———. Normal Taxes and Surtaxes. 26 U.S.C. § 191 (repealed 1981).

———. Outer Continental Shelf Lands Act. 43 U.S.C. § 1331 et seq.

———. Rules & Regulations of National Parks, Reservations, and Monuments; Timber; Leases. 16 U.S.C. § 3.

———. Water Pollution Prevention and Control. Permits and Licenses. 33 U.S.C. 1341 et seq.

———. Water Pollution Prevention and Control. Research and Related Programs. 33 U.S.C. § 1251 et seq.

U.S. Constitution.

U.S. Council on Environmental Quality. NEPA and Agency Planning. 40 C.F.R. pt. 1501 (2008).

———. Terminology and Index. 40 C.F.R. pt. 1508 (2008).

U.S. Department of Commerce. National Oceanic and Atmospheric Administration. Coastal Zone Management Program Regulations. 15 C.F.R. pt. 923 (2009).

———. National Oceanic and Atmospheric Administration. Federal Consistency with Approved Coastal Management Programs. 15 C.F.R. pt. 930 (2009).

———. National Oceanic and Atmospheric Administration. Consideration of the national interest in facilities. 44 Fed. Reg. 18,608 (March 28, 1979).

———. Notice of Withdrawal of the Waimanu Valley National Estuarine Research Reserve from the National Estuarine Research Reserve System. 61 Fed. Reg. 32,774 (June 25, 1996).

U.S. Dept. of the Interior. Joint Regulations. Northwestern Hawaiian Islands Marine National Monument. 50 C.F.R. § 404.1 et seq.

———. Native American Graves Protection and Repatriation Regulations. 43 C.F.R. pt. 10 (2008).

U.S. Environmental Protection Agency. 404 Program Definitions; Exempt Activities Not Requiring 404 Permits. 40 C.F.R. pt. 232 (2009).

———. Approval and Promulgation of Implementation Plans. 40 C.F.R. pt. 52 (2009).

———. Effluent Guidelines and Standards. 40 C.F.R. pt. 401 (2009).

———. National Primary and Secondary Ambient Air Quality Sources. 40 C.F.R. pt. 50 (2009).

———. Requirements for Preparation, Adoption, and Submittal of Implementation Plans. 40 C.F.R. pt. 51 (2009).

U.S. Federal Emergency Management Agency. National Flood Insurance Program. 44 C.F.R. Parts 59–79.

U.S. Fish & Wildlife Service. Endangered and Threatened Wildlife and Plants. 50 C.F.R. pt. 17 (2009).

———. National Wildlife Refuge System. 50 C.F.R. § 25.11 et seq.

U.S. Internal Revenue Service. Qualified Conservation Contributions. 26 C.F.R. § 1.170A-14 (2008).

———. Qualified Rehabilitated Building; Expenditures Incurred after Dec. 31, 1981. 26 C.F.R. § 1.48-12 (2008).

U.S. National Park Service. Concession Contracts. 36 C.F.R. § 51.1-.2.

———. Leasing of Properties in Park Areas. 36 C.F.R. § 18.1 et seq.

———. National Register of Historic Places. 36 C.F.R. pt. 60 (2008).

———. Permits. 36 C.F.R. § 1.6.

U.S. President. Exec. Order No. 10530. 19 Fed. Reg. 2709 (May 10, 1954).
———. Exec. Order No. 10960. 26 Fed. Reg. 7823 (Aug. 21, 1961).
———. Exec. Order No. 11508. 35 Fed. Reg. 2855 (Feb. 10, 1970).
———. Exec. Order No. 11724. 38 Fed. Reg. 16837 (June 25, 1973).
———. Exec. Order No. 11954. 42 Fed. Reg. 2297 (Jan. 7, 1977).
———. Exec. Order No. 11988. 42 Fed. Reg. 26951 (May 25, 1977).
———. Proclamation No. 8031. 71 Fed. Reg. 36443 (June 26, 2006).

Primary Authorities

STATE STATUTES/RULES AND REGULATIONS

California. Development Agreements. CAL. GOV'T CODE tit. 7, div. 1, ch. 4, art. 2.5.
Hawaii. Constitution.
———. Department of Business, Economic Development and Tourism. Aloha Tower Development Corporation. HAW. CODE R. § 15-26-1 to -201 (Weil 2005).
———. Department of Business, Economic Development & Tourism. Land Use Commission. HAW. CODE R. § 15-15-1 et seq. (Weil 2005).
———. Department of Hawaiian Home Lands. HAW. CODE R. tit. 10 (Weil 2005).
———. Department of Health. Environmental Impact Statement Rules. HAW. CODE R. § 11- 200-1 et seq. (Weil 2005).
———. Department of Health. Environmental State Revolving Funds. HAW. CODE R. § 11-65-1 et seq. (Weil 2005).
———. Department of Health. Water Pollution Control. HAW. CODE R. § 11-55-1 et seq. (Weil 2005).
———. Department of Health. Water Quality Control. HAW. CODE R. § 11-54-1 et seq. (Weil 2005).
———. Department of Land & Natural Resources. *The Hawaii State Plan: Conservation Lands State Functional Plan* (1991).
———. Department of Land & Natural Resources. Conservation District. HAW. CODE R. § 13- 5-1 et seq. (Weil 2005).
———. Department of Land & Natural Resources. Division of State Parks. HAW. CODE R. § 13-146-1 et seq. (Weil 2005).
———. Department of Land & Natural Resources. Natural Areas Reserves System. HAW. CODE R. § 13-209-1 et seq. (Weil 2005).
———. Department of Land & Natural Resources. Rules and Practices and Procedure Relating to Burial Sites and Human Remains. HAW. CODE R. § 13-300-1 et seq. (Weil 2005).
———. Department of Land & Natural Resources. Rules Governing Standards for Archaeological Inventory Surveys and Reports. HAW. CODE R. § 13-276-1 et seq. (Weil 2005).
———. Department of Land & Natural Resources. The Hawaii and National Registers of Historic Places Programs. HAW. CODE R. § 13-198-1 et seq. (Weil 2005).
———. Division of Aquatic Resources. Waikiki Marine Life Conservation District. HAW. CODE R. § 13-36-1 to -4 (Weil 2005).
———. Housing and Community Development Corporation. State Assisted Land and Housing Development. HAW. CODE R. § 15-174-1 et seq. (Weil 2005).

———. Legislature. 2050 Sustainability Plan for Hawai'i. Act 8, 2005 Haw. Laws 1st Sp. Sess., (effective July 1, 2005).

———. Legislature. Acquisition of Resource Value Lands. Haw. Rev. Stat. ch. 173A (2008).

———. Legislature. Aloha Tower Development Corporation. Haw. Rev. Stat. ch. 206J (2009).

———. Legislature. Coastal Zone Management. Haw. Rev. Stat. ch. 205A (2008).

———. Legislature. Concessions on Public Property. Haw. Rev. Stat. ch. 102 (2009).

———. Legislature. Conservation and Resources. Conservation Districts. Haw. Rev. Stat. § 183C-1 et seq. (1993).

———. Legislature. Conservation of Aquatic Life, Wildlife, and Land Plants. Haw. Rev. Stat. § 195D-5.1 (1993).

———. Legislature. Conveyance Tax. Haw. Rev. Stat. ch. 247 (2009).

———. Legislature. Environmental Impact Statements. Haw. Rev. Stat. ch. 343 (2008).

———. Legislature. Executive and Administrative Departments. Haw. Rev. Stat. ch. 26 (2009).

———. Legislature. Federal Flood Insurance. Haw. Rev. Stat. § 46-11 (2009).

———. Legislature. General Jurisdiction and Powers. Haw. Rev. Stat. ch. 46 (2009).

———. Legislature. General Powers and Limitations of the Counties. Haw. Rev. Stat. § 46-1.5 (2009).

———. Legislature. General Provisions. Haw. Stat. Rev. § 46 (2008).

———. Legislature. General Provisions. Historic Preservation. Haw. Rev. Stat. § 6E (2008).

———. Legislature. Hawaii Community Development Authority. Haw. Rev. Stat. ch. 206E (1993).

———. Legislature. Hawaii Housing Finance and Development Administration. Haw. Rev. Stat. ch. 201H (2009).

———. Legislature. Hawaii Public Housing Authority. Haw. Rev. Stat. ch. 356D (2009).

———. Legislature. Hawaii State Planning Act. Haw. Rev. Stat. § 226 et seq. (2008).

———. Legislature. Impact Fees. Haw. Rev. Stat. § 46-141 et seq. (2008).

———. Legislature. Land Use Commission. Haw. Rev. Stat. ch. 205 (2009).

———. Legislature. Marine Life Conservation Program. Haw. Rev. Stat. § 190.1 et seq. (1993).

———. Legislature. Natural Area Reserves System. Haw. Rev. Stat. ch. 195 (2008).

———. Legislature. Office of Hawaiian Affairs. Haw. Rev. Stat. ch. 10 (2009).

———. Legislature. Parks and Playgrounds for Subdivisions. Haw. Rev. Stat. § 46-6 (2009).

———. Legislature. Public Lands, Management & Disposition of. Haw. Rev. Stat. ch. 171 (2009).

———. Legislature. Real Property Tax Law. Haw. Rev. Stat. § 246 (2008).

———. Legislature. Reclamation of Lands. Haw. Rev. Stat. ch. 173 (2009).

———. Legislature. State Building Code and Design Standards. HAW. REV. STAT. §
107-21 through -29 (2009).

———. Legislature. State Parks. HAW. REV. STAT. ch. 184 (2009).

———. Legislature. Urban Renewal Law. HAW. REV. STAT. ch. 53 (2009).

———. Legislature. Water Pollution. HAW. REV. STAT. § 342D-11 (1993).

Illinois. Annexation Agreements. 65 ILL. COMP. STAT. 5/11-15.1 et seq. (West
1993).

Primary Authorities

COUNTY ORDINANCES/RULES AND REGULATIONS

City and County of Honolulu.

———. *Additional Boards, Commissions and Committees.* HONOLULU, HAW., REV. ORDI-
NANCES ch. 3 (2008).

———. Department of Planning and Permitting. *Development/Sustainable Communities Plan* (1999–2004).

———. Department of Planning and Permitting. *Land Use Ordinance.* HONOLULU,
HAW., REV. ORDINANCES ch. 21 (2008).

———. Department of Planning and Permitting. *Primary Urban Center Development
Plan* (2004).

———. Department of Planning and Permitting. *Subdivision Rules and Regulations.*
Honolulu (1973).

———. *Development Plans.* HONOLULU, HAW., REV. ORDINANCES ch. 24 (2008).

———. *General Plan.* Honolulu (2006).

———. *North Shore Sustainable Communities Plan.* Honolulu (2000).

———. *Revised Charter of the City and County of Honolulu* (2000).

———. *Revolving Special Funds, Housing Mortgage Loans and Fees.* HONOLULU, HAW.,
REV. ORDINANCES ch. 6 (2008).

———. *Special Management Area.* HONOLULU, HAW., REV. ORDINANCES ch. 25
(2008).

———. *Subdivision of Land.* HONOLULU, HAW., REV. ORDINANCES ch. 22 (2008).

County of Hawai'i.

———. *Hawai'i County Charter* (2000).

———. *Hawai'i County Code* (1975).

———. *Hawai'i General Plan* (2005).

———. *Special Management Area Rules of the County of Hawai'i.*

County of Maui.

———. *Charter of the County of Maui* (2003).

———. Department of Public Works. *Subdivision Processing Guidelines* (2008).

———. *Kaho'olawe Community Plan 5.* 1992.

———. *Maui County Code.* Ordinance no. 1941 § 1. 1990 (as amended).

———. Maui County Council. *Wailuku-Kahului Community Plan* (2002).

———. *Maui County General Plan.* Ordinance no. 2039. September 27, 1991.

———. Maui County Planning Department. *Wailuku Redevelopment Plan* (Feb.
2000).

———. *Maui Planning Commission Rules.* Art. II, § 12 200 et seq. (2004).

County of Kaua'i.
———. *Comprehensive Zoning Ordinance* (August 1972, as amended).
———. *Heritage Resources Maps.* Ordinance no. 3.1.1. (2000).
———. *Kaua'i County Charter* (1969).
———. *Kaua'i County Code.*
———. *Kaua'i County Subdivision Ordinance.*
———. *Policy.* Ordinance no. 1.4.1. (2000).
———. *Special Management Area Rules and Regulations.* Planning Commission Rules §§ 1.4 A, 1.4-C, 1.4-I, 5.0, 8-10 (1984).
———. *The General Plan.* Ordinance no. 753. (2000).

Cases

Adolph v. Fed. Emergency Mgmt. Agency, 854 F.2d 732 (5th Cir. 1988).
Ako v. OHA, 87-1 Haw. Legal Rep. 87-537 (1st Cir. Ct. 1987).
Alexander v. Block, 660 F.2d 1240 (8th Cir. 1981).
Allen v. City and County of Honolulu, 58 Haw. 432, 571 P.2d 328 (1977).
Aluli v. Brown, 602 F.2d 876 (9th Cir. 1979).
Am. Petroleum Inst. v. Knecht, 609 F.2d 1306 (9th Cir. 1979).
Amoco Oil Co. v. Vill. of Schaumburg, 661 N.E.2d 380 (Ill. App. Ct. 1995).
Art Neon Co. v. City & County of Denver, 488 F.2d 118 (10th Cir. 1973).
A-S-P Assocs. v. City of Raleigh, 258 S.E.2d 444 (N.C. 1979).
Babbitt v. Sweet Home Chapter of Cmtys. for a Great Or., 515 U.S. 687 (1995).
Baltica Constr. Co. v. Planning Bd. of Franklin Twp., 537 A.2d 319 (N.J. App. 1987).
Batch v. Town of Chapel Hill, 387 S.E.2d 655 (N.C. 1990).
Bd. of County Comm'rs of Boulder Co. v. Homebuilders Ass'n of Metro. Denver, No. 95SC479, 1996 WL 700564 at *4 (Colo. 1996).
Berman v. Parker, 348 U.S. 26 (1954).
Bldg. Indus. Ass'n of Cent. Cal. v. City of Patterson, 171 Cal. App. 4th 886 (2009).
Bloom v. City of Fort Collins, 784 P.2d 304 (1989).
Brescia v. Edends-Huff, Civ. No. 08-1-0107 (D. Haw. Oct. 2, 2008).
Brescia v. N. Shore Ohana, 115 Haw. 477, 168 P.3d 929 (2007).
Cal. Coastal Comm'n v. Granite Rock Co., 480 U.S. 572 (1987).
California v. Norton, 150 F. Supp. 2d 1046 (N.D. Cal. 2001).
Candlestick Prop. v. San Francisco Bay Conservation & Dev. Comm'n, 89 Cal. Rptr. 897 (Ct. App. 1970).
Carlino v. Whitpain Investors, 453 A.2d 1385 (Pa. 1982).
Carlsmith, Carlsmith, Wichman & Case v. CPB Props., Inc., 64 Haw. 584, 645 P.2d 873 (1982).
Carr v. Alta Verde Indus., Inc., 931 F.2d 1055 (5th Cir. 1991).
Casey v. Mayor & City Council of Rockville, 929 A.2d 74 (Md. 2007).
Cederberg v. City of Rockford, 291 N.E.2d 249 (Ill. App. Ct. 1973).
Christopher Lake Dev. Co. v. St. Louis County, 35 F.3d 1269 (8th Cir. 1994).
Citizens for Prot. of N. Kohala Coastline v. County of Hawaii, 91 Haw. 94, 979 P.2d 1120 (1999).
City & County of Honolulu v. Attractions Haw., Civ. No. 01-1-03622-12 (D. Haw. Jan. 13, 2006).

City of Annapolis v. Waterman, 745 A.2d 1000 (Md. 2000).

City of Cuyahoga Falls v. Buckeye Cmty. Hope Found., 538 U.S. 188 (2003).

City of Eastlake v. Forest City Enters., 426 U.S. 668 (1976).

City of Los Angeles v. Gage, 274 P.2d 34 (Cal. Ct. App. 1954).

City of W. Hollywood v. Beverly Towers, 805 P.2d 329 (Cal. 1991).

Clark v. City of Albany, 904 P.2d 185 (Or. Ct. App. 1995).

Commercial Builders of N. Cal. v. City of Sacramento, 941 F.2d 872 (9th Cir. 1991).

Concerned Area Residents for the Env't v. Southview Farm, 34 F.3d 114 (2d Cir. 1994).

Country Meadows W. P'ship v. Vill. of Germantown, 614 N.W.2d 498 (Wis. Ct. App. 2000).

County of Hawaii v. Ala Loop Homeowners, 120 Haw. 256, 203 P.3d 676 (2009).

County of Hawaii v. C&J Coupe Family Ltd., 120 Haw. 400, 208 P.3d 713 (2009).

County of Kauai v. Pac. Standard Life Ins. Co., 65 Haw. 318, 653 P.2d 766 (1983).

Cummings v. City of Waterloo, 683 N.E.2d 1222 (Ill. App. Ct. 1997).

Curtis v. Bd. of Appeals, 90 Haw. 384, 978 P.2d 822 (1999).

Dalton v. City & County of Honolulu, 51 Haw. 400, 462 P.2d 199 (1966).

Defenders of Wildlife v. Bernal, 204 F.3d 920 (9th Cir. 2000).

Denning v. County of Maui, 52 Haw. 653, 485 P.2d 1048 (1971).

Dolan v. City of Tigard, 512 U.S. 374 (1994).

DuRant v. S.C. Dep't of Health & Envtl. Control, 604 S.E.2d 704 (S.C. Ct. App. 2004).

Dur-Bar Realty Co. v. City of Utica, 394 N.Y.S.2d 913 (App. Div. 1977).

Ehrlich v. Culver City, 12 Cal. 4th 854 (1996).

Embassy Real Estate Holdings, LLC v. D.C. Mayor's Agent for Historic Pres., 944 A.2d 1036 (D.C. 2008).

Envtl. Def. v. Duke Energy Corp., 549 U.S. 561 (2007).

Exxon Corp. v. Train, 554 F.2d 1310 (5th Cir. 1977).

Fasano v. Bd. of County Comm'rs of Wash. County, 507 P.2d 23 (Or. 1973).

Foreman v. State, 387 N.E.2d 455 (Ind. Ct. App. 1979).

Fortier v. City of Spearfish, 433 N.W.2d 228 (S.D. 1988).

Frisella v. Town of Farmington, 550 A.2d 102 (N.H. 1988).

Garneau v. City of Seattle, 147 F.3d 802 (9th Cir. 1998).

GATRI v. Blane, 88 Haw. 108, 962 P.2d 367 (1988).

Giger v. City of Omaha, 442 N.W.2d 182 (Neb. 1989).

Goffinet v. County of Christian, 357 N.E.2d 442 (Ill. 1976).

Goldblatt v. Town of Hempstead, 369 U.S. 590 (1962).

Golden v. Planning Bd. of Ramapo, 285 N.E.2d 291 (N.Y. 1972).

GST Tucson Lightwave, Inc. v. City of Tucson, 949 P.2d 971 (Ariz. Ct. App. 1997).

Haw. Hous. Auth. v. Midkiff, 467 U.S. 229 (1984).

Hawaii v. Gordon, 373 U.S. 57 (1963).

Hawaii v. OHA, 129 S.Ct. 1436 (2009).

Headwaters, Inc. v. Talent Irrigation Dist., 243 F.3d 526 (9th Cir. 2001).

Hernando County v. Budget Inns of Fla., Inc., 555 So.2d 1319 (Fla. Dist. Ct. App. 1990).

Herron v. Mayor & City Council of Annapolis, 388 F. Supp. 2d 565 (D. Md. 2005).

Holmdel Builders Ass'n v. Twp. of Holmdel, 583 A.2d 277 (N.J. 1990).

Home Builders Ass'n of Cent. Ariz., Inc. v. Riddel, 510 P.2d 376 (Ariz. 1973).

Home Builders Ass'n v. City of Scottsdale, 930 P.2d 993 (Ariz. 1997).

Honolulu Waterfront Ltd. v. Aloha Tower Dev. Corp., 692 F. Supp. 1230 (D. Haw. 1988).

Hoohuli v. Ariyoshi, 631 F. Supp. 1153 (D. Haw. 1986).

Idaho Rural Council v. Bosma, 143 F. Supp. 2d 1169 (D. Idaho 2001).

In the Matter of Stoeco Dev., Ltd., 621 A.2d 29 (N.J. Super. Ct. App. Div. 1993).

Just v. Marinette County, 201 N.W.2d 761 (Wis. 1972).

Ka Paakai o ka Aina v. Land Use Comm'n, 94 Haw. 31, 7 P.3d 1068 (2000).

Kahana Sunset Owners Ass'n v. County of Maui, 86 Haw. 66, 947 P.2d 378 (1997).

Kailua Cmty. Council v. City & County of Honolulu, 60 Haw. 428, 591 P.2d 602 (1979).

Kaiser Hawaii Kai Dev. Co. v. City & County of Honolulu, 70 Haw. 480, 777 P.2d 244 (1989).

Kalorama Heights Ltd. v. D.C. Dep't of Consumer & Regulatory Affairs, 655 A.2d 865 (D.C. 1995).

Kamaole Pointe Dev. LP v. County of Maui, 2008 WL 5025004 (D. Haw. Nov.25, 2008).

Kansas-Lincoln, L.C. v. Arlington County Board, 66 Va. Cir. 274 (Cir. Ct. 2004).

Kapiolani Park Pres. Soc'y v. City & County of Honolulu, 69 Haw. 569, 751 P.2d 1022 (1988).

Kelly v. 1250 Oceanside Partners, Civ. No. 00-1-0192K (D. Haw. Sept. 9, 2003).

Kelo v. City of New London, 545 U.S. 469 (2005).

Kenneth H. Hughes, Inc. v. Aloha Tower Dev. Corp., DPR No. 07-0459-A (April 29, 2009) (arbitrator's partial final decision and award).

Kepoo v. Kane, 106 Haw. 270, 103 P.3d 939 (2005).

Keystone Bituminous Coal Ass'n v. DeBenedictis, 480 U.S. 470 (1987).

Kilauea Neighborhood Ass'n v. Land Use Comm'n, 7 Haw. App. 227, 751 P.2d 1031 (1988).

Kleppe v. New Mexico, 426 U.S. 529 (1976).

Kozesnik v. Twp. of Montgomery, 131 A.2d 1 (N.J. 1957).

Krahl v. Nine Mile Creek Watershed Dist., 283 N.W.2d 538 (Minn. 1979).

Lafferty v. Payson City, 642 P.2d 376 (Utah 1982).

Lakeview Dev. Corp. v. City of South Lake Tahoe, 915 F.2d 1290 (9th Cir. 1990).

Lanai Co. v. Land Use Comm'n, 105 Haw. 296, 97 P.3d 372 (2004).

Leroy Land Dev. Corp. v. Tahoe Reg'l Planning Agency, 939 F.2d 696 (9th Cir. 1991).

Life of the Land, Inc. v. City Council of Honolulu, 60 Haw. 446, 592 P.2d 26 (1979).

Life of the Land, Inc. v. City Council of Honolulu, 61 Haw. 390, 606 P.2d 866 (1980).

Lingle v. Chevron U.S.A., Inc., 544 U.S. 528 (2005).

Loggerhead Turtle v. County Council of Volusia County, 148 F.3d 1231 (11th Cir. 1998).

Lucas v. S.C. Coastal Council, 505 U.S. 1003 (1992).

Lum Yip Kee Ltd. v. City & County of Honolulu, 70 Haw. 179, 767 P.2d 815 (1989).

MacGibbon v. Bd. of Appeals of Duxbury, 255 N.E.2d 347 (Mass. 1970).

Mahaulepu v. Land Use Comm'n, 71 Haw. 332, 790 P.2d 906 (1990).

Mahuiki v. Planning Comm'n of Kauai, 65 Haw. 506, 654 P.2d 874 (1982).

Marblehead v. City of San Clemente, 277 Cal. Rptr. 550 (1991).

Mauna Kea Anaina Hou v. Bd. of Land & Nat. Res., Civ. No. 04-1-397 (D. Haw. Aug. 3, 2006).

McCarthy v. City of Manhattan Beach, 264 P.2d 932 (Cal. 1953).

Meegan v. Village of Tinley Park, 288 N.E.2d 423 (Ill. 1972).

Modjeska Sign Studios, Inc. v. Berle, 373 N.E.2d 255 (N.Y. 1977).

Morgan v. Planning Dep't, County of Kauai, 104 Haw. 173, 86 P.3d 982 (2004).

Morris County Land Improvement. Co. v. Parsippany-Troy Hills, 193 A.2d 232 (N.J. 1963).

Morrison Homes Corp. v. City of Pleasanton, 130 Cal. Rptr. 196 (Ct. App. 1976).

N. Cal. River Watch v. City of Healdsburg, 496 F.3d 993 (9th Cir. 2007).

N.M. Cattle Growers Ass'n v. U.S. Fish & Wildlife Serv., 248 F.3d 1277 (10th Cir. 2001).

Nectow v. City of Cambridge, 277 U.S. 183 (1928).

Neighborhood Bd. No. 24 (Waianae Coast) v. State Land Use Comm'n, 64 Haw. 265, 639 P.2d 1097 (1982).

Nollan v. Cal. Coastal Comm'n, 483 U.S. 825 (1987).

O'Malley v. Village of Ford Heights, 633 N.E.2d 848 (Ill. App. Ct. 1994).

OHA v. Bd. of Land & Natural Res., No. 95-0330-01 (Haw. Sup. Ct. 1998).

OHA v. Hous. & Cmty. Dev. Corp. of Haw., 117 Haw. 174, 177 P.3d 884 (2008), *rev'd and remanded sub nom. Hawaii v. OHA*, 129 S. Ct. 1436 (2009).

OHA v. O'Keefe, Civ. No. 02-00227, slip op (D. Haw. Jul. 15, 2003).

OHA v. State, 96 Haw. 388, 31 P.3d 901 (2001).

Palila v. Hawaii Dep't of Land & Natural Res., 639 F.2d 495 (9th Cir. 1981).

Pardee Construction Co. v. City of Camarillo, 690 P.2d 701 (Cal. 1984).

Parking Ass'n of Georgia, Inc. v. City of Atlanta, 515 U.S. 1116 (1995).

Pele Def. Fund v. Estate of James Campbell, Civ. No. 89-089 (D. Haw. Aug. 26, 2002).

Pele Def. Fund v. Paty, 73 Haw. 578, 837 P.2d 1247 (1992).

Penn Cent. Transp. Co. v. City of New York, 438 U.S. 104 (1978).

Penn. Coal Co. v. Mahon, 260 U.S. 393 (1922).

Pronsolino v. Nastri, 291 F.3d 1123 (9th Cir. 2002).

Public Access Shoreline Haw. v. Haw. County Planning Comm'n, 79 Haw. 425, 903 P.2d 1246 (1995).

Rapanos v. United States, 547 U.S. 715 (2006).

Rebman v. City of Springfield, 250 N.E.2d 282 (Ill. App. Ct. 1969).

Rice v. Cayetano, 528 U.S. 495 (2000).

Rumson Estates, Inc. v. Mayor & City Council of Fair Haven, 828 A.2d 317 (N.J. 2003).

Rybachek v. EPA, 904 F.2d 1276 (9th Cir. 1990).

S. Kemble Fischer Realty Trust v. Bd. of Appeals of Concord, 402 N.E.2d 100 (Mass. App. 1980).

San Remo Hotel v. City & County of San Francisco, 41 P.3d 87 (Cal. 2004).

Santa Margarita Area Residents Together v. San Luis Obispo County Bd. of Supervisors, 100 Cal. Rptr. 2d 740 (Ct. App. 2000).

Save Sunset Beach Coal. v. City & County of Honolulu, 102 Haw. 465, 78 P.3d 1 (2003).

Scrutton v. County of Sacramento, 79 Cal. Rptr. 872 (Ct. App. 1969).

Sec. of the Interior v. California, 464 U.S. 312 (1984).

Sierra Club v. Dep't. of Transp., 115 Haw. 299, 167 P.3d 292 (2007).

Sierra Club v. Office of Planning, 109 Haw. 411, 126 P.3d 1098 (2006).

Sills v. Walworth County Land Mgmt. Comm., 648 N.W.2d 878 (Wis. Ct. App. 2002).

Sprenger, Grubb & Associates, Inc. v. City of Hailey, 903 P.2d 741 (Idaho 1995).

State v. Hanapi, 89 Haw. 177, 970 P.2d 485 (1998).

Stop H-3 Ass'n v. Dole, 870 F.2d 1419 (9th Cir. 1989).

Subaru of New England v. Bd. of Appeals of Canton, 395 N.E.2d 880 (Mass. App. Ct. 1979).

Texas Landowners Rights Ass'n v. Harris, 453 F. Supp. 1025 (D.D.C. 1978).

Texas Manufactured Housing Ass'n v. City of Nederland, 101 F.3d 1095 (5th Cir. 1996).
T-Mobile USA, Inc. v. County of Haw. Planning Comm'n, 106 Haw. 343, 104 P.3d 930 (2005).
Town of Longboat Key v. Lands End Ltd., 433 So.2d 574 (Fla. Dist. Ct. App. 1983).
Town v. Land Use Comm'n, 55 Haw. 538, 524 P.2d 84 (1974).
Trustees of OHA v. Bd. of Land & Nat. Res., 87 Haw. 471, 959 P.2d 841 (Haw. Mar. 12, 1998) (mem).
Trustees of OHA v. Yamasaki, 69 Haw. 154, 737 P.2d 446 (1987).
Turner v. County of Del Norte, 101 Cal. Rptr. 93 (Ct. App. 1972).
Turnpike Realty Co. v. Town of Dedham, 284 N.E.2d 891 (Mass. 1972).
Twin Lakes Dev. Corp. v. Town of Monroe, 801 N.E.2d 821 (N.Y. 2003).
United States v. Brown, 552 F.2d 817 (8th Cir. 1977).
United States v. Irizarry, 98 F. Supp. 2d 160 (D.P.R. 2000).
United States v. Parish of St. Bernard, Civ. No.'s 81-1808 and 81-1810 (E.D. La. 1981).
Unlimited v. Kitsap County, 750 P.2d 651 (Wash. App. 1988).
Van Cleave v. Village of Seneca, 519 N.E.2d 63 (Ill. App. Ct. 1988).
Ventura County v. Gulf Oil Corp., 601 F.2d 1080 (9th Cir. 1979).
Vill. of Euclid v. Ambler Realty Co., 272 U.S. 365 (1926).
Vill. of Orlando Park v. First Fed. Sav. & Loan Ass'n, 481 N.E.2d 946 (Ill. App. Ct. 1985).
Watch v. Harris, 603 F.2d 310 (2d Cir. 1979).
Weinberger v. Romero-Barcelo, 456 U.S. 305 (1982).
Youngblood v. Bd. of Supervisors, 586 P.2d 556 (Cal. 1978).

Books, Reports, Articles, Online Sources

Advisory Council on Historic Preservation. *Protecting Historic Properties: A Citizen's Guide to Section 106 Review.* Washington, D.C.: ACHP, 2002.
Aloha Tower Development Corporation. "Aloha Tower project area plan," 26-3 to 26-4 (2006), http://www.alohatower.org/areaplan.pdf (last visited Nov. 28, 2009).
Alterman, Rachelle. "Evaluating linkage and beyond." 32 WASH. U. J. URB & CONTEMP. L. 3 (1988).
AM. JUR. 2D, vol. 63c. *Public Lands* (2009).
Apoliona, Haunani. "2007 State of OHA address" (Dec. 17, 2007). KAWAI OLA, Jan. 2008, at 7. *Available at* http://www.oha.org/pdf/kwo08/kwo0801.pdf (last visited Nov. 20, 2009).
Applegate, John S., and Jan G. Laitos. *Environmental Law: RCRA, CERCLA and the Management of Hazardous Waste.* New York: Foundation Press, 2005.
Arakawa, Lynda. "EIS exemption bill moves on." HONOLULU ADVERTISER, Mar. 9, 2008, at A33.
———. "New affordable housing finished." HONOLULU ADVERTISER, Sept. 21, 2007. http://the.honoluluadvertiser.com/article/2007/Sep/21/ln/hawaii7092 10344.html (last visited Nov. 20, 2009).
Ariyoshi, George R. "Hawaii 2050." HAW. BUS., May 2006, http://www.hawaiibusiness. com/Hawaii-Business/May-2006/Hawaii-2050/ (last visited Nov. 28, 2009).
Auer, Michael J. *Preservation Tax Incentives for Historic Buildings.* Washington D.C.:

U.S. Dept. of the Interior, National Park Service, Heritage Preservation Services, 2004.

Babcock, Richard F. *The Zoning Game: Municipal Practices and Policies.* Madison: University of Wisconsin Press, 1966.

Bail, Lisa A., Maren Calver, Robert D. Harris, Lea Hong, Naomi U. Kuwaye, and Paul J. Schwind. "Emerging environmental and land use issues." HAWAII BAR JOURNAL (June 2005).

Bergeson, Lynn L. *FIFRA: Federal Insecticide, Fungicide, and Rodenticide Act.* Chicago: American Bar Association, 2000.

Bernardo, Rosemarie. "Under new management." HONOLULU STAR-BULLETIN, Sept. 29, 2007. http://starbulletin.com/2007/09/29/news/story03.html (last visited Nov. 20, 2009).

Bernstein, Leonard A., Philip H. Myers, and Daniel Steen. "Flood insurance reform act engulfs mortgage lenders." 112 BANKING L.J. 238 (1995).

Bettman, Alfred. "The constitutionality of zoning." 37 HARV. L. REV. 834 (1924).

Blaesser, Brian W., and Christine M. Kentopp. "Impact fees: The second generation." 38 WASH. U.J. URB. & CONTEMP. L. REV. 55 (1990).

Blake, Robert Mason, and Julian Conrad Juergensmeyer. "Impact fees: An answer to local governments' capital funding dilemma." 9 FLA. ST. U. L. REV. 415 (1981).

Boonstoppel, Robert, and Adriane Miller. "U.S. military and communities seek ways to share natural resources." 38 MD. B.J. 32 (March/April 2005).

Bosselman, Fred P. "Can the town of Ramapo pass a law to bind the rights of the whole world?" 1 FLA. ST. U. L. REV. 234 (1973).

Bosselman, Fred P., and David L. Callies. *The Quiet Revolution in Land Use Control.* Prepared for the Council on Environmental Quality. Washington, D.C.: U.S. Government Printing Office, 1973.

Bosselman, Fred P., David L. Callies, and John Banta. *The Taking Issue: An Analysis of the Constitutional Limits of Land Use Control.* Prepared for the Council on Environmental Quality. Washington, D.C.: U.S. Government Printing Office, 1973.

Bosselman, Fred P., Duane A. Feuer, and Tobin M. Richter. *Federal Land Use Regulation.* New York: Practicing Law Institute, 1977.

Bosselman, Fred P., Duane A. Feuer, and Charles L. Siemon. *The Permit Explosion.* Washington, D.C.: Urban Land Institute, 1976.

Bosselman, Fred P., and Nancy Stroud. "Legal aspects of development exactions." In *Development Exactions.* Chicago: Planners Press, 1987.

———. "Mandatory tithes: The legality of land development linkage." 9 NOVA. L.J. 381 (1985).

Breemer, J. David. "The evolution of the nexus test." 59 WASH. & LEE L. REV. 373 (2002).

Callies, David L. "A hypothetical case: Value capture/joint development techniques to reduce the public costs of public improvements." 16 URB. L. ANN. 155 (1979).

———. "Euclid." Chapter 12 *in* Gerald Korngold and Andrew P. Morris, eds., *Property Stories*, 2d ed. New York: Foundation Press, 2009.

———. "Grand Central Station: Landmark preservation law." HAW. ARCHITECT, Oct. 1978, at 11.

———. "Impact fees, exactions and paying for growth in Hawaii." 11 U. Haw. L. Rev. 295 (1989).

———. "The interplay between land use and environmental law." 23 Pace Envtl. L. Rev. 685 (2006).

———. "Land use: Herein of vested rights, plans and the relationship of planning and controls." 2 U. Haw. L. Rev. 167 (1979).

———. *Public Use and Public Purpose, After* Kelo v. New London. Newark, N.J.: LexisNexis, 2008.

———. "The quiet revolution revisited." 46 J. Am. Plan. Ass'n 135 (1980).

———. "The quiet revolution revisited: A quarter century of progress." 26 Urb. Law. 197 (1994).

———. *Regulating Paradise: Land Use Controls in Hawaii.* Honolulu: University Press of Hawai'i, 1984.

———. "Takings: Physical and regulatory." 15 Asia Pac. L. Rev. 77 (2007).

Callies, David L., ed. *Takings: Land Development Conditions and Regulatory Takings after* Dolan *and* Lucas. Chicago: ABA, 1996.

Callies, David L., and Calvert G. Chipchase. "Water regulation, land use and the environment." 30 U. Haw. L. Rev. 49 (2007).

Callies, David L., Daniel J. Curtin Jr., and Julie A. Tappendorf. *Bargaining for Development: A Handbook on Development Agreements, Annexation Agreements, Land Development Conditions, Vested Rights, and the Provision of Public Facilities.* Washington, D.C.: Environmental Law Institute, 2003.

Callies, David L., Robert H. Freilich, and Thomas E. Roberts. *Cases and Materials on Land Use,* 5th ed. St. Paul, Minn.: West, 2008.

Callies, David L., and Malcolm Grant. "Paying for growth and planning gain: An Anglo American comparison of development conditions, impact fees and development agreements." 23 Urb. Law. 221 (1991).

Callies, David L., Nancy C. Neuffer, and Carlito P. Caliboso. "Ballot box zoning: Initiative, referendum and the law." 39 Wash. U.J. Urb. & Contemp. L. 53 (1991).

Callies, David L., and Julie A. Tappendorf. "Unconstitutional land development conditions and the development agreement solution: Bargaining for public facilities after *Nollan* and *Dolan.*" 51 Case W. Res. L. Rev. 663 (2001).

Caputo, Drew. "A job half finished: The Clean Water Act after 25 years." 27 Envtl. L. Rep. 10 (1997).

Carlton, Jim. "Hot properties: Private 'inholdings' in federal preserves." Wall St. J., July 28, 2004, at B1.

Cartensen, Vernon R. *The Public Lands: Studies in the History of the Public Domain.* Madison: University of Wisconsin Press, 1963.

Chang, Lester. "Attention focused on state park cabin leases." Garden Isle, Nov. 3, 2001 http://www.kauaiworld.com/articles/2001/11/05/news (follow the "Advanced Search Options" hyperlink and type in keywords from article title) (last visited Nov. 22, 2009).

———. "Land board to move on Koke'e plan today." Garden Isle, Jan. 15, 2005. http://www.kauaiworld.com/articles/2005/01/14/news (follow the "Advanced Search Options" hyperlink and type in keywords from article title) (last visited Nov. 22, 2009).

————. "State may end leases of prized Koke'e cabins." GARDEN ISLE, Oct, 3, 2003. http://www.kauaiworld.com/articles/2003/10/03/news (follow the "Advanced Search Options" hyperlink and type in keywords from article title) (last visited Nov. 22, 2009).

————. "State reviewing Koke'e-Waimea Canyon park." GARDEN ISLE, Oct. 30, 2001. http://www.kauaiworld.com/articles/2001/10/31/news (follow the "Advanced Search Options" hyperlink and type in keywords from article title) (last visited Nov. 22, 2009).

Chassis, Sarah. "The Coastal Zone Management Act." 46 J. OF THE AM. PLAN. ASS'N 145 (April 1980).

Cheng, Norman. Comment. "Is agricultural land in Hawai'i "ripe" for a takings analysis?" 24 U HAW. L. REV. 121 (2001).

Chinen, Jon. *The Great Mahele: Hawaii's Land Division of 1848.* Honolulu: University of Hawai'i Press, 1958.

City & County of Honolulu, Department of Planning & Permitting. "Guidelines on processing a subdivision application (rev. 2005), http://honoluludpp.org/downloadpdf/engineering/subappguide.pdf. (last visited Nov. 28, 2009).

————. "Interactive GIS maps and data." http://gis.hicentral.com/ (last visited Nov. 21, 2009).

————. "Zone change application instructions." http://www.honoluludpp.org/downloadpdf/planning/ZoneChangeApp.pdf (last visited Nov. 21, 2009).

————. Press release. "Mayor approves Waimea Valley resolution" (Apr. 3, 2006). http://www.honolulu.gov/refs/csd/publiccom/honnews06/mayorapproves waimeavalleyresolution.htm (last visited Nov. 16, 2009).

Cody, Betsy A. *Major Federal Land Management Agencies: Management of Our Nation's Lands and Resources.* Congressional Research Services Report 95-599. May 15, 1995.

Cornford, Tom. "Planning gain and the government's new proposals on planning obligations." 2002 J. PLAN. & ENV'T. L. 796.

Costonis, John J. "The disparity issue: A context for the Grand Central Terminal decision." 91 HARV. L. REV. 402 (1977).

Creamer, Beverly. "Manoa flood may cost $80M." HONOLULU ADVERTISER, Dec. 7, 2004. http://the.honoluluadvertiser.com/article/2004/Dec/07/ln/ln03p.html (last visited Nov. 8, 2009).

Curtin, Daniel J. Jr. "Protecting developers' permits to build: Development agreement in practice in California and other states." 18 ZONING & PLAN. L. REP. 85 (1995).

Da Silva, Alexandre. "Park officials put brakes on Haleakala tour rides." HONOLULU STAR-BULLETIN, Oct. 4, 2007. http://archives.starbulletin.com/2007/10/04/news/story03.html (last visited Nov. 22, 2009).

Dator, Jim, Michael Hamnett, Devin Nordberg, and William S. Pintz. *Hawaii 2000: Past, Present and Future.* Prepared for the Hawaii Office of Planning, Department of Business, Economic Development and Tourism. Honolulu: Social Science Research Institute, University of Hawai'i, Dec. 1999.

Daws, Gavan. *Shoal of Time: A History of the Hawaiian Islands.* New York: Macmillan, 1968.

Daysog, Rick. "Church project in need of disinterment permit." HONOLULU ADVER-
    TISER, June 13, 2009, at B1.
———. "Kawaiahaʻo church center's fundraising costs questioned." HONOLULU
    ADVERTISER, May 29, 2009, at A1–A2.
———. "OHA asks for study of burials." HONOLULU ADVERTISER, June 9, 2009, at
    B1.
Dayton, Kevin. "Big push to erect telescope in Isles." HONOLULU ADVERTISER, Aug.
    10, 2008, at A1.
Delafons, John. Land-Use Controls in the United States. 2nd ed. Cambridge: MIT Press,
    1969.
Delaney, John J. "Vesting verities and the development chronology: A gaping dis-
    connect?" 3 WASH. U. J.L. & POL'Y 603 (2000).
Dinell, Tom. "Land use zoning in a developing state: A brief critique of Hawaiʻi's
    Land Use Law." 2 THIRD WORLD PLAN. REV. 195 (1980).
Dowling, Michael B., and Joseph A. Fadrowsky III. Note. "Dolan v. City of Tigard:
    Individual Property Rights v. Land Management Systems." 17 U. HAW. L. REV.
    193 (1995).
Dunham, Allison. "Flood control via the police power." 107 U. PA. L. REV. 1098
    (1959).
EDAW, Inc. Revisions to the Kakaako Community Development District Mauka Area Plan
    and Rules. SUPPLEMENTAL ENVIRONMENTAL IMPACT STATEMENT PREPARATION
    NOTICE 2-1. Honolulu: EDAW, Inc. (Dec. 2007).
Eddins, Todd W., and Jerilynn S. Ono Hall. "Kaiser Hawaii Kai Development Co. v. City
    and County of Honolulu: Zoning by initiative in Hawaii." 12 U. HAW. L. REV. 181
    (1990).
Editorial. "Car dealership not ideal urban renewal." HONOLULU ADVERTISER, Jan.
    26, 2004, at A6.
Eilperin, Juliet. "Hawaiian marine reserve to be world's largest: Bush to designate
    national park in Pacific waters." WASH. POST, June 15, 2006, at A01.
Fassler, Richard C. "The winners and losers in Kakaako Makai fiasco." HONOLULU
    STAR- BULLETIN, May 14, 2006, http://archives.starbulletin.com/2006/05/14/
    editorial/special3.html (last visited Nov. 20, 2009).
Federal Emergency Management Agency. "National Flood Insurance Program:
    Program description (2002)." http://www.fema.gov/library/viewRecord.
    do?id=1480 (follow the "View / Download / Print" hyperlink).
———. "Community Status Book Report: Hawaii – Communities Participating in
    the National Flood Program." http://www.fema.gov/cis/HI.pdf (last visited
    February 1, 2010).
"Federal land sales stir up turf dispute." CONSERVATION FOUNDATION LETTER (May
    1982).
Finnegan, Tom. "Bill tackles Kokee cabins flap." HONOLULU STAR-BULLETIN, May 5,
    2008. http://archives.starbulletin.com/2008/05/05/news/story04.html#cxb
    (last visited Nov. 22, 2009).
Finnell, Gilbert L. Jr. "Coastal land management: An introduction," 1978 AM. B.
    FOUND. J. 153 (1978).
Fiorino, Daniel. The New Environmental Regulation. Boston: MIT Press, 2006.
Flynn, Rory. "Seeing through the fog of 'fake farms.'" HAW. REP., Jan. 30, 2007.

http://www.hawaiireporter.com/story.aspx?71b94b7f-385a-45e5-9f82-f8966a07f4e0 (last visited Nov. 28, 2009).

Frank, James E., and Robert M. Rhodes, eds. *Development Exactions.* Washington, D.C.: Planners Press, 1987.

Frankel, David Kimo. *Protecting Paradise: A Citizen's Guide to Land & Water Use Controls in Hawai'i.* Kailua: Dolphin Printing & Publishing, 1997.

Freilich, Robert H. *From Sprawl to Smart Growth.* Chicago: American Bar Association, 2000.

Freilich, Robert H., and David W. Bushek, eds. *Exactions, Impact Fees and Dedications: Shaping Land-Use Development and Funding Infrastructure in the* Dolan *Era.* Chicago: State and Local Government Law Section, ABA, 1995.

Freilich, Robert H. and Michael M. Shultz. *National Model Subdivision Regulations: Planning and Law.* Chicago: APA Planners Press, 1995.

Freilich, Robert, and S. Mark White. *21st Century Land Development Code.* Chicago: APA Planners Press, 2008.

Gardin, Stefanie. U.S. Army Garrison, Hawaii. "Partnership preserves Hawaii's Waimea Valley." Fall 2006, http://aec.army.mil/usaec/newsroom/update/fall06/fall0602.html (last visited Nov. 20, 2009).

Garner, John F., and David L. Callies. "Planning law in England and Wales and in the United States." 1 ANGLO-AM. L. REV. 292 (1972).

Gomes, Andrew. "A new look for Kaka'ako." HONOLULU ADVERTISER, May 17, 2009, at A5.

———. "Affordable condo going up in Salt Lake." HONOLULU ADVERTISER, Sept. 21, 2007, http://the.honoluluadvertiser.com/article/2007/Sep/21/bz/hawaii 709210323.html (last visited Nov. 28, 2009).

———. "Affordable housing in Hawai'i back on the map." HONOLULU ADVERTISER, Feb. 25 2007, at F1.

———. "Affordable housing tower will break ground." HONOLULU ADVERTISER, Mar. 13, 2007, at C1.

———. "Affordable townhouses on tap down-home prices." HONOLULU ADVERTISER, Aug. 25, 2006, http://the.honoluluadvertiser.com/article/2006/Aug/25/bz/FP608250330.html (last visited Nov. 28, 2009).

———. "Kaka'ako on the rise." HONOLULU ADVERTISER, Oct. 30, 2005, at F1.

Goodin, Charles C. "The Honolulu development plans: An analysis of land use implications for Oahu." 6 U. HAW. L. REV. 33 (1984).

Grady, Denise. "Even good health system is overwhelmed by tsunami." N.Y. TIMES, Jan. 9, 2005, at 10.

Griffith, Charles T. Note. "The National Flood Insurance Program: Unattained purposes, liability in contract and takings." 35 WM. & MARY L. REV. 727 (1994).

Gross, Joel M., and Lynn Dodge. *Clean Water Act: Basic Practice Series.* Washington, D.C.: American Bar Association, 2005.

Haar, Charles M., and Jerold S. Kayden, eds. *Zoning and the American Dream: Promises Still to Keep.* Chicago: Planners Press, 1989.

Haar, Charles M., and Michael C. Wolf. *Land-Use Planning: A Casebook on the Use, Misuse, and Re-Use of Urban Land,* 4th ed. Boston: Little, Brown & Co., 1989.

Hagman, Donald G. "Estoppel and vesting in the use of multi-land permits." 11 Sw. U. L. REV. 545 (1979).

Hagman, Donald G., and Dean Misczynski. "The quiet federalization of land-use controls: Disquietude in the land markets." REAL ESTATE APPRAISER (Sept./ Oct. 1974).

Haleakalā National Park. *Downhill Bicycle Tour Safety Stand Down Documents.* Washington, D.C.: National Park Service, 2007.

Haleakalā National Park. *Special Use Permits.* Washington, D.C.: National Park Service.

Hall, Taylor. "Big Island project may get second chance." HONOLULU ADVERTISER, June 6, 2009, at B5.

Hao, Sean. "Ancient burial likely in transit path." HONOLULU ADVERTISER, June 22, 2008, at A13.

Harrigan-Lum, June F., and Arnold L. Lum. "Hawaii's TMDL program: Legal requirements and environmental realities." 15 NAT. RESOURCES & ENV'T 12 (2000–2001).

Hawai'i Community Services Council and Hawai'i Institute for Public Affairs. *Hawai'i State Policy & the Nonprofit Sector: Optimizing the Relationship between Nonprofits and Government.* Honolulu, 2002. http://hawaii.gov/dbedt/main/ about/annual/2002-reports/2003-state-policy.pdf (last visited on January 5, 2010).

Hawai'i Department of Land & Natural Resources. Division of State Parks. "Hawai'i state parks: A visitor's guide to park resources and recreational activities." http://www.hawaiistateparks.org/pdf/brochures/Hawai'i_State_Parks_ Guide.pdf (last visited Nov. 22, 2009).

Hawai'i Department of Land & Natural Resources. "Legacy Land Conservation Program projects." http://hawaii.gov/dlnr/dofaw/llcp/legacy-land-conserva tion-program-projects new (last visited Nov. 20, 2009).

Hawai'i Military Installations map. U.S. Army, 652nd Engineers Battalion; State of Hawai'i. January 1979.

Hawai'i Sustainability Task Force. "Hawai'i 2050 Sustainability Plan: Charting a course for Hawai'i's sustainable future" (2008). *Available at* http://www. hawaii2050.org/images/uploads/Hawaii2050_Plan_FINAL.pdf (last visited Dec. 16, 2009).

Helund, Nancy. "Kakaako Makai needs protection of HB 2555." HONOLULU STAR-BULLETIN, June 15, 2006, at A12.

Herke, John. Note. "Teething pains at 25: Developing meaningful enforcement of the National Flood Insurance Program." 7 TUL. ENVTL. L.J. 165 (1993).

Heyman, Ira M., and Thomas K. Gilhool. "The constitutionality of imposing increased community costs on new suburban residents through subdivision exactions." 73 YALE L.J. 1119 (1964).

Hibbard, Benjamin H. *A History of the Public Land Policies.* Madison: University of Wisconsin Press, 1965.

Ho, J. Mikilani. *Pana O'ahu: Sacred Stones, Sacred Lands.* Honolulu: University of Hawai'i Press, 1999.

Hong, Lea, Mark Fox, and Black McElheny. "Environmentalists, army join forces on preservation.: U.S. Army INCOM-Pacific Region, May 21, 2009. http://www. incom.pac.army.mil/news/article.aspx?id=44.

Hoover, Will. "Waimea Valley preserved." HONOLULU ADVERTISER, Jan. 14, 2006.

http://the.honoluluadvertiser.com/article/2006/Jan/14/ln/FP601140338. html (last visited Nov. 22, 2009).

Horwitz, Robert H., Judith B. Finn, Louis A. Vargha, and James W. Ceaser. *Public Land Policy in Hawaii: An Historical Analysis.* Report No. 5. Honolulu: University of Hawai'i, Legislative Reference Bureau, 1969.

Hosoda, Lyle S. "Development agreement legislation in Hawai'i: An answer to the vested rights uncertainty." 7 U. HAW. L. REV. 173 (1985).

Houck, Oliver A. *The Clean Water Act TMDL Program: Law, Policy, and Implementation.* Washington, D.C.: Environmental Law Institute, 2002.

———. "Rising water: The National Flood Insurance Program and Louisiana." 60 TUL. L. REV. 61 (1985).

———. "Tales from a troubled marriage: Science and law in environmental policy." 17 TUL. ENVTL. L.J. 163 (2003).

Indigenous Mapping Network. "Kānaka Maoli scholars against desecration—Second statement on Naue." March 24, 2009, http://indigenousmapping.net/ newitem.html?start=25 (scroll down to "Kānaka Maoli Scholars Against Desecration") (last visited Dec. 29, 2009).

Johnson, Eric J., and Edward H. Ziegler, eds. *Development Agreements, Analyses, Colorado Case Studies, Commentary.* Denver: Rocky Mountain Land Use Institute, 1993.

Johnston, John D. Jr. "Constitutionality of subdivision exactions: The quest for a rationale." 52 CORNELL L.Q. 871 (1967).

Jones, William K. "Confiscation: A rationale of the law of takings." 24 HOFSTRA L. REV. 1 (1995).

Juergensmeyer, Julian Conrad. *Funding Infrastructure: Paying the Costs of Growth through Impact Fees and Other Land Regulation Charges.* Lincoln Institute of Land Policy Monograph 85-5 (Feb. 1985).

Juergensmeyer, Julian Conrad, and Robert M. Blake. "Impact fees: An answer to local government's capital funding dilemma." 9 FLA. ST. U. L. REV. 415 (1981).

Juergensmeyer, Julian Conrad, and Thomas E. Roberts. *Land Use Planning and Control Law,* 2d ed. St. Paul, Minn.: West, 2002.

Kaho'olawe Island Reserve Commission. "Kaho'olawe History: Hanau hou he 'ula 'o Kaho'olawe—Rebirth of a Sacred Island." http://www.kahoolawe.hawaii. gov/history.shtml (last visited Dec. 29, 2009).

Kakesako, Gregg K. "People wonder . . . Why Waimea?" HONOLULU STAR-BULLETIN, Oct. 6, 2000. http://starbulletin.com/2000/10/06/news/story4.html (last visited Dec. 22, 2009).

Kamakau, Samuel Manaiakalani. *Ka Po'e Kahiko: The People of Old.* Honolulu: Bishop Museum Press, 1991.

Kanahele, Edward L. H. *Ancient Sites of Oahu.* Honolulu: Bishop Museum Press, 1991.

Kapiolani Park Preservation Society. "Historical context." http://www.kapiolani park.org/about/history.html (last visited Nov. 28, 2009).

Kayden, Jerold S., and Robert Pollard. "Linkage ordinances and traditional exactions analysis." 50 LAW & CONTEMP. PROBS. 127 (Winter 1987).

Kea, Jody Lynn. Comment. "Honolulu's Ohana Zoning Law." 13 U. HAW. L. REV. 505 (1991).

Keith, Lynton. "The Hawaii State Plan revisited." 7 U. HAW. L. REV. 29 (1985).

Kennedy, Joseph. OHA. "Valley of the priests: Highlights of Waimea Valley's extraordinary history." http://www.oha.org/index.php?Itemid=225&id=180&option
=com_content&task = view (scroll down to the "Valley of the Priests" article)
(last visited Nov. 20, 2009).

Kessler, Glen. "Powell pledges long-term aid; Confirmed death toll from tsunami
rises to 147,000." WASH. POST, Jan. 8, 2005, at A14.

Kubota, Gary T. "Parking fee increase opposed." HONOLULU STAR-BULLETIN, June
2, 2009. http://www.starbulletin.com/news/20090602_Parking_fee_increase_
opposed.html (last visited Nov. 22, 2009).

Kubota, Lisa. "Controversy over Kapiolani Park activities." KGMB9 News Hawaiʻi,
Nov. 25, 2007.

Kuykendall, Ralph S. *The Hawaiian Kingdom 1778–1854: Foundation and Transformation.* Honolulu: University of Hawaiʻi Press, 1938.

Lachman, Beth E., Anny Wong, and Susan A. Resetar. *The Thin Green Line: An Assessment of DoD's Readiness and Environmental Protection Initiative to Buffer Installation
Encroachment.* Santa Monica, Cal.: RAND Corp., 2007.

Laitos, Jan G., and Thomas A. Carr. "The transformation on public lands." 26 ECOL-
OGY L.Q. 140 (1999).

Larsen, David J. *Development Agreement Manual: Collaboration in Pursuit of Community
Interests.* Prepared for the California League of Cities Institute of Local Self-
Government. Sacramento, 2002.

Leone, Diana. "State, Kokeʻe cabin lessees debate terms." HONOLULU STAR-BULLE-
TIN, July 26, 2008, at B5.

———. "Largest U.S. coral reef gets vast government protection." HONOLULU STAR-
BULLETIN, June 15, 2006, at A1.

Lo, Catharine. "Waimea indivisible: Who will save the valley?" HONOLULU WEEKLY,
Nov. 30– Dec. 6, 2005, at 6.

Lockhart, William J. "External threats to our national parks: An argument for substantive protection." 16 STAN. ENVTL. L.J. 3 (1997).

Lowry, G. Kem Jr. "Policy-relevant assessment of coastal zone management programs." 7 COASTAL ZONE MGMT. J. 2 (1980).

MacKenzie, Melody Kapilialoha. *Native Hawaiian Handbook.* Honolulu: University
Press of Hawaiʻi, 1991.

Magin, Janis L. "Hawaiʻi edges closer toward unified State Building Code."
PAC. BUS. NEWS, Mar. 2, 2007. http://pacific.bizjournals.com/pacific/sto
ries/2007/03/05/focus1.html (last visited Nov. 28, 2009).

Maloney, Frank E., and Dennis C. Dambly. "The National Flood Insurance Program:
A model ordinance for implantation of its land management criteria." 16 NAT.
RESOURCES J. 665–736 (1976).

Mandelker, Daniel R. *Environmental and Land Control Legislation.* Indianapolis:
Bobbs-Merrill, 1976.

———. *Land Use Law,* 4th ed. Charlottesville, Va.: LEXIS, 1997.

Mandelker, Daniel R., and Thea A. Sherry, "The national Coastal Zone Management Act of 1972." 119 URB. L. ANN. 7 (1974).

Mandelker, Daniel R., D. Netsch, P. Salsich, J. Wegner, S. Stevenson, and J. Griffith.
State and Local Government in a Federal System, 5th ed. New York: LexisNexis, 2004.

Marcus, Alan L., and George H. Abrams. "Flood insurance and flood plain zoning as compatible components: A multi-alternative approach to flood damage reduction." 7 NAT. RESOURCES LAW. 581 (1974).

Maui County Department of Planning. "Wailuku Redevelopment Plan frequently asked questions." http://www.mauicounty.gov/faq.aspx (scroll down to "Wailuku Redevelopment Plan" section) (last visited Nov. 20, 2009).

Mayer, Phil. "Native claim opener set for Saturday." HONOLULU STAR-BULLETIN, Jan. 6, 1982, at A12.

McGaffrey, Karen. "Water pollution control under the national pollutant discharge elimination system." *In* Mark A. Ryan, ed., *The Clean Water Act Handbook*, 2d ed. Chicago: Section of Environment, Energy, and Resources, ABA, 2003.

McKinley, James C. Jr. "Three weeks after storm, a grim task of recovery." N.Y. TIMES, Oct. 5, 2008, at A20.

Meltz, Robert, Dwight H. Merriam, and Richard M. Frank. *The Takings Issue: Constitutional Limits on Land Use Control and Environmental Regulation*. Washington, D.C.: Island Press, 1998.

Merriam, Dwight. *The Complete Guide to Zoning*. New York: McGraw-Hill, 2004.

Merriam, Dwight H., and Mary Massaron Ross. *Eminent Domain Use and Abuse:* Kelo *in Context*. Chicago: ABA Publishing, 2006.

Meshenberg, Michael J. *The Language of Zoning: A Glossary of Words and Phrases*. Chicago: American Society of Planning Officials, 1976.

Moss, Elaine, ed. *Land Use Controls in the United States: A Handbook on the Legal Rights of Citizens*. Natural Resources Defense Council. New York: Dial, 1977.

Munger, Lisa Woods. *Hawaii Environmental Law Handbook*, 3rd ed. Honolulu: Government Institutes, 2000.

Myers, Barry Lee, and Jeffery K. Rubin. "Complying with the Federal Disaster Protection Act." 7 REAL EST. L. J. 116 (1978).

Myers, Phyllis. *Zoning Hawaii: An Analysis of the Passage and Implementation of Hawaii's Land Classification Law*. Washington, D.C.: Conservation Foundation, 1976.

National Park Service. "Director's Order #53: Special park uses," § 4 (Apr. 4, 2000–Dec. 31, 2006). http://www.nps.gov/policy/DOrders/DOrder53.html (last visited Nov. 22, 2009).

National Trust for Historic Preservation. *State Tax Credits for Historic Preservation: A State-by-State Summary*. Washington, D.C.: NTHP, 2007.

"New Orleans mayor backs building plan." WASH. POST, Mar. 20, 2006, at A03.

Nicholas, James C. "Impact exactions: Economic theory, practice, and incidence." 50 LAW & CONTEMP. PROBS. 85 (1987).

Nicholas, James C., and Dan Davidson. "Impact fees in Hawaii: Implementing the state law." 50 LAW & CONTEMP. PROBS. 85 (1987).

Nicholas, James C., Arthur C. Nelson, and Julian Conrad Juergensmeyer. *A Practitioner's Guide to Development Impact Fees*. Chicago: Planners Press, 1991.

Nicholson, Sheryl L. Comment. "Hawai'i's ceded lands." 3 U. HAW. L. REV. 101 (1981).

O'Connor, Jim E., and John E. Costa. "Large floods in the United States: Where they happen and why." U.S. Geological Survey Circular 1245 (2003). http://pubs.usgs.gov/circ/2003/circ1245/pdf/circ1245.pdf.

Office of Environmental Quality Control. *A Guidebook for the Environmental Review Process*. Honolulu, 2004.

OHA. *Grant of Conservation and Access Easement* (Jun. 30, 2006).

OHA Public Information Office. "Protection of Wao Kele o Puna celebrated." Aug. 27, 2007. http://www.oha.org/index.php?Itemid=224&id=398&option=com _content&task=view.

Orebech, Peter, Fred Bossleman, Jes Bjarup, David Callies, Martin Chanock, and Hanne Petersen. *The Role of Customary Law in Sustainable Development.* Cambridge: Cambridge University Press, 2005.

Owens, David W. "The zoning variance: Reappraisal and recommendations for reform of a much-maligned tool." 29 COLUM. J. ENVTL. L. 279 (2004).

Pang, Gordon Y. K. "Huge Kapolei mall project on track despite Hawaii's economy." HONOLULU ADVERTISER, Mar. 12, 2009. *Available at* http://the.honolulu advertiser.com/palm/2009/Mar/12/ln/hawaii903120339.html (last visited Jan. 5, 2010).

Pavelko, Thomas M. "Subdivision exactions: A review of judicial standards." 25 J. URB. & CONTEMP. L. 269 (1983).

Platt, Rutherford H. "The National Flood Insurance Program: Some midstream perspectives." 42 J. AM. INST. PLANNERS 304 (July 1976).

Porter, Douglas R., and Lindell L. Marsh, eds. *Development Agreements, Practice, Policy and Prospects.* Washington, D.C.: Urban Land Institute, 1989.

Powell, Frona M. "Challenging authority for municipal subdivision exactions: The ultra vires attack." 39 DEPAUL L. REV. 635 (1990).

Pukui, Mary Kawena. *ʻŌlelo Noʻeau: Hawaiian Proverbs and Poetical Sayings.* Honolulu: Bishop Museum Press, 1983.

Purcell, Madalyn. Comment. "Residential use of Hawaii's conservation districts." 14 U. HAW. L. REV. 633 (1992).

Reynolds, Osborne M. Jr. "Self-induced hardship in zoning variances: Does a purchaser have no one but himself to blame?" 20 URB. LAW. 1 (1988).

Ripley, J. Douglas. "Legal and policy background." *In Conserving Biodiversity on Military Lands: A Guide for Natural Resources Managers,* NatureServe, 2008. *Available at* http://www.dodbiodiversity.org/Full_Publication_Conserving_Biodiversity _on_Military_ Lands.pdf (last visited Nov. 14, 2009).

Rivkin, David B. Jr., Lee A. Kasey, and Mark DeLaquil. *EPA's NSR Enforcement Policy: An Improvident Regulatory Endeavor?* Washington, D.C.: The Federalist Society, 2006.

Roberts, Thomas E., ed. *Taking Sides on Takings Issues.* Chicago: ABA Press, 2003.

Rodgers, William H. Jr. *Environmental Law,* 2d ed. St. Paul, Minn.: West Publishing, 1994.

Roehrig, Nathan. Comment. "Urban type residential communities in the guise of agricultural subdivisions." 25 U. HAW. L. REV. 199 (2002).

Rohan, Patrick J. *Zoning and Land Use Controls.* Matthew Bender & Co. (Eric Damian Kelly ed.), 2006.

Ruhl, J. B. "Farms, their environmental harms, and environmental law." 27 ECOL. L.Q. 263 (2000).

Saarnio, Robert. "Legal framework for historic preservation in Hawaii: National Historic Preservation Act / Preservation 101." *Historic Preservation: Easements, Tax Incentives and Litigation,* Lorman Education Services, June 18, 2008 at 6–7.

Salzman, James, and Barton H. Thompson Jr. *Environmental Law and Policy*, 2d ed. Washington, D.C.: Foundation Press, 2007.

Sanburn, Curt. "*I luna a'e:* OHA at the end of a decade." Ka Wai Ola O OHA, Sept. 1991, at 14, http://www.oha.org/pdf/OHA10yrHistory/KWO0991YR10PRT5.pdf (last visited Nov. 28, 2009).

Sanburn, Curt. "OHA: The beginning—part one." Ka Wai Ola O OHA, Apr. 1991, at 13. http://www.oha.org/pdf/OHA10yrHistory/KWO0491YR10PRT1.pdf (last visited Dec. 22, 2009).

Sax, Joseph L. "Helpless giants: The national parks and the regulation of private lands." 75 Mich. L. Rev. 239 (1976).

Schaefers, Allison, and Stewart Yerton. "A&B subsidiary gets big Kakaako project." Honolulu Star-Bulletin, Sept. 15, 2005, at A1.

Scheuer, Jonathan. Presentation to Lambda Alpha International Hawai'i Chapter (Nov. 16, 2007).

Schoettle, Susan P., and David G. Richardson. "Nontraditional uses of the utility concept to fund public facilities." 25 Urb. Law. 519 (1993).

Scott, Randall W., David J. Bower, and Dallas D. Miner. *The Management and Control of Growth*. Washington, D.C.: Urban Land Institute, 1975.

"Settlement agreement between OHA and the State of Hawai'i." Exhibit A at 5, 9, Jan. 17, 2008. *Available at* http://www.oha.org/pdf/080117_settlement_signed.pdf.

Siegan, Bernard H. "Non-zoning in Houston." 13 J.L. & Econ. 71 (1970).

Singer, Saul Jay. "Flooding the Fifth Amendment: The National Flood Insurance Program and the 'takings' clause." 17 B.C. Envtl. Aff. L. Rev. 323 (1990).

Smith, Alan F. "Uniquely Hawaii: A property professor looks at Hawaii's land law." 7 U. Haw. L. Rev. 1 (1985).

Spann, Bryant J. Note. "Going down for the third time: Senator Kerry's reform bill could save the drowning National Flood Insurance Program." 28 Ga. L. Rev. 593 (1994).

"Sprawl vs. farms." Honolulu Weekly, Feb. 13, 2008. http://honoluluweekly.com/cover/2008/02/sprawl-vs-farms/ (last visited Nov. 14, 2009).

Sproat, Kapua D. "The backlash against PASH: Legislative attempts to restrict Native Hawaiian rights." 20 U. Haw. L. Rev. 321 (1998).

Stanbro, Joshua. "Hawai'i State tax fund a reality." The Trust for Public Land, Dec. 2005. http://www.tpl.org/tier3_print.cfm?folder_id=269&content_item_id=20300&mod_type= 1 (last visited Nov. 20, 2009).

Starritt, Sam D., and John J. McClanahan. "Land-use planning and takings: The viability of conditional exactions to conserve open space in the Rocky Mountain west after *Dolan v. City of Tigard*." 114 S. Ct. 2309 (1994), 30 Land & Water L. Rev. 415 (1995).

State of Hawai'i. *State of Hawaii Coastal Zone Management and Final Environmental Impact Statement*. Honolulu: DBEDT (2004).

State of Hawai'i Department of Business, Economic Development & Tourism. *State of Hawai'i Data Book 2004*. Honolulu: DBEDT (2005).

———. *State of Hawai'i Data Book 2007*. Honolulu: DBEDT (2008).

———. *State of Hawai'i Data Book 2008*. Honolulu: DBEDT (2009).

State of Hawai'i Department of Land & Natural Resources. *Memorandum of Agreement between the Department of Natural Resources, State of Hawai'i and the Office of Hawaiian Affairs*. Honolulu: DLNR (June 27, 2006).

———. "Division of State Parks." http://www.hawaiistateparks.org/ (last visited Nov. 22, 2009).

State of Hawai'i Department of Taxation. *Annual Report 2007–2008*.

State of Hawai'i Historic Preservation Division. *Statewide Historic Preservation Plan for the State of Hawaii*. Honolulu, 2001.

State of Hawai'i Legislative Auditor. *Financial Audit of the Department of Land and Natural Resources* (report submitted to the governor). Apr. 2000.

Strong, Ann Louise. *Land Banking: European Reality, American Prospect*. Baltimore: Johns Hopkins University Press, 1979.

Suarez, Adrienne. Comment. "Avoiding the next Hokulia: The debate over Hawai'i's agricultural subdivisions." 27 U. Haw. L. Rev. 441 (2005).

Sullivan, Paul M. "Customary revolutions: The law of custom and the conflict of traditions in Hawaii." 20 U. Haw. L. Rev. 99 (1998).

Taylor, William David III. Comment. "He who calls the tune must pay the piper: Compensation for regulatory takings of property after *First English Evangelical Lutheran Church v. County of Los Angeles*." 53 Mo. L. Rev. 69 (1988).

TenBruggencate, Jan. "Federal disaster relief on way." Honolulu Advertiser, May 3, 2006, at B1.

Toll, Seymour I. *Zoned American*. New York: Grossman Publishers, 1969.

Trust for Public Land. "3716 acres protected." Apr. 2, 2008. http://www.tpl.org/tier3_cd.cfm?content_item_id=22107&folder_id=269 (last visited Nov. 16, 2009).

———. "Wao Kele o Puna now protected." http://www.tpl.org/tier3_cd.cfm?content_item_id=21822&folder_id=269 (last visited Dec. 22, 2009).

———. "Coastal bluff on Oahu's north shore protected." June 27, 2007. http://www.tpl.org/tier3_cd.cfm?content_item_id=21669&folder_id=269 (last visited Nov. 20, 2009).

Tsai, Michael. "Saving Chinatown." Honolulu Advertiser, Dec. 14, 2005, at 1E.

"Tsunamis and the United States: The past . . . .." Wash. Post, Jan. 9, 2005, at B02.

Tuohy, Matt. *Victory in the Valleys: At Honolulu's Doorstep, Moanalua is Forever Wild*. Hawaiian Islands Program, Issue I (2008).

U.S. Army Environmental Command. Army Compatible Use Buffer Program: Year end summary FY07. http://aec.army.mil/usaec/acub/docs_acub/eoys-fy07.pdf (last visited Jan. 5, 2010).

U.S. Army Garrison, Hawai'i. "Pupukea-Paumalu protected." June 27, 2007. http://www.25idl.army.mil/pressrelease/20070606.pdf (last visited Nov. 28, 2009).

U.S. Department of Agriculture. State and Private Forestry, Coop. Forestry. "Forest Legacy Program implementation guidelines" (2003). http://www.fs.fed.us/spf/coop/library/fpl_guidelines.pdf.

U.S. Department of Commerce. "Service assessment: Hurricane Katrina, August 23–31, 2005" 1 (2005). http://www.weather.gov/om/assessments/pdfs/Katrina.pdf (last visited Jan. 5, 2010).

U.S. Department of Defense. *Military Property Requirements in Hawai'i (MILPRO-HI)*. Apr. 1979.

———. *Project FRESH—Facility Requirements Evaluation, State of Hawai'i*. Jan. 1973.

U.S. Department of the Interior, National Park Service. "National Register of Historic Places." http://www.nps.gov/history/nr/owners.htm.

————. U.S. Geological Survey. "Federal lands and Indian reservations: Hawaii." *Map in The National Atlas of the United States of America.* Washington, D.C.: USGS, 1970.

U.S. Fish & Wildlife Service. America's national wildlife refuges (2007). http://www.fws.gov/refuges/pdfs/factsheets/FactSheetAmNationalWild.pdf (last visited Nov. 22, 2009).

————. Copy of Special Conditions on Special Use Permit No. 12522-98001, issued on June 15, 1998 (in author's file).

————. Copy of Special Conditions on Special Use Permit No. HUL-93-55779, issued to Robert Crane (fax received July 26, 2005).

————. Copy of Special Conditions on Special Use Permit No. 12516-04023, issued to Hawai'i Forest and Trail on May 1, 2004 (fax received July 26, 2005).

————. "Kīlauea Point National Wildlife Refuge: About us." http://www.fws.gov/kilaueapoint/aboutus.html (last visited Dec. 21, 2009).

————. "Refuge list by state: Hawai'i. http://www.fws.gov/refuges/profiles/ByState.cfm?state=HI (last visited Jan. 5, 2010).

————. National Wildlife Refuge System. "How long has the federal government been setting aside lands for wildlife?" http://www.fws.gov/refuges/about/acquisition.html (last visited Nov. 22, 2009).

————. National Wildlife Refuge System. "Welcome to the National Wildlife Refuge System." http://www.fws.gov/refuges/ (last visited Nov. 22, 2009).

U.S. General Services Administration. "Federal real property profile." Table 16 at page 19 (2004). http://www.gsa.gov/gsa/cm_attachments/GSA_DOCUMENT/Annual Report FY2004 Final_R2M-n11_0Z5RDZ-i34K-pR.pdf (last visited Nov. 22, 2009).

U.S. Office of Management and Budget. *Procedures for Reports on Federal Property in Hawai'i.* Budget Circular No. A-52. Washington, D.C.: OMB, Nov. 14, 1960.

Ushijima, Douglas. "*Mahaulepu v. Land Use Comm'n:* A symbol of change; Hawaii's Land Use Law allows golf course development on prime agricultural land by special use permit." 13 U. HAW. L. REV. 205 (1991).

Valla, Brenda. "Linkage: The next stop in developing exactions." 2 GROWTH MGMT. STUD. NEWSL. No. 4 (June 1987).

Van Dyke, Jon M. *Who Owns the Crown Lands of Hawai'i?* Honolulu: University of Hawai'i Press, 2007.

"Various aspects of flood plain zoning." Note. 55 N.D. L. Rev. 429 (1979).

Walden, Andrew. "Big Island superstore ban rejected." HAW. FREE PRESS, Oct. 19, 2007. http://www.hawaiireporter.com/story.aspx?36a593b3-efee-4f28-9084-7b4d108a559a (last visited Nov. 28, 2009).

Weaver, Clifford L., and Richard F. Babcock. *City Zoning: The Once and Future Frontier.* Chicago: APA Planners Press, 1979.

Wegner, Judith Welch. "Moving toward the bargaining table: Contract zoning, development agreements, and the theoretical foundations of government land use deals." 65 N.C. L. REV. 957 (1987).

Weyeneth, Robert R. *Kapiolani Park: A History.* Honolulu: Kapiolani Park Preservation Society, 2002.

Wolf, Michael Allan. *The Zoning of America: Euclid v. Ambler.* Lawrence: University Press of Kansas, 2008.

Wu, Nina. "Developer awarded $1.2M." HONOLULU STAR-BULLETIN, May 12, 2009, at 20.

"Zoo fence art, fairs at Kapiolani allowed." HONOLULU STAR-BULLETIN, May 26, 2009, at 6.

Index

About the Author

DAVID L. CALLIES is Benjamin A. Kudo professor of law at the University of Hawai'i where he teaches land use, state and local government, and real property. A graduate of DePauw University, the University of Michigan Law School (J.D.), and the University of Nottingham (LL.M.), and a past foreign fellow and present life member of Clare Hall, Cambridge University, he is an elected member of the College of Fellows of the American Institute of Certified Planners (FAICP), the American College of Real Estate Attorneys (ACREL), and the American Law Institute (ALI). He is the author or co-author of seventeen books.

Production Notes for Callies / *Regulating Paradise*

Cover design by Wilson Angel

Text design and composition by Santos Barbasa with
display type in Rockwell and text type in
New Baskerville

Printing and binding by The Maple-Vail Book Manufacturing Group

Printed on 50# Glat Offset D37, 400 ppi